SMALL &
CONTAINER
GARDENING

SMALL &
CONTAINER
GARDENING

A practical guide to gardening in small spaces

PETER MCHOY & STEPHANIE DONALDSON

HERMES
HOUSE

This edition published by Hermes House an imprint of

Anness Publishing Limited

© Anness Publishing Limited 2001
Hermes House
88–89 Blackfriars Road
London SE1 8HA

Publisher Joanna Lorenz
Managing Editor Judith Simons
Project Editor Mariano Kälfors
Designers Patrick McLeavy & Partners, Bill Mason, Janet James and Ian Sandom
Photographers John Freeman, Debbie Patterson,
Janine Hosegood and Marie O'Hara
Jacket Designer Nigel Partridge
Production Controllers Ben Worley and Joanna King

Printed and bound in Spain by Mateu Cromo, S.A Madrid

CONTENTS

Introduction	6
THE SMALL GARDEN	8
ELEMENTS OF DESIGN	12
Planning Your Garden	14
Difficult Sites	38
FEATURES AND STRUCTURES	56
The Garden Floor	58
Forming Boundaries	84
Finishing Touches	102
Rock and Water Gardens	126
CHOOSING PLANTS	140
Beds and Borders	142
Planning Borders	148
Maintaining Beds and Borders	180
Plants for a Purpose	188
The Kitchen Garden	220
THE CONTAINER GARDEN	230
GETTING STARTED	234
Decorating Containers	270
THE PLANTING PROJECTS	276
Colour Schemes for Containers	278
Seasonal Planters	328
Edible Collections	378
Scented Collections	394
Difficult Situations	408
Inspirational Containers	418
The Young Container Gardener	448
Indoor Containers	462
PLANT GUIDE	484
GARDENER'S RECORDS	486
INDEX	504
ACKNOWLEDGEMENTS	512

Introduction

Small gardens can be a blessing in that they do not require a lot of hard work to create and maintain. But this is no reason to settle for a patch of lawn and a few hardy plants. Your garden is very much a part of your home it pays to give it the kind of attention that you would the inside of your house.

The hard landscaping (paving, fences, paths, walls) gives the garden its design. Hedges or careful screening can hide a garden shed or the place where garden refuse is stored, and at the same time add interest to the garden. It is important to keep the design simple, as most of a small garden can be seen at a glance; however, it is an advantage if the garden does not show all its attractions at once. Individual features or focal points like benches, urns, birdbaths, lights or well-placed containers arranged singly or in groups, draw the eye and add an extra dimension to the garden.

Choice of the right plants can enhance the general landscaping, providing the flesh, shape and texture of the garden. The size of plants is also important in a small garden. Taller plants can be used for architectural effects and give the garden height, but plants that are too big can overpower a small garden. Tiny plants, planted in the cracks or paving stones or walls, add texture and colour.

Plants maintain the visual interest in the garden. By choosing the appropriate plants you can ensure that your garden is a picture all year round. Bulbs provide colour in spring with welcome signs that a new year is beginning. Berries and foliage attract the birds and turn into autumnal reds

and browns, evergreens keep the interest going in winter, annuals and perennials make up a kaleidoscope of colour, or enhance a colour-themed garden, throughout the year.

Containers also play their part in year-round visual interest. By planning their planting carefully, not only do they provide colour and interest in their own right, but by placing them in a flower bed after a plant has finished flowering or in a newly empty space, they can continue to delight the viewer. Apart from creating beautiful displays outside, planting in containers is also an easy and extremely versatile way to bring the garden inside.

Plants have other purposes too. They can be planted for shade or shelter, as screens for privacy, for

their scent, to attract butterflies and birds to the garden, and to harvest fruit and vegetables for the home, or herbs for the cook.

The small garden can be designed to be one that is easily maintained, an ongoing hobby or a challenge. It can also become a place to sit out on a summer's day, a play space for children or an outdoor room. Whether you are a novice or an experienced gardener and plantsman, this book will help you make the garden of your dreams a reality.

BELOW: *A garden can be many things, but ultimately it is a place of relaxation. A vibrant display of plants on the wall and potfulls of plant colour creates an instant and irresistible al fresco room.*

OPPOSITE: *Family gardens have to be multi-purpose. If you do lots of entertaining, then a barbecue and seating area is likely to be a priority. A bright or colourful tablecloth will transform a drab table in an instant. Add a few pots of seasonal plants for that finishing touch.*

The Small Garden

• Planning your Garden • Difficult Sites
• The Garden Floor • Forming Boundaries
• Finishing Touches • Rock and Water
Gardens • Beds and Borders • Planning
Borders • Maintaining Beds and Borders
• Plants for a Purpose • The Kitchen Garden

Gardening in small spaces

SMALL GARDENS CAN STILL HAVE A BIG IMPACT, and this book shows you how to get the best from a limited area. Size is comparative of course, and if your gardening is confined to a tiny backyard or a balcony, even a small town garden can seem large. On the other hand, a medium-sized country garden may appear small to the owner of a large estate. But whether you garden on a rooftop, or you have a fairly typical small town garden or a larger plot that simply seems small to you, this book offers ideas and solutions.

Making the most of a small space depends partly on design and partly on planting. If you want a low-maintenance garden the emphasis should be on hard landscaping and the use of ground cover and low-maintenance plants. If you are a plant collector, a design with the emphasis on planting space will be important . . . but choosing the right plants in proportion to the available space is vital.

You will find lots of ideas for redesigning a small garden, from initial ideas to execution. But sometimes only minor modifications to your existing garden are necessary for a transformation, and the section on features and structures has plenty of thought-provoking ideas that you might like to consider.

Choosing appropriate plants can be the key to ensuring a small garden design works well. In the third section of the book you will find hundreds of recommended plants, arranged by use or purpose – from plants for colour theme beds and borders, and those providing colour in the cold months, to those grown for shade (a particular problem in small gardens) or fragrance. Many plants have more than a single role, of course, so to avoid repetition and to make space for more plants, multiple entries have been thoroughly cross-referenced.

Size is especially important in a small garden, so we have given an indication of likely heights and spreads. In the case of herbaceous plants these are typical dimensions after a couple of years, but for slower-growing trees and shrubs they are the probable size after 10–15 years. Bear in mind, however, that dimensions can be no more than a crude guide. Heights can vary greatly, according to soil, position, and local climate. Some trees and shrubs can be kept compact by regular pruning – for example, buddleias and eucalpytus are both too tall for a small garden if left unpruned, but will make compact shrubs with a good shape if cut back severely each spring.

Although you will find plenty of suggestions in the following pages, attractive gardens are not designed to a rigid formula, and there is always room for individual interpretation – and even eccentricity. Some gardens are designed to shock, some are traditional in concept, a few are strictly formal, and many are a compromise between formality and informality. There are as many garden styles as there are tastes, and the only criterion for success is whether the result pleases you personally.

Design does not become easier with decreasing size: rather, it becomes more difficult and demanding. A large garden tends to look good anyway, with the odd weedy bed going almost unnoticed among the overall impression of large lawns, stately trees and shrubs. In a small garden long vistas are out of the question and the use of trees and large shrubs is often severely limited. Every part of the garden comes under the spotlight, and errors of judgement are often emphasized.

All these handicaps can be overcome, however, and, as the illustrations in this book show, you can still make a big impact with a small garden.

OPPOSITE: *Pots and containers are a good means of incorporating herbs in a very confined space.*

Elements of Design

Attractive small gardens seldom just happen, they are designed. And despite the apparent contradiction, the smaller the garden, the more important good design becomes. A small garden can be taken in almost at a glance, and the difference between good and bad design, attention to detail or neglect, is immediately obvious. In a small garden there is always the temptation to try to cram in many more features than there is really space for. Keep the design simple, stick to a style, and follow the suggestions in this section for making a plan to scale. Then check the effect by marking out the shapes in the garden before you start work.

This way you will be assured success.

ABOVE: *Sometimes accommodating essentials, such as this tool shed, attractively can become a problem. Careful screening can help minimize their impact.*

OPPOSITE: *A small garden should not lack impact. Provided it is well planted and has some strong focal points, it becomes easy to ignore the limitations of size.*

Planning Your Garden

Some successful gardens are worked out on the ground, in the mind's eye, perhaps visualized during a walk around the garden, or conceived in stages as construction takes place. This approach is for the gifted or very experienced, and it is far better to make your mistakes on paper first.

A major redesign can be time-consuming and expensive, especially if it involves hard landscaping (paving, walls, steps, etc). However, simply moving a few plants is rarely enough to transform an uninspiring garden into something special. It is worth having a goal, a plan to work to, even if you have to compromise along the way. Bear in mind that you may be able to stagger the work and cost over several seasons, but having a well thought out design ensures the garden evolves in a structured way.

Use the checklist opposite to clarify your 'needs', then decide in your own mind the *style* of garden you want. Make a note of mundane and practical considerations, like where to dry the clothes and put the refuse, plus objects that need to be screened, such as a compost area, or an unpleasant view.

Unattractive views, and necessary but unsightly objects within the garden, such as toolsheds, are a particular problem because they can dominate a small garden. Well-positioned shrubs and small trees can act as a screen. To improve the outlook instantly use a large plant in a tub.

ABOVE: *In this garden the bird table helps to draw the eye away from the practical corner of the garden.*

LEFT: *Make a small garden look larger than it really is by ensuring the sides are well planted and creating a striking focal point.*

OPPOSITE: *Shape and form can be as important as colour in creating a stylish garden.*

LABOUR-SAVING TIPS

- To minimize cost and labour, retain as many paths and areas of paving as possible, but only if they don't compromise the design.
- If you want to enlarge an area of paving, or improve its appearance, it may be possible to pave over the top and thus avoid the arduous task of removing the original.
- Modifying the shape of your lawn is easier than digging it up and relaying a new one. It is simple to trim it to a smaller shape if you want a lawn of the same area, and if you wish to change the angle or shape, it may be possible to leave most of it intact, and simply lift and relay some of the turf.

LEFT: Strong lines and several changes of level give this small garden plenty of interest. In this kind of design, the hard landscaping is more important than the soft landscaping (the plants).

CHOICES CHECKLIST

Before you draw up your design, make a list of requirements for your ideal garden. You will almost certainly have to abandon or defer some of them, but at least you will realize which features are most important to you.

Use this checklist at the rough plan stage, when decisions have to be made . . . and it is easy to change your mind!

Features

Barbecue	☐
Beds	☐
Borders, for herbaceous	☐
Borders, for shrubs	☐
Borders, mixed	☐
Birdbath	☐
Changes of level	☐
Fruit garden	☐
Gravelled area	☐
Greenhouse/conservatory	☐
Herb garden	☐
Lawn (mainly for decoration)	☐
Lawn (mainly for recreation)	☐
Ornaments	☐
Patio/terrace	☐
Pergola	☐
Pond	☐
Raised beds	☐
Summerhouse	☐
Sundial	☐
Vegetable plot	☐
Plus	☐

Functional features

Compost area	☐
Garage	☐
Toolshed	☐
Plus	☐

Necessities

Children's play area	☐
Climbing frame	☐
Sandpit	☐
Swing	☐
Clothes dryer	☐
Dustbin area	☐
Plus	☐

Choosing a style

Before sitting down with pencil and paper to sketch out your garden, spend a little time thinking about the style that you want to achieve. In many gardens plants and features are used for no other reason than that they appeal; an excellent reason, perhaps, but not the way to create an overall design that will make your garden stand out from others in the street.

The styles shown in the following six pages are not exhaustive, and probably none will be exactly right for your own garden, but they will help you to clarify your thoughts. You should know roughly what you want from your garden before you start to design it.

FORMAL APPROACH

Formal gardens appeal to those who delight in crisp, neat edges, straight lines and a sense of order. Many traditional suburban gardens are formal in outline, with rectangular lawns flanked by straight flower borders, and perhaps rectangular or circular flower beds cut into them. Such rigid designs are often dictated by the drive for the car and straight paths laid by the house builder.

Although the gardens shown here are all very different, what they have in common is a structure as important as the plants contained within it. The designs are largely symmetrical, with no pretence at creating a natural-looking environment for the plants.

The very size and shape of most small gardens limits the opportunities for natural-looking landscapes, so a formal style is a popular choice.

Parterres and knot gardens

Parterres and knot gardens often appeal to those with a sense of garden history, though in a small garden the effect can only ever be a shadow of the grand designs used by sixteenth-century French and Italian gardeners.

Parterres are areas consisting of a series of shaped beds, or compart-

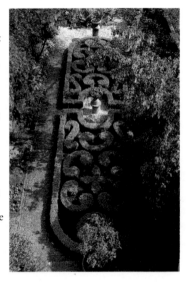

ABOVE: *A knot garden. This kind of garden is not colourful, but the strong lines and formal shape, backed by a variety of greens, make it a restful place to relax.*

LEFT: *This small, enclosed courtyard garden balances a central focal point with a boundary that features this dramatic entrance.*

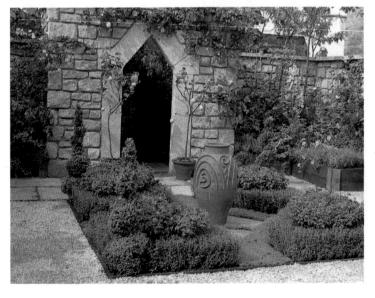

ments, that fit together to form a pattern, often quite complex, on the ground. They were designed, often, to be viewed from the upper windows of grand houses.

Knot gardens, originally designed to be viewed from above, are similar but low-growing clipped hedges are used to form the geometric and often interwoven designs. The space between hedges can be filled with flowers or, more historically correct, coloured sands or gravel, or even crushed coal if black appeals.

These are expensive gardens to create, slow to establish, and labour-intensive to maintain, but the results can be stunning. This kind of garden is unsuitable for a young family.

Formal herb gardens
Herb gardens are popular features and are much easier to create than knot gardens. Illustrations of both old and new herb gardens in books will often give you ideas for designs.

Rose gardens
A formal rose garden is easy to create, and it will look good even in its first season. To provide interest throughout the year, edge the beds with seasonal flowers and underplant the roses with spring bulbs or low-growing summer flowers.

Paved gardens
A small garden lends itself to being paved throughout. By growing most plants in raised beds or in containers, less bending is involved and many of the smaller plants are more easily appreciated. Climbers can be used to make the most of vertical space, and if you plant in open areas left in the paving, the garden can still look green.

Courtyard gardens
Space can be at a real premium in the heart of a town, but you can turn your backyard into an oasis-like courtyard garden, with floor tiles and white walls that reflect the light. Add some lush green foliage, an 'architectural' tree or large shrub, and the sound of running water. Although the plants may be few, the impact is strong.

Traditional designs
A small formal garden, with a rectangular lawn, straight herbaceous border, and rose and flower beds is still a popular choice with gardeners looking for the opportunity to grow a wide variety of plants such as summer bedding, herbaceous plants, and popular favourites such as roses. The design element is less important than the plants.

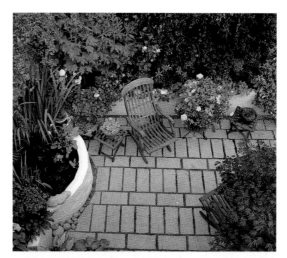

LEFT: *The use of white masonry paint can help to lighten a dark basement garden or one enclosed by high walls.*

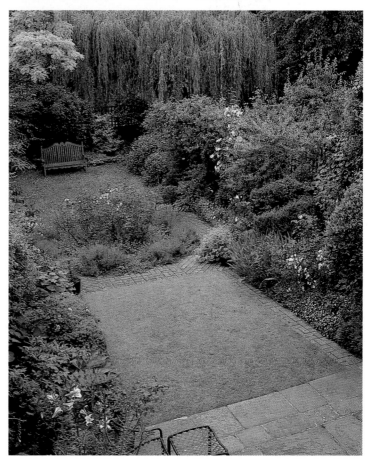

BELOW: *This long, narrow plot has been broken up by strong lines: a useful design technique.*

Informal effects

The informality of the cottage garden and the 'wilderness' atmosphere of a wild garden are difficult to achieve in a small space, especially in a town. However, with fences well clothed with plants so that modern buildings do not intrude, an informal garden can work even here.

Cottage gardens

The cottage garden style is created partly by design and the use of suitable paving materials (bricks for paths instead of modern paving slabs), and also by the choice of plants.

Relatively little hard landscaping is necessary for a cottage garden – brick paths and perhaps stepping-stones through the beds may be enough. It is the juxtaposition of 'old-fashioned' plants and vegetables that creates the casual but colourful look associated with this type of garden.

Mix annuals with perennials – especially those that will self-seed such as calendulas and *Limnanthes douglasii*, which will grow everywhere and create a colourful chaos. If flowers self-sow at the edge of the path, or between other plants, leave most of them to grow where they have chosen to put down roots.

Plant some vegetables among the flowers, and perhaps grow decorative runner beans up canes at the back of the border.

Wildlife gardens

A small wildlife garden seems almost a contradiction in terms, but even a tiny plot can offer a refuge for all kinds of creatures if you design and plant with wildlife in mind.

Wildlife enthusiasts sometimes let their gardens 'go wild'. However, this is not necessary. A garden like this one looks well kept and pretty, yet it provides long vegetation where animals and insects can hide and find

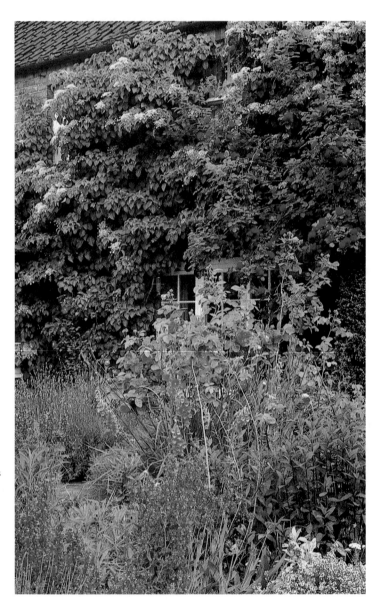

RIGHT: *The house itself will inevitably dominate a small garden, especially when you look back towards it. Covering the walls with climbers will help it to blend in unobtrusively.*

food. There is water to attract aquatic life, and flowers and shrubs to bring the butterflies and seeds for the birds.

An orchard can also be a magnet for wildlife of many kinds.

Woodland gardens

A woodland effect is clearly impractical for a very tiny garden, but if you have a long, narrow back garden, trees and shrubs can be used very effectively. Choose quick-growing deciduous trees with a light canopy (birch trees, *Betula* species, are a good choice where there's space,

RIGHT: *The woodland effect can be delightfully refreshing on a warm spring or summer day, but works best with trees that have a tall canopy that allows plenty of light to filter through. Although a pond is attractive in this situation, care will have to be taken to remove leaves in the autumn.*
BELOW: *A pretty pond is a super way to attract wildlife, and looks especially good if well integrated into the garden like this one.*

but they can grow tall). Avoid evergreens, otherwise you will lose the benefit of the spring flowers and ferns that are so much a feature of the traditional woodland garden.

Use small-growing rhododendrons and azaleas to provide colour beneath the tree canopy, and fill in with ground cover plants, naturalized bulbs such as wood anemones and bluebells, and plant woodland plants such as ferns and primroses.

Use the woodland effect to block out an unattractive view or overlooking houses. As an added bonus it is low-maintenance too.

Rocks and streams

Rock or water features alone seldom work as a 'design'. They are usually most effective planned as part of a larger scheme. Combined, however, rocks and water can be used as the central theme of a design that attempts to create a natural style in an informal garden.

Meandering meadows

Instead of the rectangular lawn usually associated with small gardens, try broadening the borders with gentle sweeps, meandering to merge with an unobstructed boundary if there is an attractive view beyond. If the distant view is unappealing, take the border round so that the lawn curves to extend beyond the point of view. Use shrubs and lower-growing border plants to create the kind of border that you might find at the edge of a strip of woodland.

Bright beds and borders

If plants are more important than the elements of design, use plenty of sweeping beds and borders, and concentrate heavily on shrubs and herbaceous plants to give the garden shape. Allow plants to tumble over edges and let them grow informally among paving.

If you want to create a strong sense of design within such a plant-oriented small garden, use focal points such as ornaments, garden seats or birdbaths.

Distant influences

Professional garden designers are frequently influenced by classic styles from other countries, especially Japan, but amateurs are often nervous of trying such designs themselves. Provided you start with the clear premise that what pleases you is the only real criterion of whether something works, creating a particular 'foreign' style can be great fun. Adapt the chosen style to suit climate, landscape and the availability of suitable plants and materials.

Japanese gardens

'Real' Japanese gardens are for the purist who is prepared to give the subject much study. Raked sand and grouped stones have special meaning for those briefed in the Japanese traditions, but can be enigmatic to untrained Western eyes.

Many elements from the Japanese style can be adapted for Western tastes, however, and many gardeners are happy to introduce the essential visual elements without concern for deeper meanings. This style is easily adapted to a small space, and the uncluttered appearance makes a confined area appear larger.

Stone and gravel gardens

Although stones and rocks are widely used in Japanese gardens, they can also be key components in creating a garden which is more reminiscent of a dry river bed in an arid region – the sort of garden that you might find in a rocky, semi-desert area.

This kind of garden needs minimal maintenance, and if you choose drought-tolerant plants it should look good even in a very dry summer.

Stone gardens appeal to those with a strong sense of design, and an adventurous spirit, rather than to plant-lovers. Although the plants play a vital role in the drama of the scene, opportunities for using a wide range of plants is limited.

Gravel gardens are also a practical choice where space is limited. You can add some large boulders or rocks as focal points, and plants can be used much more freely. It is easy to plant through the gravel, and a wide range of plants can be grown in groups or as isolated specimens.

LEFT: *You don't need a lot of plants to create a Japanese-style garden. Strong hard landscaping and the restrained use of plants is a hallmark of the Japanese garden style.*

OPPOSITE TOP: *The use of formal water, painted wall and patio overhead gives this garden a Mediterranean atmosphere.*

OPPOSITE: *The dry gravel slope and the use of plants like yuccas help to create the illusion of a garden in a warm, dry climate.*

Mediterranean gardens

The illusion of a Mediterranean garden is most easily achieved in a backyard 6r tiny walled garden. The effect is difficult to achieve if you view neighbouring homes and gardens over a low fence – guaranteed to kill any self-deception as to location!

Paint the walls white, or a pale colour, to reflect the light and create a bright, airy feeling. If possible include alcoves in which you can place plants, or build ledges on which you can stand pots.

Pave the area with bricks, terracotta-coloured pavers or tiles – but steer clear of paving slabs. Use plenty of decorative terracotta pots and tubs.

The illusion is completed by using plenty of appropriate plants, such as pelargoniums, oleanders, bougainvilleas, and daturas (brugmansias). Stand pots of large cacti and succulents outdoors too.

The success of this kind of garden owes less to its structural design than to the use of appropriate plants, ornaments, and garden furniture.

Exotic effects

You can give your garden an exotic appearance by concentrating on exotic-looking plants that are hardier than

their appearance might suggest. Grow them in pots on the patio (which will enable you to move the tender kinds to a greenhouse or conservatory, or just a sheltered position, if you garden in a cold area), or in a gravel garden.

Tough, spiky plants to consider for this kind of garden are many of the hardy yuccas, and phormiums if they grow in your area without protection. Add some agaves such as *A. americana* if you live in a very mild area.

Palms are associated with warm climates, but some are tough enough to withstand moderately severe winters. *Trachycarpus fortunei* is particularly reliable. Just a few well-chosen plants can create images of far-away places.

Getting the details right

One of the most difficult tasks when planning a small garden is working out how best to use the available space. For most of us, it is the decorative features – the plants themselves – that take priority. But functional features are important, too, and it is best to allocate space for these first.

Once the fundamentals have been dealt with, it is much easier to decide where you want to have planting areas. Within this framework, you will be able to transform the space into a decorative outdoor room that you will want to use for much more of the year than just the few summer months.

Practical considerations

You will probably have decided that you want somewhere to sit. This need not necessarily be next to the house. For example, if evening is the time of day when you will most often be able to sit outside, and there's a spot at the far end of your garden that catches the evening sun, then it makes sense to site your seating area here.

If you have children, you will probably want somewhere for them to play. Common sense dictates that this is near the house, to make supervision easier. Try, if you can, to include a sandpit – children will be thrilled with one just 1m (3ft) square; if there is just a little more space, there will be room enough for a small play house.

Although there is a temptation to banish such mundane essentials as the tool shed and the compost bins to the bottom of the garden, with a long site this will not be very practical. Consider giving them a more central position, suitably screened from view all round.

Plan out in your mind the best place for each of these features in much the same way as you might plan your kitchen, where you also need to make the best possible use of the available space to make it efficient to work in and comfortable to be in.

RIGHT: *By dividing up the spaces, you can create visual depth. These two spectacular box orbs help to define a vista and lend perspective to the arbour at the end.*

Making changes

Once these priorities are fixed, it will be much easier to work out the layout of the garden. This is important, even if you don't have the resources for new paving and landscaping, at least for the foreseeable future. For example, there may be a flower bed just where you feel it would be best to create a seating area. With the garden layout left as it is, you would continually

ABOVE: *This wall hides part of the garden, offering privacy, while the archway frames a statue, bringing perspective to the whole space.*

BELOW: *Secret places can be created in even the smallest of spaces. This pathway winds through plantings in a tiny 3m (10ft) plot.*

ABOVE: *Even the smallest of spaces may be transformed with decorative touches such as pots of colourful primulas in a wooden holder.*

have to bring furniture in and out when you need it. That is no more comfortable than a living room would be if you had to bring in a chair every time you wanted to sit down. However, with a few little changes, like simply turfing over the flower bed, you can organize the garden so it is ready for relaxation any time you want.

Planning for privacy

Privacy and shelter are essential requirements for relaxation in the garden but, especially in built-up areas, they can be difficult to achieve. Try fixing trellis on top of walls and fences to create extra height. You can then grow decorative climbers to provide a wonderful natural wallpaper. You could plant fast-growing conifers such as thuja, although you should always check their potential final height or you could end up deeply overshadowed, if not overlooked.

Seating areas in particular need privacy. Even if you live in the middle of the country, you will feel much more comfortable if you site these where, at least on one side, there is the protection of a wall of some sort. This could be the garden boundary wall, a hedge, or even a trellis screen to lend a more intimate feel.

Overhead screens

If you are closely overlooked, you may also want to create privacy from above. One of the most successful ways of doing this is to put up a pergola and let it become entwined with vines or other climbers. That way, you have a 'roof', which filters the natural light and allows a free flow of fresh air.

Creating the right atmosphere

Creating the right mood for your garden depends on stimulating the senses: sight, sound, touch, taste and smell, all of which are supplied free of charge by nature. And simply by being outside, you are closer to nature, so it should be even easier to bring atmosphere to the garden than to anywhere else in your home. For many people, the garden is just as important as any room in the house.

Sight and sound
You will find a wealth of suggestions for stimulating the senses throughout the following pages. These ideas can be set against the visual delights provided by the plants themselves. As well as the sound of birdsong and buzzing insects, you can add the music of wind chimes or the evocative trickling of water in even the smallest plot.

Smells galore
The outdoors also provides the most glorious fragrances, both sweet – from flowers such as roses, honeysuckle, and jasmine – and aromatic – from lavender and piquant herbs. Remember that scent develops in the warmth of the sun, so choose a sunny spot and that after a spring or summer shower, the air can smell heavenly.

Touch and taste
Touch, too, can be stimulated as it is impossible to walk through a garden without being touched by – or reaching out to touch – some of the plants. This is especially pleasing if they have interesting textures. Plan for a variety of these, using plants with fleshy, frondy and feathery leaves. Finally, eating out in the garden completes the sensory picture.

ABOVE: *A pretty Victorian-style wire plant stand, filled with flowering plants, brings flashes of bright white high up in the middle of a largely green planting area.*

LEFT: *The sound of trickling water enhances any outdoor area, and a water feature need not take up a large amount of space. Water flows over this wall-mounted, cast-iron shell.*

ABOVE: *A courtyard is set out as an outdoor room, with a cherry tree suggesting pretty 'wallpaper' and blossom forming a carpet.*

ABOVE: *Brick-shaped paviours set into a tiny lawn, then decorated with urns mimic the vistas set out on the floors of classical gardens.*

A hint of romance

The most romantic gardens hint at intimacy. They could literally be enclosed outdoor rooms, such as courtyards, balconies or roof gardens, which automatically offer intimacy. If your space is rather larger, you can add romantic interest by creating hidden places. This isn't difficult, even in the smallest garden. You can put a door in the fence or wall to hint at another space beyond; put up an archway to give the feeling of moving from one area to another; or add a trellis screen to section off an eating area or enclose a garden seat.

Creating an illusion

As well as creating intimacy, these dividing tactics also give the illusion of space. Adding an archway or screen means you are able to see beyond into another area, which lends perspective to the whole space, giving it structure and shape. However light the resulting screening is, it hints at secret places and romance.

LEFT: *A series of basic motifs painted over stripes of vibrant colours gives simple pots a rich Mexican look.*

Focal points

Focal points are an essential part of good garden design, relevant whatever the size of garden. They help to take the eye to a favourable part and away from the less favourable. They can also act as signposts to lead the eye around the garden and placed at the end of the garden they can lead the eye into the distance, thus making the garden seem larger than it is in reality.

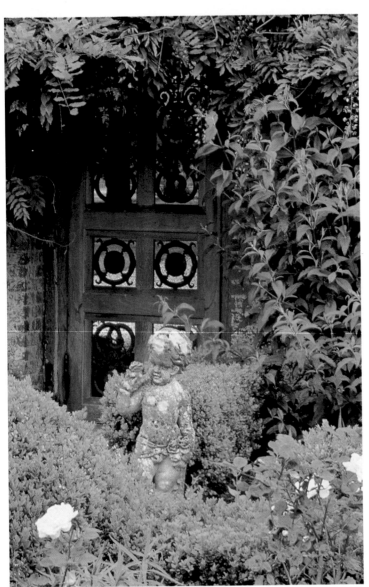

Adding interest to lawns

An expanse of even a well-kept lawn may look bare and a little boring, especially if all the interest is in the beds and borders around the edges. It can be useful to create a focal point within the lawn, but this often works best if offset to one side or towards one end of the lawn, rather than in the centre. Position it where you want to take the eye to an attractive view, or use it to fill an area that lacks interest. Try to avoid placing the focal point against a background that is already busy or colourful; otherwise one will fight against the other for attention.

Birdbaths and sundials

A sundial is a popular choice for a focal point on the lawn, but should be placed in a sunny position if it is to look in the least credible. A birdbath is another favourite option, and is especially delightful if it is close to the house where the visiting birds can be seen and enjoyed.

Statues and plants

In a small garden, a spectacular focal point such as a statue can be used to dominate a corner of the garden so that the limitations of scale and size become irrelevant for the moment. Bear in mind that plants can be used as well as inanimate objects. While a well-placed ornament or figure will serve as a simple focal point, when used in conjunction with plants, the effect can be particularly striking.

LEFT: *An exquisite, weathered wood and metal door makes a decorative garden entrance while the statue draws the eye towards the doorway.*

RIGHT: *A formal geometric pond with its oriental overtones makes a charming focal point in a terraced town garden.*

FAR RIGHT: *An enchanting little pond, complete with fountain and cherub, mimics designs on a much grander scale.*

Gateways and arches

Gateways and arches make excellent focal points in a garden, and can add a feeling of mystery and promise from whichever side you view them. Both gateways and arches work best if the areas on either side of them are laid out in contrasting styles or are visually very different to each other. In a long, narrow garden, for example, you could produce a series of arches or gates, taking the eye further on into a journey of exploration.

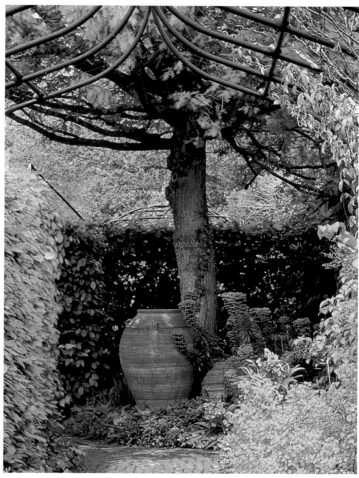

ABOVE: *A tripod can be used to draw the eye to the end of the garden. Once fully grown this Clematis 'Jackmanii' will cover it completely.*

RIGHT: *Beneath this metal walkway, Greek pithoi in a bed of euphorbia and hellebores are used to great effect as a focal point.*

Screens and disguises

Unless you are extremely fortunate, there will be a certain view or some objects within the garden that you really want to hide. Focal points can be used to take the eye away from some of them, but others will require some form of screening or disguise. A little bit of trickery can even be used to make the garden look a different shape – to shorten the appearance of a long thin site, for example, or to give apparent depth to a garden that is wide but shallow.

Living screens
Many common hedging plants can be allowed to grow taller than normal to form a shrubby screen. Space the plants further apart than for a hedge, so that they retain a shrubby shape, and clip or prune only when it is necessary to keep within bounds. Avoid a formal clipped shape unless you are screening within a very formal garden. Most hedging plants will grow to twice their normal hedge height if you give them more space and do not restrict them by frequent clipping and pruning.

Matching screen and setting
Choose plants appropriate to the setting. In a Japanese-style garden, many of the tall bamboos will make an excellent screen for, say, a garage wall or oil storage tank. Use shrubby plants in a garden where there are lots of shrubs, and especially if the shrub border can be taken up to the screening point. On a patio, a climber-covered trellis may look good.

Urban solutions
In town gardens, and particularly in the case of balcony and roof gardens, the problem is to minimize the impact of surrounding homes, offices and factories. These usually require impracticably huge walls to mask the view, which would also make the garden excessively dark. In a very small garden, trees may not be a practical solution for this type of screening either, although in a larger one they will probably provide the answer.

ABOVE: *Dense planting at the end of the garden suggests that the property goes further, even if the path leads nowhere in particular.*

A sensible compromise is to extend the wall or fence with a trellis, or similar framework, along which you can grow climbers. This will not block out the view completely, but it will soften the harsh impact of buildings and help to concentrate the eye within the garden by minimizing the distractions beyond. The boundary itself will be given extra height and interest.

Boundaries and beyond
A combination of plants and hard landscaping is often the most satisfactory way to screen a view beyond a boundary. Trees are a particularly pleasing solution. Even if they lose their leaves in winter, the network of branches is often sufficient to break up the harsh outline of buildings and beyond, and in summer – when you spend more

time in the garden and require more privacy – the canopy of foliage will usually block out most of the view. Trees are a particularly good solution if the aspect is such that most of the shadow falls away from your garden rather than over it.

Optical illusions

Although there are limits to how much you can change the site of your garden physically, it is possible to employ some optical tricks with which to alter its appearance.

A long, straight view will be foreshortened by a tall object or bright colours at the far end of it. If, on the other hand, the distant end has a scaled-down ornament and misty, pale colours, the ornament will appear to be further away.

Using colour and mirrors

A straight lawn can be narrowed towards the further end to make it seem longer, and the effect can be enhanced by using a bright splash of colour near the beginning. If your garden is wide but not very deep, you can give an impression of enhanced depth by positioning a mirror almost opposite the entrance and surrounding it with plants. As you step outside, you seem to see an entrance to another, hidden part of the garden.

If the area is surrounded by walls, they can be painted white (for extra light), green (to blend in), or with a floral mural where the planting is sparse. Shaped trellises can be added to give the impression of a distant perspective rather than a flat wall, and a false doorway with a *trompe l'oeil* vista disappearing away behind it can be wonderfully effective at enlarging a confined space.

OPPOSITE: *Here, painted square trellis has been used as a screen, dividing off one part of the garden from another.*

RIGHT: *A floral arbour makes a rich decorative frame for a piece of statuary, creating a very theatrical effect and hiding an unsightly view.*

ABOVE: *A cleverly positioned mirror will reflect the plants back into the garden, suggesting that it is larger than it actually is.*

ABOVE: *An ordinary, wooden-slat garden door leads from an alleyway to a tiny but enchanting city garden.*

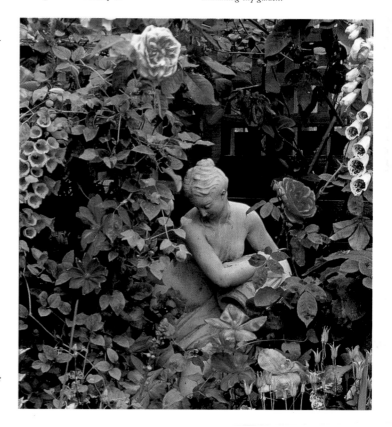

Utilities and storage

The need to find room for less attractive bits and pieces of the garden – such as the dustbins (garbage cans) and the compost heap – is a fact of life, but utilities like these need not be on show. With a little imagination, they can be completely disguised or made to blend in with their surroundings. Storage space will also be needed for the amount of practical paraphernalia that gardening brings, from tools and pots and planters to potting compost (soil mix), seeds and string.

In an ideal world, dustbins (garbage cans) and recycling containers would be beautiful in themselves, but, unfortunately, in reality they are seldom an attractive sight. They are necessary, however, and they do need to be accessible. You can ignore your dustbins (garbage cans) or spend a little time and effort blending them in, by painting them to co-ordinate with the overall scheme (if this is feasible), using a screen of plants to hide them, or camouflaging them with a plant-covered trellis.

RIGHT: A wire shelving unit, intertwined with clematis, makes a delightful garden detail that also serves a practical purpose.

BELOW: Shelving can be used for purely decorative purposes outside as well as in, no matter how small the garden.

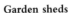

Compost bins

Compost is an invaluable aid for any gardener, no matter how small or large the plot. Material for composting can simply be piled in a heap in a corner and left to rot, but a manufactured container certainly looks more appealing. Various kinds of compost containers are available from garden centres. Those made of plastic tend to resemble rubbish bins (garbage cans), so why not treat them in the same way, either decorating them or screening them with plants. An alternative is to make your own container from suitably treated timber, painted to match the house or the rest of the garden furniture. The design can be very simple, with timber slats fixed to corner posts, or more imaginative – such as a compost bin in the shape of a traditional beehive!

Garden sheds

Garden sheds are the classic means of storing tools and equipment. Most gardens can accommodate one, although smaller gardens may be restricted to a mini-shed or tool store (cabinet), which can be as small as 30cm (12in) deep and so can be tucked into a corner. The shed need not be an eyesore: if painted and decorated it can become an attractive part of the garden architecture. Alternatively, you can camouflage the shed with plants climbing up a trellis. Fix the trellis to timber battens using catches rather than screws, so you will be able to remove both climbers and trellis when the shed needs another coat of preservative.

All-weather shelves

Another solution is to put your goods on show. Garden pots can be very attractive and, displayed on all-weather shelves, can become part of the decorative appeal of the garden. This is an excellent solution for very small gardens and patios, all of which still need space for practical elements.

Instead of buying ready-made garden shelving, you could build

RIGHT: Every available space should be utilized in a small garden. Here, a box on a shelf has been used to grow a few vegetables.

BELOW RIGHT: These well-filled borders help to draw the attention away from a storage shed hidden in the corner of the garden.

BELOW: French baker's shelves against a house wall make a garden nursery for growing seedlings on – and do not take up much room.

your own from timber and treat it with exterior-quality paint. Old metal shelves can be given a new life using car spray paint or specially manufactured metal paint, which can even be sprayed straight over rust.

All shelves should be fixed firmly to the garden wall – avoid fixing to the house wall as this could lead to damp (moisture) problems. Once fitted, use shelves for displays, to store tools, or for bringing on young seedlings, which can look delightful potted up in ranks of terracotta.

Basic patterns

Having decided on the *style* of garden that you want, and the *features* that you need to incorporate, it is time to tackle the much more difficult task of applying them to your own garden. The chances are that your garden will be the wrong size or shape, or the situation or outlook is inappropriate to the style of garden that you have admired. The way round this impasse is to keep in mind a style without attempting to recreate it closely.

If you can't visualize the whole of your back or front garden as, say, a stone or Japanese garden, it may be possible to include the feature as an element within a more general design.

STARTING POINTS
If you analyse successful garden designs, most fall into one of the three basic patterns described below, though clever planting and variations on the themes almost always result in individual designs.

Circular theme
Circular themes are very effective at disguising the predictable shape of a rectangular garden. Circular lawns, circular patios, and circular beds are all options, and you only need to overlap and interlock a few circles to create a stylish garden. Plants fill the gaps between the curved areas and the straight edges.

Using a compass, try various combinations of circles to see whether you can create an attractive pattern. Be prepared to vary the radii and to overlap the circles if necessary.

Diagonal theme
This device creates a sense of space by taking the eye along and across the garden. Start by drawing grid lines at 45 degrees to the house or main fence. Then draw in the design, using the grid as a guide.

Rectangular theme
Most people design using a rectangular theme – even though they may not make a conscious effort to do so. The device is effective if you want to create a formal look, or wish to divide a long, narrow garden up into smaller sections.

Circular theme

Diagonal theme

Rectangular theme

Circular theme

Diagonal theme

Rectangular theme

Measuring up

Whether designing a garden from scratch or simply modifying what you already have, you need to draw a plan of the garden as it is. A drawn plan will enable you to see the overall desi clearly, and to experiment with different i before committing yourself to a definite o

HOW TO MEASURE THE SITE

YOU WILL NEED:

- One, or ideally two, 30m (100ft) tape measures (unless your garden is very short). Plasticized fabric is the best material as linen stretches and steel is difficult to manipulate.
- A steel rule about 1.8m (6ft) long (to measure short distances).
- Pegs to mark out positions, and meat skewers to hold one end of the tape in position if working alone.
- Clip-board and pad or graph paper.
- A couple of pencils, sharpener and an eraser.

1 Make a rough visual sketch by eye. It does not have to be accurate, but try to keep existing important features roughly in proportion. Leave plenty of space on the plan for adding dimensions. If necessary, use several sheets of paper, and indicate where they join.

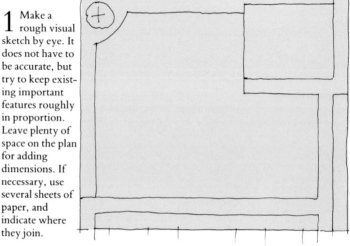

2 Choose a base line from which to start measuring. Make it a long, straight edge from which the majority of other points can be measured. A long fence or a house wall are often convenient starting points. From the straight edge or base line, measure off key points, such as the positions of windows, doors, any outbuildings, and so on. Measure out at right angles to establish the distances from the base line to the important features so that you can build the outline plan. Most key points on your plan can be established by measuring again at right angles from these right angles if necessary.

HOW TO MAKE
A SCALE DRAWING

1 To make a scale drawing, choose a scale that enables you to fit the garden (or at least a self-contained section of it) onto the one sheet of graph paper. Buy large sheets of graph paper if necessary. For most small gardens, a scale of 1:50 (2cm to a metre or ¼in to 1ft) is about right. If your garden is large, try a scale of 1:100. Draw your base line in first, then transfer the scale measurements. When the right-angle measurements have been transferred, draw in the relevant outlines.

DON'T MAKE WORK

When measuring your plot, don't waste time measuring and plotting the position of features that you have no intention of retaining in your replanned garden. If you intend to remove an unsightly tree or large shrub, or to pull down a garden shed that has seen better days, leave them off your plan – they will only clutter and confuse.

SLOPES AND
CONTOURS

In a large garden, slopes are often significant and may have to be taken into account. You can generally ignore gentle slopes in a small garden, or make a mental note of them.

HOW TO USE TRIANGULATION

It may not be possible to position some features or key points simply by measuring a series of right angles. These are best determined by a process known as triangulation. Using a known base, perhaps the corners of the house, simply measure the distance from two points to the position to be established. By transferring the scale distances from the two known points later, the exact position can be established. To transfer the triangulated measurements, set a compass to each of the scale distances in turn, and scribe an arc in the approximate position. Where the second arc intersects the first one, your point is established.

To fix position of tree, measure to A, then to B. Strike arcs on a scale drawing with compasses set at these measurements. Where the arcs cross shows the position of the tree in relation to the house.

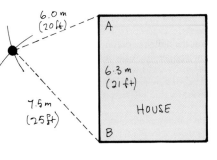

Creating the design

The most off-putting part of drawing up the design is the blank sheet of paper. Once this is overcome, producing alternative plans becomes fun, and there is the satisfaction of marking out the space to see the final effect in the garden. Just follow the stages below.

Stage 1: the basic grid

With the measurements transferred to graph paper you should already have a plan of your garden, showing any permanent structures and features that you want to retain.

Now superimpose onto this grid the type of design you have in mind – one based on circles, rectangles or diagonals, for example. If you are sure of the type of layout you want, draw these directly onto your plan in a second colour. If you think you might change your mind, draw the grid on a transparent overlay. For most small gardens, grid lines 1.8–2.4m (6–8ft) apart are about right.

Using an overlay, or a photocopy of your plan complete with grid, mark on the new features that you would like to include, in their approximate positions. You might find it helpful to cut out pieces of paper to an appropriate size and shape so that you can move them around.

Stage 2: the rough

Using an overlay or a photocopy, start sketching in your plan. If you can visualize an overall design, sketch this in first, then move around your features to fit into it. If you have not reached this stage, start by sketching in the features you have provisionally positioned – but be prepared to adjust them as the design evolves.

You will need to make many attempts. Don't be satisfied with the first one – it may be the best, but you won't know this unless you explore other options.

Don't worry about planting details at this stage, except perhaps for a few important plants that form focal points in the design.

Stage 3: the detailed drawing

Details such as the type of paving should be decided now – not only because it will help you to see the final effect, but also because you need to work to areas that use multiples of full blocks, slabs or bricks if possible. Draw in key plants, especially large trees and shrubs, but omit detailed planting plans at this stage.

Trying it out

Before ordering materials or starting construction, mark out as much of the design as possible in the garden. Use string and pegs to indicate the areas, then walk around them. If possible take a look from an upstairs window. This will give a much better idea of the overall design and whether paths and sitting areas are large enough.

Use tall canes to indicate the positions of important plants and new trees. This will show how much screening they are likely to offer, whether they may become a prob in time. By observing the shadow at various parts of the day, you'll know whether shade will be a problem – for other plants or for a sitting-out area.

CONSTRUCTION

You can employ a contractor to construct the garden for you, but many gardeners prefer to get hel with the main structural features, such as patios and raised beds, and do the rest of the work themselves to keep the cost down. Even the 'heavy' jobs are well within the ability of most gardeners with modest DIY skills. For more information see the next section.

Difficult Sites

DIFFICULT SITES AND PROBLEM SHAPES CAN BE A
challenge, but one that can be met with a little
determination and a touch of inspiration. Some
ways to tackle a selection of special areas are
suggested in the following pages.

If your garden is little more than a roof or a
balcony, or your house has been wedged in on a
building plot that is perhaps L-shaped, or even
triangular, traditional garden design techniques
might seem difficult to apply.

Many of the design ideas outlined in the
previous chapter can still be applied, however,
although you may require an alternative design
strategy for specific areas.

Patios usually feature as an element in a larger
overall design, but in turn have to be designed
themselves. Difficult sites like slopes, windy

ABOVE: *When your front
garden is as tiny as this,
compensate by making the
most of vertical space with
climbers and windowboxes.*

LEFT: *High walls, which
would otherwise have
dominated this garden, are
balanced by strong vertical
lines. Even the tops of the
walls have been put to good
use!*

alleys and passageways between houses demand thoughtful planning and appropriate plants.

Front gardens present a special problem, not because of size or shape, but because a large portion of the garden is usually dedicated to the car – often there is a broad drive to the garage or a hard standing area where the vehicle is left for long periods. Legal restrictions about what you can do with your front garden can be another potential problem – especially on estates where the developers or local authority want to maintain an 'open plan' style.

If conditions really are too inhospitable for permanent plants, or the space too limited for a 'proper' garden, containers can provide the answer. Use them creatively, and be prepared to replant or rotate frequently so that they always look good, whatever the time of year.

Unpromising backyards and basements can be transformed as much by a coat of masonry paint, a few choice plants, and some elegant garden furniture and tubs, as by an extensive – and expensive – redesign. Imagination and inspiration are the keynotes for this type of garden design.

In this chapter you will find many solutions to specific problems like these, and even if your particular difficulty is not covered exactly, you should be able to find useful ideas to adapt.

ABOVE: *This long, narrow plot has been broken up into sections, with an angled path so that you don't walk along the garden in a straight line.*

LEFT: *Roof gardens are always cramped, but by keeping most of the pots around the edge it is possible to create a sense of space in the centre.*

Unusual shapes

Turn a problem shape to your advantage by using its unusual outline to create a garden that stands out from others in your street. What was once a difficult area to fill will soon become the object of other gardeners' envy because of its originality.

Long and narrow – based on a circular theme
This plan shows a design based on a circular theme. The paved area near the house can be used as a patio, and the one at the far end for drying the washing, largely out of sight from the house. Alternatively, if the end of the garden receives more sun, change the roles of the patios.

Taking the connecting path across the garden at an angle, and using small trees or large shrubs to prevent the eye going straight along the sides, creates the impression of a garden to be explored.

Long and narrow – based on diagonal lines
This garden uses diagonals to divide the garden into sections, but the objective is the same as the circular design. It avoids a straight path from one end of the garden to the other, and brings beds towards the centre to produce a series of mini-gardens.

Long and tapered to a point
If the garden is long as well as pointed, consider screening off the main area, leaving a gateway or arch to create the impression of more beyond while not revealing the actual shape. In this plan the narrowing area has been used as an orchard, but it could be a vegetable garden.

Staggering the three paved areas, with small changes of level too, adds interest and prevents the garden looking too long and boring. At the same time, a long view has been retained to give the impression of size.

Corner sites

Corner sites are often larger than other plots in the road, and offer scope for some interesting designs. This one has been planned to make the most of the extra space at the side of the house, which has become the main feature rather than the more usual back or front areas.

Curved corner sites

Curved corner gardens are more difficult to design effectively. In this plan the house is surrounded by a patio on the left-hand side, and a low wall partitions the patio from the rest of the garden, making it more private. For additional interest, the drive is separated from the gravel garden by a path. Gravel and boulders, punctuated by striking plants such as phormiums and yuccas, effectively marry the straight edges with the bold curve created by the corner site.

Square and squat

A small square site like this offers little scope for elaborate design, so keep to a few simple elements. To give the impression of greater space the viewpoint has been angled diagonally across the garden. For additional interest, the timber decking is slightly raised creating a change of level. In a tiny garden a small lawn can be difficult to cut, but you could try an alternative to grass, such as chamomile, which only needs mowing infrequently.

A variety of styles have been used in this plan, a combination of diagonals and circles – both of which counter the basic rectangle of the garden itself.

L-shaped

L-shaped gardens offer plenty of scope. Even in a small garden, the opportunity to walk around and explore an area that cannot be seen from one place is a considerable plus-point. This plan shows the clever use of focal points – a tree seat and a seat at the far end – to create a reason to explore the garden. The patio area is partially covered with overhead beams and separated from the rest of the garden by raised flowerbeds.

Planning patios

The majority of small garden patios are little more than a paved area adjoining the back of the house, usually with little sense of design and often boring for most of the year. Your patio can be a key focal point that looks good in all seasons. A patio needs careful designing. It should be an attractive feature in its own right yet still form an integrated part of the total garden design.

Siting a patio

The natural choice for a sitting-out area is close to the house, especially if you plan a lot of outdoor eating. It's convenient, and forms an extra 'room', a kind of extension to the home, with a good view of the rest of the garden.

However, this spot may be shady for much of the day, in a wind tunnel created by adjacent buildings, or simply not fit in with your overall garden design.

Be prepared to move the patio away from the main building to gain

ABOVE: *Consider alternatives to paving slabs – bricks, clay and concrete pavers.*
BELOW: *The clever patio overhead makes this area function like an extra room.*

shelter or sun or if it suits your design. Using a position at one side of the garden, or even at the end, may give you more privacy from neighbours or a better view of the garden.

Choosing a shape

Most patios are rectangular – the logical shape for most gardens – but feel free to express yourself in a way that suits the overall design. A circular or semi-circular patio can form part of a circular theme. However, a round patio in a small garden designed around rectangles is likely to look incongruous.

Setting the patio at an angle to the house retains the convenience of straight lines, yet creates a strong sense of design. Consider using this shape on a corner of the house.

Patio boundaries

A clearly defined boundary will emphasize the lines of a design based on a rectangular grid. A low wall, designed with a planting cavity, will soften the hard line between paving and lawn.

High walls should be used with caution as a patio boundary, but occasionally they can be useful on one or perhaps two sides of the patio as a windbreak or privacy screen. A screen block wall will break up the space less than a solid wall, blocks or bricks. Planting suitable shrubs in front of the wall will soften the impact and help to filter the wind.

Changes of level

If the garden slopes towards the house a change of level helps to make a feature of a patio. Use a few shallow

LEFT: *Patios don't have to be by the house. A cosy corner of the garden can even be more appealing.*

steps to act like a 'doorway' to the rest of the garden.

A raised patio is a practical solution if your garden slopes away from the house. This creates a vantage point, a terrace from which you can overlook the rest of the garden. On a flat site, simply raising the level by perhaps 15cm (6in) can be enough to give the patio another dimension.

Paving materials

The choice of paving sets the tone of the patio: brash and colourful, muted but tasteful, integrated or otherwise. Do not be afraid to mix materials. Single rows of bricks will break up a large area of slabs. Choose any combination of materials that is appropriate for the setting.

BELOW: *A patio at its best where plants and people meet. The use of bricks instead of large slabs gives the illusion of size.*

If the patio is close to the house, choose bricks or pavers that match the house bricks closely. The facing bricks used for the house may be unsuitable for paving, but you should be able to achieve a close match.

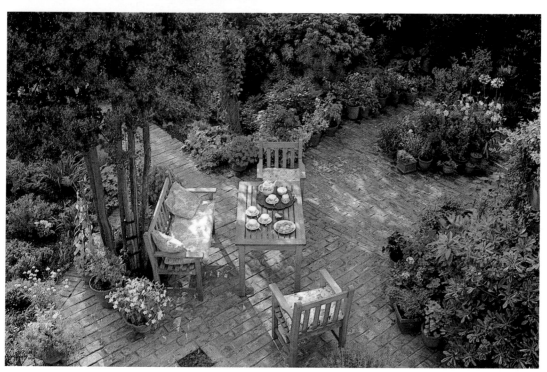

Finishing touches to patios

It is the finishing touches such as collections of containers and pergolas that turn a patio from a hard, flat and rather uninteresting area into a spot where you can enjoy relaxing.

Patio pergola

The overhead beams of a pergola help to give the patio an enclosed, integrated appearance that effectively extends the home. They provide excellent support for climbers that can bring useful shade as well as beauty. Avoid covering the whole patio with a thick canopy of climbers, however, as you will be searching for the sun, and spattered in drips after a summer shower.

Grape vines are good climbers for an overhead support, particularly as they lose their leaves in autumn, so you will get full winter sun. A relative with larger leaves and lovely autumn colour is *Vitis coignetiae*.

Floor joists are ideal for overhead beams, but they will need to be securely fixed to the house or garden wall using joist hangers. Use a cold chisel to remove some of the mortar

RIGHT: If you can position your patio away from the house, it may be necessary to construct a free-standing overhead feature.

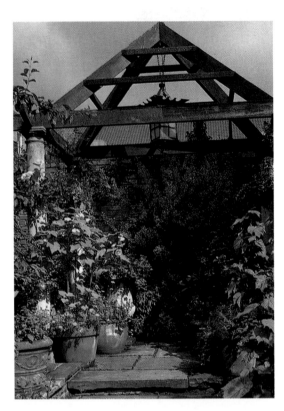

between the bricks, to make room for the joist hanger. Insert the hanger and mortar it into position. Once set, you can position the beam and nail it into place through the holes in the hanger.

Depending on the span of the pergola, you will need at least one cross-beam supported on posts. Use sturdy posts, together with ground anchors and supports to keep the timber out of contact with damp ground and prolong its life.

If you want permanent shade, or always to be screened from overlooking windows, you can fix reed or rush matting to the overhead beams. First you will need to nail timber battens on top of the beams, arranging them at right-angles. Then lay lengths of reed or rush matting,

ABOVE: *Joist hangers are used to secure sawn timber to the house for a patio overhead.*

GETTING THE HEIGHT RIGHT

Patio beams should always be high enough to give plenty of clearance beneath them when clothed with plants. Even plants trained and tied in regularly may have shoots that cascade downwards, and this is especially hazardous with thorny plants such as climbing roses. If the beams are used as hanging basket supports in an area where you will be walking, make sure the bottom of the basket will be above head height. As a guide, a clearance of about 2.4m (8ft) should be the minimum in most instances.

or pieces of bamboo screen, across the battens. Use carpet tacks or small nails to fix the shading into position.

Built-in features

A built-in barbecue blends with the garden in a way that a free-standing one cannot, and it will probably be used more often. Build it from bricks or blocks, depending on the material used in nearby buildings; include a sheet of mild steel, on which to burn the charcoal, and a grill on which to place the food.

It is not essential to cement the bricks or blocks in place, but do prepare the site before you begin, making sure it is both flat and firm. Lay a flat bed of bricks on the ground, then position the metal sheet. Lay two layers of bricks around three sides, leaving the front open. Be sure to stack the bricks so that the joints are staggered between the layers. Position the grill, then top with another two or three layers of bricks to provide some protection from the wind.

Built-in seats not only save space, they also give the patio a well-designed, sophisticated look. A few bright cushions give hard bench seats comfort and colour.

Planting spaces

Most people fill the space in their patio with plant containers, partly for

ABOVE: Even on a tiny patio, there is room to create levels. Here, raised beds are built in white-painted brick to match the garden walls.

BELOW: This irregularly paved area is softened by the addition of a collection of container-grown, largely pink and white plants.

convenience, but planting directly into the ground makes watering less of a chore. Permanent plants such as shrubs and small trees are best grown in the ground whenever possible. Some manufacturers make paving slabs that are designed to form a series of planting holes.

Raised beds

Building a raised bed, either against the house wall, or to form the patio boundary, enables you to bring far more plants into the patio area, especially useful in very small plots, where the patio is the garden. Build the bed from bricks, concrete blocks, or old railway sleepers, but be sure to provide a solid foundation. Place a layer of rubble then one of gravel in the bed, to provide good drainage, then fill with a suitable potting compost (soil mix), depending on the plants you want to grow.

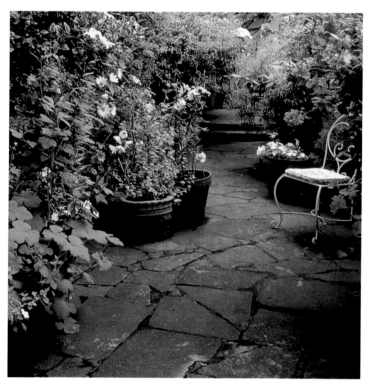

Front gardens

Front gardens greet visitors and can give delight
to passers-by. Unfortunately they are difficult to
design well if you have to accommodate a
driveway for the car, and possibly a separate path
to the front door. Even enthusiastic gardeners
with delightful back gardens are often let down
by an uninspired front garden. We have taken
four typical front gardens and shown how they
can be improved. Pick ideas from any of these
that you think could enhance your own space.

EXAMPLE ONE
This is a typical design for a front
garden: a rectangular lawn is edged
with a flower border used mainly for
seasonal bedding, and bordered by a
hedge. The redesigned garden
concentrates on softening the harsh
demarcation between drive and
ornamental section. Plants now play a
more prominent role, and the
emphasis is on informality instead of
angular lines.

Problems
● The drive isn't part of the garden
design, and this makes the area left for
plants and grass look even smaller.
● The soil close to the base of a hedge
is often dry and impoverished, so
bedding plants don't thrive.

Solutions
● Most of the lawn has been dispensed
with, and the flower beds enlarged
and planted with low-maintenance
shrubs. Plenty of evergreens have been
used to provide year-round interest.
● Gravel has been used for the drive,
and extended to form a broad and
informal sweep to the front door. Not
everyone likes gravel as a surface to
walk on, however, and pavers could
have been used instead. If plenty of
plants cascade over the edge, the
widening sweep would still look soft
and attractive.

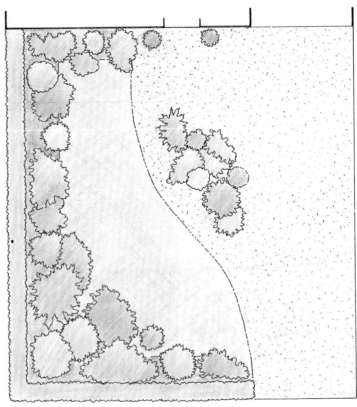

EXAMPLE TWO

Tall conifers along the drive dominate the garden and will continue to do so even after redesigning it. Remove trees that are too large rather than attempt to design around them.

Problems
- Tall hedges offer privacy, but here the scale is out of proportion, and depending on the aspect may keep out too much light.
- Rose beds are popular, but the small circular bed in the lawn looks incongruous with the rectangular design and can be difficult to mow around.
- Narrow, straight-edged beds around the edges make the lawn seem even smaller.

Solutions
- The concrete drive has been paved with bricks or brick-like pavers.
- A central planting strip has been left to break up the expanse of paving.
- The tall, dark hedge has been replaced with an attractive white ranch fence. The gravelled area beneath is planted with alpines.
- Climbing roses are planted by the house walls instead of a central weeping rose. They provide a fragrant welcome in summer.
- Existing borders remain to minimize the reconstruction.
- Small shrubs such as hebes and lavenders have been used, along with low-growing perennials like *Stachys lanata* (syn. *S. byzantina* or *S. olympica*) and *Bergenia cordifolia*, instead of seasonal bedding plants.
- A small deciduous tree, a crab apple, replaces the large conifer in the bottom corner. The area beneath can be planted with spring-flowering bulbs such as crocuses and snowdrops.
- The small circular bed has been enlarged and filled with gravel, as a base on which to stand pots.
- The narrow bed has been filled in with grass removed when the new paving in front of the house was laid. Bricks or blocks form a crisp edge.

Front gardens

EXAMPLE THREE

Gardens don't come much more
boring than this: a concrete drive,
small narrow flower bed in front of
the window and along the edge of
the garden, and a single flowering
cherry tree.

   The solution for this garden was a
simple one, as the redesigned garden
shows. The cottage-garden style
includes plants of all kinds which
grow and mingle happily together
with minimum intervention.

   Besides being a short cut to the
front door, the stepping stones
encourage exploration of the garden
and its plants. You actually walk
through the planting, which cascades
and tumbles around the paving slabs.
The garden design has been reversed,
with plants forming the heart of the
garden rather than peripherals around
the edge.

Problems

● Although the cherry is spectacular
in flower, and provides a show of
autumn colour, it is only attractive for
a few weeks of the year. Its present
position precludes any major redesign
and so it is best removed.
● Unclothed wooden fences add to
the drab appearance.
● Small flower beds like these lack
impact, and are too small for the
imaginative use of shrubs or
herbaceous perennials.

Solutions

● The lawn and tree have been
removed, and the whole area planted
with a mixture of dwarf shrubs,
herbaceous perennials, hardy annuals,
and lots of bulbs for spring interest.
● Stepping-stones have been
provided for those who want to take a
short-cut (they also make access for
weeding easier).
● The fences have been replaced with
low walls so that the garden seems
less confined.

EXAMPLE FOUR

This garden is a jumble of shapes and angles, and lacks any sense of design. With its new look, the old curved path has been retained because its thick concrete base and the drain inspection covers within it would have made it difficult to move, but all the other lines have been simplified and more appropriate plants used.

Problems

• Rock gardens are seldom successful on a flat site, and although small rock beds in a lawn can be made to resemble a natural rock outcrop, in this position the rocks can never look convincing.

• The tree here is young but will grow large and eventually cast considerable shade and dominate the garden.

• Small beds like this, used for seasonal bedding, are colourful in summer but can lack interest in winter. This curve sits uneasily with the straight edge at one end and the curve of the path at the other.

Solutions

• The rock garden has been paved so that the cultivated area is not separated by the drive.

• Gravel replaces the lawn. This needs minimal maintenance and acts as a good foil for the plants.

• Dwarf and medium-sized conifers create height and cover. By using species and varieties in many shades of green and gold, and choosing a range of shapes, this part of the garden now looks interesting throughout the year.

• Stepping-stones add further interest. Because it isn't possible to see where the stepping stones lead to from either end (the conifers hide the route), a sense of mystery is added and this tempts the visitor to explore.

• The existing path has been retained but covered with slate crazy-paving it looks more interesting.

• A pond creates a water feature.

• The awkward, narrow curving strip has been turned into a 'stream', with circulating water flowing over a cascade into the pond at one end.

Basement gardens and backyards

Some gardens are not just small, they are gloomy too because they are below street level, or hemmed in by tall walls. Because there is little that can be done to alter this sort of garden structurally, it is best to direct any efforts towards improving the environment and devising a strategy that helps plants survive, or at least ensure lots of lush-looking plants to flourish despite the handicaps. Not all of the techniques shown here will be applicable to your own garden, but most of them can be adapted to suit even the most unpromising site.

Using lighting

Garden lights can extend the hours of enjoyment you derive from your garden, and you don't need many of them for a lot of impact in a small area. You can illuminate most of the space – useful if you often entertain in the evening – or use just one or two spotlights to pick out dramatic elements in the design. Some can be swivelled so that you can highlight different features. For subtle lighting, a cheaper and pretty option is to use lanterns which hold candles.

Painting the walls

In a garden enclosed by walls or fences, you need to do everything possible to reflect light and make the background bright and cheerful. Painting the walls a pale colour will improve things dramatically.

Using trellis

Trellis can be used as a decorative feature in its own right, or as a plant support. If you want to make a feature of it, paint it white, but if it is used primarily as a plant support, make sure it has been treated with a non-toxic preservative. Enclose unsightly downpipes in a trellis 'box' over which you can grow an evergreen climber such as ivy.

Adding water features

The sound of running water is refreshing on a summer's day, and in a small area you only need a trickle to do the job. A wall spout (with a tiny pool at ground level, from which the

ABOVE: *Ferns thrive in shady positions where many other plants would languish. If you can provide moisture from a water feature, so much the better.*
RIGHT: *Even the tiniest basement garden or backyard has space for a water feature.*

water is recirculated) or a self-contained wall fountain is ideal.

Introducing wind chimes

Wind chimes both look and sound good. Choose one primarily for the sound it makes.

Training wall shrubs

Cover some of the walls with climbers, but try espalier or fan-trained fruit trees or espalier pyracanthas too.

Furnishing in style

White-painted furniture looks bright in a small, enclosed garden, but don't add too much furniture or the area will look cluttered rather than elegant.

Using containers with character

If the area is small, make everything work for its space. Instead of plastic containers, use interesting old kitchen utensils, or other unexpected holders, but be sure to add drainage holes to prevent waterlogging.

Focal points in shade

Basement areas and enclosed backyards are often inhospitable for plants – the light is poor and the walls keep off much of the rain. If, in addition, you have a tree that casts shade, even the shade-loving plants will struggle. Use these positions for ornaments or make them into focal points.

Planting ferns

Ferns do well in a cool, shady spot, so use them freely in those areas too dull for bright summer flowers. Try a collection of hardy ferns – they won't look dull if you nestle an attractive ornament among them, or include white flowers, perhaps backed by a white wall. On a hot summer's day the space will be an oasis of coolness and tranquillity.

Growing white-flowered plants

Use pale flowers if the area lacks direct sun. You won't be able to use plants that need strong sun light, but fortunately some of the best white-flowering plants are shade-tolerant. Try white varieties of impatiens and white nicotianas, for example. White flowers will show up more brilliantly than coloured ones in a dull spot.

Introducing exotics

Gardens enclosed by walls can be hot and sunny too, and being sheltered provides the ideal environment for many exotic plants to grow successfully. Try a few bold houseplants to create a tropical effect.

LEFT: Use wall pots and half baskets to make a dominant wall more interesting. They will be more effective staggered rather than in straight rows.

LEFT BELOW: White flowers, like this nicotiana, show up well in darker corners.

Making the most of steps

Open railings can be used as supports for attractive climbers, planted in pots at the base of the steps, but always keep them trimmed so that slippery leaves do not trail across the steps or obstruct the hand-rail. If the steps are very wide, place pots of bright flowers on the steps themselves to produce a ribbon of colour. Do not obstruct the steps. If there is no space on the steps, use a group of containers filled with flowers at the top and bottom of the stairway.

Fixing windowboxes and wall baskets

Use windowboxes lavishly – not only beneath windows but fixed to walls too. Windowboxes, wall pots and half-baskets can all bring cascades of colour to a bare wall. Stagger the rows instead of placing them in neat and tidy lines.

Capturing the scents

An enclosed garden is an ideal place in which to grow scented plants – the fragrances are held in the air instead of being carried off on the wind. Use plenty of aromatic plants, especially big and bold plants like daturas, and those with a heavy perfume such as evening-scented nicotianas and night-scented stocks.

Roof gardens

Despite the obvious handicaps, many people manage to create verdant planted areas on the top of roofs and tall buildings. If they are not overlooked, roof gardens can prove to be very private. However, there are potential structural limitations that must be checked out before you progress with any construction or planting plans. Never construct a roof garden without seeking professional advice from a structural engineer on whether the roof is able to take the weight.

You might be advised that it is safe, or told to keep the weight to certain areas – perhaps to the parapet wall – but you should abandon any idea of a roof garden if advised that it would be unsafe. Sometimes additional strengthening can be added, but this is a major and potentially expensive job.

RIGHT: Euonymus *fortunei 'Emerald 'n Gold'*, provides thick, vividly coloured cover, perfect for adding brightness to a roof garden.

BELOW: *Mock orange (*Philadelphus*) is one of the most popular of fragrant shrubs. The combination of pure white flowers and the sweet perfume suggest purity and innocence.*

WIND-TOLERANT PLANTS

Calluna vulgaris (Scotch heather)
Cornus alba (red-barked dogwood)
Cotinus coggygria (smoke bush)
Erica carnea (Alpine heath, winter heath)
Euonymus fortunei varieties
Hippophäe rhamnoides (sea buckthorn)
Hydrangea macrophylla
Hydrangea paniculata 'Grandiflora'
Lavatera olbia (tree mallow)
Lonicera pileata (honeysuckle)
Mahonia aquifolium (Oregon grape)
Olearia × *haastii*
Pachysandra terminalis
Pernettya mucronata
Philadelphus (mock orange)
Spiraea japonica
Tamarix tetrandra (tamarisk)

The shape of the roof will largely determine your design. Usually raised beds are built around the edge, with a sitting area in the centre. Pots can be used to provide variety within the paved area.

The roof is one place where artificial grass does have a place in the garden. Paving is heavy, artificial grass light. And it adds a touch of much-needed colour.

Keeping weight down

Do everything possible to keep down the weight. Avoid thick, heavy paving stones – if you do use paving, choose the thinnest. Use lightweight, loam-free potting composts (soil mixes), and plastic or glass-fibre containers rather than terracotta or wood.

Watering

Plants in containers need frequent watering in warm or windy weather. Carrying water to the rooftop is unappealing, and getting out a hosepipe (garden hose) to connect to a tap indoors is also cumbersome. Give some thought to installing an automatic watering system.

Using windbreak screens

A windbreak of some kind is likely to be an essential feature of a roof garden, since gusting wind and turbulence can play havoc with plants – and people. A windbreak screen can also be invaluable in providing privacy and in masking many of the unattractive features that a rooftop presents.

A structure that is partly permeable to the wind is much more effective than a solid one, where localized turbulence is created as the wind hits it and is deflected. Black windbreak netting becomes almost invisible if it is strung between two posts and then hidden behind a painted trellis, especially if plants are then grown up the trellis.

This form of windbreak is both effective and does not take up much room – an important consideration when space is at a premium.

ABOVE: *A roof garden can be quite spectacular, especially if the building is strong enough to take structural features such as those shown here.*

RIGHT: *Trellises provide privacy and shelter from the wind and can be fairly light which avoids increasing the weight.*

Using plants for protection

Where more room is available, a screen of tall, wind-tolerant shrubs installed along the most vulnerable side will act to shelter the area behind them. Many plants will tolerate this kind of exposure, while still providing colour and interest throughout the year. For a permanent screen, it is important to use mainly evergreen plants, although some of the tough deciduous shrubs can be included to add variety.

With this barrier in place, the effect of the wind should be considerably reduced, allowing you to complete a decorative planting scheme. As far as the space will allow, plan for a staggered effect, using tall plants or small shrubs at the back, next to the windbreak screen, and moving through to ever smaller perennials and annuals. At the front, you should end up with a relatively warm, sheltered space, which is ideal for less resilient plants – delicate spring bulbs, for example.

Balconies and verandas

For someone without a garden, a balcony may be their entire 'outdoor room', a 'garden' to enjoy from indoors when the weather is inclement. Even more than a patio, the balcony or veranda is an outdoor extension of the home.

The area is usually small, so the money you are prepared to spend on gardening will go a long way. Splash out on quality flooring and furniture, and ornate containers, which will create a classy setting for your plants.

Choosing flooring

The floor will help to set the tone and style, and it can make or mar a tiny 'garden' like this.

Paving slabs are best avoided: they are heavy, frequently lack the kind of refinement that you can achieve with tiles, and the size of individual slabs may be too large to look 'in scale' for the small area being covered.

Think of the veranda or balcony floor as you might the kitchen or conservatory floor – and use materials that you might use indoors. Quarry tiles and decorative ceramic tiles work well, and produce a good visual link with the house. Make sure ceramic tiles are frostproof however. Tiles are relatively light in weight, and their small size is in proportion to the area.

Timber decking is another good choice for a veranda.

The problem of aspect

Aspect is an important consideration. Unlike a normal garden, or even a roof garden, the light may be strong and intense all day, or there may be constant shade, depending on position. Balconies above may also cast shade.

If the aspect is sunny, some shade from above can be helpful. Consider installing an adjustable awning that you can pull down to provide shade for a hot spot. Choose sun-loving plants adapted to dry conditions for this situation – your indoor cacti and

RIGHT: *Roof gardens and balconies are often improved if you lay a wooden floor and create a timber overhead.*

succulents will be happy to go outside for the summer.

If the aspect is shady for most of the day a lot of flowering plants won't thrive. You may have to concentrate on foliage plants, though some bright flowers, such as impatiens and nicotiana, do well in shade.

Countering the wind

Like roof gardens, balconies are often exposed to cold and damaging winds. The higher a balcony the greater problem wind is likely to be.

To grow tender and exotic plants, provide a screen that will filter the wind without causing turbulent eddies. A trellis clothed with a tough evergreen such as an ivy is useful, or use screens of woven bamboo or reeds on the windiest side – these not only provide useful shelter and privacy, but make an attractive backdrop for plants in containers.

Adding colour round the year

Create a framework of tough evergreens to clothe the balcony or veranda throughout the year, and provide a backdrop for the more colourful seasonal flowers.

Use plenty of bright seasonal flowers in windowboxes or troughs along the edge, with trailers that cascade down over the edge.

In the more sheltered positions, grow lots of exotic-looking plants, and don't be afraid to give lots of your tough-leaved houseplants a summer holiday outside.

Pots of spring-flowering bulbs extend the season of bright flowers, but choose compact varieties – tall daffodils, for example, will almost certainly be bent forward as wind bounces back off the walls.

Add splashes of colour with cut flowers. In summer choose long-lasting 'exotics' such as strelitzias and anthuriums.

ABOVE: *In mild areas or a sheltered position, you can turn your balcony into a tropical garden.*

RIGHT: *Turn your balcony into an outdoor room where many indoor plants thrive in summer.*

Features and Structures

Overall garden design is important, but it is individual features that make a garden special. Major structural decisions, such as the type of paving to use, the shape of the lawn, or how to define the boundaries, have a significant impact, but even small details like ornaments and garden lights can lift a small garden above the ordinary. The use of containers is especially important in a small garden – on a tiny balcony they may *be* the garden. Use them imaginatively, choosing containers that are decorative, and grouping them for added interest.

ABOVE: *Create the urge to explore with small paths that lead to features such as seats and ornaments.*

OPPOSITE: *The garden floor is important, whether paving or a lawn, but it is features, like this arbour and its seat, that give the garden character.*

The Garden Floor

THE GARDEN FLOOR – LAWN, PAVING, PATHS, even areas of gravel or ground cover plants – can make or mar your garden. These surfaces are likely to account for more area than the beds and borders. Although they recede in importance when the garden is in full bloom, for much of the year they probably hold centre stage.

Removing existing paths and paved areas presents a practical problem. If they are laid on a thick bed of concrete you will probably have to hire equipment to break up the surface. Provided these areas do not compromise your design too much, it is much easier to leave as many as you can in position. Consider paving over the top with a more sympathetic material. It should be relatively easy to extend the area if you want to.

Lawns are more easily modified than paths and paved areas. At worst you can dig them up and resow or relay them. If you simply want to change the shape, you can trim off surplus grass or lift and relay just part of the lawn.

ABOVE: *Paths can be both functional and attractive, often giving the garden shape and form.*

OPPOSITE: *Hard land-scaping, such as bricks, combined with soft landscaping, such as lawns, can look very harmonious if designed with integration in mind.*

OPPOSITE ABOVE: *A brick edging marks the boundary between lawn and border, and serves the practical purpose of making mowing easier.*

LEFT: *Areas like this would soon become weedy if not densely planted. Here hostas suppress the weeds, and Soleirolia soleirolii spills over onto the path.*

Timber decking is very popular in some countries, seldom used in others. Much depends on the price of timber locally, and to some extent the climate, but decking should always be on your list of options.

There are useful alternatives to grass for areas that are not used for recreation or are seldom trodden on. Ground cover plants not only suppress weeds in flower beds, but can replace a lawn where the surface does not have to take the wear and tear of trampling feet. Inset stepping-stones to protect the plants. Where the garden is *very* small, low-growing ground cover may be much more practical than a lawn that is almost too tiny to cut with a mower.

Lawns

The lawn is often the centrepiece of a small garden, the canvas against which the rest of the garden is painted. For many gardeners this makes it worth all the mowing, feeding and grooming that a good lawn demands. If your lawn has to serve as a play area too, be realistic and sow tough grasses, and settle for a hard-wearing lawn rather than a showpiece. It can still look green and lush – the important consideration from a design viewpoint. Instead of aiming for a bowling-green finish, the shape of the lawn or a striking edging could be its strong visual message.

Working with circles

Circular lawns can be very effective. Several circular lawns, linked by areas of paving, such as cobbles, work well in a long, narrow garden.

If the garden is very small, all you will have space for is a single circular lawn. If you make it the centrepoint with beds around it that become deeper towards the corner of the garden, you will be able to combine small trees and tall shrubs at the back with smaller shrubs and herbaceous plants in front. To add interest, include a couple of stepping-stone paths that lead to a hidden corner.

Using rectangles

Rectangular lawns can look boring, but sometimes they can be made more interesting by extending another garden feature – such as a patio or flower bed – into them to produce an L-shaped lawn.

Alternatively, include an interesting feature such as a birdbath or sundial (often better towards one side or end of the lawn than in the middle). A water feature is another good way to break up a boring rectangle of grass.

An angled lawn

If you have chosen a diagonal theme for your design, you will probably want to set your lawn at an angle to the house so that it fits in with the

ABOVE RIGHT: *A sweeping lawn can help to create a sense of perspective.*
RIGHT: *This lawn would look boring with straight edges. The curves add style.*

other features. The same rectangle of lawn becomes much more interesting when set at an angle of about 45 degrees. By lifting and patching the lawn, you may be able to achieve this without having to start from scratch.

Creating curves

A sweeping lawn with bays and curves where the flower borders ebb and flow is very attractive. It is difficult to achieve in a small garden. However, you can bring out a border in a large curve so the grass disappears around the back. You may be able to do this by extending the border into an existing rectangular lawn.

Changing height

If you have to create an impression in a small space, try a raised or sunken lawn. The step does not have to be large – 15–23cm (6–9in) is often enough. If making a sunken lawn, always include a mowing edge so that you can use the mower right up to the edge of the grass.

ABOVE: *Sunken lawns make a bold feature.*

KEEPING A TRIM EDGE

Circular lawns must be edged properly. Nothing looks worse than a circle that isn't circular, and of course constant trimming back will eat into the lawn over the years. To avoid this, incorporate a firm edging, such as bricks placed on end and mortared into position, when you make the lawn.

Where the edges are straight use proprietary lawn edging strips.

HOW TO CREATE A MOWING EDGE

If flowers tumble out of your borders, or there is a steep edge that makes mowing difficult, lay a mowing edge of bricks or paving slabs.

1 Mark out the area of grass to be lifted using the paving as a guide. Lift the grass where you want to lay the paved edge. To keep the new edge straight, use a half-moon edger against the paving slab. Then lift the grass to be removed by slicing it off with a spade.

2 Make a firm base by compacting gravel or a mixture of sand and gravel where the paving is to be laid. Use a plank of wood to ensure it is level. Allow for the thickness of the paving and a few blobs of mortar.

3 It is best to bed the edging on mortar for stability, but as it will not be taking a heavy weight just press the slabs onto blobs of mortar and tap level (use a spirit-level to double-check).

Making a new lawn

You can make a new lawn using either seed or turf (sod). Each method has its advantages and disadvantages. Your choice will depend largely on how long you – and your family – can bear to wait before you use the lawn, and how much money you are prepared to spend.

SOWING A NEW LAWN

The advantage of growing a lawn from seed is that it is usually less expensive than laying turf (sod) and you can choose the grass seed mixture to suit your own particular needs. Seed companies usually offer a range of mixtures for specific purposes, such as play areas or under shade, but they can be expensive. The main disadvantage of using seed is that it can take the best part of a year for the lawn to established.

Thorough ground preparation is essential for a quality lawn, and this should start several weeks before sowing. You can sow in either spring or autumn, as long as the ground is warm and not too dry.

1 Dig the ground well, and remove any difficult or deep-rooted perennial weeds. Rake the soil level. Use pegs marked with lines 5cm (2in) down from the top as a guide.

2 Allow the soil to settle for a week, then consolidate it further by treading evenly to remove air pockets. Shuffle your feet over the area, first in one direction then at right angles.

3 Rake the soil to produce a fine soil for sowing seeds. Allow weed seeds to germinate. Hoe them off or use a weedkiller that leaves the ground safe for replanting within days.

4 Use string to divide the site into strips 1m (1yd) wide, and use a pair of canes to mark off a 1m (1yd) length. Move the canes along the strips as you sow.

5 Use a small container that holds enough seed for a square metre or square yard (make a mark on it if the amount only partly fills it). Scatter the seeds as evenly as possible.

6 For a large area, it is worth hiring a seed distributor. Check the seed delivery rate on paper first. Rake the seed into the soil surface and use a water sprinkler to keep the soil moist.

LAYING A LAWN FROM TURF (SOD)

Turf (sod) provides the best method of creating a lawn quickly – you can use it within a few months – and soil preparation is a little less demanding. You will usually find that it is a more expensive option than growing a lawn from seed, but many gardeners are happy to pay a premium for the convenience.

1 You should dig and consolidate the soil as described for seed, but there is no need to wait a few weeks to allow weeds to emerge – the turf (sod) will prevent weed seeds germinating. Start by laying the turf (sod) along a straight edge.

2 Use a plank to stand on while you lay the next row, as this will help to distribute your weight. Stagger the joints from row to row, to create a bond as if you were laying bricks. If using a long roll of turf (sod), there will be fewer joints. Make sure that these do not align.

3 Tamp down each row of turf (sod) (you can use the head of a rake as shown), then roll the plank forwards to lay the next row.

4 Brush sieved sandy soil, or a mixture of peat and sand, into the joints. This will help to bind the turves (pieces of sods) together

5 Shape edges when the lawn is laid. Lay a hose or rope to form the shape for a curved edge, or use a straight-edged piece of wood for a straight edge, and trim with a half-moon edger.

Weed-free paths and lawns

A weed-filled lawn will spoil your garden, but with modern weedkillers it is quite easy to eliminate weeds to leave your grass looking like a lawn rather than a mown wildflower meadow. It's easy, too, to clear garden paths of unsightly weeds – and to keep them that way.

Killing weeds in lawns and paths
The only place where weeds are really acceptable is in a specially designated wildlife corner, although some people find daisies and other so-called weeds in the lawn a very attractive feature. Generally, however, weeds have to be controlled, and pulling them up by hand is a time-consuming job that few of us enjoy. It is even more frustrating if they grow back again within a few days.

The method on the opposite page shows how easily you can deal with weeds in the lawn. Paths can also be kept weed-free for a season using one of the products sold for the purpose. Most of these contain a cocktail of chemicals which act

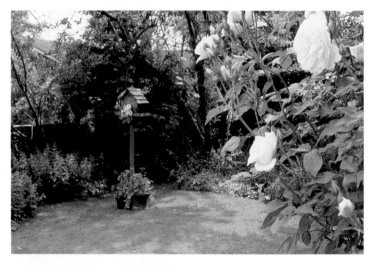

quickly to kill existing weeds and others that prevent the growth of new ones for many months. A single application should be enough to keep the path clear of weeds for a long time. It is a good idea to use an improvised shield to prevent the weedkiller being blown by the wind onto the flowerbeds while you are applying it to the paths.

ABOVE: *This garden illustrates the beauty of a well-maintained lawn that is free of weeds. The lawn in this garden is the perfect spot for a bird house, which will attract many local birds, and possibly squirrels, all year round. The addition of a couple of rose bushes adds elegance and interest to this very pretty garden.*

LEFT: *The most beautiful and expensive of paths can be marred by weeds. Either make sure they are mortared between the joints, or use a path weedkiller to keep them smart.*

KILLING WEEDS IN LAWNS

This method ensures a weed-free lawn with as little as one application a year.

1 Weeds in lawns are best controlled by a selective hormone weed-killer, ideally in mid- or late spring. These are usually applied as a liquid, using a dribble bar attached to a watering-can. To ensure even application, you should mark out the lawn with string lines, spacing them the width of the dribble bar apart.

2 Always mix and apply the weedkiller as recommended on the packet by the manufacturer. There are a number of different plant hormones used, some killing certain weeds better than others, so always check that the product is recommended for the weeds you most want to control. When mixed, simply walk along each strip slowly enough for the droplets from the dribble bar to cover the area evenly.

3 If your lawn also needs feeding, you can save time by using a combined weed and feed. The most efficient way to apply these products – which are likely to be granular rather than liquid – is with a fertilizer spreader.

4 If you only have a few trouble-some weeds in a small area, it is a waste of time and money treating the whole lawn. For this job a spot weeder that you dab or wipe onto the offending weed should work very well.

WORDS OF WARNING

Weedkillers are extremely useful aids, but they can be disastrous if you use the wrong ones, or are careless in their application.

• Always check to see whether it is a total or selective weedkiller.
• If selective, make sure it will kill your problem weeds – and make sure it is suitable for applying to the area you have in mind. Lawn weedkillers should be used only on lawns.
• Don't apply liquid weed-killers on a windy day.
• For greater control, use a dribble bar rather than an ordinary rose on watering-cans.
• Keep a watering-can specially for applying weed-killers, otherwise residues may harm your plants.
• Avoid run-off into flowerbeds, and if necessary use a shield while applying a weedkiller.

Caring for lawns in autumn

Autumn is a good time to prepare your lawn for the year ahead, and the best time to tackle any long-term improvements. Tasks such as raking out lawn debris as well as feeding and aerating will improve the quality of your lawn greatly if they are carried out every year.

1 Over the years, grass clippings and debris form a 'thatch' on the surface of your lawn. This affects growth of the grass and should be removed with a lawn rake.

2 If grass growth is poor, the soil beneath may have become compacted, preventing oxygen reaching the plant roots. You can aerate the lawn by pushing the prongs of a garden fork about 15cm (6in) into the ground.

3 Brush a soil improver into the holes made by the fork. Use sand or a mixture of fine soil and sand if the ground is poorly drained. Alternatively, use peat or a peat-substitute, or very fine, well-rotted garden compost if the ground is sandy.

4 If your lawn is in poor condition and needs reviving, apply an autumn lawn feed. It is essential that you use one formulated for autumn use, as spring and summer feeds will contain too much nitrogen.

5 You can tidy an uneven lawn edge at any time, but doing it in autumn will mean one less job to do at busier times of year. Use a half-moon edger against a board held in position with your feet. This is not an annual job.

MECHANICAL AIDS

Working on large areas such as lawns can be exhausting and back-breaking work. Raking out thatch is a particularly tiring job. If you have a fairly large lawn area, it is definitely worth investing in a powered lawn rake. This will remove the thatch both rapidly and efficiently for you.

You can also take the sheer drudgery out of aerating your lawn by using a hollow-tined aerator that removes a core of soil effortlessly and efficiently.

If you need to remove a large quantity of leaves from your lawn in the autumn, you also might prefer to invest in a special leaf sweeper or blower.

Collecting and composting leaves

Never waste the leaves that accumulate in your garden. They will make excellent garden compost if you collect them and allow them to rot down.

In addition, if they are left on the ground, they can damage areas of grass as well as smother other small plants on the edges of beds and borders.

1 Don't let leaves lie for long on your lawn. The grass beneath them will turn yellow and be prone to disease. On a small lawn, rake them up with a lawn rake.

2 The leaves that build up on paths and drives are best brushed up with a broom or besom.

DON'T LET LEAVES SMOTHER SMALL PLANTS

If you let leaves lie for long on small plants such as alpines, they may begin to rot due to the lack of light and free movement of air. The leaves will also provide a haven for slugs and other pests that may eat your plants. Wait until most of the leaves have fallen from the trees, then go around and pick them off vulnerable plants.

3 You can buy special tools to lift the leaves without too much bending, but using two pieces of wood is also an effective method of lifting them once they have been brushed into a heap.

4 Leaves can be added to the compost heap, but some leaves rot down slowly, so it is best to compost large quantities on their own. Rotted leaves are also a useful addition to potting composts (soil mixes).

Naturalizing bulbs

Many spring- and autumn-flowering bulbs look delightful naturalized in a lawn. Planted at random among the grass and left undisturbed, they soon form large colonies, and will flower year after year. One possible drawback is that you won't be able to cut the lawn for several weeks after flowering, until the leaves have died down – although some people may see this as an advantage.

What to plant?

If you are lucky enough to have space in your garden to naturalize bulbs in lawn or an area of longer grass, then choose those bulbs that will multiply and flower freely. These include an array of spring-flowering bulbs such as crocuses, daffodils (*Narcissus*), snowdrops (*Galanthus*), small fritillaries (*Fritillaria*) and winter aconites (*Eranthis hyemalis*). Even planting just a few early-flowering tulips can create a spectacular swathe of bright colour. Although tulips look spectacular growing within the lawn, avoid planting them too close together because their broad leaves can smother the grass beneath.

Naturalizing is also an ideal way of growing colchicums: these are leafless at flowering time in autumn (the leaves appear later in the spring) and the grass will help to disguise the bare stems. Despite this these delightful plants are well worth growing for their large goblet-shaped, usually pink or white, flowers.

You can use a number of different bulbs, or grow just one type, and choose flowers all of the same colour, or an eye-catching mixture. Even if you decide to limit yourself to the familiar daffodils and crocuses, there are many different kinds of these bulbs to choose from, so you will have plenty of choice.

A variety of methods

There are several different ways of naturalizing bulbs. You can dig individual planting holes in the grass (satisfactory for just a few bulbs), or lift strips of turf (sod) to expose a larger area of soil for planting. Alternatively, if you have a lot of bulbs to plant over a wide area, then individual planting holes may be more appropriate than creating larger excavations to take a group of bulbs.

For more delicate bulbs, which won't be able to compete with strong-growing turf (sod), the best method is to plant them in bare but well-cultivated ground and sow a fine grass seed over the top.

HOW TO NATURALIZE SMALL BULBS IN GRASS

1 If you have a lot of small bulbs, such as crocuses and winter aconites, to plant in a limited area, it is best to lift sections of turf (sod) and plant the bulbs underneath. Use a spade to slice beneath the grass, then roll it back for planting.

2 Loosen the soil with a fork first as it will be very compacted, and work in a slow-acting fertilizer such as bonemeal.

3 Scatter the bulbs randomly. Very small ones can be left on the surface; larger ones are best buried slightly. Cover the bulbs with twice their own depth of soil. Roll back the grass, firm it well, and water.

DIVIDING ESTABLISHED CLUMPS

1 Naturalized bulbs and those left in borders for years will eventually need dividing to stop overcrowding, which will lead to deteriorating results. Lift very large clumps when the leaves have just died back, or any time when the bulbs are dormant.

2 Separate the clump into smaller pieces and then replant. You do not have to separate the clump into individual bulbs.

WHICH WAY UP

It is of great importance to check that a bulb is the right way up when planted, with the growing point upwards. Most bulbs have a very obvious top and bottom and present no problem. Others, especially corms and tubers, can cause confusion because they lack an obvious growing point. If you are in any doubt, it is best to plant them on their side – the shoot will grow upwards and the roots down.

A few bulbs that do have an obvious top are planted on their side because the base tends to rot in wet soil – although these are rare exceptions. *Fritillaria imperialis* is sometimes planted this way, and it is always worth planting vulnerable bulbs on a bed of grit or coarse sand to encourage good drainage around the base.

HOW TO NATURALIZE LARGE BULBS IN GRASS

1 Large bulbs such as daffodils are easier to plant using a bulb planter, which takes out a core of soil. Scatter the bulbs randomly over the surface so that the display will look natural.

2 Push the bulb planter into the soil, twisting it a little if the ground is hard, then pull it out with the core of soil. Place the bulb at the bottom of the hole.

3 Crumble some soil from the bottom of the core. Drop some of this into the hole to fall around the bulb and make sure it is not suspended in a pocket of air. Then press the core back into position.

Grass substitutes

Grass is still the best form of living carpet for a large lawn subject to wear, but small areas are ideal for experimenting with those alternatives to grass that will give your garden a highly individual touch.

None of the plants described will form such a hard-wearing lawn as grass, but they have their own attractions. Bear in mind that you can't use a normal selective lawn weedkiller on these broad-leaved plants, so be prepared for some hand weeding. On a small-scale, however, this is manageable, and a price worth paying if you fancy a lawn with a difference.

Scent with chamomile

This classic grass substitute has been used for centuries to make an attractive, pale green lawn. The fact that it is aromatic when walked on combined with an ability to tolerate a reasonable amount of wear, makes it an excellent choice for a small, ornamental area. But, like the other plants suggested here, chamomile is not a practical proposition for a children's play area.

What it looks like Chamomile has small, feathery, aromatic leaves and white daisy flowers, though the non-flowering 'Treneague' is preferable as flowers spoil the close carpeted effect. It spreads rapidly by creeping stems, which is one reason that it makes such a good substitute for grass.

How to sow or plant You can sow seed, but the best lawns are established from young offshoots or cuttings of a non-flowering variety. If you buy seed, start them off in seed trays to produce young plants to put out later. If you buy young plants or offshoots by post they will probably arrive in a plastic bag – larger specimens from a garden centre will

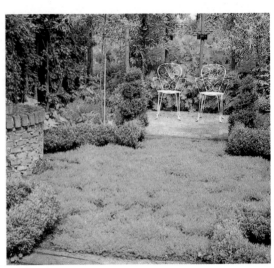

RIGHT: *For an attractive-looking lawn in a small area not subject to heavy wear, chamomile is ideal.*

BELOW: *Thyme is tough enough to grow between paving, where it is often crushed underfoot.*

be pot-grown but you will pay more.

Plant 23cm (9in) apart – closer if you have a lot of seed-raised plants or cuttings of your own. Close spacing will achieve quicker cover, but the final result is unlikely to be any better. If you are growing from seed, start off under glass in early spring, and plant out in late spring, rather than sow directly in the open ground like grass.

Trim with the mower set high to encourage the development of sideshoots if the plants do not seem to be making enough bushy side growth. You will have to mow flowering forms occasionally to keep the plants compact.

You may find chamomile under

one of its two widely used Latin names *Chamaemelum nobile* or *Anthemis nobilis*.

Thyme

Thyme is another popular alternative to grass for a small area, but be sure to choose the right kind of thyme. The culinary species is too tall and bushy for this purpose. Choose the more prostrate *Thymus serpyllum*.

Thymes are good for dry soils, and do well in alkaline (chalky) areas. Unfortunately they tend to become woody and straggly after about four or five years. Cuttings are easy to root, however, so periodic replanting should not be an expensive task.

What it looks like Thymes have small, aromatic leaves, and *T. serpyllum* has low, spreading growth 5cm (2in) high. Clusters of tiny purple, white, pink, red, or lavender flowers appear in summer.

How to sow or plant Plant about 23cm (9in) apart. You can raise your own plants from seed (sow in trays, not directly into the soil).

HOW TO PLANT A THYME LAWN

1 Prepare the ground thoroughly by digging over the area and levelling it at least a month before planting. Dig out any weeds that appear. Hoe off seedlings. Rake level.

2 Water the plants in their pots, then set them out about 20cm (8in) apart, in staggered rows (a little closer for quicker cover, a little further apart for economy but slower cover).

3 Knock the plant from its pot and carefully tease out a few of the roots if they are running tightly around the edge of the pot.

5 Water the ground thoroughly and keep well watered for the first season.

4 Plant at their original depth, and firm the soil around the roots before planting the next one.

ABOVE: *Clover – in this case wild white – makes a novel lawn, as gardeners usually spend so much time trying to eliminate it.*

Clover

If clovers seem to thrive better than the grass in your existing lawn, eliminate the grass and try a clover lawn – it will probably look greener than grass in dry weather! You will, of course, still have to weed, to remove non-clover seedlings.

What it looks like The three-lobed leaves of the clover are well known. The white or purple flowers should not be a feature of a clover lawn – mow the plants before they are tall enough to flower.

How to sow or plant Clover is sown in-situ, on ground cleared of weeds, ideally in spring. You can sometimes buy clover seed from companies specializing in wild flower seeds. White clover (*Trifolium repens*) is a good one to sow for a lawn.

Cotula

There are several low-growing species of cotula that can be used for a lawn. In some countries they are regarded as lawn weeds, in others lawns are sometimes created for them. They are worth a try if you are prepared for a rampant plant that may need curtailing.

What it looks like Cotulas are low-growing plants, with divided, fern-like leaves. The creeping stems root as they grow. Masses of small yellow flowers are produced in mid summer.

How to sow or plant Plant about 10–15cm (4–6in) apart. *Cotula coronopifolia* is the one usually used as a grass substitute. The cheapest way is to sow seed, but this is only likely to be available from suppliers dealing in the less common plants.

Imaginative paving

Most small gardens have a patio or at least a paved area close to the house. Often it is the main feature around which the remainder of the back garden is arranged. It can be the link that integrates home and garden. At its worst, paving can be boring and off-putting; at its best it can make a real contribution to the overall impact of the garden.

On the following pages you will find a selection of popular paving materials, with suggestions for use, and their advantanges and disadvantages. Always shop around because the availability and price of natural stones vary enormously, not only from country to country, but also from area to area.

Even the availability of man-made paving will vary from one area to another. Choosing the material is only part of the secret of successful paving – how you use it, alone or combined with other materials, is what can make an area of paving mundane or something special.

LEFT: *Bricks and pavers often look more attractive if laid to a pattern such as this herringbone style.*

Colour combinations
Your liking for bright and brash colour combinations will depend on the effect you want to create. Be wary of bright colours though – they can detract from the plants, although they will mellow with age.

Sizing up the problem
In a small garden, large-sized paving units can destroy the sense of scale. Try small-sized paving slabs (which are also easier to handle), or go for bricks, pavers, or cobbles.

Mix and match
Mixing different paving materials can work well, even in a small space. Try areas or rows of bricks or clay pavers with paving slabs, railway sleepers with bricks, in fact any combination that looks good together and blends with the setting. Avoid using more than three different materials, however, as this can look too fussy in a small garden.

Paving patterns
You can go for a completely random pattern – crazy-paving is a perfect example – but most paving is laid to a pre-planned pattern using rectangular paving slabs or bricks. Look at the brochures for paving slabs. These usually suggest a variety of ways in which the slabs can be laid.

Although a large area laid with slabs of the same size can look boring, avoid too many different sizes, or complex patterns in a small space. Simplicity is often more effective.

Bricks and clay pavers are often the best choice for a small area, because their small size is more likely to be in harmony with the scale of the garden. The way they are laid makes a significant visual difference, however, so choose carefully.

The stretcher bond is usually most effective for a small area, and for paths. The herringbone pattern is suitable for both large and small areas, but the basket weave needs a reasonably large expanse for the pattern to be appreciated.

Stretcher bond

Herringbone

Basket weave

HOW TO LAY PAVING

1 Excavate the area to a depth that will allow for about 5cm (2in) of compacted hardcore topped with about 3–5cm (1–2in) of ballast, plus the thickness of the paving and mortar. As an alternative to hardcore topped with ballast, you can use 5cm (2in) of scalpings. Check the depth of the foundation before laying the paving. If adjoining the house, make sure that the paving will end up below the damp-proof course.

2 Put five blobs of mortar where the slab is to be placed – one at each corner, and the other in the middle.

3 Alternatively, cover the area where the paving is to be laid with mortar, then level.

4 Position the slab carefully, bedding it on the mortar.

5 Use a spirit-level to ensure that the slab is level, but use a small wedge of wood under one end to create a slight slope over a large area of paving so that rainwater runs off freely. Tap the slab down further, or raise it by lifting and packing in a little more mortar. Position the level over more than one slab (place it on a straight-edged piece of wood if necessary).

6 Use spacers of an even thickness to ensure regular spacing. Remove these later, before the joints are filled with mortar.

7 A day or two after laying the paving, go over it again to fill in the joints. Use a small pointing trowel and a dryish mortar mix to do this. Finish off with a smooth stroke that leaves the mortar slightly recessed. This produces an attractive, crisp look. Wash any surplus mortar off the slabs before it dries.

Paving materials

There are plenty of paving materials from which to choose, so spend time looking through brochures and visit garden centres and builders' merchants before you come to a decision.

PAVING SLABS
Rectangular paving slabs

The majority of paving slabs are based on a full-sized slab 45 × 45cm (18 × 18in) or 45 × 60cm (18 × 24in). Half and quarter slabs may be a little smaller in proportion to allow for mortar joints. Thickness may vary according to make, but provided you mix only those made by the same manufacturer this won't matter.

A *smooth* surface can be boring, slippery, and a little too much like public paving, but many have a *textured* finish. Textures vary. A riven finish usually looks like natural stone, an exposed aggregate finish has exposed gravel to give a natural-looking non-slip finish.

Slabs imprinted with a section of a larger pattern are usually unsatisfactory in a small area. As quite a large area of paving is usually required to complete the pattern, they only emphasize the space limitations.

Shaped paving slabs

Use shaped slabs with caution. Circular slabs are useful for stepping-stones, but are difficult to design into a small patio. Hexagonal slabs also need a fairly large area to be appreciated. Special half-block edging pieces are usually available to produce a straight edge.

Paved and cobbled finish slabs

Some designs are stamped with an impression to resemble groups of pavers or bricks, some containing as many as eight basket-weave 'bricks' within the one slab. They create the illusion of smaller paving units, and are very effective in a small area.

RIGHT: *Bricks, unlike clay pavers, are laid with mortared joints. This can emphasize the design.*

TOP LEFT: *Slabs like this are particularly useful for a small area because they give the illusion of smaller paving units.*

TOP RIGHT: *Paving slabs with a riven finish look convincingly like real weathered stone.*

MIDDLE LEFT: *Paving slabs will always weather. Pale colours like this will soon look darker, while bright colours will become muted.*

MIDDLE RIGHT: *Hexagonal paving slabs can be attractive, but are not usually satisfactory in a very small area.*

BOTTOM: *Rectangular shapes like this can be used alone, or integrated with other sizes to build up an attractive design.*

Planting circles

A few manufacturers produce paving slabs with an arc taken out of one corner. Four of these placed together leave a circular planting area for a tree or other specimen plant.

BRICKS AND PAVERS

Bricks and pavers are especially useful for a small garden. You can create an attractive design even in a small area, and you may be able to obtain them in a colour and finish that matches your home, which will produce a more integrated effect.

Always check that the bricks are suitable for paving, however, as some intended for house building will not withstand the frequent saturation and freezing that paths and patios are subjected to. After a few seasons they will begin to crumble. Clay pavers, on the other hand, have been fired in a way that makes them suitable for paving. Concrete pavers and blocks are another option, though these are usually more suitable for a drive than a small patio.

Rectangular pavers

Clay pavers look superficially like bricks but are designed to lock together without mortar. They are also thinner than most bricks, though this is not obvious once they have been laid. Concrete pavers or paving blocks are laid in a similar way and are more attractive than concrete laid in-situ for a drive. They can look a little 'municipal'.

Interlocking pavers and blocks

Concrete pavers or blocks are often shaped so that they interlock. Interlocking clay pavers may also be available.

Bricks

Bricks require mortar joints – they won't interlock snugly like clay pavers. On the other hand you may be able to use the same bricks for raised beds and low walls, giving the whole design a more planned and well-integrated appearance.

To use bricks economically, lay them with their largest surface exposed, not on edge. This excludes the use of pierced bricks (which have holes through them). It does not matter if they have a frog (depression) on one side, provided this is placed face-down.

Setts and cobbles

Imitation granite setts, which are made from reconstituted stone, and cobbles, which are natural, large, rounded stones shaped by the sea or glaciers, are both excellent for small areas of irregular shape. Their size makes them much easier to lay to a curve. Bed them into a mortar mix on a firm base.

Tiles

Quarry and ceramic tiles are appropriate for small areas near the house, or to create a patio that looks just that little bit different. Always make sure ceramic tiles are frostproof. Lay them on a concrete base that has been allowed to set, and fix them with an adhesive recommended by the supplier or manufacturer.

LEFT: *Hard paving comes in many forms. The top row shows (from left to right) natural stone sett, clay paver, clay brick, artificial sett. The centre row shows a typical range of concrete paving blocks. The bottom row illustrates some of the colours available in concrete paving slabs.*

Paths and path materials

As with any other garden structure, paths should be designed to suit the purpose they are to serve. There are a wide range of materials on the market to suit every need so shop around before deciding which you require.

Practical paths should be functional first and attractive second. Drives for cars and paths to the front door must be firmly laid on proper foundations. And don't skimp on width – it is extremely frustrating for visitors if they have to approach your door in single file. It might be better for the route to take a detour, perhaps forming an L-shape with the drive, if there isn't enough space for a wide path directly to the door.

Internal paths, used to connect one part of the garden to another, can be more lightly constructed, and are softened with plants.

Casual paths, which often lead nowhere and are created for effect, such as stepping-stones through a flower bed, can be lightly constructed and much less formal in style.

RIGHT: *Although the gaps between these paving slabs have been filled with chipped bark in this example, you could also use gravel.*

BELOW: *Paving can reflect artistic ambitions.*
BELOW RIGHT: *Victorian-style rope edging.*

Bricks and pavers
These are ideal materials for internal garden paths that have to be both practical and pretty. Complex bonding patterns are best avoided unless the path is very wide.

Paving slabs
By mixing them with other materials the look of paving slabs can be much improved. A narrow gravel strip either side can look smart, and the gravel can be extended between the joints to space out the slabs. The slab-and-gravel combination is ideal if you need a curved path.

A straight path can be broken up with strips of beach pebbles mortared between the slabs. Tamp them in so that they are flush with the surrounding paving.

Crazy-paving

Use this with caution. In the right place, and using a natural stone, the effect can be mellow, and harmonize well with the plants. Be more wary of using broken paving slabs – even though they are cheap. Coloured ones can look garish, and even neutral slabs still look angular and lack the softness of natural stone.

Path edgings

Paths always make a smarter feature with a neat or interesting edging. If you have an older-style property, try a Victorian-style edging. If it is a country cottage, try something both subtle and unusual, like green glass bottles sunk into the ground so that just the bottoms are visible. Or use bricks: on their sides, on end, or set at an angle of about 45 degrees.

CREVICE PLANTS

Plants look attractive and soften the harsh outline of a rigid or straight path. They are easy to use with crazy-paving or any path edged with gravel. It may be necessary to excavate small holes. Fill them with a good potting mixture. Sow or plant into these prepared pockets.

Some of the best plants to use for areas likely to be trodden on are chamomile, *Thymus serpyllum* and *Cotula squalida*. For areas not likely to be trodden there are many more good candidates, such as *Ajuga reptans* and *Armeria maritima*.

HOW TO LAY CLAY OR CONCRETE PAVERS

The method of laying clay or concrete pavers described in the following steps can be used for a drive or a patio as well as a path.

1 Excavate the area and prepare a sub-base of about 5cm (2in) of compacted hardcore or sand and gravel mix. Set an edging along one end and side first, mortaring into position, before laying the pavers.

2 Lay a 5cm (2in) bed of sharp sand over the area, then use a straight-edged piece of wood stretched between two height gauges (battens fixed at the height of the sand bed) to strike off surplus sand and provide a level surface.

3 Position the pavers, laying 2m (6½ft) at a time. Make sure they butt up to each other, and are firm against the edging. Mortar further edging strips into place as you proceed.

5 Brush more sand into the joints, then vibrate or tamp again. It may be necessary to repeat this once more.

4 Hire a flat-plate vibrator to consolidate the sand. Alternatively, tamp the pavers down with a club hammer over a piece of wood. Do not go too close to an unsupported edge with the vibrator.

Decorative floors

A single surface of one kind of paving is likely to look flat and dull in anything but the smallest of patios. To create a much more interesting view, you might like to introduce some variation and texture – either with different decorative paving materials, or by using plants.

Often, it simply is not practical to go for major change, and you may feel you are stuck with a stretch of uniform concrete slabs. But there are ways to improve the situation – perhaps by removing some of the slabs to increase the planting areas around the perimeter and within the main paving areas. Or you could use decorative detailing to disguise parts of a less than pretty surface.

Ornamental paving

Coloured tiles have been used to create decorative floors down the centuries. It is likely that tiles laid in an intricate mosaic pattern over the whole patio will be overpowering, especially in a very small garden, and put up fierce competition with the plants. However, you can turn an ordinary paved area into something quite distinctive by replacing one or two of the paving slabs with panels of different coloured ceramic tiles. Arrange them in geometric patterns, forming squares, oblongs, or triangles, depending on the layout of the rest of the space. If you have the room you could extend the paved area by adding two rows of tiles around the perimeter; lay them diagonally in alternating colours – perhaps one row in terracotta, the other in cream, again depending on the design of the rest of the paving.

Pebbles

Pebbles are another decorative material with a centuries-old tradition. Their natural colours and smoothly rounded forms can be used to make exquisite textural panels within concrete or brick paving. Again, geometric shapes are most commonly seen but, in the hands of an artist given enough space, they can become elaborate works of art.

Floor planting

One way of softening uninspired areas of large concrete paving is to replace some of the slabs with mini-gardens. Try planting a miniature herb lawn that releases its aroma as you brush past. Chamomile (the non-flowering variety 'Treneague') and thyme are particularly effective. Or you can plant with larger herbs, such as lavender or sage. Low-growing flowers, such as alyssum, violets, pinks or any of the alpines, can offer a subtle but effective splash of floor-level colour.

If the ground allows, you can encourage small plants to grow between the paving stones, but you will need to be selective. While self-seeded violas can look enchanting, thistles are not so appealing.

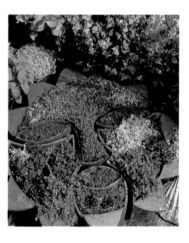

ABOVE: *This ceramic sun makes an original floor feature. Planted with low-growing plants, it looks like a rich green tapestry.*

BELOW: *The clay-tiled floor and brick retaining walls make an evocative home for a herb garden and a focal point within the garden.*

MAKING A MINIATURE PEBBLE CIRCLE

This very simple mosaic, which is made from pieces of slate and old terracotta as well as a few beach pebbles and stones, can be used as an eye-catching, decorative detail anywhere in the garden.

1 Prepare a smooth circular area to the size you want the pebble circle to be. Mark out the area for the finished circle using a simple pair of compasses. These can be made from two small pieces of wood linked by a piece of string the length of the radius of the circle.

2 Add sufficient water to a sand and cement mix in order to achieve a crumbly consistency. Using a mortar trowel, smooth the cement over the circle.

3 Working quickly before the cement sets, press in the vertical border of slates.

4 Working in concentric rings, add a circle of old terracotta and another of slates, then a 'wheel' of pebbles and terracotta.

RIGHT: *Tessellated tiles rescued from a crumbling city pathway, which were destined for a builder's skip, make an enchanting detail in a flowerbed.*

Timber decking

Timber decking creates a distinctive effect, and will make a refreshing change from ordinary paving for the patio area. As with paving, the material used should be in proportion to the size of the garden, so the width of the planks is important. Wide planks look best in a large garden, but in a small, enclosed area narrower planks are usually preferable.

Different designs can be achieved by using planks of different widths and fixing them in different directions, as illustrated here, but on the whole it is best to keep any pattern fairly simple. Leave a small gap between each plank, but not so large that high-heeled shoes can slip into it.

The construction method and timber sizes must reflect the size of the overall structure and its design – especially if built up over sloping ground. In some countries there are building codes and regulations that may have to be met. If in doubt, seek professional help with the design, even if you construct it yourself.

All timber used for decking must be thoroughly treated with a wood preservative. Some preservatives and wood stains are available in a range of colours, and this provides the opportunity for a little creativity. Dark browns and black always look good and weather well, but if you want to be more adventurous choose from reds, greens and greys.

If you want your decking to have a long life, special pressure-treated timber is the best choice. However, the range of colours available is bound to be less extensive.

Parquet decking

The easiest way to use timber as a surface is to make or buy parquet decking. Provided the ground is flat panels are easy to lay and can look very pleasing. Bed them on about 5cm (2in) of sand over a layer of gravel, to ensure free drainage beneath. If you already have a suitable concrete base to use, you can lay them directly onto this.

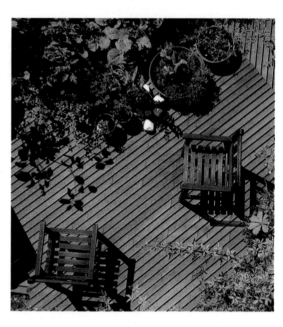

LEFT: *Timber decking makes a refreshing change from paving slabs or bricks, and can give the garden a touch of class.*

Patterns of Timber Decking

Ground cover with plants

If you want to cover an area of ground with a living carpet simply for texture, and don't expect to walk on the area, suitable ground cover plants are the answer.

To use ground cover plants like this, rather than simply as a means to suppress weeds in a flower bed, they must be evergreen, compact, and grow to a low, even height.

HOW TO PLANT CLUMP-FORMING GROUND COVER

1 Clear the ground of weeds first, and be especially careful to remove any deep-rooted or difficult perennial weeds.

2 Add plenty of garden compost or rotted manure, then rake in a controlled-release fertilizer. Add these before laying a mulching sheet.

3 Cover the area with a weed-suppressing mulching sheet. You can use a polythene sheet, but a special woven mulching sheet is much better.

4 Make crossed slits through the sheet where you want to plant. Avoid making the slits too large.

5 Excavate planting holes and firm in the plants. If necessary tease a few of the roots apart first.

6 Water thoroughly, and keep well watered. Remove the sheet once the plants are well established.

GROUND COVER PLANTS

Some of the best plants for the job are *Armeria maritima*, bergenias, *Cotoneaster dammeri*, *Euonymus fortunei* varieties, *Hypericum calycinum*, and *Pachysandra terminalis*. If you want flowers as the main feature, heathers are difficult to better.

HOW TO PLANT CREEPING GROUND COVER

The mulching sheet method is a good way to get clump-forming plants such as heathers off to a good start, but don't use it for those that creep and root, such as ajugas and *Hypericum calycinum*. Plant these normally but apply a loose mulch about 5cm (2in) thick to cover the soil.

Gravel gardens

Gravel is an inexpensive and flexible alternative to paving or a lawn, although it is not suitable for a patio. It blends beautifully with plants, needs little maintenance, and can be used in both formal and informal designs. It is also a useful 'filler' material to use among other hard surfaces, or in irregularly shaped areas where paving will not easily fit and a lawn would be difficult to mow.

LEFT: *Gravels naturally vary considerably in colour.*

Types of gravel

Gravel comes in many different shapes, sizes and colours. Some types are angular, others rounded, some are white, others assorted shades of green or red. All of them will look different in sun or shade, when wet or dry. The subtle change of colour and mood is one of the appeals of gravel. The gravels available will depend on where you live, and which ones can be transported economically from further afield. Shop around first going to garden centres and builders merchants to see what is available in your area before making your choice.

Gravel paths

Gravel is often used for drives, but it is also a good choice for informal paths within the garden. It conforms to any shape so is useful for paths that meander. However, it is not a good choice for paths where you will have to wheel the mower.

HOW TO LAY A GRAVEL PATH

1 Excavate the area to a depth of about 15cm (6in), and ram the base firm.

2 Provide a stout edge to retain the gravel. For a straight path, battens secured by pegs about 1m (3ft) apart is an easy and inexpensive method.

3 First place a layer of compacted hardcore. Add a mixture of sand and coarse gravel (you can use sand and gravel mixture sold as ballast). Rake level and tamp or roll until firm.

4 Top up to the required height with the final grade of gravel. In small gardens, the size often known as pea gravel looks good and is easy to walk on. Rake and roll repeatedly until the surface is firm and stable.

If the path is wide, it is a good idea to build the gravel up towards the centre slightly so that puddles do not form after heavy rain.

Gravel beds

Gravel can be used as a straight substitute for grass and requires much less maintenance. You can even convert an existing lawn very simply by applying a weedkiller to the grass, laying edging blocks around the edge, then topping up with gravel.

Informal gravel beds still require some kind of edging restraint to prevent the gravel from spreading. If the bed is surrounded by a lawn, simply make sure that the gravelled area is about 5cm (2in) below the surrounding grass.

Other practical ways to prevent the gravel from scattering onto beds and other unwanted areas are to create a slightly sunken garden or to raise the surround slightly with a suitable edging.

Informal gravel areas often look especially effective if some plants are grown through the gravel – either in beds with seamless edges where the gravel goes over them, or as individual specimen plants.

HOW TO LAY A GRAVEL BED

1 Excavate the area to the required depth – about 5cm (2in) of gravel is sufficient in most cases.

2 Level the ground. Lay heavy-duty black polythene or a mulching sheet over the area. Overlap strips by about 5cm (2in).

3 Then tip the gravel on top and rake level.

4 To plant through the gravel, draw it back from the planting area and make a slit in the polythene. Plant normally, enriching the soil beneath if necessary.

5 Firm in and pull back the polythene before re-covering with gravel.

Forming Boundaries

MOST OF US HAVE AN INSTINCTIVE DESIRE TO mark our territory with a very visible boundary. It gives us a sense of privacy and the illusion of security, but above all it marks out our plot of land, the area in which we create our own very special paradise.

The problem with a small garden is that the boundary forms a large part of the garden, and the chances are that you will see it from whichever direction you look. In a large garden the boundary often merges into the background, but in a small one it can easily dominate.

Tall walls can be an asset – the walled town garden has many of the treasured attributes of an old walled country garden – but drab wooden fences and large overgrown hedges pose real problems if you want to make your garden look smart and stylish.

Don't take your boundary for granted, and never assume it can't be improved. Replacing a fence or grubbing up a long-established hedge are not projects to be tackled lightly – they can be expensive or labour-intensive. Never make changes until you have consulted neighbours that

LEFT: *This is an excellent example of a combination boundary – a wooden picket fence supported on a low wall, with an escallonia flowering hedge growing through it.*

OPPOSITE ABOVE: *Walls make secure boundaries, but to prevent them looking oppressive cover with climbers, and if possible create a view beyond, as this attractive gate has done.*

OPPOSITE: *A wall as tall as this can easily dominate a small garden, but by treating it boldly and using it as a feature it becomes an asset.*

are affected. The boundary may belong to them, in which case it is not yours to change unilaterally. Even if it is legally yours to replace, the courtesy of discussing changes with others affected will go a long way to helping you remain on good terms with your neighbours.

Although you are unlikely to want to exceed them in a small garden, there may be legal limitations on boundary height, perhaps laid down in the terms of the contract when you bought the property. In some countries there may be restrictions placed by the highways authority on road safety grounds.

Restrictions are most likely in front gardens – some 'open plan' estates, for example, may have limitations on anything that might infringe the integrated structure of the gardens.

None of these restrictions need inhibit good garden design, but it is always worth checking whether any restrictions exist before erecting or planting a new boundary.

Hedges for small gardens

Many of the classic hedges, like beech, yew, and tall conifers like × *Cupressocyparis leylandii*, and even the privet (*Ligustrum ovalifolium*) have strictly limited use in a small garden. In small gardens the emphasis should be on plants that have much to offer or compact growth. The hedges suggested here are just some of the plants that could be used to mark your boundary without being dull or oppressive. Be prepared to experiment with others.

Clipped formality

The classic box hedge (*Buxus sempervirens*) is still one of the best. It clips well and can be kept compact, but choose the variety 'Suffruticosa' if you want a really dwarf hedge like those seen in knot gardens. A quick-growing substitute is *Lonicera nitida*, and there's a golden form that always looks bright – but be prepared to cut frequently. Some of the dwarf berberis stand close clipping – try the red-leaved *Berberis thunbergii* 'Atropurpurea Nana'. Yew (*Taxus baccata*) is also excellent for formal clipping, and it can be kept compact enough for a small garden.

Colourful informal hedges

If you want to cut down on clipping, and want something brighter and more colourful than most foliage hedges, try the grey-leaved *Senecio* 'Sunshine' or the golden *Philadelphus coronarius* 'Aureus' (unfortunately sheds its leaves in winter). *Viburnum tinus* can also be kept to a reasonable height, and provided you avoid pruning out the new flowers it will bloom in winter. Many of the flowering and foliage berberis also make good 'shrubby' hedges. These will lack a neatly clipped profile, but pruning and shaping is normally only an annual job.

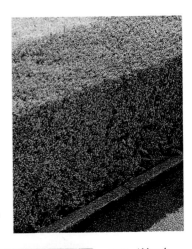

ABOVE: *Although Lonicera nitida needs frequent clipping, it makes a neat formal hedge.*

LEFT: *Many shrub roses can make an attractive flowering hedge in summer, but do not plant them too close to the edge of a path otherwise their thorny stems may be a nuisance.*

Using roses

Roses make delightful – and often fragrant – boundaries, but they have shortcomings. Their summer beauty is matched by winter ugliness, and they are not a good choice for a boundary where passers-by may be scratched by thorns. You can use a row of floribunda (cluster-flowered) roses, but the shrubby type are usually preferred for this job.

Old-fashioned lavender and rosemary dividers

Both these herbs make excellent informal flowering hedges, with the merit of being evergreen too. You could try the shorter lavender in front of the taller rosemary. Both become untidy with age, so replace the plants when it becomes necessary.

Other flowering hedges

Forsythia is one of the most popular flowering hedges, but careful pruning is required to achieve consistent flowering on a compact hedge. There are plenty of alternatives, including the shrubby potentillas, berberis like *B. × stenophylla*, with bold flowers, though this one can take up a lot of space, and even tall varieties of heathers if you just want a boundary marker rather than a barrier.

ABOVE: *Box is one of the classic plants to use for clipped formality. This is a glaucous form.*

HOW TO PLANT A NEW HEDGE

1 Prepare the ground very thoroughly. Excavate a trench – ideally about 60cm (2ft) wide – and fork in plenty of rotten manure or garden compost.

2 Add a balanced fertilizer at the rate recommended by the manufacturer. Use a controlled-release fertilizer if planting in the autumn.

3 Use a garden line, stretched along the centre of the trench, as a positioning guide. If the area is windy or you need a particularly dense hedge, plant a double row of trees. Bare-root plants are cheaper than container-grown plants, but only separate them and expose the roots once you are ready to plant. Only the most popular hedging plants are likely to be available bare-root, and for many of the plants suggested you will have to plant a single row of container-grown plants.

4 Use a piece of wood or a cane cut to the appropriate length as a guide for even spacing. Make sure the roots are well spread out. If planting container-grown plants, tease out some of the roots that are running around the edge of the root-ball.

5 Firm the plants in well and water thoroughly. Be prepared to water the hedge regularly in dry weather for the first season. Keep down weeds until the hedge is well established, then it should suppress the weeds naturally.

Garden walls

Except for special cases, such as basement flats and the need for privacy or screening in a difficult neighbourhood, high walls are inappropriate for a small garden. However, low walls up to about 1–1.2m (3–4ft) are a useful alternative to a hedge, particularly if you want to avoid regular trimming. Although the rain shadow and shade problems remain the same for a wall as a hedge, a wall will not impoverish the soil in the same way as a hedge.

Low walls
A low wall, say 30–60cm (1–2ft) tall, will serve the same demarcation function as a taller one, but in more appropriate scale for a small garden, and shrubs planted behind it are more likely to thrive. Modest garden walls like this are much easier to construct than tall ones, which may need substantial reinforcing piers, and are well within the scope of a competent garden handyman to build.

Brick walls
Plain brick walls can harmonize with the house, but generally look dull from a design viewpoint. A skilled bricklayer can often add interest by laying panels or strips to a different pattern. The choice of brick and the capping will also alter the appearance. Some are capped with bricks, others have special coping tiles. These all add to the subtle variety of brick walls.

Block walls
Many manufacturers of concrete paving slabs also produce walling blocks made from the same material. These are especially useful for internal garden walls and raised beds. They are often coloured to resemble natural stone, but brighter colours are available if you want to match the colour scheme used for the paving. Bear in mind that colours will weather and become much more muted within a couple of years.

ABOVE: *An interesting brick wall.*
RIGHT: *A wall like this makes a solid and secure boundary without making the garden appear too enclosed.*

Screen block walls

Screen block walls (sometimes called pierced block) are most frequently used for internal walls, perhaps around the patio or to divide one part of the garden from another, but they can also be used to create a striking boundary wall too.

These blocks have to be used with special piers and topped with the appropriate coping. They are useful if you want to create a modern image, or perhaps the atmosphere of a Mediterranean garden.

Mixing materials

Some of the smartest boundary walls are made from more than one material. Screen blocks look good as panels within a concrete walling block framework. Screen blocks can also be incorporated into a brick wall, and help to let light through and to filter some of the wind. Panels of flint or other stone can be set into an otherwise boring tall brick wall.

ABOVE: *Dry stone walls are not difficult to build provided you keep them low, and you can plant into the sides for extra interest.*

BELOW: *Walls can be colourful . . . if you create planting areas. The summer bedding plants used here are replaced at the end of the season with bulbs and spring bedding plants to use the planting areas to their full advantage.*

Cavity walls

Low cavity walls that can be lined with plants soon become an eye-catching feature. Pack them with colourful summer flowers, or plant with permanent perennials such as dwarf conifers, which maintain interest throughout the year (but be sure to choose truly dwarf conifers for this). If you plant cascading forms such as nasturtium or trailing lobelia, the effect can be really stunning. For a spring display, try aubrietia and the yellow *Alyssum saxatile*, with a few dwarf spring-flowering bulbs.

Dry stone walling

Dry stone walls are more often used for retaining banks or as internal dividers, but in an appropriate setting this kind of wall makes an attractive boundary. This type of wall looks best where dry stone walls are part of the natural landscape.

The great advantage of a dry stone wall – which is assembled without mortar – is the ability to plant in the sides. This can provide a home for many kinds of alpines.

Walls with a difference

The larger and taller the wall, the more imaginative you should be when designing it. Try incorporating an alcove for an ornament, or a panel into which you can set an artistic piece of wrought-iron that can be viewed against the green of a neighbouring field or garden.

Wall building materials

Most builders' merchants stock a good range of bricks, the majority are suitable for garden walls, but if you need a lot of bricks – enough to justify ordering direct – get in touch with a few brick companies. Their expertise can be invaluable, and most will be able to offer you a wide choice.

Buying bricks is something most of us do only rarely, so professional advice is especially useful. The author's experience, however, suggests that you can't always depend on the advice of a builder's merchant. Shop around until you find someone who really appears to have a knowledgeable passion for bricks – they will tell you about all the different finishes and colours available, and most importantly will know whether a particular brick is suitable for the job you have in mind. *Always* explain what you want your bricks for: a building, a garden wall, wall of a raised bed, or for paving. Some bricks which are perfectly suitable for house walls may be very unsuitable for paths or garden walls.

If you need a lot of bricks (many hundreds), it may be better, and cheaper, to buy direct from a brick manufacturer if they will deal with the general public.

ABOVE: *Bricks come in many colours and finishes, and these are just a small selection from the many kinds available. Names of bricks vary from country to country, but whatever names are used you are likely to have a good choice.*

MASONRY MORTAR

A suitable mortar for bricklaying can be made from 1 part cement to 3 parts soft sand. Parts are by volume and not weight. Cement dyes can be added to create special effects, but use coloured mortar cautiously.

Common bonds

Expert brick-layers may use more complicated bonds, but for ordinary garden walls – and especially those that you are likely to lay yourself, perhaps for a low boundary wall or for a raised bed within the garden – it is best to choose one of the three bonds illustrated below.

Running bond or stretcher bond This is the simplest form of bonding, and is used for walls a single brick wide – or where you want to create a cavity, such as a low wall with a planting space.

Flemish bond This is another way to create a strong bond in a wall two bricks wide. The bricks are laid both lengthways and across the wall within the same course.

English bond This is used for a thick wall the width of two bricks laid side by side – useful where strength is needed for a high wall. Alternate courses are laid lengthways then across the wall.

HOW TO LAY BRICKS AND BLOCKS

Although bricks are being laid here, the same principles apply to laying walling blocks.

1 All walls require a footing. The one shown here is a for a low wall just one brick wide: for larger and thicker walls the dimensions of the footing will have to be increased.

Excavate a trench about 30cm (12in) deep, and place about 13cm (5in) of consolidated hardcore in the bottom. Drive pegs in so that the tops are at the final height of the base. Use a spirit-level to check levels.

2 Fill with a concrete mix of 1 part cement, 2½ parts sharp sand and 3½ parts 2cm (¾in) aggregate, and level it off with the peg tops.

3 When the concrete has hardened for a few days, lay the bricks on a bed of mortar, also place a wedge of mortar at one end of each brick to be laid. For stability, always make a pier at each end, and at intervals of about 1.8–2.4m (6–8ft) if the wall is long. Here two bricks have been laid crossways for this purpose.

4 For subsequent courses, lay a ribbon of mortar on top of the previous row, then 'butter' one end of the brick to be laid.

5 Tap level, checking constantly with a spirit-level.

6 The wall must be finished off with a coping of suitable bricks or with special coping sold for the purpose.

Boundary fences

Fences have the great merit of being more instant than hedges and less expensive than walls. That is the reason they are so often chosen by builders for new properties, and why they are frequently chosen again when the original fences come to the end of their useful life.

Closeboard and panel fences are popular, but predictable and a little boring. There are plenty of styles to choose from, however, so select a fence appropriate to your garden design yet practical for the purposes you have in mind.

If you want privacy or animal-proofing, you will have to opt for one of the solid styles, but if it is just a boundary-marker that is needed there are many attractive fences that look stylish and won't appear oppressive in a small garden.

The names of particular fence types can vary from country to country. If you do not recognize any of the names here check with the illustrations.

Closeboard

Closeboard fencing is erected on site by nailing overlapping feather-edged boards to horizontal rails already secured to stout upright posts. It is a strong, secure fence, but not particularly attractive – especially viewed from the side with the rails.

Panels

Prefabricated panels are quick and easy to erect and a popular choice for that reason. Panels are usually about 1.8m (6ft) long and range in height from about 60cm (2ft) to 1.8m (6ft), generally in 30cm (1ft) steps. The interwoven or overlapping boards are sandwiched between a frame of sawn timber. The woven style is not as peep-proof as overlapping boards.

Interlap or hit-and-miss

This combines strength and a solid appearance with better wind-filtering than a solid fence (which can create turbulent eddies that can be damaging

ABOVE: *Closeboard fencing well covered with climbing roses.*

ABOVE: *Wattle or woven fences make an attractive background for plants.*

ABOVE: *A low wooden fence is not obtrusive and can look very attractive.*

to plants). It is constructed from square-edged boards that are nailed to the horizontal rails on alternate sides. Overlapping the edges gives more privacy, while spacing them further apart can look more decorative.

Picket

Picket fences look good in country gardens, but can also be a smart choice for a small town garden. Narrow, vertical pales are nailed to horizontal timbers, spaced about 5cm (2in) apart. You can make them yourself or buy kits with some of the laborious work done for you. The simplest shape for the top of each pale is a point, but you can make them rounded or choose a more ornate finial shape. A picket fence can be left in natural wood colour, but they look particularly smart painted white. Because they are usually relatively low, and you can see plenty of garden through the well-spaced pales, they don't dominate the garden in the same way as a tall, solid fence.

Ranch-style

Ranch-style fences consist of broad horizontal rails fixed to stout upright posts. They are usually quite low, and frequently consist of just two or three rails. White-painted wood is a popular material, but wipe-down plastic equivalents are very convincing and easy to maintain. For a small garden they provide a clear boundary without becoming a visual obstruction. Also, rain and sun shadows are not created in the way that occurs with more solid fences.

Post and chain

This is the least obtrusive of all fences. Purely a boundary marker, it will do nothing to deter animals or children, or keep balls out of the garden, but it is a good choice if you want a fence that is hardly noticeable. You can use wooden, concrete or plastic posts and metal or plastic chains. Choose a white plastic chain if you want to make a feature of the fence, black if you want the chain to recede and blend into the background.

Chain link

Chain link is not an aesthetic choice, but it is highly practical and an effective barrier for animals. It is probably best to have a contractor erect a chain link fence, as it needs to be tensioned properly. You may like the fact that you can see through it, especially if the view beyond is attractive, but you may prefer to plant climbers beside it to provide a better screen. Choose tough evergreens such as ivy if you want year-round screening.

Bamboo

Bamboo is a natural choice if you've created an oriental-style garden, but don't be afraid to use this type of fence for any garden style if it looks right. Bamboo fences come in many shapes and sizes, and the one you adopt will depend partly on the availability and cost of the material and partly on your creativity and skill in building this kind of fence.

ABOVE: *A fence like this just needs a supply of bamboo and skill at tying knots!*

LEFT: *A white picket fence can make the boundary a feature of the garden.*

How to erect a fence

Many gardeners prefer to employ a contractor to erect or replace a fence. They will certainly make lighter work of it with their professional tools for excavating post holes, and a speed that comes with expertise, but some fences are very easy to erect yourself. Two of the easiest are panel and ranch-type fences, which are illustrated in simple steps below.

HOW TO ERECT A PANEL FENCE

1 Post spikes are an easier option than excavating holes and concreting the post in position. The cost saving on using a shorter post and no concrete will go some way towards the cost of the spike.
   Use a special tool to protect the spike top, then drive it in with a sledge-hammer. Check periodically with a spirit-level to ensure it is absolutely vertical.

2 Once the spike has been driven in, insert the post and check the vertical again.

3 Lay the panel in position on the ground and mark the position of the next post. Drive in the next spike, testing for the vertical again.

4 There are various ways to fix the panels to the posts, but panel brackets are easy to use.

5 Insert the panel and nail in position, through the brackets. Insert the post at the other end and nail the panel in position at that end.

6 Check the horizontal level both before and after nailing, and make any necessary adjustments before moving on to the next panel.

7 Finish off by nailing a post cap to the top of each post. This will keep water out of the end grain of the timber and extend its life.

HOW TO ERECT A RANCH-STYLE FENCE

1 Although ranch-style fences are easy to erect the posts must be well secured in the ground. For a wooden fence, use 12.5 × 10cm (5 × 4in) posts, set at about 2m (6½ft) intervals. For additional strength add intermediate posts. A size of 9cm (3½in) square is adequate for these.

Make sure the posts go at least 45cm (18in) into the ground.

2 Concrete the posts into position, then screw or nail the planks in position, making sure fixings are rust-proof. Use a spirit-level to make sure the planks are horizontal. Butt-join the planks in the centre of a post, but try to stagger the joints on each row so that there is not a weak point in the fence.

3 Fit a post cap. This improves the appearance and also protects the posts. Paint with a good quality paint recommended for outdoor use.

ABOVE LEFT: *Panel fences are easily erected and provide a peep-proof barrier, but are best clothed with plants to soften the effect.*
ABOVE: *Ranch-style fences make an unobtrusive barrier – ideal where the garden merges into the countryside.*

THE PLASTIC ALTERNATIVE

There are many plastic ranch-style fences. They will vary slightly in the way they are assembled. Detailed instructions should come with them, however, and you should have no difficulty.

The 'planks' are sometimes available in different widths – 10cm (4in) and 15cm (6in) for example – and these help to create different visual appearances. Gates made from the same material are also available from some manufacturers.

Posts are usually concreted into the ground, and the cellular plastic planks are push-fitted into slots or special fittings. Special union pieces are used to join lengths, and post caps are usually glued and pushed into position.

White ranch fencing needs to be kept clean to look good, and plastic can simply be washed when it looks grubby.

Trelliswork

Trellis usually makes a much more decorative boundary than a fence. It is not so solid, allowing glimpses of what lies on the other side, and provides a framework for all but the most tender climbers and ramblers. Trellis can also lend height to boundary walls where extra privacy is needed and it can be used to decorate the walls themselves. The decorative aspect is especially valuable where the walls or fences are less than beautiful, or where you would like to add a little extra texture.

Shapes and sizes

Trellis is wonderfully versatile garden feature and comes in a wide variety of panel shapes and sizes. As well as the basic rectangular panels, there are also panels with pointed, convex or concave tops, and even with integral 'windows', all of which should provide you with plenty of scope for being creative. To finish off the supporting posts, there is also an extensive choice of attractive finials in shapes such as globes, acorns, pineapples and obelisks. A coat or two of exterior-quality paint or coloured wood stain – applied to the posts and panels – will immediately give a more finished and highly individual appearance that can also be enjoyed during the winter.

Improvised trellis

The trellis, of course, does not have to be ready-made. Old gates, an old window frame, metal panels or panels made from vines or other organic materials can serve the same purpose as ordinary trelliswork. These also look good in themselves, before being dressed up with climbing plants.

HOW TO ERECT A TRELLIS FENCE

The key to erecting a trellis fence is to make certain that it is firmly planted in the ground. In all but the most sheltered positions, it will come under enormous pressure from the wind and will work loose unless you have ensured the posts are firmly bedded in the concrete.

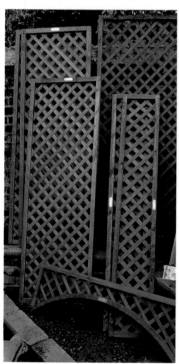

ABOVE: *Ready-made trellis panels in a variety of shapes and sizes can be used to create trellis fencing and even a trellis arbour.*

1 Start by digging a hole for the first supporting post. Make it at least 60cm (2ft) deep, deeper in light soils.

2 Put the post into the prepared hole and partly fill the hole with dry-mix concrete. Use a spirit-level to check that the post is upright and not sloping. Adjust the position if necessary and then continue filling the hole, tamping the concrete mix down firmly as you work, to hold the post still.

3 Continue filling the hole with concrete, ramming it down well. Frequently check that the post is still upright. It should now be firm enough in the ground so that you can work on it and, once the concrete has set or 'cured', will be permanently secure.

4 Lay the trellis panel on the ground first of all, so that you can work out where the next post hole should be dug. Dig the hole for the post, again to a depth of at least 60cm (2ft).

5 Nail the panel to the first post. You will need to ask someone to support the free end for you.

6 Place the second post in its hole and nail the panel to it, checking that the tops of the two posts are level and the panel is horizontal. Fill the second hole with dry-mix concrete, tamping down as you proceed. Check that the post is upright and adjust its position if necessary.

7 Repeat the steps by digging the third post hole, nailing on the second panel, positioning and nailing the third post, and so on, until the length of trellising is complete. This is more accurate than putting in all the posts and then fixing all the panels, when, inevitably, some gaps will be too large and some too small.

Fixing trellis to walls

Wooden trellis clothed with colourful climbers is an attractive method of decorating an expanse of plain brick or plastered wall. If the trellis itself is pleasing to look at, perhaps with a painted or stained finish, you may want to make it into a feature in itself. If this is the case, it is best to use only a few plants in order to avoid covering it over completely.

Securing trellis

It is essential that the trellis is fixed securely to the wall, preferably with screws. It should be held a short distance from the brickwork or masonry, so that the stems of the climbing plants can easily pass up behind it. This can be simply achieved by using spacers – wooden battens (wooden laths) will do – between the trellis and the wall.

Easy access

If the wall is a painted one, or might need future attention for other reasons, it is sensible to make the trellis detachable. The best method is to fix hinges along the bottom edge of the trellis panel, and a catch to the top edge. This allows the framework to be gently eased away from the wall, bringing the climber with it, so that any maintenance work can take place. Alternatively, the trellis can be held in position by a series of clips or catches, although it will not be as easy to manipulate as one that is held on hinges.

TRELLIS SCREENS

Free-standing trellis panels also offer an effective method of screening or dividing one part of the garden from another. Or you can use them simply as a means of supporting climbers, perhaps in a bed or border, or throughout the garden to define its major routes. Erect the panels as described for a trellis fence, making sure they are bedded firmly in the ground.

ABOVE: Rosa 'Dublin Bay' here climbs up a wooden trellis secured to the wall. The rose is fragrant and flowers over a very long period.

HOW TO FIX TRELLIS TO A WALL

If you want to fix a series of trellis panels to a boundary wall, simply fit them close together, one butting up to the other. This method is equally suitable for fixing a single panel, to the front wall of the house for example.

1 Mark the position of the trellis. Drill holes in the wall for fixing the spacer battens (laths) and insert plastic or wooden plugs. On a low wall, you will need two battens (laths) at the top and base. For trellis more than 1.2m (4ft) high, allow for an additional batten (lath) halfway up.

2 Drill corresponding holes in the spacer battens (laths) and secure each to the wall with screws, checking with a spirit-level that it is horizontal. Use battens (laths) that hold the trellis at least 2.5cm (1in) from the wall.

3 Drill and screw the trellis to the battens (laths), first fixing the top and then working downwards. Check that the trellis is not crooked.

4 The finished trellis should be tightly fixed to the wall, so that the weight of the climber, and any wind that blows on it, will not pull it away from its fixings.

See-through boundaries

The best boundary of all might be no boundary . . . at least none that you can see. The ha-ha, once popular with the great landscape gardeners of the past, was a successful way of achieving this. The boundary is a deep, wide ditch that can't easily be seen from within the garden, so the garden appears to continue into the rolling countryside beyond.

The ha-ha is not a technique easily adapted to a small modern garden, and totally inappropriate if you overlook a townscape instead of pleasant green fields. However, the principle of being able to blur the margin between your garden and your neighbour's garden, or perhaps open countryside if you are fortunate enough to have the option, is one worth pursuing.

Ditches
A ditch sounds an unattractive feature. However, if one happens to run along one of your boundaries it might be possible to make a feature of it, rather than trying to hide it. Try planting it with bog plants, and landscape it into your garden, perhaps with a pond and an extended bog garden linking the two.

Some people even try to create a ditch, using a liner that restricts water loss and flooding it with water periodically. Provided the view of the garden beyond is attractive, this is a sure-fire way to give your small garden an open style only normally associated with larger gardens.

Shared gardens
Like-minded gardening enthusiasts sometimes design their gardens so that they appear to be linked. Usually this is done by taking the lawn through a gap in the boundary and using shrubs or mixed borders that start in one garden and end in the next. This can work surprisingly well, and although each is responsible for his own area the illusion is that the garden goes on beyond.

If this seems too 'communal', the same effect can be achieved by making lawns and borders meet yet still retain an unobtrusive fence, such as a widely spaced post and rail fence, or even a few simple strands of wire – which can be almost invisible from a distance.

Alternatively, consider linking gardens with an attractive gate. You don't have to use it, but it will look as though there is more garden beyond to be explored.

Shrubby solutions
Although a continuous lawn is the best way to link adjoining gardens and make them look larger, you can instead agree to abolish the fence and both plant shrubs in a bed along the boundary. Even if a relatively narrow strip is used in each garden, the

ABOVE: *A window in the wall can immediately transform a potentially boring area of brick into a real focus point.*

impression will be of a much larger and more substantial shrub border with no sign of obtrusive fences.

Claire-voyée
The term means literally 'clear view', and came into use after the lawless Middle Ages in Europe when it became less necessary to enclose one's property with a solid wall, and apertures were cut in walls to allow the countryside beyond to be viewed from within.

If you have a view that is worth framing, you can introduce a claire-voyée 'window' in the wall of even a tiny garden.

Brightening up fences and walls

If replacing an existing old fence or wall simply isn't practical because of the time and expense involved, consider ways to camouflage or brighten up the old one.

RIGHT: *Old fences discolour and look drab and shabby with age. This is one way to transform a dull fence.*

Climbers

Climbers present one of the most pleasing ways to cover an unsightly wall or fence, but always make sure the fence is firm in its foundations first . . . otherwise the extra weight and wind resistance will just bring it down sooner and you will have to untangle the climber and repair the fence anyway.

For year-round cover, tough evergreens such as ivies are justifiably popular. They can be slow to establish, but ultimately provide dense cover and can easily be clipped back once or twice a year to prevent the shoots encroaching beyond their territory.

For summer-only cover, try the vigorous hop (*Humulus lupulus*), especially in its very attractive golden form 'Aureus'. Once established one plant will cover a large area of fence.

For flowers some of the clematis can be very successful, though winter's an unattractive time. Tall-growing species such as *Clematis montana* sound unlikely candidates, but they will run along the fence and cascade down each side instead of climbing, and the pink *C. m. rubens* looks particularly splendid.

BELOW: *Vigorous clematis such as C. montana will cover a fence with blooms in late spring and early summer.*

Trained trees

Trained fruit trees can transform a tall wall or fence and turn it into a real feature when laden with flowers or fruit. Even in winter the bare stems of a fan or espalier tree can look dramatic, especially if picked out against a white-painted wall.

Training from scratch is difficult and time-consuming, and it is worth buying ready-trained trees.

A coat of paint

A drab old wall can be transformed with a coat of masonry paint. White reflects the light well, but any pale colour can look pleasing, particularly when contrasted with greenery.

Grow striking plants like phormiums or yuccas in front so that their strong profiles are picked out against the background, or stand groups of containers so that they are backed by the painted wall.

Framed effects

Fences are more difficult to paint as a backdrop for plants, and you must be careful about paint seeping through to your neighbour's side, but a little localized painting could work well.

Try a large white circle within which you can frame a striking plant as a focal point. Instead of painting the actual fence, try cutting out a large wooden circle and painting that – then pin it to the fence.

Finishing Touches

A SMALL GARDEN SHOULD BE FULL OF SURPRISES, packed with finishing touches that compensate for the lack of scope offered by limited size.

Many of the focal point techniques used in large gardens can be scaled down and applied on a small scale, and even in a small space the garden can express the owner's sense of fun and personality in the little extras that are grafted onto the basic design.

The whole area can be made to work, every corner can be exploited with devices if not plants, and a degree of flexibility can be built in that makes variety a real possibility.

ABOVE: *A seat like this suggests a gardener with a strong sense of design.*

OPPOSITE ABOVE: *Ornaments have been used to excellent effect here. A sundial commands centre stage and the eye is taken across the garden to a figure which adds light and life.*

OPPOSITE BELOW: *Figures usually look best framed by plants.*

LEFT: *This quiet corner has been transformed by white-painted trellis and a seat.*

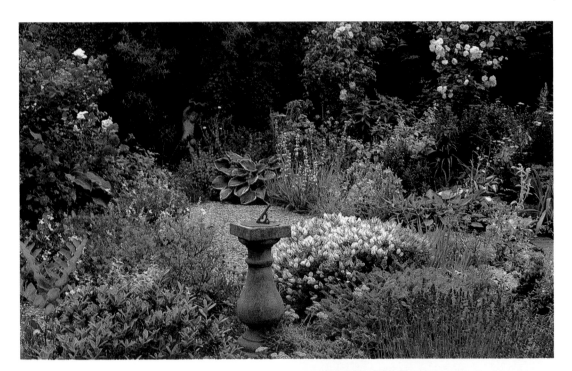

In a large garden most ornaments, furniture and fixtures like garden lights are a static part of the design. In a small garden a slight rearrangement of the furniture, the changed position of a light, or the simple exchange of one ornament for another according to mood and season means that the garden need never be predictable despite limitations of size.

Ornaments in particular can set a tone for the garden: serious or frivolous, classic or modern. They suggest the owner's taste . . . and even sense of humour. Just as the painting on the living-room wall or the ornaments on the sideboard can tell you a lot about the occupier, so garden ornaments reveal the personality of the garden maker.

Garden lighting can be practical and even a useful security measure, but it also offers scope for artistic interpretation. Experiment with spotlights in various positions and discover the dramatically different effects created by the use of light and shadows from different angles.

Arches and pergolas are a more permanent element of the garden's design, but they don't have to be planned in at the design stage and are easily added to an existing garden.

Pergolas and arches

A sense of height is important even in a small garden. Unless there is vertical use of plants or upright garden features, the centre of the garden will be flat. Attention will pass over the centre and go instead to the edges of the garden: exactly the lifeless effect you want to avoid.

Small trees, wall shrubs and climbers can provide the necessary verticals, but if these are in short supply an arch or pergola may be the answer.

Traditionally, and especially in cottage gardens, they have been made from rustic poles, but where they adjoin the house or link home with patio, sawn timber is a better choice. The various constructions described here are free-standing, and usually used as plant supports. Their visual effect is to take the eye to further down the garden.

If a pergola or arch seems inappropriate, similar construction techniques can be used to create an intimate arbour.

HOW TO ASSEMBLE AN ARCH

The simplest way to make an arch is to use a kit, which only needs assembling.

1 First establish the post positions, allowing 30cm (1ft) between the edge of the path and post, so that plants do not obstruct the path.

2 Fence spikes are the easiest way to fix the posts. Drive them in using a protective dolly. Check frequently with a spirit-level. Insert the posts and tighten the spikes around them. Alternatively, excavate four holes, each to the depth of 60cm (2ft).

3 Position the legs of the arch in the holes. Fill in with the excavated earth, and compact.

4 Lay the halves of the overhead beams on a flat surface, and carefully screw the joint together with rust-proof screws.

5 Fit the overhead beams to the posts – in this example they slot into the tops of the posts and are nailed in place.

HOW TO JOIN RUSTIC POLES

Rustic arches and pergolas look particularly attractive covered with roses or other climbers. You can be creative with the designs, but the same few basic joints shown here are all that you will need.

1 To fix horizontal poles to vertical ones, saw a notch of a suitable size for the horizontal piece to fit snugly.

2 If you have to join two horizontal pieces, saw two opposing and matching notches so that one sits over the other, and secure them.

3 To fix cross-pieces to horizontals or uprights, remove a V-shaped notch using a chisel if necessary to achieve a snug fit, then nail into place with rust-proof nails.

4 Use halving joints where two pieces cross. Make two saw cuts half way through the pole, then remove the waste timber with a chisel.

5 Secure the joint with a nail. For extra strength, paint the joint with woodworking adhesive first.

6 Bird's mouth joints are useful for connecting horizontal or diagonal pieces to uprights. Cut out a V-shaped notch about 3cm (1in) deep, and saw the other piece to match. Use a chisel to achieve a good fit.

7 Try out the assembly on the ground, then insert the uprights in prepared holes and make sure these are secure before adding any horizontal or top pieces. Most pieces can be nailed together, but screw any sections subject to stress.

ABOVE: *Rustic poles are an appropriate choice for a feature such as this.*

Temporary supports for climbers

When trying to add height to your garden, it is not always desirable to have fixed screens or supports. Growing climbers against temporary structures allows a much more flexible garden design, letting you easily ring the changes from year to year, even from one season to the next. While this is not really practical with most perennial climbers, especially those that might take several years to establish themselves, it is entirely possible with annuals.

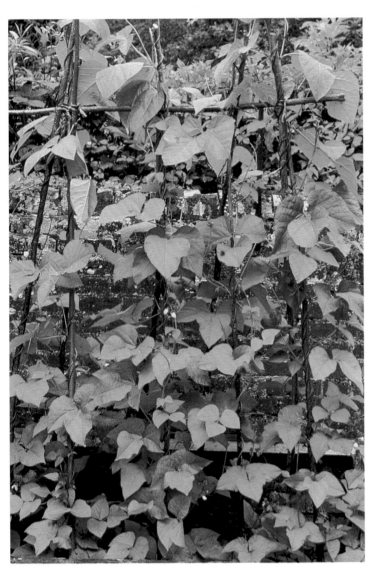

Temporary supports can often serve two functions at once: to provide an attractive screen as well as a support for vegetables. Thus, peas and beans make good traditional subjects, while more novel ideas include climbing marrows (squash), courgettes (zucchini), gourds and cucumbers.

Choosing materials

Temporary supports are easy to make and a variety of materials can be used. Many are rustic in nature, such as pea-sticks simply pushed into the ground or traditional bean poles tied together in a row or wigwam (tepee). More modern materials include plastic netting held on poles or a metal frame. However, do try to make the supports as attractive as you can: they will often be fully in view until the early summer, when the plants start growing strongly, and won't be completely covered until midsummer.

Supporting perennials

Temporary structures can also be used for a few perennials that are cut to the ground each year, such as the everlasting pea (*Lathyrus latifolius*) or some of the clematis that are either herbaceous or are pruned back almost to ground level each year. Since the latter can grow quite tall, they can be supported by large branches stuck in the ground, to imitate small trees.

LEFT: *A typical bean row, with the scarlet-flowered runner beans climbing up poles that have been tied together for support. The poles can be kept for several seasons before replacing.*

ABOVE: *Climbing plants can be grown more horizontally than usual. It is an ideal way to utilize space after the spring flowers have faded.*

ABOVE RIGHT: *A framework of hazel sticks have been woven into an attractive dome. The burgundy clematis that is growing over it is resplendent with flowers.*

RIGHT: *Sweet peas growing up a temporary screen of pea-sticks. Hazel (*Corylus avellana*) is one of the best types of wood, but any finely branched sticks will do.*

ANNUAL CLIMBERS

Asarina
Cobaea scandens (cup-and-saucer vine, cathedral bells)
Eccremocarpus scaber (Chilean glory flower)
Ipomoea (morning glory)
Lablab purpureus (syn. *Dolichos lablab*)
Lagenaria (gourds)
Lathyrus odoratus (sweet peas)
Mina lobata (syn. *Ipomoea lobata*)
Rhodochiton atrosanguineum
Thunbergia alata (black-eyed Susan)
Tropaeolum majus (nasturtium – climbing varieties)
Tropaeolum peregrinum (syn. *T. canariense*) (canary creeper)

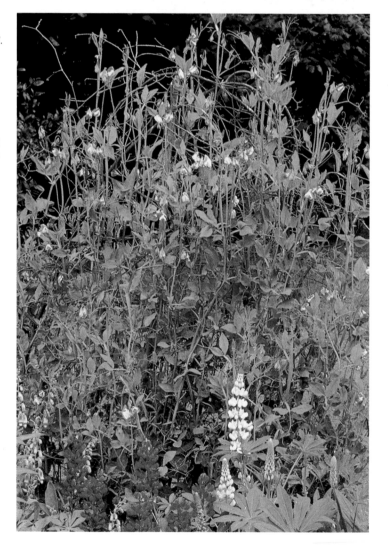

Growing climbers through trees

Trees and shrubs make wonderful natural supports for climbers, often providing conditions that are similar to those in the plant's natural habitat. In the wild, particularly in dense woodland or forests, many climbers may grow to 50m (160ft) or more as they grow ever upwards in their search for light, but in the garden supports of this height are rarely necessary – or even available. If they were, the flowers of the climbers using them would be out of sight.

Good partners

Smaller supports are required for cultivated climbers in the garden, and a large apple tree is usually the highest used. Clematis and roses will scramble through its branches, creating huge fountains of flowers. On a more modest scale, even dwarf shrubs can be used to support some low-growing climbers.

Two in one

One of the advantages of growing climbers through shrubs is that it is possible to obtain two focuses of interest in one area. This is particularly valuable for shrubs that flower early, as these tend to be fairly boring for the rest of the year. Through these it is possible to train a later-flowering climber to enliven the area further on in the season. Clematis are particularly good for this, especially the late-flowering forms, such as the viticellas. These can be cut nearly to the ground during winter, so that when the shrub itself is in flower early in the next season, it is relatively uncluttered with the climber.

Roses and fruit

A fruit tree that has come to the end of its fruiting life can be given new appeal if you grow a rose through it. However, it is important to remember that old trees may be weak and the extra burden of a large rose, especially in a high wind, may be too much for it to bear.

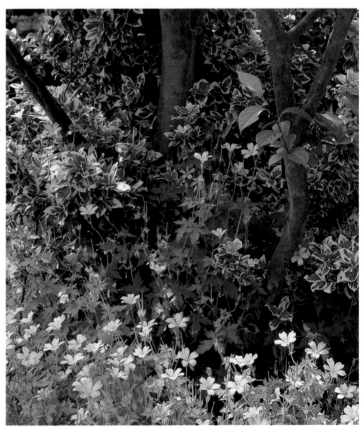

BELOW: *Scrambling plants can provide vertical interest through the summer. Here,* Euonymus fortunei *'Emerald Gaiety' scrambles up a tree with* Geranium × oxonianum *below.*

CLIMBERS FOR GROWING THROUGH TREES

Clematis (vigorous kinds)
Hydrangea petiolaris (climbing hydrangea)
Humulus (hop)
Lonicera (honeyuckle)
Polygonum baldschuanicum (syn. *Fallopia baldschuanica*) (Russian vine)
Rosa (roses – vigorous varieties)
Vitis coignetiae (crimson glory vine)

HOW TO GROW A CLIMBER THROUGH A TREE OR SHRUB

1 Any healthy shrub or tree can be chosen. It should preferably be one that flowers at a different time to the climber. Choose companions that will not swamp each other. Here, a low *Salix helvetica* is to be planted with a small form of *Clematis alpina*. The two will make a delicate mix, especially the blue clematis flowers against the silver foliage.

2 Dig the planting area at a point on the perimeter of the shrub and prepare the soil by adding well-rotted organic material. For clematis, choose a position on the shady side of the plant, so that its roots are in shade but the flowers will be up in the sun. Dig a hole that is bigger than the climber's rootball and plant it. Most plants should be planted at the same depth as they were in their pots but clematis should be 5cm (2in) or so deeper.

3 Using a cane, train the clematis into the bush. Once the clematis has become established, you can remove the cane. Spread the shoots of the climber out so that the it spreads evenly through the shrub, not just in one area.

4 If possible, put the climber outside the canopy of the shrub or tree, so that it receives rain. However, it is still important to water in the new plant and, should the weather be dry, continue watering until the plant has become established.

CLIMBERS SUITABLE FOR GROWING THROUGH SHRUBS

Clematis (small varieties)
Cobaea scandens (cup-and-saucer vine, cathedral bells)
Eccremocarpus scaber (Chilean glory flower)
Hedera (ivy)
Ipomoea (morning glory)
Jasminum (jasmine - climbing species)
Lathyrus odoratus (sweet pea)
Lonicera (honeysuckle - climbing species)
Passiflora (passion flower)
Stephanotis floribunda (Madagascar jasmine)
Tropaeolum majus (nasturtium – climbing varieties)
Tropaeolum peregrinum (syn. *T. canariense*) (canary creeper)

Simple pillars

A very effective way of creating vertical emphasis in a border or a small garden is to grow a climber up a single pole, which is usually called a pillar.

Whether solitary or in groups, these can look very elegant and also make it possible to grow a large number of climbers in a relatively small space.

Using pillars
A surprising number of climbers are suited to growing up pillars. Most climbing roses, for example, look particularly good in this situation, although it is probably best to avoid vigorous climbers or rambling roses.

Temporary or permanent
An advantage of using pillars is that they are both inexpensive and simple to erect as well as to take down. They can be permanently positioned in a border, but if you want to be able to remove them in winter, when the plants have died down, set each post in a collar of concrete or a metal tube, so you can simply lift it out when the time comes.

Pillared walkway
If space is available, a very attractive walkway can be created by using a series of pillars along a path. Enhance this further by connecting the tops with rope, along which swags of climbers can grow. This is a delightful way of growing roses and creates a romantic, fragrance-filled route through the garden. The effect is suitable for formal designs, but is so soft and flowing that it gives a very relaxing feel.

CLIMBERS FOR PILLARS

Clematis
Eccremocarpus scaber (Chilean glory flower)
Humulus (hop)
Lonicera (honeysuckle)
Rosa (roses)
Solanum jasminoides (potato vine)
Tropaeolum (nasturtium)

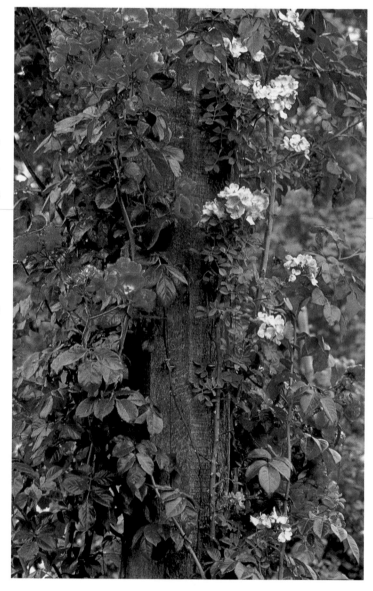

RIGHT: *Single-post pillars help to break up what would, otherwise, be a dull, rather two-dimensional border. Although it is only a thin structure, when clothed with a climber it becomes a well-filled out, irregular shape, as this* Rosa *'American Pillar' shows.*

OPPOSITE: *Although single-post pillars are rather slim, they can accommodate more than one climber. Here, there are two roses,* Rosa *'American Pillar' and* R. *'Kew Rambler'.*

HOW TO ERECT A SIMPLE PILLAR

1 Dig a hole at least 60cm (2ft) deep. Put in the post and check that it is upright. Backfill with earth, ramming it firmly down as the hole is filled. In exposed gardens, fill the hole with concrete to give the pillar a more solid fixing.

2 Plants can be tied directly to the pillar, but a more natural support is provided using wire netting, secured with nails or staples. Plants such as clematis will then be able to climb by themselves, with little attention from you other than tying in wayward stems.

3 Plant the climber a little way out from the pole, to avoid the compacted area. Lead the stems to the wire netting and tie them in, to get them started. Self-clingers will now make their own way, but plants such as roses will need to be tied in as they climb. Twining plants such as hops can be grown up the pole without the wire.

Tripods and hoops

Tripods and hoops can provide a means of raising the level of the planting in a small garden, without creating an imposing barrier. They also provide a useful opportunity for growing climbers – even edible climbers – in beds and borders or other areas where space is limited.

Using tripods

Tripods can be formal, made to a classic design, or they can be made from more natural-looking rustic poles. The former are better where they are still partly on show when the climber is in full growth. The latter, in spite of their informal charm, are more suitable for carrying heavy, rampant climbers that will eventually cover them completely.

More formal designs can be bought complete, ready to be installed in the garden. A rustic-pole tripod is much more basic and can easily be constructed by most gardeners. Tripods can be made to any height, to suit the eventual height of the plants and the visual aspects of the site.

Climbers for tripods

Although any type of climber can be grown up a tripod, self-clingers would not be so good because there is not enough flat surface to which they can attach themselves. Tripods are ideal for carrying two or more climbers at once. If possible, choose plants that flower at different times. Alternatively you could choose two that flower at the same time but look particularly well together.

Using hoops

Training a climber over hoops allows you to direct the growth of the plant, thus helping to keep its final height in proportion to the border in which it is growing. Most climbers are suitable for this purpose, although very vigorous plants are best avoided; they will soon outgrow their allotted space, no matter however much training you do.

1 Position three posts in the ground. The distance apart will depend on the height: balance the two to get a good shape. You can drive the posts into the ground, but the tripod will be more secure if you dig holes at least 60cm (2ft) deep, insert the posts and ram the earth back in. Fill the holes with dry-mix concrete.

2 Nail cross-pieces between the posts. These will not only help support the plants but also give the structure rigidity. Rails 40–45cm (15–18in) apart should be sufficient for tying in stems. If you want more support for self-clingers, wrap a layer of wire netting around the structure. The plants will soon hide it.

3 Nail the pieces on first and then cut them to the right length. Alternatively, cut to length and then drill holes in the appropriate places before nailing to the poles.

4 Plant the climbers in and around the tripod. Avoid the area close to the poles as the earth here may be hard or replaced with concrete. Dig in well-rotted organic matter first.

TRAINING A CLIMBER OVER HOOPS

Bending the new young growth of a climber into curving arches encourages flowering buds to form along the whole length of the stem, rather than just at the tip, as happens if the branch grows upwards.

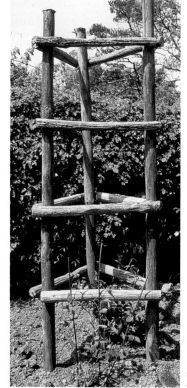

5 Water all the plant in well. If the weather continues dry, keep watering until the plants have become established.

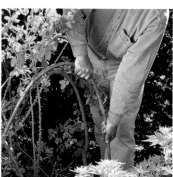

1 In early spring, use lengths of a pliable wood (hazel is ideal) to make a series of hoops around the climber. Bend each length carefully so that it does not crack, and push both ends of each one into the ground.

2 Allow each hoop to overlap the previous one.

6 The finished tripod will look raw at first, but will soon weather and become covered in plants.

3 Sort out the long shoots of the climber and carefully bend them over and then tie them to a convenient point on the hoop. In some cases it may be easier to tie the shoot to a stem that has already been tied down.

4 Initially the overall effect will look rather untidy, but gradually the leaves will turn to face the light and the plant will produce new buds all along the upper edges of the curved stems. Each year, remove a few of the older stems and tie in all the new ones. After a few years, you will need to replace the hoops with new ones.

Using ornaments

Ornaments can be used around the garden in much the same way as around the house. Choose them simply because you like them, because they will look good in a particular position, or as a device for attracting attention and admiration.

In a small garden their use as a focal point is paramount. Large focal points are impractical or can only ever be few in number, but small ornaments, birdbaths, sundials, and attractive urns can be used liberally. The only 'rule' is not to have more than a couple in view at once, as they will then compete for attention rather than taking centre stage. There is no limit to the number you can use in a small garden provided they form part of a journey of discovery. Use them among plants that you only discover from a particular viewpoint, or around a corner that is not visible from where you viewed the previous focal point.

Never let ornaments detract from major focal points that form part of the basic design, and don't allow the garden to look cluttered. Aim for simplicity with surprises.

Sundials

Whole books are written about sundials, and purists expect them to be functional. Setting them up accurately not only demands a sunny spot but quite a lot of calculations too, with compensation for geographical position. Most of us, using the sundial simply as an ornament, are happy to go out at noon on a sunny day in summer and align the gnomon to give the appropriate reading. It won't be accurate as the seasons change, but then you are unlikely to be using it to decide when it is time to leave for the office.

Accuracy may not be important, but a sunny position is. The whole object of a sundial is lost in a shady

RIGHT: A bird bath is a better choice than a sundial for a position often in shade.

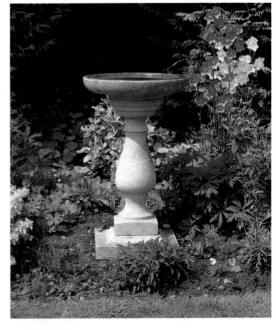

BELOW: A chimney pot makes an unusual plinth for a sundial.

spot, where a birdbath would serve a similar design function without looking incongruous.

Choose the plinth carefully – they vary in style and height (you could even build your own from bricks) and go for a fairly low plinth if the area available is quite small.

The best place for a sundial is as a centrepiece for a formal garden, perhaps in the centre of a herb garden with paths radiating out from the centre. The lawn is another practical choice, but if the lawn is small, consider placing the sundial to one side rather than in the centre.

Birdbaths

The positions suggested for a sundial are also appropriate for a birdbath, but birdbaths are much more useful for shady positions – though not too close to trees, otherwise they become filled with leaves and debris. A birdbath can even look effective in a flower border, with much of the plinth covered by flowers, or try it as a patio ornament if you want the pleasures of watching the birds drinking from it and bathing.

Sculptures

The use of sculptures and artistic objects demands confidence. Few people react adversely to a sundial or birdbath, but sculptures or artistic ornaments that generate admiration in one person can be abhorrent to another. This should never deter anyone from using ornaments that please them, but they are bound to be somewhat more difficult to place in a small garden.

Human figures

Busts sound unlikely ornaments for a small garden, but provided they aren't too large they can look great in an alcove or on a plinth in a dull corner. Small figures can sometimes work well if surrounded by clever planting.

Animal figures

Animal figures are always a safe bet, especially if set among the plants, or even on the lawn.

Abstract ornaments

Abstract ornaments should be used with restraint – they make a considerable impact. Too many will tend to make the area look more like an art gallery than a garden.

Wall masks, plaques and gargoyles

These are great for relieving a dull wall, but are almost always best set amid the leaves of a climber such as ivy. The foliage frames the feature, and emphasizes its roles as an unusual focal point.

Gnomes

You probably love them or hate them, and that is the problem with using gnomes. One or two little people cleverly used with restraint can be very effective and add a sense of fun, but usually either they are banished from the garden or there is a whole army of them. The problem with the latter approach is that the garden will simply appear as a setting for a gnome collection.

Plinths and pedestals

Plinths are essential for raising a sundial, birdbath or bust to an appropriate height, but they can look stark in a small garden. Make more of a feature of a plinth by planting some low-growing plants around the base, and then use a few tall ground cover plants that can gradually stretch up around the base.

A plinth can look severe on a lawn and mowing around it can be difficult. Try setting one in a gravel bed with alpines around the base, or leave the bed as soil and plant thymes or other low-growing aromatic herbs.

ABOVE: *Small animal figures creeping out from the plants add a sense of fun.*

ABOVE: *This kind of ornament needs careful placing in a small garden – always take time to consider position.*

RIGHT: *Figures are often more exciting when they are discovered among the plants.*

Garden lighting

Garden lights not only make your garden look more dramatic as dusk falls, they also extend the hours during which you can enjoy it. If you like entertaining in the garden on summer evenings, or just want to sit and relax, lights will add another dimension to the space.

When illuminating your garden you are not attempting to fill the garden with floodlights, but rather to use spotlights to pick out a particular tree, highlight an ornament, or bring to life the droplets of a cascade or fountain.

You don't even need elaborate mains lighting. Low-voltage lighting supplied from a transformer indoors is perfectly adequate for most lighting jobs in a small garden.

Lighting beds
Summer bedding looks good with pools of light thrown downwards onto the beds. If you find the lights obtrusive during the day, choose a low-voltage type that is easy to move around. Simply push the spiked supports into the bed when you want to use the garden in the evening.

Picking out plants
Use a spotlight to pick out one or two striking plants that will form focal points in the evening. The white bark of a birch tree, perhaps underplanted with white impatiens, the tall ramrod spikes of red hot pokers (kniphofias), or a spiky yucca, make excellent focal points picked out in a spotlight. Tall feathery plants, such as fennel, also illuminate well.

Spotlighting ornaments
Ornaments and containers full of plants also make striking features to pick out in a spotlight.

Before highlighting an ornament, try moving the beam around. Quite different effects can be achieved by directing it upwards or downwards, and side lighting creates a very different effect to straight-on illumination.

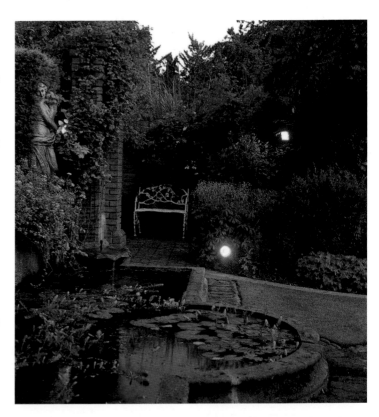

ABOVE: *An illuminated garden can become magical as dusk falls, and you will derive many more hours of pleasure from being able to sit out in the evening.*

Illuminating water
Underwater lighting is popular and you can buy special sealed lamps designed to be submerged or to float, but the effect can be disappointing if the water is murky or if algae grows thickly on the lenses. A simple white spotlight playing on moving water is often the most effective.

THINKING OF THE NEIGHBOURS

There is a problem with using garden lights in a small garden: you have to consider neighbours. It is unsociable to fix a spotlight where the beam not only illuminates your favourite tree but also falls on the windows of your neighbour's house. If you direct beams downwards rather than upwards, the pools of light should not obtrude.

WHEN PROFESSIONAL ADVICE IS NEEDED...

Low voltage lighting is designed for DIY installation, but 110-120 AC/DC demands special care. If you are going to wire your garden, use special outdoor fittings, and be aware of any regulations concerning the depth cables have to be buried and the protection required; you may be able to do the wiring yourself. But if in the slightest doubt use a professional electrician. If you want to keep the cost down, offer to do the labouring, such as digging trenches, yourself.

LEFT: *The best garden lighting is not obtrusive or unattractive during the day, and throws off white light when illuminated.*

HOW TO INSTALL LOW-VOLTAGE LIGHTING

1 A low-voltage lighting kit will come with a transformer. This must always be positioned in a dry place indoors or in a garage or outbuilding.

2 Drill a hole through the window frame or wall, just wide enough to take the cable. Fill in any gaps afterwards, using a mastic or other waterproof filler.

3 Although the cable carries a low voltage and you will not be electrocuted, it is still a potential hazard if left lying on the surface where someone might trip over it. Unless the lights are to be positioned close to where the cable emerges from indoors, run it underground in a conduit

4 Most low-voltage lighting systems are designed so that the lamps are easy to position and to move around. Many of them can just be pushed into the ground wherever you choose to place them.

Candle power

Candles must surely offer the most romantic outdoor lighting. The light they cast is soft, natural and flattering. Sitting near candles in the garden evokes campfires. They are also very practical for outside as they are eminently portable and they don't rely on electricity, so avoiding the problem of trailing cables. Candlelight is perfect for the table but, in various forms, can also provide subtle illumination throughout the garden itself, while flares can add that extra sparkle.

Candles

There are many forms of candlelight. Ordinary indoor candles can simply be taken outside, candelabra and all, for a candle-lit dinner. Ones containing beeswax burn more slowly than those made solely of paraffin wax, and they give off a lovely honey scent.

Lanterns

If the weather is a touch breezy, use a lantern or some other holder that protects the flame from the elements. Choose lanterns that can take a substantial size candle, otherwise you will be forever jumping up and down to light yet another. Also, check that the metalwork is robust, as some aluminium (aluminum) lanterns collapse once the lit candle melts the solder holding it together.

ABOVE: *Garden flares, 'planted' around the garden, provide a surprising amount of light. Many are also scented to discourage insects, which is of benefit when eating outdoors.*

LEFT: *A large, glass, hanging lantern makes enchanting lighting for dinner al fresco. Lotus-like flower candles float above a bed of shells, looking like an exotic lily pond.*

As well as lanterns, you could also try Victorian nightlights, tumbler-like glass containers that hang on wires, huge glass hanging lanterns, and candles in garden pots or galvanized buckets, which – once they burn down below the rim – have the added advantage of being protected from the wind.

Garden flares

Candles that are specially designed to cope with the outside elements are garden flares, which produce a huge flame and can burn for up to three hours. The light they give off is surprisingly bright, which makes them ideal for general lighting around the entertainment area or for lighting the route along pathways. This is particularly useful for any guests that do not know the garden as well as you do.

Position with care

The main danger from outdoor candles and garden flares is that the wind blows the flames, so it is important to position them well away from any furniture or foliage.

GILDED POTS

Ordinary terracotta pots, gilded and filled with candle wax, offer the most enchanting outdoor lighting. Make several pots in assorted sizes to group on tables, patios, walls and outdoor shelves.

1 Prime each pot with red oxide primer. Allow to dry for three to four hours.

2 Apply a coat of water-based gold size and allow to dry for about 30 minutes or until the size becomes transparent.

3 Lay pieces of gold Dutch metal leaf carefully onto the size, smoothing each one with a cloth or soft-bristled brush. Brush off any excess leaf.

4 Apply a coat of amber shellac to seal the metal leaf and allow to dry for 30 minutes.

5 To age the pots, tint a little white acrylic paint with aqua acrylic. Thin with water and brush on and rub off with a cloth. Allow to dry. For the candle, suspend the wick in the pot by tying it to a stick laid across the pot, ensuring it reaches the bottom. Melt the wax in a double boiler. Pour into the pot. Allow to set overnight.

Illuminate a warm summer night in your garden with candlelight. These pretty gilded pots will add a sparkle to the evening.

Furnishing the garden

A few seats and a table make the garden an inviting place to eat, or to sit and relax. Unfortunately where space is at a premium every item has to be chosen and placed with care. Built-in seats, and especially tree seats, are a good choice for a small garden.

Portable furniture
Furniture that can be moved is useful for a quick scene change and helps to prevent your garden becoming predictable. It is surprising how effective a canvas 'director's chair' can look on a summer's day, and it is quick and easy to fold up and store when not in use.

Built-in
Built-in furniture saves space and helps prevent a small garden looking cluttered. The best place for built-in seating is the patio, where it can often be designed along with the rest of the structure. White-painted planks look smart, and can quickly be trans- formed with cushions to look elegant as well as feel comfortable.

Built-round
A tree seat makes an eye-catching garden feature, and this is one occasion when the advice not to have a seat beneath a tree can be ignored! White paint will help the seat to stand out in the shade of its branches.

Wrought and cast iron
Genuine cast and wrought iron furniture is expensive and very heavy, but alloy imitations are available with all the charm of the original but at a more manageable price and weight. White is again a popular colour, but bear in mind that although this type of furniture can stand outside through- out the year, it will soon become dirty. Cleaning the intricate patterns isn't easy. Colours such as green look smart yet don't show the dirt.

Use cushions to add patches of colour, and to make the chairs less uncomfortable to sit on!

LEFT: *White-painted metal furniture looks tasteful and can help enliven a dull corner of the garden.*

BELOW: *A charming wooden seat.*

BELOW LEFT: *A reconstituted stone seat has a timeless appeal that beckons you to sit and rest.*

Wooden seats and benches
Timber seats can be left in natural wood colour to blend with the background or painted so that they become a focal point. White is popular, but green and even red can look very smart. Yacht paint is weather-resistant.

Plastic
Don't dismiss plastic. Certainly there are plenty of cheap and nasty pieces of garden furniture made from this material, but the better pieces can look very stylish for a patio in the setting of a modern garden.

HOW TO MAKE A TREE SEAT

1 Start by securing the legs in position. Use 3.8cm × 7.5cm (1½in × 3in) softwood, treated with a preservative. You will need eight lengths about 68cm (27in) long. Concrete them into position.

2 Position the legs about 38–45cm (15–18in) apart in two rows about the same distance either side of the trunk.

3 Cut four pieces of 2.5 x 5cm (1 × 2in) softwood for the cross-bars. Allow 7.5cm (3in) over-hang at each end. Drill and screw these to the posts.

4 Then, cut slats to the required length (the number will depend on the size of your seat). Allow for a 2.5cm (1in) space between each slat. Paint the slats and cross-bars with white paint (or a wood preservative or stain if you prefer), and allow to dry before final assembly. Test the spacing, using an offcut of wood as a guide, and when satisfied that they are evenly spaced on the cross-bars, mark the positions with a pencil. Then glue and nail into position.

Decorating garden furniture

Co-ordinating furniture with its surroundings helps to give the garden a feeling of harmony. By painting or staining furniture, you can also keep the costs down, as you can pick up bargain pieces from junk shops or rejuvenate old kitchen chairs that are due for replacement. Whether you opt for a simple decorative finish or one that is more elaborate, the key to success lies in the preparatory work you do.

Practicality

If garden furniture is to be left outside all year, bear in mind that any decorative finish will have to be able to withstand a lot of beating from the weather – frosts, strong winds, torrential rain, and the blistering sun of high summer. For this reason, it is best to use exterior-quality products: they are less likely to peel and flake, their colours are less likely to fade, and they are specifically designed to protect the surface they are covering. However, you can achieve a reasonably hard-wearing finish using paints made for interior use, then finishing with several coats of a polyurethane varnish.

Compatibility counts

Whatever you plan to paint or stain, it is important to use compatible primers, undercoats and varnishes, otherwise they may react against each another. So, if you intend to use a water-based product, make sure that you also prime and finish using water-based products; similarly,

ABOVE: *This colourful, plastic-covered chair offers indoor comfort outside. Its bright green framework and pink floral pattern provide a witty contrast to the Louis XIV style.*

LEFT: *An old Lloyd loom chair has been given a fresh look with two vivid shades of blue spray-on car paint.*

ABOVE: *Clashing Caribbean colours in pink and tangerine make for a lively look in a brightly coloured garden.*

ABOVE: *This simply shaped chair has been given a bright, modern finish to team with the painted shed behind.*

ABOVE: *The same chair has been decorated with a traditional Tyrolean design. The colours complement the colours of a summer garden.*

acrylics should be kept together and oil-based products should be kept together.

Also, ideally, you should stick to one manufacturer's products for each job as that will ensure compatibility. When you are not able to do this, it would be wise to test a small, hidden area first to see how the different products behave.

Working outdoors

If you have to paint outdoors, it is a good idea to choose a dry, warm day – preferably after several similar days and with the prospect of more to come. The reasons for this carefulness are clear. If the surface is damp, the paint will not adhere properly. If the surface is hot, from baking sun, it will blister. If frost is about, it will 'lift' the paint.

Preparatory work

It really is important to make sure the surface you are working on is properly prepared first, following the instructions given by the manufacturer of the product you are using.

Smooth wood

Most garden furniture is made from smooth-planed wood. There are three types of product you can use to paint these: exterior gloss, exterior woodstain, and exterior varnish, which comes in a clear, matt or gloss finish as well as in a wide selection of colours. Most woodstains – as the name implies – come in wood colours, although some specialist manufacturers produce coloured stains too. Garden furniture is usually bought ready-treated with a preservative that you can simply paint over. However, check this is the case before you buy.

Wash the surface with a proprietary paint cleaner or a mild detergent, then rinse thoroughly. Rub down with wet and dry paper. Allow to dry out completely, then paint on a coat of exterior primer. Allow to dry, then rub down and apply an undercoat. Allow to dry, then rub down and apply exterior gloss paint. Always allow plenty of drying time between each stage, taking the manufacturer's specified time as the minimum.

If you would prefer a finish that allows the grain of the wood to show through, you can choose either a woodstain or a varnish. The colour in woodstains penetrates the wood; varnish, even if it is a stained varnish, sits on top. These products are usually applied directly to the clean, dry wood.

Metal

Metal tables and chairs (as well as gates and railings) can be painted with exterior-quality gloss paint. Brush previously painted metal with a wire brush to clean it and remove any loose paint and metal badly eroded by rust. Then dust off. Treat rust with a rust cure and prime any new or bare metal with the appropriate metal primer, then allow to dry before applying the top coat. There are also special metal paints available in aerosol and brush-on versions that can be applied straight over the metal without priming, even if truly rusty. However, it is worth removing any loose rust first with a wire brush.

Entertaining outdoors

Entertaining friends in the garden is one of the joys of summer. Pleasant company and beautiful surroundings rarely fail to induce a feeling of well-being and relaxation, and serving food that you have grown yourself brings deep satisfaction.

The food can be simple, with freshly picked salads, fruits or vegetables and meat or fish grilled or barbecued with fresh herbs, the aroma complementing the scent of the herbs growing in the nearby beds.

ABOVE: *Lunch taken outside in the summer can be a memorable occasion. Attractive garden furniture and a pretty flower arrangement create a suitably restful ambience for eating outdoors.*

However informal the occasion, your guests will feel more comfortable if the eating area is sheltered, rather than completely in the open. If it is not next to the house, it will need to be screened by hedges or trellis to lend some privacy. You don't need a large space – just think how cramped restaurants can be, yet, once seated, you feel comfortable.

Awnings and umbrellas
Shade and shelter are important, but they needn't be permanent fixtures. You can put up a capacious sun umbrella or a prettily striped awning to provide temporary shade – allowing you to dine outside even in the middle of the day in high summer.

Stimulating the senses
Once the eating area is established, try to incorporate something that stimulates each of the senses. Place a handsome specimen plant within view, or position the chairs to look onto a pleasant vista. Nature will offer plenty to please your ear: summer birdsong, the hum of bees and whisper of trees and shrubs gently stirred by a breeze can be enhanced by the tinkling of wind chimes. A water feature can offer the relaxing sound of a trickling stream.

For fragrance, site plants with richly perfumed blooms near the seating area. Old-fashioned roses are hard to beat or try aromatic lavender and rosemary. Many flowers exude their scent at night. Summer jasmine and tobacco plants (*Nicotiana*) are two favourites. For touch, you can plant a contrast of textures from feathery

CLIMBERS FOR ARBOURS

Clematis (some fragrant)
Hedera (ivy – evergreen)
Humulus (hop – dies back in the winter)
Lonicera (honeysuckle – many fragrant)
Polygonum baldschuanicum (syn. *Fallopia baldschuanica*) (Russian vine – very vigorous)
Rosa (roses – many fragrant)

ABOVE: *Original Edwardian awnings like this one come with a lightweight metal frame that is easily erected and the awning is slipped over.*

ABOVE: *In the summer, a couple of potted strawberry plants are transformed into a centre-piece when contained in a wire jug.*

love-in-a-mist (*Nigella*) and shapely ferns to rich succulents. Finally, taste can be stimulated by nearby aromatic herbs or fragrant fruits such as strawberries and blackberries.

Decorating the table

Decorating the table can be effortless. Outdoor table decorations are the very easiest to put together because they are at their most successful when they complement their surroundings. So plunder the garden and then combine the ingredients with flair. You may cut a few flowers, adding foliage or even fruit and vegetables. Or you may simply gather together some of the smaller pots from around the garden. For an evening meal, add soft lighting, such as provided by candles, and the scene will be enticingly set.

Arbours

An arbour – a simple framework over which climbers are trained to create a shady outdoor room – can provide the perfect setting for entertaining friends. It can be just big enough to take a couple of chairs or bench, but best of all is an arbour large enough to accommodate a table and several chairs, where you can sit and linger over *al fresco* meals.

Designing an arbour

The structure can be of metal or wood, or the arbour can have brick or stone piers with a wooden roof. The design may be triangular, semi-circular, rectangular or octagonal – any shape, in fact, that fits the site.

Most climbers are suitable for clothing the arbour; but if you do not like bees, it is best to stick to climbers grown for their foliage rather than their flowers.

Solid construction

An arbour may have to remain in place for many years, so make sure you build it well. Take trouble to use timbers treated with preservative (not creosote, which may kill the climbers) and make certain that it is a strong design, well supported in the ground. As with similar structures that are covered in heavy climbers, the wind can wreak havoc on weak construction.

Rock and Water Gardens

ROCK AND WATER FEATURES ADD AN EXTRA
dimension to any garden, but imagination is
needed to get the best from them in a small area.
The vast majority of rock and water plants thrive
best in a sunny position, and it may be difficult to
find a suitable site in a small garden. If you can't
find a spot that is in the sun for at least half the
day – and preferably longer – it might be better to
choose a water feature that depends less on plants
for its effect, and to grow your rock plants in
other ways, such as between paving and in raised
beds or a gravel garden.

Very small ponds are much more difficult to
'balance' biologically than large ones, and green
water is often a problem for much of the year. If
the garden is very tiny choose a bubble fountain,
wall spout, or container pond instead.

Rock gardens look best on a natural slope or built to look like a natural outcrop of rocks in a large lawn. Most small gardens offer neither opportunity. Combining a rock feature with the pond is often the most satisfactory solution. You can create the raised ground from the soil excavated for the pond.

Rock plants – or alpines if you prefer the label – offer huge scope for an enthusiastic gardener with a passion for plants but without the space to grow many. You can plant dozens in the space taken by just one medium-sized shrub, and even the tiniest garden can be home for hundreds of plants.

Be careful with the choice of water plants. Some irises and rushes are compact, others are rampant and will soon make a take-over bid. There are waterlilies that need deep water and a large surface area, others that will be happy in 23cm (9in) of water and will make do with a much smaller surface area.

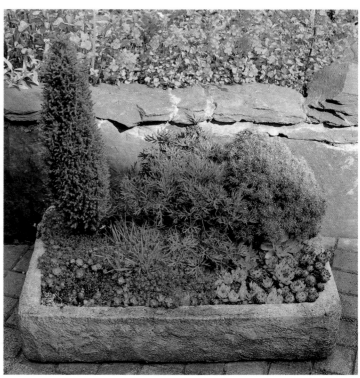

TOP: Sedum spurium 'Atropurpureum'.
ABOVE: Campanulas – here growing through Asplenium scolopendrium – are popular rock plants.
RIGHT: This sink garden contains more than half a dozen different plants in less space than a single shrub would normally occupy.
OPPOSITE: Raising the edges of this pond has emphasized its role as the centre of attention.
OPPOSITE ABOVE: Various species of dianthus do well in a rock garden and always have a special appeal.

Ponds and water features

Making a pond is very easy nowadays – most flexible liners are strong and long-lasting, and pre-formed pools are as near as you can get to buying an instant pond off the shelf. If you don't have space for a 'proper' pond, make one in a barrel or shrub tub.

If you want to grow plants and keep fish, choose a bright position for your pond, one that receives sun for at least half the day. Avoid overhanging trees, they not only cast shade but shed leaves too, which can pollute the water.

Fountains and cascades
Introduce a cascade if you build a rock garden with your pond. A simple low-voltage submersible pump linking the head of the cascade with a hose is usually adequate for a small cascade with a modest flow of water.

Fountains need a large area of water, otherwise drift will cause a gradual drop in the water level. Be aware that the disturbed surface does not suit waterlilies and some other aquatic plants. A simple bubble or geyser type of jet is often more appropriate than a high, ornate jet in a small garden.

ABOVE: *You don't need a large garden to enjoy the sight and sound of moving water, as this attractive feature shows.*

Wall features
In a courtyard or a basement garden enclosed by walls, a wall fountain is often the best choice. You don't need a great gush of water.

You can fix a spout that pours water into a reservoir at the base of the wall to be recirculated through a hidden pump; alternatively buy one that is self-contained with water simply trickling into an integrated dish beneath the spout.

Miniature ponds
If you've no room for a proper pond, make one in a half-barrel or even a plastic shrub tub. Sink it into the ground, half-sink it into the soil, or have it free-standing, perhaps on a paved area such as the patio. Container ponds are not suitable for fish, but you can grow an interesting small collection of aquatic plants in them, including miniature waterlilies.

HOW TO MAKE A POND USING A LINER

1 Mark out the shape of your pond with a piece of rope, hosepipe or by sprinkling sand. Then remove the grass and excavate the soil to the required depth, leaving a shallow ledge about 23cm (9in) wide at about that depth from the top.

2 Remove the grass or soil around the edge if you plan to pave it. Allow for the thickness of the paving plus a bed of mortar. Check levels and remove extra soil from one side if necessary. The water surface needs to be level to the sides of the pond.

3 Remove sharp stones and large roots, then line the pool with about 1cm (½in) of damp sand – it should stick to the sides if they slope slightly. Use a polyester mat (from water garden specialists) or old carpet instead of sand if the soil is stony.

HOW TO INSTALL A PRE-FORMED POND

1 Transfer the shape of your pool to the ground by inserting canes around the edge. Use a hosepipe or rope to define the shape.

2 Excavate the hole to approximately the right depth, and following the profile of the shelves as accurately as possible.

3 Place a straight-edged piece of wood across the top and check that the edges are level. Measure down to check the depths.

4 Place the pool in the hole and add or remove more soil if it does not sit snugly. Also remove any sharp stones. Check that it is absolutely straight with a spirit-level.

5 Remove the pond and line the shape with sand. Backfill so that the pond shape fits the hole snugly.

6 Run water in from a hose, and backfill and firm again as the water rises. Check the levels frequently as the backfilling often tends to lift the pool slightly.

4 Drape the liner over the hole, anchoring the edges with bricks. Run water into the pool from a hose. As the weight of water takes the liner into the hole, release the bricks occasionally. Some creases will form but are not usually noticeable.

5 Trim the liner, leaving an overlap around the edge of about 15cm (6in), to be covered by the paving.

6 Bed the paving on mortar, covering the edge of the liner. The paving should overlap the edge of the pool by about 3cm (1in). Finish off by pointing the joints with mortar.

How to plant a pond

The best time to plant a pond is between mid spring and early summer, when new growth is vigorous yet the plants are not too large. However, most plants can be introduced either earlier or later. Tender floaters such as *Eichhornia crassipes* and *Salvinia braziliensis* should not be introduced while there is a reasonable risk of frost.

HOW TO PLANT WATERLILIES

1 Waterlilies and other deep-water plants can be planted in the same mesh baskets used for marginal plants, but for the more vigorous waterlilies an old washing-up bowl provides more root-run. Plant as for marginals (see below).

2 Cover the soil surface with gravel. There may be space to insert a few oxygenating plants around the edge. These will probably spread and root elsewhere, but it will get them off to a good start.

3 Lower the bowl into the water. If planting early, before the leaf stalks are long, rest the bowl on a couple of bricks for a week or two, then lower to its final position. Different varieties should be planted at different depths.

HOW TO PLANT MARGINALS

1 Use a pond planting basket, and line it with a piece of hessian (sometimes sold for the purpose by water garden specialists) or a piece of horticultural fleece. Fill the container with a soil for aquatics. Insert the plant and carefully firm the soil around the roots.

2 Cover the surface with gravel. This will help to protect the soil from erosion and fish are less likely to stir it up. Gently lower the basket into the water so that it sits on the marginal shelf with about 5cm (2in) of water above the soil.

Six of the best marginals
- *Caltha palustris*
Yellow flowers in spring.
- *Houttuynia cordata*
Small white flowers in summer. Green leaves with red stems, but 'Chameleon' has multicoloured foliage.
- *Iris laevigata*
Mainly blue, white or pink flowers, depending on variety, in summer.
- *Juncus effusus* 'Spiralis'
Stems spirally twisted like corkscrew.
- *Pontederia cordata*
Spikes of pale blue flowers in summer and autumn.
- *Scirpus* 'Zebrinus'
Leaves transversely banded white and green.

ABOVE: *A well-planted pond has both deep-water plants like waterlilies and marginal plants around the edge.*
BELOW: *Caltha palustris is one of the easiest marginal or bog-garden plants to grow.*

Three of the best oxygenating plants
- *Elodea canadensis*
Not much to see – tightly packed small green leaves on submerged stems. Excellent oxygenator, but will require thinning out several times each season.

- *Myriophyllum* (several species)
Dense whorls of feathery green foliage that rises above the water. Can spread rapidly once established.
- *Tillaea recurva*
Bright green, almost moss-like growth just below surface.

Six of the best waterlilies for a small pond
- 'Froebelli' – Red.
- 'James Brydon' – Red.
- *Laydekeri lilacea* – Pink.
- 'Paul Hariot'
Yellow deepening to copper-red with age.
- *Pygmaea helvola*
Yellow, very small and suitable for miniature ponds.
- 'Rose Arey' – Pink.

Other deep-water aquatics
- *Aponogeton distachyos*
Slightly scented white flowers from spring to autumn.
- *Orontium aquaticum*

DON'T FORGET THE DRY-SIDE

With a natural pond, the soil by the water's edge is usually very moist. The soil immediately behind a pre-formed or liner pool will be as dry as in the rest of the garden. But there are many plants that are associated with water that will tolerate dry soil, even though they may prefer it moist. Make the most of these to give the illusion of a bog garden or natural edging to an informal pond. Plants to include are astilbes, hostas, *Iris sibirica*, *I. pseudacorus*, mimulus, many primulas, and hemerocallis.

Poker-like flowers with bright yellow tips in mid and late spring.

Floaters to try . . . and to avoid
Two good floaters that are unlikely to become uncontrollable are *Stratiotes aloides* and *Azolla caroliniana*. The latter spreads quickly but winter knocks it back except where winters are very mild (in cold areas it is worth overwintering a few plants in a frost-free place to start the colony again the following year).

Avoid any species of *Lemna* (duckweed). They not only spread rapidly but are very difficult to eradicate.

Routine pond maintenance

Although informal ponds tend to look after themselves, there are various routine measures you should undertake to help promote a healthy balance of plants and to encourage other species to inhabit the pond. Checking the water level and looking for any leaks are all-important tasks. Keeping the water clear of algae and other highly invasive plants means that the pond's other inhabitants – the ones you want to be there – get the best possible chance to thrive.

Maintaining the water level

You will need to fill up the water in the pond periodically, particularly in summer. Allowing the level to drop too much may expose the liner to the potentially harmful rays of the sun. Fill the pond in the evening with a hose. If you can raise the end of the hose above the water level, the resultant agitation will help to oxygenate the water and will be beneficial to any fish in the pond.

Checking for leaks

Some gardeners like to drain and refill the pond annually, although this is not a good idea if you keep fish, while others do it every two or three years. However, it is only necessary to drain a pond if a leak develops in the liner itself. The tell-tale sign that there is a leak is a dramatic drop in the water level, but before you drain the pond, check the edges to make sure that the liner has not collapsed at any point. If part of the liner has slipped below the desired water level, build it up again from behind, then fill the pond with fresh water.

If you are sure there is a leak, press all around the liner with your hands to locate it (the soil behind the hole will feel soft and boggy), then drain the pond to below the level of the leak. You will then need to repair the liner, using a repair kit appropriate to the type of liner material.

ABOVE: *As the water evaporates, particularly during the summer, use a hosepipe to increase the water level of the pond.*

RIGHT: *The excavated soil from this informal pool in a suburban garden has been used to make a raised bed, which is retained with local stone and log edging.*

ABOVE: *This duckweed should be removed before it spreads. It is very hardy and spreads so quickly that you need to check for it regularly.*

ABOVE: *If you leave a lettuce leaf on the surface of the water overnight, it will trap water snails that can be disposed of in the morning.*

Keeping the water clear

Most informal ponds are self-maintaining once the balance of plant and insect life is established, and you should have no major problems with water clarity.

Algal growth sometimes develops in spring and summer, however, where waterlilies and other plants with floating leaves are not mature enough to cover the required area (between 50 and 70 per cent of the water surface).

The problem may also be due to an insufficiency of oxygenating plants, but if the pond is a new one, or if you have just replaced all the water, it usually clears of its own accord. Otherwise, check the pool for dead or decaying leaves and flowers, and remove them. To clear the water quickly, use an ultraviolet clarifier.

In a formal pool where the water itself is the prime feature, eliminating algae may require more regular intervention. You can keep the water clear in a variety of ways. If the pool supports no plant or wildlife whatsoever, you can add any proprietary cleaning agent such as the chlorine that is usually used in swimming pools.

If you keep fish in a pond with plants, you may need to add an ultra-violet clarifier to keep the water clear.

Pond weeds

You are almost bound to have problems with blanketweed (*Spirogyra*), a plant that grows beneath the water surface in dense strands and is most prevalent during warm weather. You may not realize you have it until it comes to the surface, where it forms unsightly masses. It is easy to remove with a long cane, and makes good composting material.

Also in summer you may notice duckweed (*Lemna*), a tiny two-leaved plant with roots that trail in the water. It will rapidly colonize a small pond: once noticed it should be removed immediately with a net.

From time to time you may need to thin oxygenating plants by pulling out clumps with your hands, but make sure you leave enough behind to ensure water clarity. It is best to thin little and often.

ABOVE: *To clear water of blanket weed, insert a cane into the water and twist it to wind the weed around it like candyfloss.*

TOP: *Lift out and tear apart any clumps of oxygenating plants that are congested, returning about a half to two-thirds to the water.*

Water snails

Water snails can be a problem, since they feed on plants and often nibble away at the undersides of waterlily leaves. You may notice them clinging to the sides of the pool. A few will not do any significant harm and may even help to control blanketweed, but you can reduce their numbers by floating a lettuce leaf on the surface of the water and leaving it overnight. Next morning, lift the leaf and dispose of any water snails that have accumulated there. The ramshorn snail (*Planorbis corneus*), however, is a beneficial mollusc, since it feeds on decaying matter at the bottom of the pond.

The pond in winter

A few end-of-season tasks are essential if you want to help your pond, and its plants and fish, remain in good condition. These include keeping the water clear of leaves and other debris, and lifting and dividing any overgrown plants. The pump, too, may need attention now: if you leave a pump in your pond in shallow water over winter, ice may damage it. Once the pump is out of the water, you may wish to have it serviced if necessary so that it will be ready for use in the spring.

PREPARING THE POND FOR WINTER

1 Protect the pond from the worst of the leaf fall with a fine-mesh net. Anchor it just above the water's surface. This may not be practical for a large pond, but is useful for a small one. Remove the leaves regularly, and eventually take the netting off.

2 If you are not able to cover your pond with a net, or don't like the appearance of one, use a fish net or rake to remove leaves regularly – not only from the surface but also from deeper water. Too many leaves in the water can pollute the pond.

3 Submerged oxygenating plants, such as *Elodea* and rampant growers like milfoil (*Myriophyllum*), will eventually clog the pond unless you net or rake them out periodically. This is a good time to thin them simply by raking out the excess.

4 Trim back dead or dying plants, especially where the vegetation is likely to fall into the water. To divide overgrown water plants, first remove them from the containers. It may be necessary to cut some roots to do so.

5 Some plants can simply be pulled apart by hand, but others will have developed such a tight mass of roots that you may find them too tangled and have to chop them into smaller pieces with a spade.

6 Discard any pieces of plant that you don't want for replanting, then pot up the others in planting baskets. Cover the surface of the basket with gravel to prevent the soil being washed away.

PROTECTING POND PUMPS

1 Remove submersible pumps from the water before penetrating frosts cause the water to freeze deeply, unless it is below the ice line and needed to sustain a biological filter, which some gardeners prefer to keep working.

2 Clean the pump thoroughly before you put it away. It will probably be covered with algae, which can be scrubbed off with a stiff brush.

3 Remove the filter and either replace it with a new one or clean it. Follow the manufacturer's instructions.

4 Make sure all the water is drained from the pump. If your pump is an external one, make sure the system is drained.

5 Read the manufacturer's instructions, and carry out any other servicing that is necessary before storing the pump in a dry place. If you need to send the pump away for a service, do it now instead of waiting until spring.

Ways to grow rock plants

If you have a sunny corner, a rock garden could be an attractive way to fill it. Alternatively, introduce rocks with a pond. A steeply sloped rock garden provides an opportunity to include a series of cascades that run through the rock garden to the pool beneath. It also solves the problem of what to do with the soil excavated during pond construction!

If your interests lie more with the exquisite beauty of the plants than with the landscaping aspects of a rock garden, there are plenty of ways to include alpines in areas other than a rock garden.

Combined with water
Rock gardens and ponds both require a sunny position to do well, and they associate well together. It is often possible to introduce a series of cascades linking a small pool at the top with the main pool below. Bury the connecting hose when constructing the rock garden, and use plenty of rocks to make the cascades look as natural as possible.

Very pleasing combined rock and water gardens can also be constructed without running water.

Island rock beds
Provided the lawn is reasonably large, and informal in shape, small rock outcrops can be created. You don't need many rocks for this kind of rock garden, just a few bold ones, carefully positioned so that they look as though they are protruding through the ground. For rocks to look convincing it is important to slope them into the ground, and for the strata to lie in one direction.

Rock plants in gravel gardens
Rock plants look good in gravel, so include them in a gravel garden or create a small flat gravel bed just for rock plants. Provide the same soil conditions as for a raised rockery, but on the flat. In addition, you can include a few rocks to create the impression of a scree.

ABOVE: *If you like alpines but don't want a rock garden, why not have a whole collection of sink gardens?*
LEFT: *A low rock bank is another easy way to grow rock plants, and is very simple to construct.*

Sink gardens
Alpines are perfect for sink gardens. Genuine stone sinks are ideal, but these are scarce and expensive. Perfectly attractive gardens can be created in imitation stone sinks.

Although you can simply plant 'on the flat' within the trough or sink, much more effective are 'landscaped' displays in which a section of rock face is created.

Raised beds
The great advantage of a raised bed for alpines is that you are better able to appreciate their beauty in miniature. You can build the beds with bricks or walling blocks, but natural stone is much better, especially if you can leave plenty of planting holes in the sides.

Peat beds
The vast majority of alpines grow happily in ordinary or alkaline soil, but a few require acid conditions. If these plants appeal, build a peat bed from peat blocks, bonding the blocks like bricks. Fill with a peaty mixture or an ericaceous potting soil and plant the alpines in your chosen arrangement.

HOW TO MAKE A ROCK GARDEN

1 The base is a good place to dispose of rubble, which you can then cover with garden soil – the ideal place for soil excavated from the pond.

2 It is best to use a special soil mixture for the top 15–23cm (6–9in), especially if soil excavated from the pond is used. Mix together equal parts soil, coarse grit and peat (or peat substitute), and spread this evenly over the mound.

3 Lay the first rocks at the base, trying to keep the strata running in the same direction.

4 Lever the next row of rocks into position. Use rollers and levers to move them.

5 As each layer is built up, add more of the soil mixture, and consolidate it around the rocks.

6 Ensure that the sides all slope inwards, and make the top reasonably flat rather than building it into a pinnacle. Position the plants, then cover the exposed soil with a thin layer of horticultural grit.

Choosing and planting

A visit to any garden centre will reveal a huge selection of plants for your rock garden. One of the delights of collecting alpines is the constant surprises as new treasures are encountered, and the ability to indulge in a wide range of plants that won't take up much space.

The plants suggested here can only be an arbitrary selection of some of the best, with the emphasis on plants that are fairly widely available.

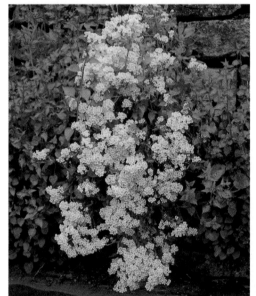

LEFT: Alyssum saxatile.

Useful for a wall
- *Acaena microphylla* (top or face)
- *Achillea tomentosa* (top)
- *Alyssum montanum* (top)
- *Alyssum saxatile* (top or face)
- *Arabis caucasica* (top or face)
- *Arenaria balearica* (top or face)
- *Aubrietia* (face)
- *Campanula garganica* (face)
- *Cerastium tomentosum* (face)
- *Corydalis lutea* (face)
- *Dianthus deltoides* (top or face)
- *Erinus alpinus* (top or face)
- *Gypsophila repens* (top or face)
- *Sedum*, many (face)
- *Sempervivum*, many (face)

BELOW LEFT: Dianthus deltoides *'Electra'*.
BELOW: Helianthemum *'Fire Dragon'*.

Try these in a trough
- *Arabis ferdinandi-coburgi* 'Variegata'
- *Aster alpinus*
- *Gentiana acaulis*
- *Hypericum olympicum*
- *Phlox douglasii*
- *Potentilla tabernaemontani*
- *Raoulia australis*
- *Rhodohypoxis baurii*
- *Sedum lydium*
- *Sempervivum* (various)

Good starter plants for a rock garden
Some of these plants are quite rampant or large – *Alyssum saxatile* and helianthemums, for example. If you are not familiar with particular plants, look them up in an encyclopedia.

- *Acaena microphylla*
- *Alyssum saxatile*

- *Antennaria dioica* 'Rosea'
- *Arabis ferdinandi-coburgi* 'Variegata'
- *Armeria maritima*
- *Campanula carpatica*
- *Campanula cochleariifolia*
- *Dianthus deltoides*
- *Dryas octopetala*

- *Erinus alpinus*
- *Gentiana acaulis*
- *Gentiana septemfida*
- *Gentiana sino-ornata*
- *Geranium subcaulescens* 'Splendens'
- *Gypsophila repens*
- *Helianthemum*

- *Hypericum olypicum*
- *Iberis sempervirens* 'Snowflake'
- *Oxalis adenophylla*
- *Phlox douglasii*
- *Phlox subulata*
- *Pulsatilla vulgaris*
- *Raoulia australis*
- *Saxifraga* (mossy type)
- *Sedum spathulifolium* 'Cape Blanco'
- *Sedum spurium*
- *Sempervivum* (various)
- *Silene schafta*
- *Thymus serpyllum* (various)
- *Veronica prostrata*

LEFT: Sempervivum ballsii.

HOW TO PLANT ALPINES

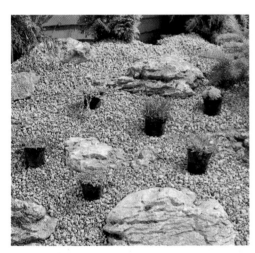

1 Position the plants while still in their pots so that you can see how they look and can move them around easily if necessary.

2 Use a trowel to take out a hole a little larger than the root-ball. You can buy narrow trowels that are particularly useful for planting in the crevices between rocks.

3 Make sure the plant is at the correct depth, then trickle gritty soil around the roots and firm it well.

4 Finish off by covering the exposed surface with more grit.

Choosing Plants

Hard landscaping (paving, walls, fences, pergolas, and so on) is what gives a garden a strong sense of design, and provides the skeleton that gives the garden its shape. But it is the soft landscaping – the plants – that provides the flesh, texture and character of the garden. The same basic design can look very different in the hands of gardeners with different ideas on the use of plants.

ABOVE: *Mixing different types of plant can be very effective. This border contains shrubs, herbaceous plants and bulbs.*

OPPOSITE: *No matter how attractive the structure of a garden, it is the plants that make it pretty.*

Beds and Borders

BEDS AND BORDERS NEED TO BE PLANNED. THE shape will affect the overall appearance, of course, but there are also practical considerations such as the amount of maintenance required, the theme to be created, as well as the crucial question of the actual plants to be used.

Formal beds and borders are normally dictated by the basic design concept, which will often determine the type of plants you can use. A formal rose garden will clearly feature roses, and only the 'filler' plants might have to be debated. A classic style with neat symmetrical beds cut into the lawn, or edged by clipped box, demands the type of formal bedding associated with this type of garden.

Herbaceous and shrub borders are much more open to interpretation, and the actual plants used will have as much affect on the overall impression created as the shape or size of the border.

In traditional large gardens there is a clear distinction between herbaceous borders and shrub borders, but few small gardens can afford this luxury and the inclusion of a 'mixed border' is the usual compromise. Here shrubs jostle for

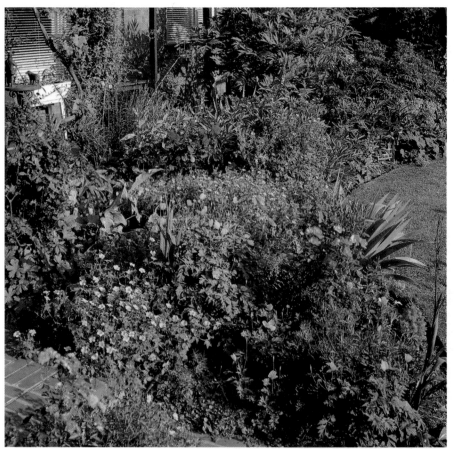

LEFT: *By curving the corners of borders in a small garden you can generate extra planting space that helps to make the garden more interesting.*

OPPOSITE ABOVE: *A garden like this, with plenty of shrubs such as roses, require little maintenance and because the hard landscaping is minimal is relatively inexpensive to create.*

OPPOSITE BELOW: *Single-sided herbaceous borders can look right in a rural setting if you have enough space. A border like this can be colourful for many months.*

position with herbaceous plants and annuals, while summer bedding plants and spring bulbs make bids for any areas of inhabitable space left. There is nothing wrong with this type of gardening: the border looks clothed long after the herbaceous plants have died down, and there will be flowers and pockets of changing interest for a much longer period than could be achieved with shrubs alone.

Colour themes are also difficult to achieve in a small garden, and although single-colour borders can be planted in a small garden, it is best to be a little more flexible. Settle for a 'golden corner' rather than a golden border, or a blue-and-silver theme for just part of a border rather than a more extensive area.

Small beds cut into the lawn do not have to be filled with summer bedding and then replaced by spring bulbs and spring bedding. Instead plant them with blocks of perennial ground cover, or use a perennial edging and plant seasonal flowers within it.

Island beds

Traditionally, low-growing seasonal plants have been grown in beds cut into the lawn – island beds – and taller herbaceous plants and shrubs placed in long borders designed to be viewed from one side. Island beds planted with herbaceous plants and shrubs bridge this divide, and provide planting opportunities that can be put to good use in a small garden.

Planting principles

Island beds are intended to be viewed from all sides, so the tallest plants usually go in the centre and the smaller ones around the edge. Don't be too rigid, however. Concentrate on creating a bed that you have to walk around to see the other side, rather than simply planting tall summer flowers like delphiniums in the centre. Shrubby plants, even medium-sized evergreens, might be better for the centre of the bed, with other lower-growing shrubs creating bays that can be filled with plants that die down for the winter. Your bed will then retain its function of breaking up a lawn and creating a

diversion that has to be explored.

Don't be afraid to plant a small tree, such as *Malus floribunda*, in an island bed, to create much-needed height.

If seasonal bedding appeals more than shrubs and border perennials, then island beds can still be used creatively for these.

The question of shape

Most people think of island beds as informal in outline, but you can introduce rectangular beds if this suits the style of your garden.

Curved beds generally look much more pleasing, however, especially if you introduce broad and narrow areas so that there are gentle bays.

Design considerations

Use an island bed to break the line of sight. By taking it across the garden, an island bed may distract attention from an uninspiring view – whether beyond the garden or simply the fence itself. Attention is directed to the sides, and as you walk around the bed, the eye is taken into the bed rather than to the perimeters.

A series of island beds can be used to divide up a long, narrow garden. Instead of the eye being taken in a straight line to the end, the beds become a series of diversions.

BELOW: *Island beds help to break up a large lawn, and create a sense of height.*

One-sided borders

Single-sided borders are useful if you want to create flowery boundaries around the perimeter and emphasize an open space within the garden, turning the garden in on itself. These borders are also useful for taking the eye to a distant focal point, and, by varying the width of the border, you can create a false sense of perspective that can appear to alter the size of the garden.

Straight and narrow beds

Most gardens have at least some straight and narrow borders around the edge of the lawn, a favourite spot for roses or seasonal bedding. If you want to cut down on the regular replanting work, plant with dwarf shrubs as backbone plants then include flowering ground cover herbaceous plants such as hardy geraniums and spring bulbs to provide flowers over a long period.

Make a border look wider by laying a mowing edge. Then use plants that will sprawl over the edge, softening the hard line and giving the impression of a wider border.

The advantages of curved borders

Straight edges are easier to mow and trim, but unless the border is wide and variation is created with the use of shrubs of various sizes, they can appear unimaginative and may take the eye too quickly along the garden, making it seem smaller. Gentle curves that create bays enable the plants to be brought further out into the garden and provide much more adventurous planting scope.

It may be possible to modify an existing straight border by cutting into the lawn. Bear in mind that mowing time is likely to be increased rather than decreased, however.

ABOVE: *Single-sided borders are the best choice for small town gardens that have high enclosing walls, especially if you can use climbers or tall plants to hide the wall.*
LEFT: *A single-sided mixed border.*

Turning corners

Don't forget that borders can turn corners. Right-angled turns seldom look satisfactory, however, so add a curve to the corner. This will give it greater depth at that point.

You can even take the border right round the garden in a continuous strip. A small square garden with a circular central lawn surrounded by border can look quite spectacular if well planted with a wide range of plants that hold interest throughout the seasons.

How to make beds and borders

If you are making a garden from scratch, areas allocated to lawns, beds and borders will be laid out accordingly, but you can often improve an existing garden by altering the shape of a border, or creating beds in what is currently a large and uninspiring lawn.

HOW TO MAKE A CURVED BORDER

HOW TO MARK OUT AN OVAL BED

For small formal beds, such as ovals and circles, it is best to sow or lay the grass over the whole area first, then cut out the beds once the grass has become established.

Start by marking out a rectangle that will contain the oval. Afterwards you can check that it is square by measuring across the diagonals, which should be the same length.

Place a peg half way along each side, and stretch a string between them. The two strings will cross at the centre point. Then cut a piece of string half the *length* of the oval and using a side peg as a pivot, insert pegs where it intersects the long string along the centre.

Make a loop from a piece of string twice the distance between one of these two pegs and the top or bottom of the oval (whichever is the furthest away).

With the loop draped over the inner pegs, scribe a line in the grass while keeping the string taut. You can make the line more visible by using a narrow-necked bottle filled with dry sand instead of a stick.

Use an edging iron to cut out the shape, then lift the grass with a spade.

1 If you want a quick and easy method, and can trust your eye for an even curve, lay hosepipe where you think the new edge should be. Run warm water through it first if the weather is cold, otherwise it may not be flexible enough to lie on the ground without awkward kinks.

2 The best way to judge whether the curves are satisfactory is to view the garden from an upstairs window, and have someone on the ground who can make further adjustments if necessary.

3 When the profile is satisfactory, run sand along the marker (dry sand in a wine bottle is a convenient method). Use an edging iron to cut the new edge, then lift the surplus grass and dig the soil thoroughly before attempting to replant.

4 An alternative and a more accurate way to achieve smooth curves is to use a stick or bottle fixed to a string attached to a peg. Use this as a pivot. By adjusting the length of the string and the position of the pivot, a series of curves can be achieved. Cut the edge as before.

How to get a neat edge

Emphasize the profile of your beds and borders, as well as your paths, by giving them a crisp or interesting edge. A mowing edge is a practical solution for a straight-edged border. Curved beds and borders usually have to be edged in other ways.

Some methods, like the corrugated edging strip and the wooden edge shown below are not particularly elegant, but they help to prevent the gradual erosion of the lawn through constant trimming and cutting back, and they maintain a crisp profile.

Using ornate or unusual edgings
For a period garden, choose a suitable edging. Victorian-style rope edging tiles are appropriate. If you live in a coastal area, consider using large seashells. If you enjoy your wine as well as your garden, why not put the empty bottles to use by forming an edging with them? Bury them neck-down in a single or double row, with just a portion showing.

TOP: *It is possible to buy a modern version of Victorian rope-edging.*
ABOVE: *Edgings such as this are useful if you want to create a formal or old-fashioned effect.*

HOW TO FIT EDGING STRIPS

Edging strips like this are available in a thin metal, soft enough to cut with old scissors, or in plastic. These strips help stop erosion of the grass through frequent edge clipping and cutting back. Although these may not be the most decorative edging strips, they are quick and easy to fit.

1 Make a slit trench along the lawn edge with a spade, then lay the strip alongside the trench and cut to length. Place the edging strip loosely into it.

2 Backfill with soil for a firm fit. Press the strip in gently as you proceed. Finish off by tapping it level with a hammer over a straight-edged piece of wood.

HOW TO FIT WOODEN EDGING ROLL

Wired rolls of sawn logs can make a strong and attractive edging where you want the bed to be raised slightly above the lawn, but bear in mind that it may be difficult to mow right up to the edge.

1 Cut the roll to length using wire-cutters or strong pliers to cut through the wires, and insert the edging in a shallow trench. Join pieces by wiring them together. Backfill with soil for a firm fit. Make sure that the edging is level, first by eye. Use a hammer over a straight-edged piece of wood to tap it down. Then check the height with a spirit-level. Adjust as necessary.

Planning Borders

THE SECRET OF A SUCCESSFUL BORDER IS PLANNING for a long period of interest. However large a border, it probably will not remain attractive for more than about a month if you plan it only with plants that flower together. Planning should include not only plants that make pleasing associations when flowering, but that look good even out of bloom. Also incorporate plants that flower at different seasons.

The risk of planting a series of plants that bloom at different times is an uncoordinated appearance, with plants in flower dotted about amid a swathe of foliage in varying stages of

ABOVE: *Hydrangeas look good in shrub borders or mixed borders, but the flower colour may vary according to the acidity or alkalinity of the soil.*

LEFT: *Don't be afraid to use a focal point like a birdbath in a border. It will be eyecatching even when the plants are not at their best.*

growth. Sadly, in a small garden there isn't space to devote to a spring border, summer border, and autumn border.

Some of these shortcomings can be overcome by planting a mixed border that clearly incorporates many different kinds of plants, and by always planting in bold groups rather than using isolated specimens.

If starting from scratch, plan your borders on paper first. In an existing border you will obviously want to retain as many plants as possible, but be prepared to uproot and move or discard those that are out of place.

Choosing plants is always difficult, but in the following pages you will find suggestions of some of the most useful for a small garden. Space precludes mention of more than a small selection of suitable plants, so add special favourites and others that suit *your* garden and *your* taste.

TOP: *A border showing a good mix of shrubs and perennials.*
ABOVE: *Hollies are useful for the back of a shrub border.*

How to plant a border

You don't have to be an artist to draw a functional planting plan. You can buy simple computer programs that will help you draw one up, but you still have to provide the plant knowledge that makes a border come alive and fulfil your own expectations. You can achieve results that are just as acceptable, and probably just as quickly, with pencil and paper.

A SCALE OUTLINE

1 Draw the outline shape of the bed and border, marking on the scale. Use graph paper so that you can easily estimate the size of a particular plant as you work.

2 Make a list of plants that you want to include. Be sure to add essential details such as height, spread, and flowering season. If you find it easier to move around pieces of paper rather than use pencil and eraser initially, cut out several pieces of paper of appropriate size, with the height and flowering period marked on. You could colour them – evergreen greens, variegated green and gold stripes, and flowering plants in the colour of the blooms.

3 Either start with a basic plan with a series of spaces to be allocated (just indicate whether tall, medium or small), or shuffle around your cut-outs until they appear to form a pleasing pattern. Don't worry about whether the plants will fill the exact shape – with time they will all grow into each other, and in the meantime you can fill the gaps with annuals.

4 When satisfied with your key plants, draw these in on a more detailed planting plan. Then fill in the gaps with other plants, not necessarily on your priority list.

If you feel sufficiently artistically inclined, you can try a profile view that will give a better idea of how the border will look – though you can only make a snapshot of how it would look in one season.

HOW TO PLANT HERBACEOUS PLANTS

GUIDELINES TO GETTING IT RIGHT

- Unless the plants are large, plant in groups of about three – a bold spash usually looks better than single plants. Using single plants just because space is limited is a common mistake – the impact is often better if you use fewer kinds but more of each.
- Take into account the likely ultimate height, but remember that plants may grow taller in one garden than another.
- As a rule place the taller plants at the back (in the centre of an island bed), with the smallest at the front. But don't follow this too slavishly unless planting formal summer bedding. A few focal point plants that stand out from the rest can be very effective.
- Consider planting the border so that different parts are at their best at different times, perhaps starting with spring flowers at one end and working through to autumn at the other.
- Use foliage plants to maintain interest throughout the border.

1 Always prepare the soil first. Dig it deeply, remove weeds, and incorporate a fertilizer and garden compost if impoverished. Most herbaceous plants are sold in pots, so space them out according to your plan. Change positions if associations don't look right.

2 Water thoroughly about half an hour before knocking the plant from its pot, then remove a planting hole with a trowel. If the roots are wound tightly around the root-ball, carefully tease out a few of them first. Work methodically from the back of the border, or from one end.

3 Firm the soil around the roots to remove any large pockets of air.

4 Always water thoroughly after planting, and keep well watered in dry weather for the first few months.

Planting for texture

Quite dramatic plantings can be achieved simply by planting blocks of the same plant – whether summer bedding, herbaceous perennials or shrubs. If the garden is seen as an area of voids and masses, blocks of colours and textures, the overall impression can be as important as individual plants. Ground cover plants are ideal for this purpose.

ABOVE: *Thyme is a useful ground cover for a sunny position, and will even tolerate being walked upon occasionally.*

CONVENTIONAL PLANTING

Many ground cover plants spread by sideways growth, sending up new plants a short distance from the parent. These are best planted like normal herbaceous or shrubby plants. Suppress weeds initially with a 5cm (2in) layer of a mulch such as chipped bark. This is also the best way to plant any kind of ground cover that forms part of a mixed border.

HOW TO PLANT GROUND COVER

If planting ground cover plants as a 'texture block', or perhaps to cover an area of ground that is difficult to cultivate, such as a steep slope, it is best to plant through a mulching sheet. You can use black polythene, but a proper mulching sheet is better as it allows water to penetrate. However, do not use the sheet method for plants that colonize by spreading shoots that send up new plants, as the sheet will prevent growth by suppressing the shoots as effectively as the weeds.

1 Prepare the ground well, eliminating weeds. Add rotted manure or garden compost, and rake in fertilizer if the soil is impoverished.
   Secure the sheet around each edge. Tuck the edges firmly into the ground and cover with soil. Make two slits in the form of a cross where you want to plant.

2 Plant through the sheet as you would normally, firming the soil around the roots.
   If you use small plants, planting with a trowel will not be a problem. Water thoroughly.

3 Although the mulching sheet will suppress weeds very effectively while the ground cover is still young and not able to do the job itself, it does not look attractive, so cover it with an ornamental mulch, such as chipped bark.

HOW TO PLANT SHRUBS

1 Most shrubs are sold in pots, and can be planted at any time of the year when the ground is not frozen or waterlogged. Space them out in their pots first, then adjust if the spacing does not look even.

2 Prepare the ground thoroughly, making sure it is free of weeds. Dig in plenty of organic material such as well-rotted manure or garden compost. Otherwise use a proprietary planting mix.

3 Excavate the hole and try the plant for size. Use a garden cane or piece of wood across the hole to make sure the plant is at its original depth. Add or remove soil as necessary.

4 Remove the plant from the pot. If the roots are tightly wound around the root-ball, carefully tease some of them free, to encourage rapid rooting.

5 Firm the plant in well to eliminate large air pockets. Gentle pressure with the heel is an efficient way to do this, or alternatively you can do this by hand.

6 Rake or hoe in a balanced fertilizer to get the plant off to a good start. In autumn use one that is slow acting or has controlled release, to avoid stimulating growth during the cold months. If planting in winter, wait until spring before adding the fertilizer. Water well, then mulch with a 5cm (2in) layer of organic material such as garden compost, cocoa shells, or chipped bark.

Rose borders

Roses (*Rosa*) used to be grown on their own in devoted borders, where their beauty and delicious scent could be admired without the distraction of other plants. However, it makes sense – particularly in a small garden, where every plant must earn its keep – to combine roses with other shrubs, herbaceous perennials, annuals and spring bulbs. These additional plants are ideal for providing interest before or after the roses have finished flowering, or as happy summer colour combinations. Below is a small selection of beautiful shrub roses, as well as possible planting companions.

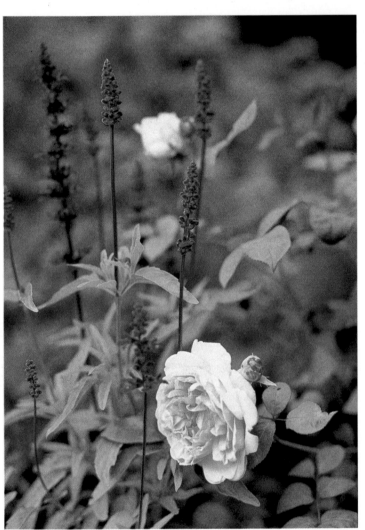

ABOVE: *Soft pink roses and scented lavender (Lavandula) make a lovely planting combination.*

Alchemilla mollis
Clump-forming perennial. Rounded, crinkly-edged leaves and sprays of small greenish yellow flowers in mid summer *45 × 45cm (18 × 18in).*

Artemisia ludoviciana
Bushy perennial. Aromatic silvery-grey lance-shaped leaves. Small silvery-white flowers in summer *90 × 60cm (36 × 24in).*

Aubrieta
Mound-forming evergreen perennial. Masses of large, violet-purple or blue flowers in spring and fresh green leaves *10 × 30cm (4 × 12in).*

Colchicum
Autumn-flowering corms. Use for late colour when many roses have ceased to be colourful. Very large crocus-shaped flowers, usually in shades of pink or mauve, sometimes white, before the leaves, in early or mid autumn. The leaves (at least twice as tall as the flowers) appear in spring and die down in summer. In flower: *10–15 × 10–20cm (4–6 × 4–8in).*

Crocus
Spring-flowering corms. Use for early colour before the roses are growing. Both large-flowered Dutch hybrids, flowering in early spring, or the smaller *C. chrysanthus* varieties, flowering in late winter or early spring, are suitable. Colours include yellow, blue, purple, and white, some being multi-coloured *8–10 × 10cm (3–4 × 4in).*

Festuca glauca
Tuft-forming semi-evergreen grass. Blue-green grassy leaves, forming

ABOVE: *Lavenders, such as this* Lavandula angustifolia, *associate happily with roses.*

ABOVE: *The fully double, peony-like flowers of* Rosa *'Constance Spry' are heavily scented.*

neat rounded clumps. Flowers in summer are insignificant. Useful in front of roses *15 × 23cm (6 × 4in).*

Galanthus nivalis
Spring-flowering bulb. This popular bulb often blooms in late winter, otherwise early spring, so use it to provide interest before the roses begin to grow again. The many varieties all have small nodding white bell flowers *10–15 × 5–8cm (4–6 × 2–3in).*

Gypsophila paniculata
Bushy perennial. Small, linear leaves on branching stems, crowned by masses of small white flowers over a long period in summer. *60–90 × 60–90cm (24–36 × 24–36in).*

Hordeum jubatum
Short-lived perennial grass, usually treated as an annual. Arching plume-like flowers spike in summer and early autumn *30–60 × 30cm (12–24 × 12in).*

Lavandula angustifolia 'Hidcote'
(syn. *L. spica* 'Hidcote Purple')
Bushy evergreen shrub. Aromatic grey-green leaves and spikes of lilac flowers from mid- to late summer *60 × 75cm (24 × 30in).*

Nepata × faassenii
Bushy, clump-forming perennial. Small grey-green leaves, topped by

loose spikes of lavender-blue flowers, at their best in early summer. Other bushy species and hybrids are also very suitable for growing with roses *45 × 45cm (18 × 18in).*

Rosa 'Bourbon Queen'
Bourbon rose. Clusters of fragrant, cup-shaped, double, magenta to rose-pink flowers, mainly in summer *2.4 × 1.5m (8 × 5ft).*

Rosa 'Cardinal de Richelieu'
Gallica rose. Compact habit with fully double, deep burgundy-purple flowers in summer *1 × 1.2m (3 × 4ft).*

Rosa 'Constance Spry'
Shrub rose. Arching habit that will climb if supported. Fully double, fragrant, pink flowers in summer *2 × 1.5m (6½ × 5ft)*

Rosa rugosa
Species rose. Wrinkled leaves and cup-shaped flowers in carmine-red from summer to autumn, followed by red to orange-red hips *2 × 2m (6½ × 6½ft).*

Viola × wittrockiana
Biennials, often treated as annuals. Pansies need no introduction, and come in a variety of colours. Some varieties flower mainly in late winter and spring, others in summer *23 × 23cm (9 × 9in).*

BELOW: *This living wall of roses provides a stunning boundary to any garden. Climbing roses quickly give dense cover, providing privacy yet adding a stunning and fragrant attraction to a garden.*

Foliage and grass borders

With the extensive range of flowering plants available, it is easy to overlook the beauty and impact of foliage. Yet many plants are more impressive in leaf than they are in flower, their colours, forms and textures providing interest at various times of year. Foliage plants – whether they be luxuriant ferns, bold hostas, spiky grasses, or fiery maples – are an essential part of any well-planned planting scheme, providing intriguing contrasts and strong architectural impact.

Acer palmatum atropurpureum
Rounded deciduous tree. Stunning red-purple, palm-like leaves that turn red in autumn *8 × 10m (26 × 30ft).*

Ajuga reptans
Semi-evergreen carpeting plant. Many variegated varieties with multi-coloured leaves. Small blue flowers in summer *10 × 30m (4 × 12in).*

Alchemilla mollis
Clump-forming perennial. Rounded, crinkly edged pale green leaves, which often hold droplets of dew or rain. Sprays of small greenish-yellow flowers in mid-summer *45 × 45m (18 × 18in).*

Cortaderia selloana 'Aureolineata'
Evergreen perennial grass. Stiff, arching, yellow-green leaves and silvery yellow plumes on erect stems in late summer *2.2 × 1.5m (7 × 5ft).*

Bergenia purpurascens
Non-woody evergreen. Large, leathery dark green leaves, turning red in late autumn. Pink flowers in spring *45 × 30cm (18 × 12in).*

Epimedium perralderianum
Evergreen carpeting plant. Heart-shaped bright green leaves with bronze markings, turning coppery-bronze in winter. Small yellow flowers in early summer *30 × 45cm (12 × 18in).*

Euonymus fortunei 'Emerald 'n' Gold'
Evergreen shrub. One of several dwarf varieties with attractive variegated foliage, in this case green and gold *60 × 120cm (24 × 48in).*

LEFT: *A tapestry of greens in high summer, the hosta in the foreground makes its mark long after the spring-flowering daphne and the peony behind have enjoyed their main period of interest.*

BELOW: *This glossy* Hosta fortunei *var.* hyacinthina *marks a bend in the path. It looks very striking planted with a yellow-leaved berberis.*

Fatsia japonica (syn. *Aralia sieboldii*)
Rounded evergreen shrub. Bold palmate leaves and architectural habit, and small white flowers in autumn, followed by black fruit *2.4 × 2.4m (8 × 8ft).*

Festuca glauca
Semi-evergreen tufted grass. Bristle-like blue-grey leaves. Small grass flowers in early and mid-summer *15 × 23cm (6 × 9in).*

Hakonechloa macra 'Alboaurea'
Deciduous grass. Forms clumps of arching narrow golden-yellow leaves from spring till autumn *30 × 30cm (12 × 12in).*

Heuchera 'Pewter Moon'
Clump-forming perennial. Grey-

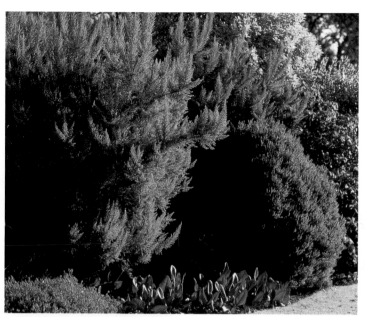

marbled, lobed leaves and large, pale pink flowers in early summer *40 × 30cm (16 × 12in)*.

Hosta hybrids
Mainly clump-forming perennials. Renowned for their bold foliage that comes in a variety of different shapes and colours such as green, golden yellow, grey-blue or variegated, and for their bell- or funnel-shaped flowers, usually in summer. *H. fortunei* var. *aureomarginata* has yellow-edged, olive-green leaves; *H.* 'Blue Moon' has blue-green foliage; *H.* 'Lemon Lime' is yellow-green; and *H. undulata* var. *undulata* has twisted leaves and white to yellow-white markings *15–100cm × 30–100cm (6–39in × 12–39in)*, according to variety.

Matteuccia struthiopteris
Deciduous fern. Erect, pale green fronds resembling shuttlecocks *1.2 × 1m (4 × 3ft)*.

Miscanthus sinensis 'Silberfeder' (syn. 'Silver Feather')
Deciduous perennial grass. Downward-arching, pale green leaves with silver midribs and erect silvery plumes in autumn on strong, erect stems *1.8 × 1.5m (6 × 5ft)*.

Pennisetum villosum (syn. P. longistylum)
Deciduous perennial grass. Flat or folded leaves and feathery green or

ABOVE LEFT: Fatsia japonica, *commonly known as the false castor oil plant, has dramatic, rich green leaves that reflect the light.*

ABOVE: *This border contains no flowers, but the impact of the planting comes from dwarf conifers and other foliage plants.*

LEFT: *The leaves of* Hakonechloa macra *'Alboaurea' become tinged with bronze-red along the margins in the autumn.*

white plumes (purple with age) on arching stems in late summer and early autumn *60 × 60cm (24 × 24in)*.

Pleioblastus auricomus (syn. P. viridistriatus)
Evergreen bamboo. Yellow, green-striped linear leaves on hollow, purple-green canes *1.5 × 1.5m (5 × 5ft)*.

Rubus cockburnianus 'Golden Vale'. Deciduous shrub. Bright golden foliage. The bare thorny stems are attractive in winter, having a white 'bloom' *100 × 100cm (40 × 40in)*.

Salvia officinalis 'Purpurascens' Evergreen or semi-evergreen dwarf shrub. Purple-flushed grey-green leaves. 'Icterina' is grey-green and yellow *60 × 75 m (2 × 2¹/₂ft)*.

Stachys lanata (syn. *S. byzantina*) Mat-forming, semi-evergreen perennial. Grey-green, furry leaves, with purple-pink flower spikes from early summer to early autumn *45 × 60cm (18 × 24in)*.

Colour themes

Colour themes can be very effective, and although it may not be practical to plant whole borders like this in a small garden, you can often use a colour theme in part of a border, devote an island bed to shades of one or two colours, or perhaps cheer up a dull corner with yellow and gold.

Mixed borders

The plants suggested here will form the foundation of a colour theme for a mixed border, but you can add to them and broaden the scope by using bulbs and annuals in appropriate colours too.

Two of the most popular colour ranges are looked at here: blue and silver, and yellow and gold, both of which are ideal for small gardens.

Blue and silver

Agapanthus hybrids
Deciduous to evergreen perennial. Light to deep blue ball-shaped flower heads mid and late summer *45 × 75cm (18 × 30in).*

Artemisia absinthium
Deciduous sub-shrub. Deeply divided silvery-grey leaves. Yellow flowers in mid and late summer *1m × 60cm (3 × 2ft).*

Artemisia ludoviciana
Herbaceous perennial. Silver-grey foliage *1m × 45cm (3ft × 18in).*

Ceanothus x *burkwoodii*
Evergreen shrub. Clusters of bright blue flowers mid summer to mid autumn *2.4 × 2.1m (8 × 7ft).*

Delphinium hybrids
Herbaceous perennial. Tall flower spikes in various shades of blue *1.8m × 60cm (6 × 2ft).*

Festuca glauca
Grass. Dense tufts of blue-grey leaves *23 × 23cm (9 × 9in).*

Hibiscus syriacus 'Blue Bird'
Deciduous shrub. Lilac-blue flowers late summer to mid autumn *2.4 × 2.4m (8 × 8ft).*

Nepeta x *faassenii*
Herbaceous perennial. Spike-like heads of lavender-blue flowers all summer. Grey-green leaves *45 × 45cm (18 × 18in).*

Perovskia atriplicifolia
Shrubby perennial. Feathery sprays of violet-blue flowers in late summer and early autumn. Grey-green leaves *1.2m × 45cm (4ft × 18in).*

LEFT: *Many ceanothus grow tall, so use them where you need bold plants for the back of a blue border. There are both evergreen and deciduous kinds of ceanothus.*

BELOW LEFT: *Grey-leaved plants are useful for filling in between blue flowers. This one is* Artemisia ludoviciana.

ABOVE: *Delphiniums are some of the best blue herbaceous border plants.*

Santolina chamaecyparissus
Evergreen shrub. Silvery, woolly
leaves on mound-forming plant.
Small yellow flowers in mid summer
45 × 45cm (18 × 18in).

Senecio 'Sunshine' (syn.
Brachyglottis 'Sunshine')
Evergreen shrub. Silver-grey foliage.
Yellow daisy-type flowers in mid and
late summer *1 × 1.2m (3 × 4ft).*

Stachys lanata (syn. *S. byzantina* or
S. olympica)
Almost evergreen herbaceous
perennial. Bold silvery leaves. Spikes
of purple flowers in mid summer
30 × 30cm (12 × 12in).

Yellow and gold

Achillea filipendulina
Herbaceous perennial. Flat heads of
lemon-yellow flowers in mid and late
summer *1 × 1m (3 × 3ft).*

Alyssum saxatile
Evergreen shrubby perennial.
Golden-yellow flowers in mid and
late spring. Grey-green leaves
30 × 45cm (12 × 18in).

Anthemis tinctoria
Herbaceous perennial. Yellow daisy-
like flowers early to late summer.
'E. C. Buxton' is lemon-yellow,
'Grallagh Gold' is deep golden-yellow
75 × 45cm (2½ft × 18in).

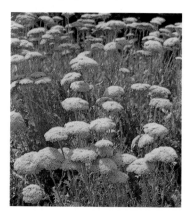

ABOVE: Achillea filipendulina *'Gold Plate',*
one of the essential plants for a yellow border.

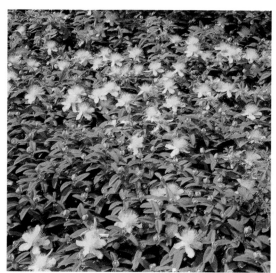

LEFT: Hypericum
calycinum *can be a*
rampant partner for
other plants, but use
it wherever you need
to create a bold splash
of yellow in an
unpromising
position.

BELOW: *Hemerocallis*
come in a range of
colours, but there are
many good yellow
varieties, such as
'Dutch Beauty'.

Berberis thunbergii 'Aurea'
Deciduous shrub. Yellow foliage,
pale yellow flowers in mid spring.
Red berries in autumn *1.2 × 1.2m*
(4 × 4ft).

Choisya ternata 'Sundance'
Evergreen shrub that is generally
planted in a somewhat sheltered
position. Yellow foliage. White
flowers in mid and late spring *1.5 ×*
1.5m (5 × 5ft).

Forsythia x *intermedia*
Deciduous shrub. Covered with
yellow flowers in early and mid
spring *2.4 × 2.1m (8 × 7ft).*

Hemerocallis hybrids
Herbaceous perennial. There are
many yellow varieties, flowering
throughout summer *1m × 75cm*
(3 × 2½ft).

Hypericum 'Hidcote'
Evergreen or semi-evergreen shrub.
Large yellow flowers from mid
summer to early autumn *1.5 × 1.5m*
(5 × 5ft).

Ligustrum ovalifolium 'Aureum'
Evergreen or semi-evergreen shrub.
Green and gold foliage *2.4 × 2.4m*
(8 × 8ft), but can be clipped to keep it
more compact.

Lonicera nitida 'Baggesen's Gold'
Evergreen shrub. Golden foliage
1.2 × 1.8m (4 × 6ft).

Philadelphus coronarius 'Aureus'
Deciduous shrub. Yellow leaves (can
become scorched in strong sun; turn
green by late summer). White flowers
in late spring and early summer *2.4 ×*
1.8m (8 × 6ft).

Potentilla fruticosa
Deciduous shrub. Many varieties
with yellow flowers all summer
1.2 × 1.2m (4 × 4ft).

Solidago hybrids
Herbaceous perennial. Sprays of
bright yellow flowers in late summer
and early autumn *30cm–1.5m ×*
30–60cm (12in–5ft × 12in–2ft),
according to variety.

Red hot borders

Creating beds and borders using such a strong, vibrant colour as red is not for the faint-hearted, but red brings warmth, drama and a touch of Mediterranean sunshine to the summer garden. Remember, too, that red-coloured foliage in the autumn and berries in the winter will bring a welcome splash of colour when the garden is, in general, rather dull. If an all-red border seems too strident for a small garden, it can, of course, be tempered with paler shades of red such as pink.

Aster novi-belgii 'Royal Ruby'
Clump-forming perennial. Semi-double flowers in rich red from late summer to mid autumn, just one of several good red varieties *50cm × 60cm (20 × 24in)*.

Camellia hybrids
Evergreen shrubs. Glossy leaves and large single or double flowers in spring, many in shades of red 'Adolphe Audusson' (blood red) is one of the most popular and widely available varieties *1.5–3m (5–10ft)*, according to variety.

Chrysanthemum hybrids
Herbaceous perennials (annual kinds are not especially suitable for hot borders). There are many hundreds of varieties, some of which appear and disappear from year to year, and may be available only in one country.

ABOVE: *Pinks and carnations (Dianthus) are available in a variety of striking colours including deep pink, scarlet and crimson.*

Consult a specialist chrysanthemum catalogue for a selection of red varieties. Garden chrysanthemums flower in autumn *60–100cm × 45–75cm (2–3ft × 1½–2½ft)*.

Crocosmia 'Lucifer'
Clump-forming perennial. Funnel-shaped, upward-facing tomato-red flowers on branched spikes in summer, and pleated, lance-shaped leaves *100 × 23cm (39 × 9in)*.

Dahlia hybrids
Tuberous-rooted perennials. Many red-flowered hybrids of variable shapes, including: peony-flowered dahlias, with semi-double blooms and pompon dahlias, with rounded

ABOVE: *Escallonias have an attractive range of flower colours from white through pink to scarlet, as this E. 'Slieve Donard' shows.*

heads. Consult a specialist catalogue for currently available red varieties. Flowers from mid summer to autumn *60cm–2m × 60–100cm (2–6½ft × 24–39in)*, according to variety.

Fuchsia hybrids
Tender deciduous shrubs (evergreen given sufficient winter warmth). Some varieties are frost-hardy. Consult a specialist fuchsia catalogue for a selection of red varieties for the garden *30–90cm × 30–90cm (1–3ft × 1–3ft)*, according to variety.

Gladiolus hybrids
Upright perennials. Tall spikes of funnel-shaped flowers, many of which are red. Look at your local

ABOVE: Crocosmia *'Lucifer' brings a splendid splash of vibrant colour to the garden with its fiery red flowers.*

garden shop (store) for red varieties, or look in the catalogues of bulb specialists *45cm–1.8m × 6–23cm (18in–6ft × 6–9in)*, according to variety.

Helenium 'Bruno'
Erect perennial. Daisy-like flowers in crimson or reddish brown, with yellow-brown centres, in late summer and early autumn *1.2m × 60cm (4 × 2ft)*.

Helianthemum 'Fire Dragon'
Spreading evergreen shrub. Grey-green leaves and saucer-shaped, orange-red flowers from late spring to midsummer *30 × 30cm (12 × 12in)*.

Hemerocallis
Evergreen perennial. Narrow, arching leaves and star-shaped tubular flowers; several varieties have red flowers *70cm × 100cm (28in × 39in)*.

Lilium hybrids
Bulbous perennials. Showy, sometimes fragrant flowers in the summer, often available in red, with species such as *L. chalcedonicum*, and hybrids like 'Fire King'. There are many more from which to choose *30cm– 2m (1–6½ft)*, according to variety.

Lobelia cardinalis
Clump-forming perennial. Slender

spikes of brilliant scarlet flowers in mid- and late summer, with reddish-bronze foliage *90 × 23cm (36 × 9in)*.

Lychnis chalcedonica
Erect perennial. Heads of small scarlet flowers in early and mid summer *100 × 30cm (39 × 12in)*.

Monarda 'Cambridge Scarlet'
Clump-forming perennial. Scarlet flowers in bushy clumps from mid to late summer *90 × 45cm (36 × 18in)*.

Papaver orientale
Border perennial. Large single flowers on tall stems above a rosette of foliage. There are many varieties, some in shades of pink, peach and white, but red shades dominate *90 × 60cm (3 × 2ft)*.

Pelargonium hybrids
Tender evergreen perennials. Numerous kinds, many of which are red. Check for red varieties in your local garden shop (store), or send for catalogues from specialist nurseries *20–60cm × 15–30cm (8–24in × 6–12in)*, according to variety.

ABOVE: *The crimson flowers and leafy stems of Helenium* 'Bruno' *are at their absolute best in late summer.*

ABOVE: Lychnis chalcedonica *bears large heads of a deep scarlet colour. It is easy to grow and loves sunlight.*

Phorium 'Dazzler'
Evergreen perennial. Sword-shaped leaves in shades of pink, red and bronze. Reddish flowers are sometimes produced in summer *1.2–1.8 × 1m (4–6 × 3ft)*.

Potentilla atrosanguinea
Clump-forming perennial. Light to deep red, yellow or orange flowers in summer to autumn *60 × 60cm (24 × 24in)*.

Rosa hybrids
Semi-evergreen or deciduous perennial shrubs and climbers. Numerous kinds, with often scented flowers in summer and autumn, many of which are red *40cm–10m × 45cm–6m (16in–30ft × 18in–20ft)*, according to variety.

Tulipa hybrids
Bulbous perennials. Many red varieties available, all flowering in spring, and in many forms. New varieties often appear, so check at your garden shop.

White borders

A border consisting predominantly of white flowers can create a stunning display. Cool, crisp, and elegant, a white planting scheme provides an air of harmony and tranquillity, and suits any style of garden, whether it is traditional or modern. White flowers combine well in a border with other colours, such as silver-leaved, soft grey-leaved or dark green-leaved plants for contrast.

Achillea ptarmica 'The Pearl'
Upright perennial. Covered in tight, double white flowers from early to late summer *75 × 60cm (30 × 24in)*.

Anemone blanda 'White Splendour'
Tuberous perennial. Forms a carpet of white daisy-type flowers in spring *10 × 15cm (4 × 6in)*.

Anemone × hybrida 'Honorine Jobert'
Upright perennial. White flowers with yellow centres, in late summer and early autumn *120 × 90cm (4 × 3ft)*.

Anthemis punctata subsp. *cupaniana*
Mat-forming perennial. Daisy-like white flowers with yellow centres in early summer *30 × 90cm (12 × 36in)*.

Chrysanthemum × superbum (syn. *C. maximum*)
Clump-forming perennial. Large white daisy-type flowers, double in some varieties, borne singly on stiff stems in summer *45–90 × 60cm (18–36 × 24in)*

Cistus hybrids
Evergreen shrubs. Summer flowers in white to pink. Whites include *C. × dansereaui* 'Decumbens' and *C. × cyprius*, with pink and yellow markings and yellow centres, and *C. × corbariensis* (syn. *C. hybridus*) with yellow centres *15cm–2m × 60cm–2m (6in–6½ft × 2–6½ft)*, according to variety.

Convolvulus cneorum
Evergreen shrub. Silvery, silky, narrow pointed leaves and white flowers with yellow centres from late spring to early autumn *75 × 60cm (30 × 24in)*.

Cormus canadensis
Ground-covering perennial. Small flowers with white bracts in late spring and early summer, sometimes followed by red berries *15cm (6in)* tall. Indefinite spread.

Cytisus multiflorus (syn. *C. albus*)
Upright then spreading deciduous shrub. A mass of pea-like white flowers in clusters from late spring to early summer *3 × 2.4m (10 × 8ft)*.

Eucryphia glutinosa
Upright deciduous or semi-evergreen tree or shrub. White, cup-shaped flowers in summer as well as striking foliage in autumn *3 × 2m (10 × 6½ft)*.

Gypsophila paniculata
Bushy perennial. Small, linear leaves on branching stems, crowned by masses of small white flowers over a long period in summer *60–90 × 60–90cm (24–36 × 24–36in)*

× Halimiocistus sahucii
Mound-forming or spreading evergreen shrub. White, saucer-shaped flowers with yellow centres in summer *45 × 90cm (18 × 36in)*.

Leucojum aestivum
Clump-forming bulbous perennial. Small white, nodding flowers in late spring *60 × 29cm (24 × 9in)*.

Lilium hybrids
Bulbous perennials. Striking, often highly fragrant flowers in summer.

ABOVE: Anthemis punctata *subsp.* cupaniana, *with its appealing daisy-like flowers, is ideal for a dry sunny garden.*

ABOVE: Chrysanthemum × superbum 'Beethoven' *is a perfect addition to a white border.*

ABOVE: *The fragrant white flowers of* Choisya ternata *are produced in profusion in late spring, with some later flowers too.*

(30in–20ft × 3–13ft), according to variety.

Phlox paniculata 'White Admiral'
Erect perennial. Fragrant white flowers from summer to autumn *90 × 80cm (36 × 32in).*

Spiraea 'Arguta'
Rounded deciduous shrub. Small white flowers in spring on arching shoots *2.4 × 2.4m (8 × 8ft).*

Syringa vulgaris 'Madame Lemoine'
Upright to spreading deciduous shrub. Conical trusses of highly fragrant white double flowers, creamy-yellow in bud, in late spring and early summer *7 × 7m (22 × 22ft).*

Viburnum plicatum
Deciduous shrub. Large heads of white flowers in late spring and early summer, followed later by red fruits *3 × 3m (10 × 10ft).*

LEFT: *In the summer the bush* Olearia × haastii *with its daisy-like flowers resembles a miniature snowy mountain. Shown in full flower, this one is delicately fronted by a variegated grass,* Phalaris arundinacea *'Picta'.*

White lilies include *L.* 'Casa Blanca', with bowl-shaped flowers; *L. longiflorum,* which are trumpet shaped; and *L. martagon* var. *album,* with reflexed petals *45cm–2m × 30–60cm (1½–6½ft × 1–2ft),* according to species or variety.

Olearia × haastii
Bushy evergreen shrub. Daisy-like white flowers with yellow centres from mid- to late summer *2 × 3m (6½ × 10ft).*

Osteospermum 'Whirligig'
Spreading evergreen subshrub. Highly unusual flowers with spoon-shaped white petals and grey-blue centres *60 × 60cm (24 × 24in).*

Philadelphus hybrids
Mainly deciduous shrubs. Fragrant white flowers in summer may be single (*P.* 'Belle Etoile'), semi-double (*P.* 'Boule d'Argent') or double (*P.* 'Virginal') *75cm–6m × 1–4m*

ABOVE: Cornus canadensis, *with its starry white flowers, followed by tight clusters of vivid red fruits, is an ideal ground-cover plant.*

Everbright evergreens

Evergreens alone can make a dull garden. They need to be relieved by plants that renew themselves, otherwise you miss the variety that comes with fresh green leaves newly emerged from their buds or the final fling of many shrubs as they go out in a blaze of colourful glory in the autumn. But a garden without evergreens is equally dull, and the clever use of them will ensure that your garden always looks good, whatever the season.

Use a few evergreens in mixed borders and beds, so that there is some height and texture in winter, or devote an area of the garden to evergreens – a heather and dwarf conifer garden can look superb. Try evergreens for focal points and specimen trees in the lawn.

When creating an evergreen bed or border, use plants in many different shades of green, and use variegated plants between plain ones.

Aucuba japonica
Large, glossy leaves. Flowers insignificant, but red berries sometimes a bonus. Choose one of the variegated varieties *1.8 × 1.8m (6 × 6ft)*.

Berberis darwinii
Small, holly-shaped leaves. Masses of attractive small orange-yellow flowers in mid and late spring *2.4 × 2.4m (8 × 8ft)*.

Bergenia hybrids
Evergreen non-woody perennial, useful as ground cover in front of shrubs. Large, rounded leaves, often tinged red or purple in winter. Pink, red or white flowers in spring *30 × 60cm (1 × 2ft)*.

Camellia hybrids
Glossy leaves and large single or double flowers, usually in shades of pink, red or white, in spring *2.4 × 1.8m (8 × 6ft)*.

Ceanothus x 'burkwoodii'
See *Colour themes*.

Choisya ternata 'Sundance'
See *Colour themes*.

ABOVE: *Erica carnea 'Myretoun Ruby' is just one of many attractive winter-flowering plants.*

OPPOSITE: *Hebes are excellent compact, rounded plants (though some are tall). This is* Hebe × franciscana *'Variegata', suitable for even the tiniest plot.*

LEFT: *Evergreens have the advantage of looking good all year, like this combination of* Elaeagnus pungens *'Maculata' with* Hebe pinguifolia *'Pagei' in front.*

Cotoneaster dammeri
Prostrate ground cover to use in front
of other shrubs. Small leaves. White
flowers in early summer, red berries
in autumn and winter *5–8cm × 1.5m
(2–3in × 5ft)*.

Elaeagnus pungens 'Maculata'
Green leaves boldly splashed with
gold in the centre. Very striking in
winter sun *2.4 × 2.4m (8 × 8ft)*.

Erica
There are many species and varieties –
look especially for varieties of *Erica
carnea* (syn. *E. herbacea*) and *E. x
darleyensis*, both winter-flowering and
lime-tolerant *30 × 60cm (1 × 2ft)*.

Escallonia macrantha
Small leaves, clusters of pink or red
flowers in summer *1.8 × 1.8m
(6 × 6ft)*.

Euonymus fortunei
Will grow along the ground or up
against a wall. Choose one of the
variegated varieties, such as 'Emerald
'n' Gold' (green and gold) *30cm ×
1.2m (12in × 4ft)* on the ground.

Hebe
Hebes make nicely shaped, usually
rounded, plants and often have
attractive flowers and sometimes
colourful or variegated foliage.
Heights can range from *30cm–1.2m
(12in–4ft)*, with similar spreads,
depending on species. Many are of
borderline hardiness where frosts can
be severe, so check with your local
garden centre to see which ones are
reliable enough for your area.

Ilex
The holly needs little introduction,
but for a small garden choose one
trained as a bush and a variegated
variety such as 'Golden King' or
'Golden Queen' (the King is female
and has berries, the Queen's male and
doesn't!) *3 × 2.4m (10 × 8ft)*.

Lonicera nitida 'Baggesen's Gold'
See *Colour themes*.

Mahonia 'Charity'
Fragrant clusters of yellow flowers
in early and mid winter *2.4 × 1.8m
(8 × 6ft)*.

Phormium hybrids
Tall, sword-shaped leaves arising
from ground level. Usually
variegated cream or shades of pink or
purple, according to variety. Of
borderline hardiness in areas where
frosts can be severe, so check with
your local garden centre about which
ones are suitable for your garden
1.2–1.8m × 1–1.2m (4–6ft × 3–4ft).

Rosmarinus officinalis
Grey-green, aromatic leaves. Small
blue flowers in spring *1.8 × 1.5m
(6 × 5ft)*.

Santolina chamaecyparissus
See *Colour themes*.

Senecio 'Sunshine'
See *Colour themes*.

BELOW: *Rosemary is pretty in flower, and in
mild areas will often start blooming in late
winter.*
LEFT: *Hollies are usually so slow-growing that
most people can find space for one. This one is
Ilex aquifolium 'Aurea Marginata'.*

Viburnum tinus
Deep to mid green leaves on tidy
bush. White flowers (tinged pink in
some varieties) from late autumn to
early spring *2.4 × 1.8m (8 × 6ft)*.

Yucca filamentosa 'Variegata'
Sword-like leaves with broad cream
and yellow margins. Large bell-
shaped flowers on tall spikes in mid
and late summer *1.2 × 1m (4 × 3ft)*.

DWARF CONIFERS

A good garden centre will have
hundreds of dwarf conifers, in a
huge range of shades, shapes, and
sizes. The permutations are
enormous, and the best way to
choose them is to go along armed
with a book or catalogue that
will give you likely sizes after,
say, 15 years, then choose
combinations that will make a
pleasing group.

Colour for the cold months

Evergreens provide winter clothes for the garden, but they don't look very dressy and they are best interspersed with plants that renew themselves. There is no substitute for flowers and fruits, which, though more transient, are all the more appreciated.

Autumn leaf colour can be as bold and bright as many flowers, but it is worth including some autumn blooms too. A few well-placed pools of late flowers will prolong summer and keep autumn at bay.

Don't overlook colourful barks and twigs in winter, which can become focal points on a sunny day.

Chimonanthus praecox
Deciduous shrub. Scented yellow flowers on bare stems in winter 2.4 × 2.4m (8 × 8ft).

Chrysanthemum
Look for varieties that flower late. Some flower well into late autumn and even early winter. Height varies with variety. Consult a specialist book or ask your garden centre for suitable varieties.

Colchicum speciosum and hybrids
Corms with large crocus-like flowers, mainly in shades of pink and mauve, single or double, in autumn. The foliage does not appear until spring 15 × 23cm (6 × 9in). The leaves can double the height.

Cornus mas
Deciduous shrub or small tree. Masses of tiny yellow flowers on bare branches in late winter and early spring 3 × 2.4m (10 × 8ft).

Crocus speciosus
Corm. Lilac–blue typical crocus flowers in mid autumn 10 × 8cm (4 × 3in).

Crocus tommasinianus
Corm, flowering between mid winter and early spring. Typical crocus flowers, usually lilac or purple in colour 8 × 8cm (3 × 3in).

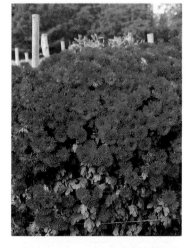

Cyclamen coum
Corm. Miniature cyclamen-shaped flowers with reflexed petals. Mainly shades of pink, but also white. Flowers early winter to early spring. Leaves often marbled silver 8 × 15cm (3 × 6in).

Cyclamen hederifolium (syn. *C. neapolitanum*).
Similar to above but flowers from late summer to late autumn.

Erica
See *Everbright evergreens*.

Hamamelis mollis
Fragrant spidery yellow flowers on bare branches in mid and late winter 2.4 × 2.4m (8 × 8ft).

ABOVE:
Chrysanthemum 'Ruby Mound'.

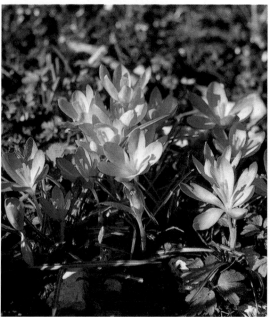

LEFT: *Long before spring crocuses are in flower, the blooms of C. tommasinianus will be putting in an appearance. These were photographed in late winter.*

Helleborus niger
Evergreen perennial border plant.
Large white flowers in mid winter
30 × 45cm (12 × 18in).

Helleborus orientalis
Evergreen perennial border plant.
Large white, pink, or purple flowers
in late winter and early spring *45 ×
60cm (18in × 2ft)*.

Iris unguicularis (syn. *I. stylosa*)
Evergreen perennial border plant.
Large blue iris flowers in winter and
early spring *30 × 45cm (12 × 18in)*.

Jasminum nudiflorum
Sprawling shrub, usually grown
against a wall or trellis. Bright yellow
flowers from late autumn to early
spring *2.4 × 2.4m (8 × 8ft)*.

Mahonia 'Charity'
See *Everbright evergreens*.

Nerine bowdenii
Heads of pretty pink, spidery flowers
on leafless stems from late summer to
early winter. The foliage appears in
spring *60 × 30cm (2 × 1ft)*.

Prunus subhirtella 'Pendula' (syn.
'Autumnalis Pendula')
Small to medium-sized drooping
deciduous tree. White flowers,
sometimes tinged pink, from late
autumn and throughout the winter in
mild spells *3 × 3m (10 × 10ft)*.

Sternbergia lutea
Bulb. Crocus-like yellow flowers in
mid and late autumn *10 × 10cm
(4 × 4in)*.

Viburnum x *bodnantense* 'Dawn'
Deciduous shrub. Small clusters of
white to pink flowers on bare stems
from late autumn to early spring
2.4 × 1.5m (8 × 5ft).

Viburnum tinus
See *Everbright evergreens*.

LEFT ABOVE: *The hellebores span winter and
spring. This is* H. orientalis guttatus.
LEFT: Iris unguicularis *can be in bloom in
mild spells right through the winter. The
plants take a few years to settle down before
flowering prolifically.*
BELOW: Nerine bowdenii *flowers in autumn,
but will sometimes continue into winter.*

COLOURFUL STEMS

A specimen tree with attractive
bark, perhaps placed in a lawn or
in an open position and
surrounded by winter-flowering
heathers, can be a winter focal
point. One of the white-bark
birches such as *Betula jacquemontii*
always looks good. If you need a
really small tree, however, try
B. pendula 'Youngii', a small
weeping tree.

In a small garden, shrubs are
more likely to be a practical
proposition, and two of the best
are *Cornus alba* 'Sibirica' (red
stems) and *C. stolonifera*
'Flaviramea' (green stems).

As a half-way house between
tree and shrub, pollard *Salix alba*
'Chermesina', a willow with
scarlet shoots. Cut the stems
hard back to a stump perhaps
1.2m/4ft tall; do this every
second year.

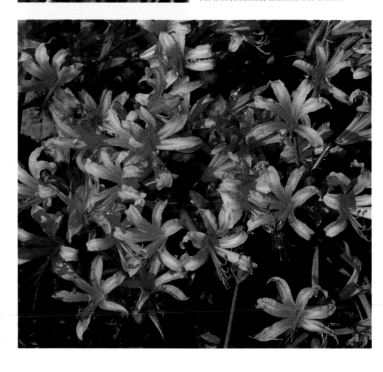

Autumn leaves and berries

Autumn tints will provide a few extra weeks of border colour at a time when every bit of interest in the garden is appreciated. Berries also add a dash of spice, and some of them will remain for many months, even through to spring in a mild winter when the birds leave them alone.

Amelanchier laevis
A small deciduous tree or large shrub. Masses of white flowers in spring, sometimes black berries in summer, rich autumn foliage colour. *A. lamarckii* is very similar *3 × 2.4m (10 × 8ft)*.

Berberis thunbergii
Deciduous shrub. Yellow flowers in spring, scarlet berries and brilliant red autumn foliage *1.2 × 1.5m (4 × 5ft)*.

Berberis wilsoniae
Deciduous shrub. Small yellow flowers in mid summer, coral red berries and red and orange foliage in autumn *1 × 1.2m (3 × 4ft)*.

Ceratostigma plumbaginoides
Deciduous sub-shrub. Clusters of small blue flowers appear from mid summer to late autumn. Leaves turn red in autumn *30 × 45cm (12 × 18in)*.

Clerodendrum trichotomum
Large deciduous shrub. Starry white fragrant flowers in late summer, followed by blue berries in crimson calyces in early and mid autumn *2.4 × 2.1m (8 × 7ft)*.

Cornus alba
Deciduous suckering shrub. Attractive autumn foliage colouring, red stems in winter *2.1 × 2.1m (7 × 7ft)*.

Cotoneaster horizontalis
Deciduous, ground-hugging shrub for front of border (can also be used against a fence or wall). Small pink flowers in early summer, followed by red berries later. Bright red foliage tints in autumn *60cm × 1.8m (2 × 6ft)*.

ABOVE: *The amelanchiers are usually grown for their white flowers in spring, but they have a second burst of colour when the leaves turn. This species is* A. laevis.

LEFT: Cornus alba *is an excellent shrub. After the brief spell of glory as the leaves colour before they fall, there is the winter-long attraction of red stems.*

Fothergilla major
Deciduous shrub. Dark green leaves,
orange-yellow or red before they fall.
Scented white flowers in late spring
1.8 × 1.5m (6 × 5ft).

Ilex
See *Everbright evergreens.*

Malus 'John Downie'
Small to medium-sized deciduous
tree. White apple blossom in late
spring. Conical yellow and crimson
crab apples in autumn *6 × 2.4m
(20 × 8ft).*

Malus tschonoskii
Deciduous tree, which though tall
is a candidate for a small garden by
virtue of its slender, pencil-like
profile. White blossom tinged pink
in late spring. Dull red fruits flushed
yellow (not a feature). Red and
yellow autumn foliage *6 × 2.1m
(20 × 7ft).*

Pernettya mucronata
Evergreen shrub. Small, sharply
pointed glossy leaves. Insignificant
white flowers in late spring. Clusters
of berries – shades of pink, red, purple
and white, according to variety – in
autumn and winter. Male and female
plants must be grown together to
ensure fruiting *1 × 1.2m (3 × 4ft).*

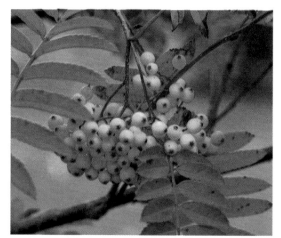

LEFT: *Most sorbus are
grown for their red or
orange berries, but
some also have white
or yellow berries, and
there is the bonus of
spectacular leaf colour
just before they fall.
This is* Sorbus
'Joseph Rock'.

Pyracantha 'Orange Glow'
Evergreen shrub, usually grown
against a wall but also an attractive
free-standing plant. White flowers in
early summer, orange-red berries in
autumn and winter. There are other
suitable species and varieties
2.4 × 2.4m (8 × 8ft).

Rhus typhina (syn. *R. hirta*)
Deciduous small tree or large shrub.
Large, divided leaves, colouring
orange-red and yellow before they fall
3 × 3.5m (10 × 12ft).

Skimmia japonica
Evergreen shrub. Fragrant creamy-
white flowers in spring, red berries in
late summer and early autumn. Male
plant needed to pollinate female
1 × 1m (3 × 3ft).

Sorbus
Many species and hybrids make small
or medium-sized trees with red or
yellow berries and good autumn
foliage colour. Good ones are *S.
aucuparia* and hybrids, *S.* 'Embley',
and *S.* 'Joseph Rock'.

ABOVE: Pernettya mucronata *is available
with pink and red berries as well as white ones.
This variety is 'Mulberry Wine'.*
RIGHT: *Skimmias have long-lasting red
berries. This one is* S. japonica *'Nymans'.*

Variety with variegation

Variegated plants make a border look lighter and more interesting when flowers are scarce, and variegated evergreens are particularly useful at times when little is flowering.

Avoid planting too many variegated plants close together. Use them between other plants with plain foliage where the leaf colouring will be shown off to advantage.

Aralia elata 'Variegata'
Deciduous shrub or small tree. Leaflets margined and marked creamy-white ('Aureovariegata' has a broad, irregular gold margin). White flowers in late summer and early autumn *3 × 2.1m (10 × 7ft)*.

Arundinaria viridistriata (syn. *Pleioblastus auricomus, Pleioblastus viridistriatus*)
Bamboo. Dark green leaves broadly striped yellow. Purplish-green canes *1m × 60cm (3 × 2ft)*.

ABOVE: Hosta fortunei albopicta.
BELOW: *Only a few variegated trees are suitable. This is* Aralia elata *'Variegata'.*

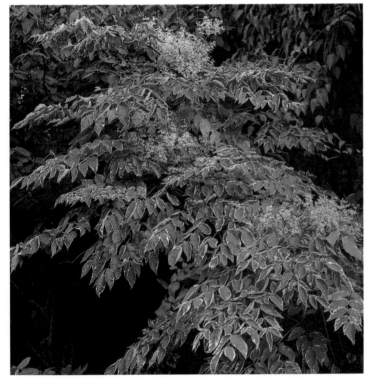

Aucuba japonica (variegated varieties)
See *Everbright evergreens*.

Buxus sempervirens 'Aureovariegata'
Evergreen shrub with small leaves striped, splashed and mottled pale yellow. 'Elegantissima' has irregular creamy-white margins *1.2 × 1m (4 × 3ft)*.

Carex morrowii 'Evergold'
Sedge
Clump-forming with grass-like leaves striped yellow along the centre *25 × 30cm (10 × 12in)*.

Cornus alba 'Elegantissima'
Deciduous suckering shrub with red stems and leaves margined and mottled with white. 'Spaethii' is similar but has gold variegation *2.1 × 1.8m (7 × 6ft)*.

Elaeagnus x *ebbingei* 'Limelight'
Evergreen shrub. Large green leaves with a central splash of deep yellow *2.4 × 2.1m (8 × 7ft)*.

Elaeagnus pungens 'Maculata'
See *Everbright evergreens*.

Euonymus fortunei (variegated varieties)
See *Everbright evergreens*.

Fuchsia magellanica 'Versicolor'
Deciduous shrub. Small fuchsia-type flower in summer and into autumn. Grey-green, white, yellow, and pink variegation. Hardy except in cold areas *1.2 × 1m (4 × 3ft)*.

Hebe x *franciscana* 'Variegata'
Evergreen shrub, not suitable for very cold areas. Small rounded leaves edged cream. Mauve-blue flowers in summer *60 × 60cm (2 × 2ft)*.

ABOVE: Pachysandra terminalis *is an excellent ground cover for shade, but the plain green form looks rather boring. 'Variegata' is much more interesting.*

LEFT: Houttuynia cordata *'Chameleon'.*

BELOW: Vinca minor *'Variegata'.*

Hostas (many variegated varieties)
Herbaceous perennial *30–60cm × 30–75cm (12in–2ft × 12in–2½ft).*

Houttuynia cordata 'Chameleon'
Herbaceous perennial. Outstandingly striking, heart-shaped foliage, variegated with shades of yellow, green, bronze and red. Small white flowers in summer *30 × 45cm (12 × 18in).*

Hypericum × moserianum 'Tricolor'
Evergreen shrub. Yellow flowers about 5cm (2in) across from mid summer to mid autumn. Green and white leaves edged pink *60 × 60cm (2 × 2ft).*

Ilex (variegated varieties)
See *Everbright evergreens.*

Iris pallida 'Variegata'
Sword-like leaves, striped creamy-white and green. Blue flowers in early summer *60 × 60cm (2 × 2ft).*

Iris pseudacorus 'Variegatus'
Sword-like leaves striped green and yellow while young, turning greener with age. Blue flowers in early summer. Although associated with water, it will grow in an ordinary border though it does best in damp soil *1m × 60cm (3 × 2ft).*

Ligustrum (variegated varieties)
See *Colour themes.*

Pachysandra terminalis 'Variegata'
Evergreen sub-shrub. Green and white leaves. Insignificant white flowers in late spring *30 × 45cm (12 × 18in).*

ABOVE: *Variegation is important in the herbaceous border. This is* Iris pallida *'Variegata'.*

Phormium hybrids
See *Everbright evergreens.*

Salvia officinalis 'Icterina'
Evergreen shrub. Grey-green leaves splashed with yellow *60 × 60cm (2 × 2ft).*

Vinca minor 'Variegata'
Evergreen prostrate shrub. Green and creamy-white leaves. Pale mauve flowers *20 × 60cm (8in × 2ft).*

Weigela florida 'Variegata'
Deciduous shrub. Leaves edged creamy-white. Pink flowers in early summer *1.5 × 1.2m (5 × 4ft).*

Yucca gloriosa 'Variegata'
See *Everbright evergreens.*

Planting for quick results

Annuals are almost instant – many are already in flower when you buy them – border perennials are respectable after a year, but shrubs can seem infuriatingly slow to mature.

Not all shrubs are slow-growers, however, so if you want your border to look well established in three years instead of five or even ten, try those suggested here.

Even those plants that grow quickly will leave gaps in the early years. In a mixed border, fill these gaps with the quicker-growing border perennials; in a shrub border add a few bushy annuals.

Bear in mind that some shrubs that grow quickly while young may continue to grow (over-enthusiastically) once they've reached what you consider a modest size. The height and spread estimates below are based on three years (though much depends on soil and climate), but the ones listed are only likely to grow a little more than this even by 10 years. Those that grow taller can be pruned back hard to restrict their size. *Buddleia davidii*, for example, will be much better if you cut it back hard each spring.

There are many more quick-growers, however, so don't assume that your scope for an almost instant border is limited solely to those listed below.

Aucuba japonica
See *Everbright evergreens*.

Buddleia davidii
Deciduous shrub. Fragrant, usually lilac-blue flower clusters at ends of arching branches, from mid summer to mid autumn. Other colours include shades of red, purple, and white *2.4 × 1.5m (8 × 5ft)*.

Caryopteris x *clandonensis*
Deciduous shrub. Narrow, grey-green leaves. Clusters of bright blue flowers in late summer and early autumn *1m × 60cm (3 × 2ft)*.

Choisya ternata
See *Colour themes*.

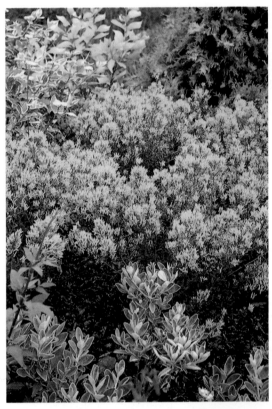

LEFT: *Tough, low-growing, quick to mature, and very bright in flower are qualities that make Genista tinctoria well worth considering. This variety is 'Royal Gold'.*

BELOW: Hypericum calycinum *grows and spreads rapidly, so don't plant it where these characteristics can become an embarrassment. The flowers are bold and beautiful.*

Cistus x *corbariensis*
Evergreen shrub. Dull green leaves wavy at the edge. Bold white flowers with a yellow mark at the base of each petal, in late spring and early summer *75 × 60cm (2½ × 2ft)*.

Cytisus x *kewensis*
Deciduous shrub. Pale yellow, pea-like flowers, in profusion in late spring. Spreading shape *45cm × 1m (18in × 3ft)*.

Philadelphus coronarius 'Aureus'
See *Colour themes*.

ABOVE: Leycesteria formosa *is quick-growing, and highly popular with birds. They love the dark purple berries.*
RIGHT: *Weigelas come in a range of colours, but mainly pinks and reds. They grow quickly and flower young and so make an excellent choice if you want fast results.*

Erica carnea
See *Everbright evergreens*.

Fuchsia magellanica
See *Variety with variegation*.

Genista tinctoria
Deciduous shrub. Deep yellow pea-type flowers all summer *75 × 60cm (2½ × 2ft)*, but height tends to be very variable.

Hebe 'Midsummer Beauty'
Evergreen shrub. Pale green leaves, slightly reddish beneath. Sprays of lavender-purple flowers from mid summer to mid autumn. Not reliably hardy in cold areas *1 × 1m (3 × 3ft)*.

Hypericum calycinum
Evergreen shrub. Large yellow, cup-shaped flowers all summer. Can be invasive *45 × 60cm (18in × 2ft)*.

Lavandula (various)
Evergreen shrub. The popular lavender. Grey-green leaves and flowers in shades of blue or purple *60 × 60cm (2 × 2ft)*.

Leycesteria formosa
Deciduous shrub. Cane-like stems forming a bamboo-like clump. Drooping flower tassels containing white flowers with claret bracts, followed by purple-black fruits *1.5 × 1m (5 × 3ft)*.

Lupinus arboreus
Short-lived deciduous shrub. Foliage and flower spikes resemble the herbaceous lupin, but the lightly fragrant flowers are much sparser. Usually yellow, but can be lilac to purple or blue. Good for a hot, dry site *1.2 × 1m (4 × 3ft)*.

Mahonia 'Charity'
See *Everbright evergreens*.

Potentilla fruticosa
See *Colour themes*.

Senecio 'Sunshine'
See *Colour themes*.

Spiraea x *bumalda* (various varieties)
Twiggy deciduous shrub. Flat flower heads, usually crimson, in late summer. Some varieties have variegated foliage *75 × 45cm (2½ft × 18in)*.

Weigela hybrids
Deciduous shrub. Funnel-shaped flowers in late spring and early summer. Mainly shades of red and pink *1.8 × 1.5m (6 × 5ft)*.

BELOW: Spiraea × bumalda *(syn. S. japonica). This is 'Anthony Waterer'.*

No fuss, low-maintenance plants

There are plenty of people who do not have a lot of time to tend to their gardens. If you want to save the cost and time involved in regularly replanting with seasonal plants, grow hardy perennials and shrubs. But if you really want to cut down on maintenance, grow only those that are undemanding, with no need to prune regularly, or to keep lifting, dividing, or hacking back.

Most shrubs will require very occasional pruning, perhaps to cut out a dead or diseased shoot, or to improve the shape if growth is not symmetrical, and sooner or later border perennials will benefit from being lifted and divided, but the plants suggested here can be left for many years without attention. They will almost thrive on neglect, yet will not get out of control.

Aucuba japonica
See *Everbright evergreens*.

Berberis thunbergii
There are many varieties, including variegated, purple-leaved and gold-leaved. Shape and height also vary with variety: *B.t. atropurpurea* 'Bagatelle', for example, makes a dwarf rounded ball of growth covered with coppery-red leaves, usually less than *45cm (18in)* tall and broad, 'Helmond Pillar' is dark purple but grows into a narrow column *1.2m (4ft)* or so high but only about *30cm (12in)* wide.

Bergenia hybrids
See *Everbright evergreens*.

ABOVE: Cotoneaster horizontalis *can be grown as ground cover or as a climber.*

ABOVE: Cotinus coggygria *is sometimes called the smoke bush because of its flower heads. It can make quite a large shrub in time, but requires minimal attention.*

Choisya ternata
Both green and golden forms (see *Colour themes*) are trouble-free plants if protected from cold winds in winter.

Cornus stolonifera 'Flaviramea'
Deciduous shrub. Green leaves turn yellow before falling. Yellowish-green winter stems *1.8 × 1.8m (6 × 6ft)*.

Cotinus coggygria
Deciduous shrub. Rounded shape with pale green leaves (there are also purple-leaved varieties) that have brilliant autumn colours. Feathery sprays of purple or pink flowers in mid summer *2.4 × 2.4m (8 × 8ft)*.

Cotoneaster
There are many cotoneasters, from ground-huggers to shrubs *3m (10ft)* or more tall. *C. horizontalis (see Autumn leaves and berries)* and *C. dammeri (see Everbright evergreens)*, are popular ground-huggers, but many others are suitable for a small garden.

Elaeagnus pungens 'Maculata'
See *Everbright evergreens*.

Erica carnea
See *Everbright evergreens*.

Fatsia japonica
Evergreen shrub. Large, hand-shaped glossy green leaves (there is a variegated variety). White, ball-shaped flower heads that appear on mature plants in mid autumn *2.4 × 2.4m (8 × 8ft).*

Griselinia littoralis
Evergreen shrub. Pale green leaves (there are variegated varieties). Not suitable for cold areas. Slow-growing *3 × 3m (10 × 10ft).*

Hebes
See *Everbright evergreens.*

Hemerocallis hybrids
See *Colour themes.*

Hibiscus syriacus
See *Colour themes*, but there are other varieties in different shades of blue, pink, and white.

Ilex
See *Everbright evergreens.*

Kniphofia hybrids
Herbaceous perennial. Large, stiff, poker-like orange or yellow flower spikes. Flowering season extends from early summer to mid autumn, according to variety *60cm–1.2m × 60cm–1.2m (2–4 × 2–4ft).*

Liriope muscari
Evergreen perennial. Clumps of broad, grassy leaves, and spikes of mauve-lilac flowers from late summer to mid autumn *45 × 30cm (18 × 12in).*

Mahonia japonica
Evergreen shrub. Glossy, dark green leaves divided into leaflets. Fragrant, lemon-yellow flowers from early winter to early spring *2.4 × 2.4m (8 × 8ft).*

Pernettya
See *Autumn leaves and berries.*

Potentilla fruticosa
See *Colour themes.*

Ribes sanguineum
Deciduous shrub. Drooping clusters of small pink or red flowers in spring *1.8 × 1.8m (6 × 6ft).*

Ulex europaeus
Evergreen shrub. Spiny growth, covered with deep yellow single or double flowers in spring. Flowers may also appear intermittently in winter *1.5 × 1.5m (5 × 5ft).*

Viburnum davidii
Evergreen shrub. White flowers in early summer. Turquoise-blue berries later if both male and female plants are planted *1 × 1.2m (3 × 4ft).*

Viburnum tinus
See *Everbright evergreens.*

Yucca
See *Everbright evergreens*, but the non-variegated form is equally suitable for a border or as a specimen plant.

ABOVE: *The kniphofias, sometimes called red-hot-pokers, are bold herbaceous border plants. Once well established they make large clumps. Some species are quite small, however, and different varieties flower at different times. Many kniphofias are unhappy in very cold areas and may need protection in some areas.*

DON'T FORGET THE DWARF CONIFERS

Conifers need negligible care, and if you choose dwarf species and varieties they will remain compact enough for a small garden. Be cautious about using them in a mixed border, however, as they seldom blend in as satisfactorily as ordinary shrubs.

Small and dwarf conifers

Dwarf conifers can provide year-round colour to a garden. They need practically no attention after their first year of growth, but in order for them to look their most effective they are best grown as a group with a variety of contrasting shapes, sizes and colours.

A good garden centre will have an wide range of dwarf and slow-growing conifers, but it is best to consult a specialist catalogue or book before you buy. Some described as dwarf may reach 2.4m (8ft) or so in time, and those described as slow-growing may eventually grow even larger. Make sure your dwarf conifers really are dwarf if space is at a premium.

Abies balsamea 'Nana'
Dwarf conifer, forming a dome-shaped bush. Has aromatic, dark green needle-like leaves and purplish blue cones. Exceptionally hardy *1 × 1m (3 × 3ft)*.

Abies cephalonica 'Meyer's Dwarf'
Dwarf conifer that forms a spreading, flat-topped mound. Needle-like leaves are glossy deep green; cones are greenish brown *50cm × 1.5m (20in × 5ft)*.

Cedrus deodara 'Golden Horizon'
Usually small, broad conifer with appealing horizontal branches hanging down at their tips. Needle-like leaves are bright yellow when young. Female cones are glaucous blue, maturing to brown *5 × 2.4m (16½ × 8ft)*.

Chamaecyparis lawsoniana 'Aurea Densa'
Small or dwarf conifer. Forms a rounded shrub with bright golden yellow, scale-like leaves, needle-like when young. Cones are glaucous or rust-brown *1.2m × 1.2m (4 × 4ft)*.

Chamaecyparis lawsoniana 'Bleu Nantais'
Dwarf conifer, forming a rounded cone shape. Bright glaucous foliage, initially needle-like, becoming scale-like *1.5 × 1.5m (5 × 5ft)*.

Chamaecyparis obtusa 'Nana Gracilis'
Small or dwarf conifer that forms a rough pyramid. Has bright glossy green scale-like leaves. Cones age from green to brown *2 × 2m (6½ × 6½ft)*.

Juniperus communis 'Compressa'
Dwarf conifer. A slow-growing dwarf with grey-green foliage, ideal for a rock garden, and can be used in small containers *60 × 15cm (24 × 6in)*.

Juniperus horizontalis
Spreading conifer forming a mat of greyish green leaves, needle-like when young, then scale-like. Blue 'berries' *30cm × 2m (1 × 6½ft)*.

Juniperus virginiana 'Sulphur Spray' (syn. *J. chinensis* 'Sulphur Spray')
Dwarf conifer that forms a spreading, flat-topped bush. Bright yellowish green scale-like leaves and bluish purple 'berries' *1 × 2m (3 × 6½ft)*.

Picea abies 'Gregoryana'
Dwarf conifer producing a dense mound of dark green needle-like leaves. Cones age from dark green to brown *60 × 60cm (2 × 2ft)*.

LEFT: Abies cephalonica *'Meyer's Dwarf'* has glossy, deep green, needle-like leaves and greenish brown resinous cones.

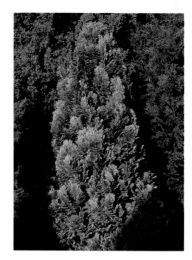

ABOVE: *The bright golden-yellow leaves of*
Chamaecyparis lawsoniana *'Aurea Densa'*
are needle-like when young, becoming scale-like.

Picea glauca var. albertiana 'Alberta Globe'
Small or dwarf, dome-shaped conifer. Blue-green needle-like leaves. Cones may not appear *1 × 1m (3 × 3ft)*.

Picea glauca var. albertiana 'Conica'
Small or dwarf conifer with a dense cone shape. Permanently juvenile, blue-green needle-like leaves. Cones may not appear *4 × 2m (13 × 6½ft)*.

Picea glauca 'Echiniformis'
Dwarf conifer, with a rounded cone shape. Needle-like leaves are blue-grey. Light green cones age to brown *1.5 × 1m (5 × 3ft)*.

Picea pungens 'Globosa'
Dwarf conifer forming a dome or mound shape. Has slightly glaucous bristle-like leaves. Green cones age to light brown *1 × 1m (3 × 3ft)*.

Picea pungens 'Montgomery'
Dwarf conifer. Forms a broad-based, cone-shaped plant, with silvery blue, bristle-like leaves. Cones age from

RIGHT: Picea abies *'Gregoryana' produces a*
virtually impenetrable mound of needle-like
leaves; the cones age from dark green to brown.

green to light brown. Slow growing *1.5 × 1m (5 × 3ft)*.

Pinus mugo 'Corley's Mat'
Dwarf conifer, forming a prostrate, spreading mat. Has long, needle-like bright green leaves, on very resinous stems. Cones are dark brown *1 × 2m (3 × 6½ft)*.

Taxus baccata 'Repandens'
Small or dwarf conifer forming a mat of spreading branches. Dark green leaves, and red 'berries' in autumn *To 60cm × 5m (2 × 16½ft)*.

Taxus baccata 'Standishii'
Small or dwarf conifer forming a slim column. Has bright yellowish green needle-like leaves on upright stems. Red 'berries' in autumn *1.5m × 60cm (5 × 2ft)*.

Thuja occidentalis 'Ericoides'
Dwarf conifer that forms a broad, sometimes rounded obelisk. Young, scale-like leaves are green in summer, turning rich brown. Cones age from yellow to brown *1.2 × 1.2m (4 × 4ft)*.

Thuja orientalis 'Aurea Nana' (syn. Platycladus orientalis 'Aurescens')
Dwarf conifer, making an egg-shaped plant. Aromatic, yellowish green, scale-like leaves, tinged bronze in

ABOVE: *The aromatic, scale-like leaves of*
Thuja orientalis *'Sieboldii', an egg-shaped*
dwarf conifer, are carried in stiff vertical plates.

autumn, are held in vertical, fan-like plates *60 × 60cm (2 × 2ft)*.

Thuja orientalis 'Rosedalis' (syn. Platycladus orientalis 'Rosedalis').
Small oval conifer. Fine, heather-like leaves, yellowish in spring, gradually turning bluish-green, then purple-blue in winter *120 × 90cm (4 × 3ft)*.

Combining heathers and conifers

Heathers and dwarf conifers are low-maintenance plants that look particularly good together, with conifers providing useful height and variation in shape, and heathers supplying seasonal colour.

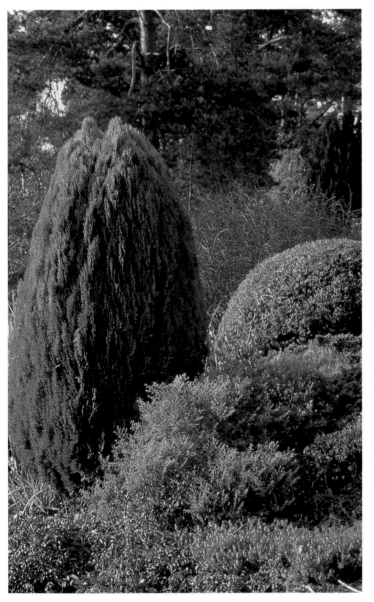

Designing a bed

Although you can make a one-sided border filled with heathers and conifers, an island bed is much more pleasing – and can be viewed from all sides. The heathers are also likely to thrive better in a more open position with plenty of sun all day – such conditions are much more akin to those of heathland.

You could design a bed for year-round interest. There are hundreds of suitable heathers and dwarf conifers that you could use, so modify the bed to suit the size of your garden and the plants available at your local garden centre.

Planting a bed like this might seem expensive initially, but bear in mind that it will probably last for decades without the need for replanting. It is a small price to pay for a really interesting, long-term, minimal-maintenance feature.

MASS PLANTING

Heathers look best when they are planted in bold natural-looking drifts. A group of perhaps ten or twenty plants of one variety will have far more impact than the same number of different varieties planted in the same area or dotted around a border. Unless the bed or border is large, choose perhaps half a dozen good varieties but plant plenty of them. This applies to both foliage and flowering varieties.

LEFT: *Some low-maintenance plants, such as these heathers and dwarf conifers in a variety of shapes and colours, are attractive all year round and need only occasional attention.*

PLANTING A CONIFER AND HEATHER MIXED BED

1 Arrange the conifers on the bed first, ensuring they look pleasing from all angles. Move them around in their containers if you are not satisfied at first. Prepare the ground thoroughly, then plant the conifers, firming them in before watering.

2 Space the heathers out around the conifers. Plant in groups or drifts of one variety at a time. Avoid planting too close together, as both heathers and conifers will spread.

BELOW: *A mixed heather and conifer bed will provide interest and at no extra upkeep. Modify the bed to suit the size of your garden and the plants available from your local garden centre.*

3 Apply a mulch of chipped bark or gravel around the plants, to hide the bare soil and make the bed look more attractive.

Maintaining Beds and Borders

Once you have designed and planted a new bed or border, much of the work will be complete. But, no matter how large or small the planting area, there will always be something to do to make it look better, so that it continues to please and delight all who see it.

Immediately after planting, the new border is bound to look bare – and it will remain this way for a while until the roots have become well established and the plants have begun to make some top growth. Applying a mulch – of bark chippings, for example – around the plants will not only make the border look more attractive, it will keep weeds down and help to retain warmth and moisture in the soil. Depending on the material used, the mulch will need to be renewed at least once a year if it is to remain effective.

The plants will need plenty of water at regular intervals, especially throughout the first growing season. Always water thoroughly, as shallow, impatient watering will encourage surface rooting instead of deeper roots, and make the plants even more vulnerable to drought. Try to water in the early morning or late in the day, when the plants are not exposed to full sun, otherwise their leaves may get scorched.

Although many perennials will support their flower stems without any extra staking or supports, some – like the sumptuous large-flowered peonies with their heavy buds and full flowers – will flop onto other plants, especially during a spring shower. Ideally, stakes or supports should be put in place when you are planting the border, even though they may look a little odd at first, when the plants are still small. Failing this, you will need to check regularly that plants aren't being flattened by the weather, or by other plants, and insert supports wherever you can.

Good preparation of the soil should have rid you of deep-rooted and creeping perennial weeds, such as dock and couch grass. Once the border is planted, you will have to remove any fresh growth carefully with a hand fork so you do not damage the border plants. Pull up any annual weed seedlings as soon as you see them – and certainly before they have a chance to flower and shed their seed, otherwise they will simply proliferate and you will have an even bigger problem to deal with next year.

Once they are established, you may want to give your plants an annual feed of a balanced fertilizer, to keep them growing well.

Last, but by no means least, you will need to go through the border regularly, removing flowers as they fade. This will stimulate the plants to produce another crop of flowers, so keeping the border in bloom over as long a period as possible.

LEFT: *This border builds up from the front but is not regimented as the heights vary along its length. It illustrates the effectiveness of using different forms, colours and leaf shapes.*

OPPOSITE: *A good combination of textures, shapes and colours is achieved here with cardoon (Cynara cardunculus) providing interesting structure with pink Salvia sclarea.*

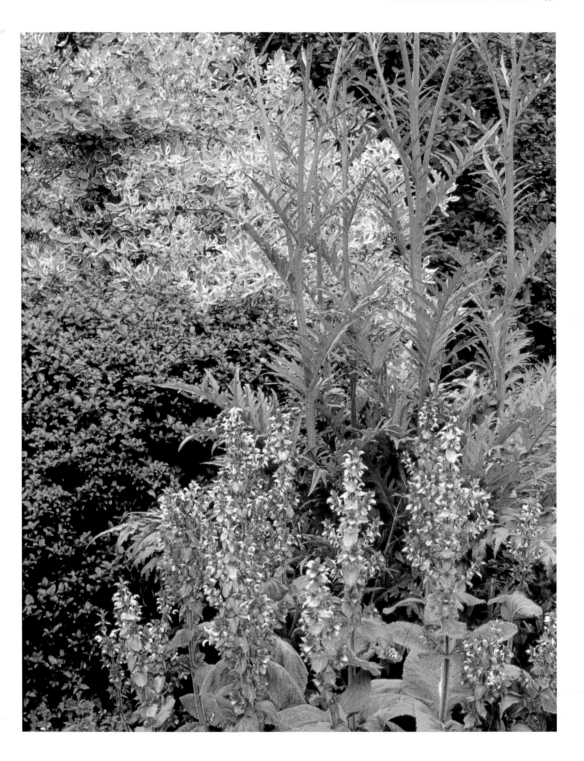

Staking border plants

Some border plants, particularly tall ones, are prone to wind damage, and sometimes a potentially beautiful plant is flattened or broken by the weather. If you stake them early, the plants will usually grow through or over the support, which will then become almost invisible.

1 Proprietary supports like this are very efficient at holding up border plants that are not particularly tall but have masses of floppy or fragile stems.

2 Proprietary supports that link together as shown are useful where you are dealing with clumps of varying sizes. They can be linked together as required.

3 Twiggy sticks pushed into the ground within and around the plant can provide a very effective means of support. Once the plant grows you won't notice them.

ABOVE: *Mixing materials breaks up a large area of garden and prevents it looking dull. A few of the plants at the back of the border are staked to protect them against adverse weather.*

4 Short canes can be used to support plants such as carnations. If you use a stout cane, loop string or twine around it as well as the plant. Use thinner split canes to keep individual flower stems or groups of stems upright.

Controlling weeds

It is never possible to eliminate weeds entirely, but you can control them. Even weeds that are difficult to eradicate can be conquered if you persist, and annual weeds will diminish in numbers if you continue to kill off the seedlings before they can flower and shed more seed. Once the weed population has been reduced, mulching and prompt action to remove any seedlings that do appear will keep the garden almost weed-free. Be prepared for the battle to be won over time.

1 Perennial weeds that have long, penetrating roots are best dug up. First loosen the roots with a garden fork, and hold the stem close to its base as you pull up the whole plant. If you do not get out all the root, new plants may grow from the pieces left behind.

2 Hoeing is one of the best forms of weed control, but it really needs to be done regularly. Slice the weeds off just beneath the soil, preferably when the ground is dry. Keep beds and borders hoed, as well as the vegetable garden.

3 Contact chemical weedkillers are useful if you want to clear an area of ground quickly and easily. Some – which normally kill only the top growth, so are better for annual weeds than for problem perennial ones – leave the ground safe to replant after a day.

4 Some weedkillers kill the whole plant, including the roots. Large areas of ground can be sprayed, but remember that you can paint some formulations onto the leaves to kill the weed without harming neighbouring plants.

5 Mulches are very effective at controlling weeds. In the vegetable and fruit garden, various forms of plastic sheeting are a cost-effective method.

6 Where appearance matters, use an organic material such as chipped bark, garden compost or cocoa shells. If the ground is cleared of weeds first, a mulch at least 5cm (2in) thick will suppress most weeds.

Mulches

Mulches can help improve growing conditions for plants. Properly applied, a mulch will not only prevent weed growth, it will also keep the soil warm and reduce the amount of moisture lost through evaporation. There are two main kinds of mulch: sheet mulches, made from various forms of plastic or rubber sheet, and loose ones, such as garden compost and chipped bark. Both have their uses, and you may want to add one of the more decorative loose mulches to make a sheet mulch visually more acceptable. This can be more cost effective than using a loose mulch alone.

Loose mulches

Most loose mulches are visually more appealing than sheet mulches, and the organic ones gradually rot down or become integrated into the soil by insect and worm activity, thus helping to improve the soil structure and fertility, and benefiting the plant in the longer term as well.

Loose mulches have to be thick in order to suppress weeds well. Aim for a thickness of at least 5cm (2in).

There is a variety of loose mulches to choose from. Grass cuttings are readily available in most gardens. They are not the most attractive form of mulch but can be used effectively at the back of borders. Bark is another ideal material as it is both effective and attractive. Do not use bark that is fresh, however, as the resin may harm the plants.

PRACTICAL POINTS

● Always prepare the ground thoroughly before laying a sheet mulch.
● Enrich the soil with plenty of organic material such as rotted manure or garden compost – you won't have an opportunity to do this later, once the mulch has been laid.
● Add fertilizer and water it in well – only liquid feeds are practical once the sheet is in position.
● Soak the ground thoroughly with water before applying the sheet.

APPLYING A LOOSE MULCH

1 Prepare the ground thoroughly, digging it over and working in plenty of organic material such as rotted manure or compost if the soil is impoverished.

2 Loose mulches will control annual weeds and prevent new perennial ones getting a foothold. You must dig up existing deep-rooted perennial weeds, otherwise they could grow up through the mulch.

3 Water the ground thoroughly before applying the mulch. Never apply a mulch to dry soil.

4 Spread the mulch thickly, but do not take it too close to the stems of the plant otherwise they may cause problems.

Sheet mulches

Black polythene (plastic) is one of the most commonly available forms of sheet mulch, and is especially effective at suppressing weeds. It does not, however, allow water to penetrate, so is best used in narrow strips such as alongside a hedge. The polythene (plastic) is simply cut to shape and laid on the surface of the soil. You will have to cut holes in the polythene (plastic) to allow water to pass through to the soil. If you find the appearance of black polythene (plastic) distasteful, it can be covered over by a thin layer of gravel.

Woven plastic sheets are more expensive than black polythene (plastic) but they do allow water to seep through, while keeping the light out, hence killing the weeds.

Butyl rubber is a very long-lasting waterproof mulch. It is expensive, but only a thin gauge is required. Butyl rubber is more suitable for the area immediately around trees or large shrubs than as cover for a large expanse of ground.

MULCHING WITH A SHEET

1 Sheet mulches are most useful in shrub beds that can be left undisturbed for some years, and are best used when the bed or border is newly planted. Always prepare the ground as thoroughly as you would if not using a mulching sheet. Make a slit around the perimeter of the bed with a spade, then push the edges of the sheet into this. For a vegetable plot you can use special plastic pegs, but these are too conspicuous for an ornamental bed.

2 Make cross-shaped planting slits in the sheet with a knife or scissors. If planting a shrub you will probably have to make slits large enough to take a spade. This won't matter as the sheet can be folded back into place.

3 Use a trowel or a spade to dig out the planting hole beneath each slit, then insert the plants and replace the soil. Fold back the cut edges of the polythene (plastic) to cover the soil, so that the sheet sits snugly around the plant.

4 Sheet mulches can also be used around individual trees and shrubs. The best way to apply the sheet is to cut a square or circle to size, then make a single slit from one edge to the centre. Slip the sheet around the tree or shrub – and the stake if there is one – and simply fold the polythene (plastic) back over the soil. It won't matter if the join is not perfect as you can hide it with a decorative mulch.

5 Although most of the sheet mulch will be hidden as the plants grow, it will initially be very conspicuous. A layer of a decorative mulch such as chipped bark or gravel will make it much more pleasant to look at.

Feeds and fertilizers

Plants need care and attention if they are to flourish. Giving them a regular feed will ensure strong growth as well as abundant flower and fruit production. A balanced intake of nutrients will also make them healthy enough to withstand pests and diseases.

Balanced nutrients

Plants need a balanced intake of nutrients to survive. These take the form of minerals and trace elements, which all keep the plant healthy. In the plant's natural environment these are available in the soil, to be taken up by the roots, along with water. They are then transported within the plant to supply the leaf cells, where photosynthesis uses energy provided by sunlight to manufacture sugars and starches – vital for a healthy plant. As the plant grows, flowers and eventually dies, the decaying material then releases nutrients back into the soil.

In the garden, where far more plants are grown closely together than in nature, the competition for nutrients becomes intense; this is exacerbated if the plant is in a pot, where the roots cannot grow into new areas in search of extra food.

Types of fertilizer

There are two types of fertilizer: organic and inorganic. The organic ones are derived from natural ingredients, such as plants (seaweed or nettles), blood, fish or bone. Some last longer than the inorganic types, and tend to become available to the plant only slowly after application. Inorganic fertilizers are mineral-based and may break down more quickly after application.

BELOW: *Maintaining a well-kept border filled with healthy looking plants that have reached their full potential is achieved by following a regular feeding regime.*

Controlled-release fertilizers

The rate at which the fertilizer is released into the soil depends on temperature, soil-organism activity, the fertilizer's solubility in water and its size (the finer the particles, the more quickly nutrients are likely to be released). Some inorganic fertilizers are called 'slow-release', which means that the particles are surrounded by a soluble coating that has a breakdown period of a number of months. The nutrients are released gradually; after this more fertilizer will be needed. 'Controlled-release' fertilizers only release their nutrients when the soil temperature is warm enough for plant growth.

Liquid fertilizers

Those fertilizers that are applied as a liquid are released to and absorbed by the plants the most quickly of all

FEEDING WEEDS

It is an irony of gardening that in feeding your plants you are also feeding the weeds. But if you get the weeds under control from the start, all the nutrients that you apply will be available to the plants you actually want to grow.

(usually within 5–7 days), and are useful as a fast-acting tonic if a plant is looking ill. This is especially true of foliar feeds, which are applied directly to the leaves rather than to the soil around the roots, and are absorbed straight into the plant's system. These can have an effect within about 3–4 days, compared with up to 21 days for a general granular fertilizer applied around the roots.

The N:P:K ratio

On the pack of fertilizer, there should be some information about the nutrients it contains. The three most important elements are nitrogen (N), phosphorus (P) and potassium (K). Nitrogen promotes healthy growth of leaves and shoots; phosphorus is needed for healthy root development; and potassium improves flowering and fruit production. Put simply, N:P:K equals shoots:roots:fruits.

The ratio is given on the back of the pack because certain plants need some elements in a greater quantity than others. A foliage plant, for example, will need more nitrogen and less potassium, as it produces leaves but not a great show of flowers or fruit, whereas a fruiting tomato plant needs a huge quantity of potassium to give a good yield.

It is often necessary to change the fertilizer through the season, particularly if you have planted heavy feeders such as vegetables. Apply more nitrogen and phosphorus in the spring to promote growth, and increase the levels of potassium as the season progresses, in order to produce a good show of flowers or fruit.

Applying fertilizer

In an established garden you can apply fertilizer in granular form as a dressing around the plants early in the season, or in soluble form as the plants are watered during the spring. For a new plant, mix fertilizer with the soil as it is replaced in the planting hole around the root-ball.

FEEDING BEDS AND BORDERS

Unless rain is expected, you should water the ground well. This will make the fertilizer active more quickly in dry conditions.

1 Most established plants benefit from annual feeding. Apply a slow- or controlled-release fertilizer in spring or early summer, sprinkling it around the bushes. Sprinkle it further out where most of the active root growth is.

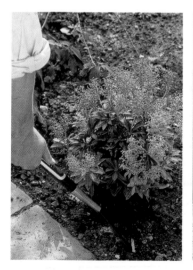

2 Hoe the fertilizer into the surface so that it penetrates the root area more quickly.

3 Unless rain is expected, you will need to water well. This will make the fertilizer active more quickly in dry conditions.

Plants for a Purpose

ONE OF THE SECRETS OF SUCCESSFUL GARDENING IS the ability to choose the right plant for a particular position or use. Plants will always thrive more readily if they are suited to the conditions. Forcing an inappropriate plant into shade if it demands sun, or planting a shade-lover in scorching sunlight, is a recipe for disappointment.

You will find plenty of ideas for plants that relish problem areas like shade or sun in the pages that follow, but sometimes the question is less which plant suits particular conditions as which fulfils a particular purpose. In the following pages you will find plants that provide the right solution, whether you want a scented shrub, climber for a pergola, or an arresting

ABOVE: *Don't be afraid to grow shrubs and plants such as lilies in pots and tubs as well as the more ubiquitous seasonal summer flowers.*

LEFT: *Climbing and rambling roses are useful for summer screens, but bear in mind that it is only seasonal cover.*

LEFT: *Clematis can be planted in shade provided they can rise above it to flower in the sun.*

OPPOSITE ABOVE: *Ivies will grow almost anywhere, in sun or shade, along the ground or up a wall or tree. Green varieties can be a trifle boring, but variegated varieties are always bright.*

BELOW: *'Exotics' can be used as focal points to bring interest to an otherwise boring area during the summer, but will probably need winter protection.*

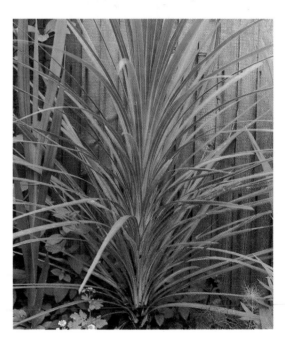

'architectural' plant as a focal point.

There are 'exotics', some of which are quite tough, other plants will only thrive during the summer months and you will either have to protect them in winter or treat them as expendable. There are also suggestions of plants to attract wildlife.

If a particular variety has been mentioned, other varieties, perhaps in different colours or with minor variations in size or shape, will almost certainly do well in the same situation. White and pale colours tend to show up better in shade, however, and where possible varieties particularly suited to the conditions have been mentioned.

Be prepared to experiment with plants, especially with those that seem to thrive in similar situations in your area, and concentrate on those that clearly do well. Do not be afraid to abandon plants that fail to live up to expectations.

The garden's aspect

The aspect of the garden is something about which you don't have any choice. Whichever direction it faces, however, there will be a range of plants suitable for growing in it. Selecting the right plants will produce a wonderful show of colour throughout the year.

Know your plants

The direction the garden faces will have a strong influence on the plants likely to thrive in it. If a plant originally hails from the warm, dry and sunny countries that border the Mediterranean, it is unlikely to grow well in a damp, shady corner. Similarly, a bog plant from a northern forest will not enjoy being placed between a south-facing wall and a path.

One of the keys to successful gardening is to match the position and the plant as closely as possible. Doing this when the plant is first acquired will save both time and money, because the plant will not have to be dug up later when it has failed to thrive and most of the growing season has been lost. A good nursery is invaluable for advice, but most plants will be labelled with the conditions they prefer.

Plants for 'morning-sun' positions

Berberis darwinii
Bergenia cordifolia
Chaenomeles × superba
Clematis montana
Clematis tangutica
Cotoneaster horizontalis
Deutzia scabra
Dodecatheon meadia
Euphorbia griffithii
Forsythia suspensa
Galanthus nivalis
Hamamelis mollis
Helleborus foetidus
Hypericum 'Hidcote'
Lonicera periclymenum
Pyracantha
Rosa rugosa
Vinca major

BELOW: *Choosing plants with interest in different seasons is vital for a small garden as this* Parthenocissus henryana *shows.*

Plants for shady positions

Akebia quinata
Berberis × stenophylla
Camellia japonica
Camellia × williamsii
Clematis alpina
Clematis 'Nelly Moser'
Choisya ternata
Crinodendron hookerianum
Digitalis
Euonymus fortunei
Garrya elliptica
Hedera colchica
Hedera helix
Hydrangea petiolaris
Ilex
Jasminum nudiflorum
Kerria japonica 'Pleniflora'
Mahonia japonica
Parthenocissus
Piptanthus laburnifolius
Tropaeolum speciosum

Plants for sunny positions
Aethionema grandiflorum
Campsis × *tagliabuana* 'Madame Galen'
Canna indica
Cistus × *pulverulentus* 'Sunset'
Dianthus
Dryas octopetala
Eccremocarpus scaber
Echinacea purpurea
Echinops ritro
Fritillaria imperialis
Geranium cinereum 'Ballerina'
Helenium 'Waldtraut'
Imperata cylindrica 'Rubra'
Lilium
Moluccella laevis
Osteospermum
Reseda odorata
Salvia officinalis 'Tricolor'
Sempervivum
Senecio (syn. *Brachyglottis*) 'Sunshine'

OPPOSITE: *Hydrangeas like this creamy petiolaris look good in borders. They prefer shade.*

ABOVE RIGHT: *Rosemary has a wonderful scent; it may also bloom late in mild weather.*

Plants for 'afternoon-sun' positions
Abelia × *grandiflora*
Campsis radicans
Ceanothus × *deleanus* 'Gloire de Versailles'
Ceanothus impressus
Cistus × *cyprius*
Crocosmia
Deutzia scabra 'Plena'
Eccremocarpus scaber
Fremontodendron 'California Glory'
Geranium 'Johnson's Blue'
Helichrysum italicum
Hosta
Humulus lupulus 'Aureus'
Kolkwitzia amabilis
Lavandula angustifolia 'Hidcote'
Lavandula stoechas
Papaver orientale
Penstemon
Rosmarinus officinalis
Vitis coignetiae

LEFT: *The large tubular flowers of* Campsis radicans, *which flowers in late summer, contrast well with the green of the foliage.*

Plants that prefer shade

Shade is perhaps the universal problem in small gardens. It is difficult to find a significantly large growing area that is not within the shade of a building or a boundary fence, wall or hedge, for at least part of the day . . . and sometimes there are areas in shade for most or all of the day. Such positions are also often very dry, for obstructions that cast shade also cast a rain shadow.

With the exception of some really difficult areas, there are nearly always some plants that will establish themselves and thrive. In these difficult spots you must be prepared to give the plants a little extra help for the first year. The soil should be enriched with organic material, such as garden compost or rotted manure and fertilizer, but above all the ground must be kept moist. Regular watering in dry spells will be almost essential for the first season. After that, all the plants mentioned here will be able to look after themselves under normal conditions.

Those plants with an asterisk are suitable for dry shade. The others are unsuitable for dry sites, and some prefer moist ground.

Ajuga reptans
Almost evergreen perennial. There are several good varieties with variegated and coloured leaves. Short spikes of blue flowers in early and mid summer *15 × 23cm (6 × 9in)*.

ABOVE: Ajuga reptans *is one of those accommodating plants that will thrive in sun or shade, and it will even grow in crevices between paving. There are many varieties that are attractively variegated.*

Astilbe hybrids
Herbaceous perennial. Fern-like divided foliage. Feathery plumes of pink, white, or red flowers *60–90 × 45cm (2–3ft × 18in)*.

Astrantia major
Herbaceous perennial. Star-like papery-looking white or greenish-pink flowers in early and mid summer *60 × 45cm (2ft × 18in)*.

★Aucuba japonica
See *Everbright evergreens*.

★Bergenia hybrids
See *Everbright evergreens*.

★Brunnera macrophylla
Herbaceous perennial. Rough, heart-shaped leaves. Sprays of blue flowers like forget-me-nots, in late spring and early summer *45 × 45cm (18 × 18in)*.

ABOVE: Astrantia major *is not an eye-catching plant from afar, but does well in shade.*

★Buxus sempervirens
See *Variety with variegation*.

Camellia
See *Everbright evergreens*.

Dicentra spectabilis
Herbaceous perennial. Ferny foliage. Pink, red or white heart-shaped flowers on arching stems in late spring and early summer *45 × 45cm (18 × 18in)*.

★Epimedium perralderianum
Evergreen perennial. Young leaves bright green marked bronze-red, changing to copper-bronze in winter. Small yellow flowers in early summer *30 × 30cm (12 × 12in)*.

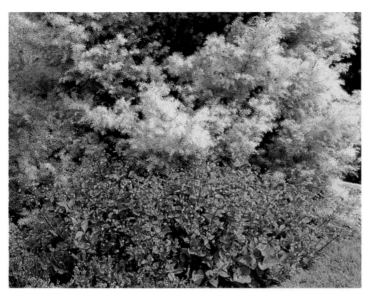

Helleborus
See *Colour for the cold months*.

Hosta
See *Variety with variegation*.

Hypericum calycinum
See *Planting for quick results*.

★*Liriope muscari*
See *No fuss low maintenance plants*.

Lonicera nitida
See *Colour themes*. The all-green species can be used, but the yellow 'Baggesen's Gold' looks brighter in a sunless position.

★*Mahonia aquifolium*
Evergreen shrub. Large, leathery divided leaves. Fragrant yellow flowers in early and mid spring *1.2 × 1.2m (4 × 4ft)*.

★*Pachysandra terminalis*
See *Variety with variegation*.

★*Ruscus aculeatus*
Evergreen sub-shrub. Strong erect stems covered with tough green 'leaves' (actually modified stalk). Inconspicuous flowers in early and mid spring, bright red berries in autumn if male and female plants are present *1 × 1m (3 × 3ft)*.

ABOVE LEFT: *Here the blue flowers of* Brunnera macrophylla *show up well against a golden conifer.*

RIGHT: Sarcococca hookeriana, *a winter-flowering plant that has unspectacular flowers but an arresting fragrance.*

Sarcococca hookeriana humilis
Evergreen shrub. Slender, lance-shaped leaves. Very fragrant small white flowers in winter *60 × 60cm (2 × 2ft)*.

Saxifraga x umbrosa
Evergreen perennial. Rosettes of green leaves from which sprays of pink flowers appear in late spring and early summer *30 × 30cm (12 × 12in)*.

Skimmia japonica
See *Autumn leaves and berries*.

Symphoricarpos albus
Deciduous shrub. Small, urn-shaped pink flowers from mid summer to early autumn. White berries like marbles from mid autumn to mid winter *1.8 × 1.8m (6 × 6ft)*.

Tiarella cordifolia
Evergreen perennial. Maple-shaped leaves, turning bronze in winter. Feathery spikes of white fluffy flowers in late spring and early summer *23 × 30cm (9 × 12in)*.

Viburnum davidii
See *No fuss, low maintenance plants*.

Vinca minor
See *Variety with variegation*.

LEFT: Symphoricarpos albus *is a vigorous, spreading shrub, which is best not planted among choice plants because of its rampant growth pattern, but it is very satisfactory for a difficult shady position.*

Fern borders

Most garden ferns flourish in a shady position, where many more flamboyant plants fail to thrive. They are fascinating and beautiful plants, and their elegance and architectural impact makes up for what they lack in colour. You can use them in a mixed border, like any other perennials, but an area devoted solely to ferns looks especially effective – and very natural.

There are many different types of attractive fern to choose from, some with bold arching shuttlecocks, others forming delicate lacy clumps. Select a mixture of shapes and sizes to make the fern border more interesting, and if you are worried about bare ground in winter, choose mainly evergreen species.

ABOVE: *The hart's tongue fern (*Asplenium scolopendrium*) is so-called because it produces long, curling leaves.*

RIGHT: *The shuttlecock fern (*Matteuccia struthiopteris*) is one of the most elegant ferns, with an attractive upright habit.*

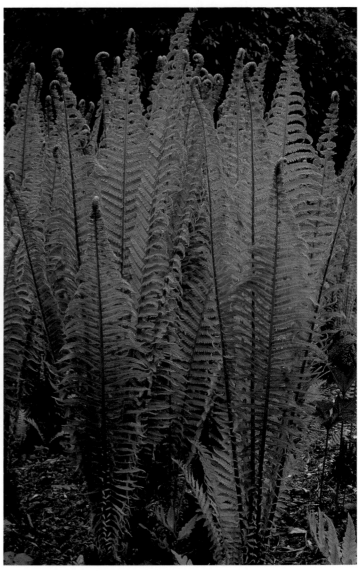

PLANTING A FERN BORDER

Ferns are easy to grow as long as they are given the right conditions. Most prefer a moist, shady or partially shady site, and it pays dividends to prepare the ground thoroughly. Spring is a good time to plant.

1 Most ferns need a moist, humus-rich soil, so fork in as much garden compost or rotted manure as possible. This is especially important if the area is shaded by trees, or a wall that also casts a rain shadow, where the soil is usually dry.

2 If the soil is impoverished, add a balanced fertilizer and rake it into the surface. If planting in late summer or winter, do not use a quick-acting fertilizer. Wait until spring to apply, or use a controlled-release fertilizer that will release the nutrients only when the weather is warm enough for growth.

3 It is very important that ferns do not dry out, especially when newly planted. Water the pots thoroughly about half an hour before planting, to make sure the root-ball is wet enough to start with.

4 Make a hole large enough to take the root-ball, but if the roots are very tightly wound round the pot, you will need to carefully tease out some of them first. This will encourage them to grow out into the surrounding soil. If the plant is in a large pot, you may have to use a spade instead of a trowel.

5 Firm in carefully to eliminate any large air pockets that could allow the roots to dry out. Then water thoroughly so that the surrounding soil is moist down to the depth of the root-ball.

6 To help conserve moisture and maintain a high level of organic matter in the soil, mulch thickly with peat moss, leaf mould or garden compost. You will need to freshen the mulch each spring.

Sun lovers

Sunny spots where the ground is moist, or where the sun is intense for just part of the day before it moves around, present no problem for the majority of plants. All except the shade-loving plants are likely to thrive. But if the position is sunny nearly all day, and the soil tends to be free-draining and dry, you need plants adapted to such bright and arid conditions.

Fortunately, those plants that do well in these positions are often bright, floriferous, and very colourful. As a general rule, grey-leaved plants are well suited to these conditions, but if in doubt check.

Most of the plants suggested here tolerate dry soil well. However, give perennials and shrubs extra attention for the first season. Once they get their roots down they should be able to survive happily in a normal year.

Achillea filipendulina
See *Colour themes.*

Agapanthus hybrids
See *Colour themes.*

Alyssum saxatile
See *Colour themes.*

Artemisia arborescens
Semi-evergreen shrub. Silvery-white, much divided leaves. Yellow flowers in early and mid summer. Not reliably hardy in cold areas *1.2 × 1.2m (4 × 4ft).*

Buddleia davidii
See *Planting for quick results.*

Caryopteris x *clandonensis*
See *Planting for quick results.*

Colutea arborescens
Deciduous shrub. Divided, pale green leaves, and yellow pea-like flowers in summer. These are followed by inflated seed pods, flushed coppery-red *2.4 × 2.4m (8 × 8ft).*

Convolvulus cneorum
Evergreen shrub. Silvery foliage. Funnel-shaped white flowers, flushed pink beneath the petals, all summer *60 × 60cm (2 × 2ft).*

Cytisus scoparius hybrids
Deciduous shrub. Green branches make it look evergreen. Pea-type flowers, in shades of yellow, red and pink, many multicoloured, in late spring and early summer *2.4 × 1.8m (8 × 6ft).*

Echinops ritro
Herbaceous perennial. Divided, prickly grey-green foliage, spherical steel blue flower heads in mid and late summer *1m × 60cm (3 × 2ft).*

ABOVE: *Osteospermums thrive in a hot, sunny situation. This one is* O. jacundum.

ABOVE LEFT: Colutea arborescens *has the bonus of interesting inflated seed pods as well as pretty yellow flowers.*

ABOVE RIGHT: Helianthemum nummularium *hybrids thrive in hot, sunny situations. They come in a variety of colours, mainly reds, pinks and yellows.*

OPPOSITE BELOW: Phlomis fruticosa *can be a rather coarse-looking plant, but it thrives in hot, dry soils.*

Eryngium variifolium
Evergreen perennial. Dark green leaves marbled white. Grey-blue flower heads with white collars, in mid and late summer *60 × 45cm (2ft × 18in)*.

Genista tinctoria
See *Planting for quick results*.

Hebe
See *Everbright evergreens*.

Helianthemum nummularium hybrids
Evergreen sub-shrub. Green or grey leaves. Masses of small flowers in shades of red, orange, yellow, pink, and white, in late spring and early summer, with a second flush later in the year if the dead flowers are trimmed off *15–23 × 60cm (6–9in × 2ft)*.

Kniphofia hybrids
See *No fuss, low maintenance plants*.

Lavandula
See *Planting for quick results*.

Nepeta x *faassenii*
See *Colour themes*.

Osteospermum hybrids
Evergreen sub-shrub. Still sometimes called *Dimorphothecas*. Large daisy-shaped flowers mainly in shades of purple, pink, and white, all summer. Not hardy in cold areas, but will tolerate frosts where the winters are not severe *30 × 60cm (12in × 2ft)*.

LEFT: Sedum spectabile *has fleshy, succulent leaves, enabling it to grow well even in a hot, sunny position.*

Perovskia atriplicifolia
See *Colour themes*.

Phlomis fruticosa
Semi-evergreen shrub. Grey-green foliage. Clusters of quaint, bright yellow flowers at the tips of shoots, in early and mid summer *75cm × 1.2m (2½ × 4ft)*.

Phormium
See *Everbright evergreens*.

Romneya coulteri
Sub-shrubby perennial. Large fragrant white flowers, *10–15cm (4–6in)* across from mid summer to mid autumn. Not recommended for cold areas *1.2 × 1.2m (4 × 4ft)*.

Rosmarinus officinalis
See *Everbright evergreens*.

Santolina chamaecyparissus
See *Colour themes*.

Sedum spectabile
Herbaceous perennial. Succulent leaves. Large, flat pink flower heads in early and mid autumn *45 × 45cm (18 × 18in)*.

Stachys lanata
See *Colour themes*.

Ulex europaeus
See *No fuss, low-maintenance plants*.

Yucca
See *Everbright evergreens*.

ANNUALS THAT LOVE THE SUN

Most hardy annuals thrive in hot, bright conditions, and especially those with daisy-like flowers that only open when it's warm and sunny. Be generous with the annuals, especially those native to sunny climates such as South Africa.

Soil

Every plant has a preference about its ideal growing conditions, and putting a plant in the right spot will mean the difference between it thriving, and looking the best it can, or merely surviving. Some plants flourish in a damp, heavy soil; others insist on a sandy, free-draining one.

Certain plants prefer to grow in soil that is higher or lower in acidity than others, while some cannot tolerate acidity at all. So, it is important to get to know the soil in your garden; you can then choose plants to suit it, which will help you achieve the best possible results.

Soil structure

Soil consists of sand, silt, clay and organic matter (humus), and the proportions in which each is present will determine the structure of the soil – its consistency and water-retaining properties. The more large sand particles it contains, the more easily water will be able to drain through it and the more quickly it will warm up in spring, allowing earlier planting. Silt particles are smaller, so water is held for longer, but they retain little in the way of nutrients. Clay particles are the smallest of all; they hold on to nutrients and water extremely well, but produce a heavy, solid soil that is cold (slow to warm up in spring, because the water has to warm up as well), and also prone to damage if it is worked when it is too wet.

The ideal soil to have is loam. This contains a perfect balance of all the elements, producing a crumbly soil, often dark in colour. It holds both moisture and nutrients well, without becoming waterlogged. This soil is rare and most gardens have a soil that favours one particle size over others.

You can improve the structure of your soil by the regular addition of organic matter, in the form of well-rotted manure or garden compost. This will add air to a heavy soil, making it easier to work, and help to keep moisture in a free-draining one.

RIGHT: *Daboecia cantabrica 'Atropurpurea',* *with its urn-shaped, dark pinkish-purple* *flowers from early summer to mid-autumn,* *creates a mat of colour, even in a small corner.*

Soil acidity

The acidity of the soil depends to a large extent on the underlying bedrock, but it can also be influenced by the amount of rainfall, the rate of drainage, and also nearby vegetation (pine trees, for example, have acid foliage).

The acidity or alkalinity of soil is usually measured on the pH scale, in units from 1 to 14. According to this, a pH of 7 indicates a neutral soil; any unit below this indicates an acid soil; any unit above it, an alkaline one. The best way to ascertain the pH level of the soil in your garden is to use a simple testing kit. It makes sense to do this before starting work on a new garden, or if some of your plants don't seem to be growing well; keen growers test their soil routinely once a year.

If your soil proves to be particularly acid, you can add a dressing of lime to make it more alkaline; if too alkaline, work in plenty of organic matter in the form of rotted manure or garden compost. However, in either case by far the best solution is to seek out plants that would naturally thrive in such soil conditions.

TESTING THE SOIL PH

Many people garden successfully without ever testing their soil, but they are probably fortunate in gardening on ground that is not deficient in nutrients, is neither too acid nor too alkaline, and receives plenty of nutrients as part of normal cultivation. If you are not as fortunate, you can easily test for pH using one of the kits available from garden centres. Always follow the instructions on the kit if they differ from the advice given here.

1 Collect the soil sample from about 5–8cm (2–3in) below the surface. This gives a more typical reading of nutrient levels in the root area. Take a number of samples from around the garden, but test each one separately.

2 With this kit one part of soil is mixed with five parts of water. Shake together vigorously in a clean jar, then allow the water to settle. This can take between half an hour and a day, depending on the soil.

3 Draw off some settled liquid from the top few centimetres (about an inch) for your test.

4 Carefully transfer the solution to the test and reference chambers in the plastic container, using the pipette provided.

5 Select the appropriate colour-coded capsule (different ones are used for each major nutrient) and empty the powder it contains into the test chamber. Replace the cap, then shake vigorously.

6 After a few minutes, compare the colour of the liquid with the shade panel that forms part of the container. The kit contains an explanation of the significance of each reading, and what – if anything – to do.

Plants for acid soils

In the wild, the most acid soils are usually found on heather moorland, or in coniferous forest. The correct term for plants which prefer acid soil is calcifuges. Plants that prefer acid soil are often wrongly referred to as ericaceous plants because many acid-loving plants belong to the family. Ericaceae include heathers (*Erica*), arbutus, kalmia and, of course, rhododendron.

Plants that prefer an acid soil tend to grow poorly on alkaline ground, often becoming chlorotic.

Some excellent garden plants grow only in acid soil, so if this is the nature of the soil in your garden, you can look forward to growing some real treasures. Acid-loving plants are often associated with the tendency to be spring-flowering, as are camellias for example, but many are renowned for their foliage colour in the autumn, and if you can grow a range of heathers it is possible to have plants in flower practically all year round.

You can check on the pH of your soil to determine its acidity by using a soil-testing kit. It takes a matter of a few minutes to discover whether or not your soil is suitable for a particular plant. As a rough guide, if your soil measures more than 6.5 on the pH scale it is unsuitable for growing acid-lovers such as rhododendrons and heathers. Of course, even if this is the case, you can always grow the plants you want in containers filled with an ericaceous potting compost (soil mix).

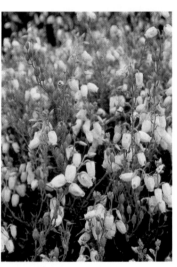

ABOVE: Daboecia cantabrica alba *is adorned with racemes of urn-shaped, white flowers from early summer to mid-autumn.*

LEFT: Azaleas are a form of rhododendron. *Many of the deciduous forms have a wonderful scent. Like other rhododendrons, they need an acid soil and shelter from hot sun.*

Berberidis corallina
Evergreen twining climber or wall shrub. Clusters of deep red flowers in summer and early autumn, against a backdrop of deep green leathery leaves. Requires a sheltered position in cold areas *3 × 3m (10 × 10ft)*.

Calluna vulgaris varieties
Low-growing evergreen shrub. Small bell-like, white to dark mauve flowers, from midsummer to late autumn. Many have colourful foliage in winter *60 × 75cm (24 × 30in)*.

Camellia hybrids
See Everbright evergreens.

Cassiope varieties
Dwarf evergreen shrub. Upright or spreading stems are densely clothed in tiny dark green leaves. Small bell-ike flowers, ranging from white to white-tinged red depending on the variety, in spring *30 × 30cm (1 × 1ft)*.

Cornus canadensis
Creeping shrub-like perennial. Forms a carpet of small white flowers in late spring or early summer. Red fruit in autumn *15cm (6in)* tall. Indefinite spread.

Daboecia cantabrica
Dwarf evergreen shrub. Tiny dark green leaves, and small urn-shaped rose-purple flowers in long slender bunches from summer to autumn *40 × 65cm (16 × 26in)*.

Epimedium grandiflorum
(syn. *E. macranthum*)
Deciduous rhizomatous perennial. Heart-shaped leaves with autumn colours. Clusters of small flowers in spring and summer. Colours vary with varieties *30 × 30cm (1 × 1ft)*.

Erica
See Everbright evergreens.

Fothergilla major
See Autumn leaves and berries.

Gentiana sino-ornata
Evergreen perennial with trailing stems. Brilliant blue trumpet-shaped flowers, striped on the outside, in autumn *15 × 30cm (6 × 12in)*.

Kalmia latifolia
Evergreen shrub. An attractive shrub

LEFT: Epimedium grandiflorum *foliage turns shades of gold, scarlet and copper in the autumn.*

BELOW: *The blood-red flowers of* Calluna vulgaris *'Dark Beauty' will last into late autumn.*

for early summer, flowering on an acid soil. Pink saucer-shaped flowers set off by glossy deep green foliage *90–120 × 120cm (3–4 × 4ft)*.

Meconopsis betonicifolia
(syn. *M. baileyi*)
Herbaceous perennial producing sky-blue flowers on tall slender stems in summer *1.2m × 45cm (4 × 1½ft)*.

Pernettya mucronata (syn. *Gaultheria mucronata*)
Evergreen shrub. Small, prickly dark green leaves, tiny white flowers in late spring and early summer, followed on female plants by large rounded berries, usually red or pink *1.2 x 1.2m (4 x 4ft)*.

Rhodohypoxis baurii
Low-growing herbaceous perennial with spear-shaped leaves. In spring and summer bears small, flattish flowers, varying from white to pale pink or red *10 × 10cm (4 × 4in)*.

Trillium grandiflorum
Rhizomatous perennial forming a dome-shaped plant. Has large, dark green leaves and white funnel-shaped flowers on short, arching stems from spring until summer *45 × 30cm (18 × 12in)*.

Plants for chalk (alkaline) soils

Although a chalk (alkaline) soil limits the range of plants you can grow, many of the loveliest garden plants thrive in chalk: clematis, honeysuckle (*Lonicera*), sweet peas (*Lathyrus*) and viburnums, as well as most bulbs. Plants that need a pH of below 7.0 are best avoided in very alkaline soils. Soil pH may vary in a single garden: it may be more alkaline near walls or patios, where lime mortar may have collected. If plants fail to thrive in these areas, replace them with chalk-loving, lime-tolerant plants.

Acanthus spinosus
Clump-forming perennial. Striking arching leaves with spiny edges, and tall spikes of white and purple tubular flowers throughout summer *1.2m × 75cm (4 × 2½ft)*.

Achillea filipendulina 'Gold Plate'
Clump-forming evergreen perennial. Flat, golden yellow flowerheads on tall

ABOVE: *The saucer-shaped, bright yellow flowers of* Potentilla fruticosa, *a deciduous shrub, last from late spring to late summer.*

RIGHT: *The leaves of* Phlomis fruticosa, *an evergreen summer-flowering shrub, have a felty surface which turns slightly yellow in autumn.*

leafy stems in late summer and early autumn *100 × 45cm (39 × 18in)*.

Anchusa azurea (syn. *A. italica*)
Clump-forming perennial. Tall spikes of bright blue flowers in early summer *100 × 60cm (39 × 24in)*.

Aquilegia alpina
Upright perennial. Clumps of ornamental, finely divided leaves and nodding blue flowers in late spring and early summer *45 × 30cm (18 × 12in)*.

Aucuba japonica
Rounded evergreen shrub. Glossy, leathery oval leaves, often toothed, and small red-purple flowers in mid spring *3 × 3m (10 × 10ft)*.

Campanula
Annuals, biennials and perennials. Mat-forming to tall, upright varieties. Many prefer an alkaline soil: *C. lactiflora*, with bell-shaped white to lavender-blue flowers, and the saucer-shaped white or blue *C. persicifolia 30–90 × 30cm (1–3 × 1ft)*, according to variety.

Caryopteris × *clandonensis* 'Heavenly Blue'
Mound-forming, deciduous sub-shrub. Silvery grey-green, lance-shaped leaves and very dark blue flowers in late summer and early autumn *1 × 1.5m (3 × 5ft)*.

Cistus hybrids
Evergreen shrubs. Eye-catching white to pink flowers in summer. *C.* × *cyprius* has white flowers with pink and yellow markings; *C. creticus* has bright pink flowers; and *C.* × *skanbergii* has pale pink blooms *15cm–2m × 60cm–2m (6in–6½ft × 2–6½ft)*, according to variety.

Delphinium
Clump-forming perennial. Tall spikes of blue on white flowers in early and mid summer *1.5m × 75cm (5 × 2½ft)*.

Deutzia scabra 'Plena'
(syn. *D. crenata* 'Flore Pleno')
Upright deciduous shrub. Arching shoots produce dense spikes of cup-shaped white flowers in summer *2.4 × 2m (8 × 6½ft)*.

Dianthus
This large group of chalk-loving plants includes dwarfs for the rock garden, border perennials, such as garden pinks and carnations, and

ABOVE: *Rock roses (*Cistus*) are fine summer-flowering plants and can cope well with drought.*

ABOVE: *This beautiful biennial* Dianthus barbatus *'Scarlet Beauty' flourishes in chalk.*

LEFT: *The fragrant flowers of lilac (*Syringa*) range from deep pink through mauve to white. This lilac is S.* × vulgaris.

Gypsophila
Semi-evergreen or evergreen perennials and annuals. Clouds of small, star- to trumpet-shaped, white or pink flowers in late spring to autumn *5cm–1.2m × 15cm–1m (2in–4ft × 6–39in)*, according to variety.

Helianthemum nummularium
Evergreen shrub. Pink, red or yellow single or double flowers over grey-green foliage in early and mid summer *15–23 × 60cm (6–9 × 24in)*.

Kolkwitzia amabilis
Erect then drooping deciduous shrub. Abundant clusters of bell-shaped, soft pink flowers in late spring and early summer *3 × 4m (10 × 13ft)*.

Lonicera × brownii (syn. *L. sempervirens*) 'Dropmore Scarlet'
Deciduous or semi-evergreen climber. Long, trumpet-shaped scarlet flowers in summer *4 × 3m (12 × 13ft)*.

biennials, such as *Dianthus barbatus*. Size depends on species.

Erysimum cheiri (syn. *Cheiranthus cheiri*)
Bushy evergreen perennial usually treated as biennial. Fragrant single or double flowers, mainly in shades of red or yellow, flowering in late spring *23–45 × 30cm (9–18 × 12in)*.

Phlomis fructicosa
Evergreen spreading shrub. Deep yellow flowers in early and mid summer, above grey-green sage-like foliage *1.2 × 1.2m (4 × 4ft)*

Potentilla fruticosa
Deciduous shrub. Dark green leaves and saucer-shaped, bright yellow flowers from late spring to late summer *1 × 1.5m (3 × 5ft)*

Scabiosa 'Butterfly Blue'
Branched perennial. Grey-green leaves and lavender-blue flowers in mid and late summer *40 × 40cm (16 × 16in)*.

Syringa vulgaris
Deciduous shrub. Fragrant single or double flowers, in shades of blue, purple, cream, and white, in late spring or early summer *3 × 2m (10 × 8ft)*.

Verbascum hybrids
Biennials and perennials. Most have tall, slim spires of flowers in summer. *V. chaixii* has felted leaves and yellow flowers with purple centres; *V. chaixii* 'Album' is white with mauve centres; and *V. phoeniceum* is smaller, with clusters of flowers surrounded by leaves *5cm–2m × 15–60cm (2in–6½ft × 6–24in)*, according to variety.

Clay soils

The ideal garden soil is a medium loam: it retains moisture yet is well drained, with a fine, crumbly texture. However, many soils have a high clay content. Clay soils are usually very fertile and retain moisture. While this is an advantage, a very heavy wet soil tends to be difficult to work, and can often mean that plants become waterlogged. Always choose plants carefully to suit your soil type: there are many excellent plants, described below, that will thrive happily in clay.

Abelia × grandiflora
Rounded, vigorous, semi-evergreen shrub. Arching shoots with glossy, dark green leaves and an abundance of fragrant, tubular white flowers with pink tinges, lasting from mid summer to mid-autumn *3 × 3m (10 × 10ft)*.

Aruncus dioicus
Clump-forming perennial. Fern-like, toothed leaves and large feathery plumes of greenish white and creamy white flowers in early and mid summer. 'Kneiffii' is a dwarf form *1–2 × 1.2m (3–6½ × 4ft)*.

Aucuba japonica
Evergreen shrub. Glossy green leaves splashed or spotted yellow, insignificant flowers, but red fruits on female plants (plant a male variety for pollination) *2.4 × 2.4m (8 × 8ft)*.

Astilbe × arendsii hybrids
Clump-forming perennials. Fern-like foliage and spikes of plume-like flowerheads in summer in various colours, including: *A.* 'Fanal', in dark crimson; *A.* 'Federsee', in deep rose-pink; and *A.* 'Feuer', in salmon-pink *50–75cm × 45cm (20–30in × 18in)*, according to variety.

Berberis × stenophylla
Arching evergreen shrub. Spiny-tipped leaves and clusters of deep yellow flowers in late spring, followed by blue-black fruit *3 × 3m (10 × 10ft)*.

Cardamine pratensis 'Flore Pleno'
Clump-forming perennial. Leaves arranged in neat rosettes and loose clusters of double, lilac flowers in late spring *20 × 50cm (8 × 20in)*.

Chaenomeles japonica
Bushy deciduous shrub. Thorny with glossy leaves and clusters of orange

ABOVE: Rodgersia pinnata *is usually grown for the impact of its deeply veined leaves.*

RIGHT: *The panicles of Astilbe 'Elizabeth Bloom' appear in summer above bronze leaves.*

to red flowers in spring, followed by yellow or yellow-tinged fruit *1 × 2m (3 × 6½ft).*

Crambe cordifolia
Clump-forming perennial. Large, dark green crinkled leaves and abundant tiny white, gypsophila-like flowers in late spring and mid summer *2.4 × 1.5m (8 × 5ft).*

Digitalis grandiflora (syn. *D. orientalis*)
Clump-forming biennial or perennial. Tall spikes of pale yellow flowers in early and mid summer *100 × 45cm (39 × 18in).*

Hemerocallis 'Burning Daylight'
Clump-forming perennial. Strap-shaped leaves, ending in a point at the tip, and bright orange, lily-like flowers in summer *1m × 75cm (3 × 2½ft).*

Humulus lupulus 'Aureus'
Perennial climber. Bright, golden yellow lobed leaves and insignificant green flowers in summer, followed by decorative 'fruit' in autumn *6m (20ft).*

Lathyrus grandiflorus
Perennial climber. Striking pink-purple and red, pea-like flowers from summer to early autumn *1.5m (5ft).*

Leucanthemum × superbum hybrids (syn. *Chrysanthemum maximum*)
Clump-forming perennials. Chrysanthemum-like flowers in white with golden centres from early summer to early autumn. Various cultivars, which are better than the species: the dwarf 'Snow Lady'; 'Wirral Supreme', with large double flowers; and 'Phyllis Smith', with single flowers with twisted petals *45–90cm × 60cm (18–36in × 24in),* according to variety.

Persicaria bistorta 'Superba' (syn. *Polygonum bistorta*)
Clump-forming, semi-evergreen perennial. Dense spires of soft pink flowers throughout summer *90 × 90cm (36 × 36in).*

Phlox paniculata
Erect perennial. White, red, mauve,

ABOVE: Phormium tenax, *a clump-forming evergreen perennial, never fails to make a statement with its robust, architectural, sword-shaped leaves.*

pink flowers in summer *75 × 75cm (30 × 30in).*

Phormium hybrids
Clump-forming evergreen perennial. Robust, upright, sword-shaped leaves in various colours *1–2.4 × 1m (3–8 × 3ft),* according to variety.

Rodgersia pinnata 'Superba'
Clump-forming perennial. Deeply veined, crinkled leaves and plumes of yellowish white, pink or red star-shaped flowers which last from mid- and late summer *100 × 75cm (39 × 30in).*

Tradescantia × andersoniana
Clump-forming perennial. Clusters of three-petalled, rich purple, blue or white flowers which last from early summer to early autumn and arching, strap-shaped leaves *50 × 50cm (20 × 20in).*

BELOW: *In mid-summer large, feathery, creamy white plumes grace the tall, tough, sturdy stems of* Aruncus dioicus, *which is a clump-forming perennial.*

Pollution-tolerant plants

Town and city gardens, particularly those alongside a main road, are often exposed to very high levels of pollution. Many plants suffer extensively from the effects, while others thrive, despite the exhaust deposits collecting on their leaves. If you live in a busy, built-up area, select plants that are suitable for the conditions (see below), and reduce the impact by planting a dense hedge of pollution-tolerant plants around the edge of the garden.

Amelanchier canadensis
Erect deciduous shrub. Orange-red foliage in autumn and star-shaped white flowers in spring, sometimes followed by blue-black fruit *6 × 3m (20 × 10ft)*.

Aucuba japonica
Rounded evergreen shrub. Glossy, leathery oval leaves, often toothed, and small red-purple flowers in mid spring *2.4 × 2.4m (8 × 8ft)*.

Berberis
Evergreen or deciduous shrubs. Attractive leaves, some holly-like and many with good autumn colour, yellow to dark orange flowers, and colourful fruit. Wide range of sizes from dwarf or mound-forming (*B. thunbergii* 'Bagatelle') to vigorous and upright (*B.* 'Goldilocks'); some are useful for hedging (*B. thunbergii*) *50cm–4m × 45cm–4m (20in–13ft × 18in–13ft)*, according to species of variety.

Buddleia davidii
Arching deciduous shrub. Dense trusses of fragrant lilac to purple flowers from summer to autumn *3 × 5m (10 × 16½ft)*.

Ceratostigma willmottianum
Spreading deciduous shrub. Dark green, purple-edged leaves that turn red in autumn, and a display of blue flowers with red-purple tubes from late summer to autumn *1 × 1.5m (3 × 5ft)*.

Chaenomeles hybrids
Deciduous shrubs. Spiny with cup-shaped flowers in pink, red, orange or white in early spring to summer, followed by edible fruit. Some suitable for ground cover or low hedging (*C. japonica*), others for a border (*C. speciosa* and *C. × superba* varieties) *1–3m × 2–5m (3–10ft × 6½–16½ft)*, according to species or variety.

ABOVE LEFT: Elaeagnus × ebbingei *'Gilt Edge' makes a good screen.*

ABOVE: Berberis *have spectacular flower displays in spring, and deciduous kinds have tinted foliage in autumn.*

Cotoneaster frigidus
Upright then spreading deciduous tree or large shrub. White, saucer-shaped flowers in summer, followed by orange-red fruit *5 × 5m (15 × 15ft)*.

Elaeagnus × ebbingei
Rounded evergreen shrub. Attractive glossy leaves, silvery beneath, and creamy, silvery white flowers in autumn *4 × 4m (13 × 13ft)*.

Elaegnus pungens
Bushy evergreen shrub. Glossy, often wavy-edged leaves and pendent, silvery white flowers in autumn, followed by brown-red fruit *4 × 5m (13 × 16½ft)*.

Forsythia × *intermedia*
Deciduous shrubs. Brilliant display of early yellow flowers. 'Lynwood' and 'Spectabilis' are popular varieties; 'Karl Sax' has leaves that turn red or purple in autumn *2.4 × 2.4m (8 × 8ft)*, according to variety.

Garrya elliptica
Upright evergreen shrub or small tree. Glossy, leathery leaves and pendulous catkins from mid winter to early spring *4 × 4m (13 × 13ft)*.

Ilex aquifolium
Usually erect evergreen shrub or tree. Spiky or smooth-edged holly leaves, and red or occasionally yellow or orange berries. While the species itself is very large, many of its varieties are suitable for a small garden *4–25m × 2.4–8m (13–80ft × 8–25ft)*, according to variety.

Leycesteria formosa
Upright deciduous shrub. Spikes of white flowers from summer to early autumn, followed by red-purple berries *2 × 2m (6½ × 6½ft)*.

Ligustrum ovalifolium
Upright evergreen or semi-evergreen shrub. Glossy green leaves and white flowers in mid summer, followed by black fruit *4 × 4m (13 × 13ft)*.

Olearia × *haastii*
Bushy evergreen shrub. Daisy-like white flowers with yellow centres in mid and late summer and glossy green leaves *2 × 3m (6½ × 10ft)*.

Osmanthus × *burkwoodii* (syn. × *Osmarea burkwoodii*)
Rounded evergreen shrub. Glossy dark green leaves and tubular white flowers in mid spring, followed by blue-black fruit *3 × 5m (10 × 16½ft)*.

Philadelphus hybrids
Mainly deciduous shrubs. Fragrant white flowers in summer may be single (*P.* 'Belle Etoile'), semi-double (*P.* 'Boule d'Argent') or double (*P.* 'Virginal') *75cm–6m × 1–4m (30in–20ft × 3–13ft)*, according to variety.

Syringa vulgaris
Deciduous shrubs. Conical trusses of fragrant flowers in late spring to early summer. Lilacs may be white,

TOP: *Ivies (varieties of* Hedera helix*) are very tough, and can be used for ground or wall cover.*

ABOVE: *The green berries of this holly,* Ilex × altaclarensis *'Lawsoniana' are yet to turn red, but they are still an attractive feature.*

LEFT: Berberis thunbergii *'Atropurpurea' has striking, marbled, reddish-purple leaves, suffused silvery pink when young.*

pink, purplish pink, blue, creamy-yellow or white *3 × 2m (8 × ft)*, according to variety.

Tamarix tetrandra
Arching deciduous shrub or small tree. Plumes of light pink flowers in mid and late spring and feathery foliage *3 × 3m (10 × 10ft)*.

Weigela florida
Spreading deciduous shrub. Funnel-shaped pink flowers in late spring and early summer *2.4 × 2.4m (8 × 8ft)*.

Plants for the tropical look

If you are trying to create a garden based on Mediterranean influences with white-painted walls and with the emphasis on hot climate flora, you will need to use plenty of plants that give the impression that they are exotic or tender when in fact they are quite frost-tolerant.

Some of the plants suggested here are only hardy enough for warm areas where frosts are light and seldom prolonged, others are really tough.

You can of course use many of them in an ordinary border, but the ones suggested here are primarily effective as part of an area reserved for the more striking plants.

If you live in a cold area and have a greenhouse, conservatory, or even a porch, grow the more vulnerable plants in large pots and move them to this protected area for winter.

Arundinaria viridistriata
See *Variety with variegation.*

Clianthus puniceus
Evergreen climbing shrub. Divided, feathery leaves, crimson-scarlet claw-shaped flowers in early summer. Will only survive outdoors in mild districts. Can reach about *3m (10ft).*

Cordyline australis
Palm-like plant with strap-like leaves at top of plant. *C. a. purpurea* has brownish-purple leaves. Where winters are mild and frost not severe it can be left in the ground and may grow into a tall tree. Elsewhere grow in a pot, where it will remain much smaller. Protect for the winter.

Fatsia japonica
See *No fuss, low-maintenance plants.*

Gunnera manicata
Huge leaves, like a giant rhubarb. In the ground it is large even for a big garden, but you can grow it in a tub or a patio pot to restrict its size. Keep very moist, and protect during the winter.

Kniphofia hybrids
See *No fuss, low-maintenance plants.*

ABOVE: Cordyline australis 'Alberti'.

Lilium hybrids
You can buy bulbs and pot up your own lilies, or buy them when they are about to bloom. These may have been dwarfed chemically and will probably make better container plants. Heights vary.

Osteospermum hybrids
See *Sun lovers.*

Phormium hybrids
See *Everbright evergreens.*

Rheum palmatum
An ornamental rhubarb that reaches 2.4m (8ft) tall in flower, but the leaves are less than half this height. White or red flowers in early summer.

ABOVE: *For the cost of a packet of seeds you can have a show like this* Ipomoea tricolor *'Heavenly Blue'.*

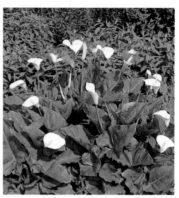

ABOVE: *Where winters are mild* Zantedeschia aethiopica *can be overwintered outside.*
TOP: *The big, bold leaves of* Rheum palmatum *look very exotic.*
LEFT: *Lilies are quite easy to grow in pots provided you choose suitable varieties.*

Yucca
See *Everbright evergreens*, but the green form can be just as effective as a variegated variety.

Zantedeschia aethiopica
Well-known white arum flowers, popular with florists. Can be kept outdoors where winters are mild, but is usually best grown in a pot and given winter protection. The growth dies down in winter.

Exotic annuals

Some annuals that are regarded as indoor plants can be grown in the garden for the summer.

Among the flowering plants, celosias are always eye-catching, whether you grow the plume-shaped varieties or those shaped like a cock's comb. A mixture will usually include shades of yellow, red, and pink. The coleus is one of the best foliage pot-plants to try outdoors *en-masse* – plants are very easy to raise cheaply from seed. The multi-coloured foliage matches the exotic croton in boldness and colour combinations. Make sure they are carefully acclimatized, and don't put them out too early.

Many half-hardy bedding plants are easily raised from seed – try large daisy-like flowers such as arctotis, with flowers in shades of red, orange and pink. Salpiglossis are always eye-catching, and with their velvety, funnel-shaped flowers in shades of red, purple, and yellow, usually prominently veined and marked, certainly have that 'exotic' look.

Portulacas and cleomes (with spidery-looking flower heads) are among the other half-hardy annuals to include. But be sure to make space for *Ipomoea tricolor*, with its big blue flowers often *10cm (4in)* or so across, which are bound to make a real feature climbing up a trellis.

Disposable houseplants

Use flowering pot-plants to add short-term colour to your patio. Plants like gerberas, and dwarfed chrysanthemums, are inexpensive and generally treated as disposable plants if used indoors. Sink the pot into the soil so that the plant is easily removed after flowering.

Architectural plants

Architectural plants may seem a contradiction in terms, for one implies the rigidity of buildings and structures, the other the informality and fluidity of plant life. The term is often a puzzle to non-gardeners, yet a plant enthusiast will know instantly when he sees an 'architectural' plant.

'Sculptural' plants

'Sculptural' is perhaps a better way to describe those plants, which, though clearly possessing all the natural beauty of any first-rate plant, also have structure and stature, and above all a shape – and perhaps texture – that an architect might be pleased to use to enhance his buildings and structures in the same way as a piece of sculpture might be used.

Some herbaceous plants, such as the acanthus, have assumed architectural status – in this case because the acanthus leaf occurs so often as a pattern in classical architecture, but also because the plant has the bold stance and distinctive profile that makes it stand out from the ordinary. Most architectural plants are trees and shrubs, however, with height as well as a distinctive outline. Use architectural plants sparingly and with careful consideration, not as part of a mixed planting but rather as you would large ornaments, as punctuation points within the garden.

Use architectural plants to make a bold statement in paved and gravel gardens, or to break up an otherwise boring area of lawn.

Acanthus spinosus
Statuesque plant with large, deeply divided leaves that are both erect and arching. Mauve and white, hooded flowers on stiff spikes in mid and late summer *1 × 1m (3 × 3ft)*.

Angelica archangelica
Biennial or short-lived perennial. Large, deeply divided, aromatic leaves on stiff, upright plant. Ball-like head of smaller clusters of yellowish-green flowers in mid and late summer *2.4 × 1m (8 × 3ft)*.

LEFT: Acanthus spinosus *is one of those plants with dramatic leaves and equally imposing flowers, and not one that will be ignored.*

BELOW: Angelica archangelica *makes a bold plant about 1.8m (6ft) tall, with large leaves and striking globular flower heads. Use it as a focal-point plant in the herb garden.*

Catalpa bignonioides 'Aurea'
Deciduous tree. The green species is far too large for a small garden, but 'Aurea' is more compact, and can be bought trained as a shrub-like multi-stemmed tree. The golden leaves are very large and handsome *4.5 × 4.5m (15 × 15ft)*.

Cordyline australis
See *Plants for the tropical look*.

Cornus controversa 'Variegata'
A small tree with wide-spreading branches spaced out to give it a layered effect. Leaves have striking silver margins *4.5 × 4.5m (15 × 15ft)*.

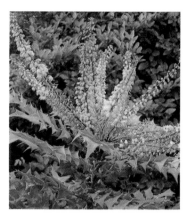

LEFT: *Daturas (now more correctly called brugmansias) are ideal for the summer patio but they have to be taken indoors for winter frost protection.*

RIGHT: *'Charity' is one of the most imposing hybrid mahonias, with bold sprays of yellow flowers blooming through the coldest months of the year.*

Crambe cordifolia
Herbaceous perennial. Normally a plant for a large garden, but sparsely planted it will make a bold statement. Enormous leaves and huge clouds of gypsophila-like small white flowers in early and mid-summer *1.8 × 1.8m (6 × 6ft)*.

Datura (syn. *Brugmansia*)
Tender shrub. Must be overwintered in frost-proof place, but often grown on patio in a large tub for summer. Large drooping leaves, big bell-shaped very fragrant flowers – usually white or cream, but there are also red and pink kinds *1.8 × 1.2m (6 × 4ft)* in tub.

Fatsia japonica
See *No fuss, low maintenance plants.*

Gunnera manicata
See *Plants for the tropical look.*

Juniperus scopulorum 'Skyrocket'
Conifer. You may also find it sold under the name of *J. virginiana* 'Sky-rocket'. Very narrow, pencil-like growth. Typical conifer foliage *4.5m × 75cm (15 × 2½ft)*.

Kniphofia
See *No fuss, low maintenance plants.*

Mahonia 'Charity'
See *Everbright evergreens.*

RIGHT: *Salix matsudana 'Tortuosa' is a small tree that can be as fascinating in winter as it is in summer.*

Paulownia tomentosa
A large tree totally unsuitable for a small garden. It can be grown as a large shrub, however, by annual hard pruning close to ground level, when the leaves become huge. Treated like this height will be about *2.4–3m (8–10ft)* and spread about *1.8m (6ft)*.

Phormium hybrids
See *Everbright evergreens.*

Salix matsudana 'Tortuosa'
A small to medium-sized tree with spiralling and twisted stems as well as contorted leaves. Seen at its best in winter when the stems are bare *4.5 × 4.5m (15 × 15ft)*.

Yucca
See *Everbright evergreens*, but a green form is just as useful as a variegated variety as an architectural plant.

Living screens

The screening plants described here are not rows of tall conifers or large windbreaks along the boundary, which are inappropriate in a small garden, but plants that you can use to screen objects within the garden and plants that you would be happy to grow as ornamentals too.

Generally, something that requires screening will need it the year round, so evergreens naturally predominate in any list of screening plants. But sometimes a summer-only screen is acceptable. For a summer screen within the vegetable plot consider Jerusalem artichokes, which provide excellent summer cover and a crop to harvest at the end of the season!

When looking for a good screening shrub, check that it is well clothed at the base. If you are prepared to erect a trellis or internal fence, many of the plants described under *Climbers and wall shrubs* will also make excellent internal screens. A trellis covered with sweet-smelling honeysuckle will make a summer screen that is pleasing to the eye and the nose. The most popular – and best – honeysuckles are deciduous, so don't expect winter cover, but some fragrant climbing honeysuckles, such as *Lonicera japonica*, are evergreen or semi-evergreen so you will have winter cover as well as summer scent – though at the price of less spectacular flowers.

Trellises and screen block walls
Sometimes it is possible to screen an unsightly object, such as a storage tank with just two or three well-chosen shrubs. Alternatively, erect a trellis or screen wall, carefully integrated as part of the garden design, then use climbers, wall shrubs or ordinary shrubs against these. This double-masking is often the most effective because you have a whole range of climbers that can be used on a trellis, including the ubiquitous but very practical and evergreen ivy, and wall shrubs such as pyracanthas.

Garage walls
Detached garages can dominate a small garden, so you probably need to soften the impact of the walls. Climbers are a natural choice, as are wall shrubs. But you could use a garage as an ideal backdrop for espalier or fan trained fruit trees.

Many evergreen shrubs will do an excellent masking job in front of a garage wall. Let hedging plants such

ABOVE: Griselinia littoralis *'Dixon's Cream'*.
LEFT: Griselinia littoralis.

as *Lonicera nitida* 'Baggesen's Gold' or a golden privet (such as *Ligustrum ovalifolium* 'Aureum') grow up untrimmed until the required height has been reached. Don't attempt to clip these like a formal hedge, but prune over-enthusiastic growth occasionally, and leave them with a natural shape.

LEFT: *For a fast-growing shrubby screen the climbing* Polygonum baldschuanicum *(syn.* Fallopia baldschuanica*) is difficult to beat.*

BELOW: Ligustrum ovalifolium *'Aureo-marginatum' (syn. 'Aureum') is a fast-growing hedging plant, much more attractive than the form with plain green leaves.*

Arundo donax
Grass. Forms tall, almost bamboo-like clump, with drooping blue-green leaves. There is also a variegated form *2.4 × 1.2m (8 × 4ft)*.

Buxus
Be careful not to choose a dwarf form if you want a taller screen. This is a classic shrub to clip to shape, and is much used for topiary as well as hedges. You could clip your screen to shape.

Griselinia littoralis
See *No fuss, low maintenance plants*.

Ilex
See *Everbright evergreens*.

Ligustrum ovalifolium 'Aureum'
See *Colour themes*.

Lonicera nitida 'Baggesen's Gold'
See *Colour themes*.

Miscanthus sacchariflorus
A large grass. Narrow, arching leaves, forming a dense clump *2.4 × 1m (8 × 3ft)*.

Polygonum baldschuanicum
Now more correctly *Fallopia baldschuanica*. Deciduous climbing shrub. A vigorous climber, but instead of using it as a screen up a trellis, try letting it grow over the eyesore itself, if it is an old shed, for example. Within a few years it will almost cover it. Profusion of small white or pale pink flowers in conspicuous sprays from mid summer to early autumn. Height and spread is usually dictated by its support.

Climbers and wall shrubs

Small gardens almost inevitably have a lot of potential space for climbers and wall shrubs. Often there are external fences or walls that can be covered, interior surfaces, such as trellises, which can be used as screens, and nearly always there are all the walls of the house. Some will be in sun for most of the day, others will remain mainly in shade, but there are plants to suit every aspect.

Where space is at a premium, the vertical space provides a wonderful opportunity to grow more plants. Climbers and wall shrubs have a small 'footprint', and if pruned or trained so that they do not encroach too far out from the support, it is usually possible to grow other plants in front of them.

The climbers suggested here are all shrubs that will form a permanent part of the garden framework, but supplement them with annual climbers for a little extra variety and colour. Most annuals can be grown up a trellis – and they should be happy in a container if there is no soil in which they can be planted.

The heights given in the following list are an indication of how tall they are likely to grow in a small garden. Many climbers grow as high and wide as their support. Some clematis will grow to more than 9m (30ft) with a suitable support – such as a tree – but settle for 1.2m (4ft) if that is the height of a fence, and grow along it instead.

Actinidia kolomikta
Climber for wall or pergola. Dark green heart-shaped leaves tipped with white and pink. Sun or partial shade *3m (10ft)*.

Ceanothus
Wall shrub. Blue flowers in late spring or early summer, or in late summer and into autumn, depending on species. Some are evergreen, others deciduous. Some are of border-line hardiness where winters are cold. Sun *3m (10ft)*.

RIGHT: *Clematis remains one of the most popular climbers. This is 'The President'.*

Clematis
An impressive deciduous climber. Use large-flowered hybrids against a trellis on a wall. Vigorous species such as *C. montana* can be grown along a fence or through a tree. Sun or partial shade. Large-flowered hybrids *3m (10ft)*.

Euonymus fortunei
See *Everbright evergreens*.

LEFT: Actinidia kolomikta.

Garrya elliptica
Evergreen wall shrub. Grown for its long catkins in late winter and early spring. Shade or sun *2.4m (8ft)*.

Hedera
The ivies need no introduction. Choose large-leaved kinds, such as *H. colchica* 'Dentata Variegata', for a pergola or arch, small-leaved varieties of *H. helix* for a wall or fence. Shade or sun *3m (10ft)*.

Humulus lupulus 'Aureus'
Herbaceous perennial climber. Golden leaves. Pergola or arch. Sun or partial shade *3m (10ft)*.

Hydrangea petiolaris
Vigorous climber. Flat heads of white flowers in early summer. Shade or partial shade. Needs tall wall or a tree *6m (20ft)*.

Jasminum nudiflorum
See *Colour for the cold months*. Shade or partial shade. Best against a wall, perhaps secured to a trellis *3m (10ft)*.

Jasminum officinale
Climber. Fragrant white flowers in summer and often into autumn. Pergola or arch *3m (10ft)*.

Lonicera x *japonica*
Evergreen climber. White or pale yellow fragrant flowers from early summer to mid autumn. 'Aureoreticulata' has yellow-veined leaves. Best supported against pergola or fence *6m (20ft)*.

Lonicera periclymenum
Deciduous climber. Very fragrant flowers, pale yellow flushed purple-red, ideal for pergola, arch, or trellis. Some varieties flower in late spring and early summer, others from mid summer to early autumn *3m (10ft)* but can grow much taller up a tree.

Polygonum baldschuanicum
See *Living screens*. Fence or wall.

Pyracantha
Wall shrub. White flowers in early summer, red or orange berries in autumn and into winter. Sun or shade *3m (10ft)*.

Rosa
Climbing and rambling roses need no description or introduction. There are many to choose from, and some are excellent for pergolas, arches, and against the wall around the door. Many are very fragrant. Sun or partial shade *3m (10ft)*.

Vitis coignetiae
Deciduous climber. Large leaves with beautiful autumn colours. Sun or shade. Will grow very tall in a tree but can be contained on a pergola.

ABOVE LEFT: Jasminum nudiflorum.
ABOVE: *Pyracantha – a good wall shrub*.
TOP: Garrya elliptica.

Wisteria
Deciduous climber, with long drooping tassels of blue or white flowers in late spring and early summer. *W. sinesis* and *W. floribunda* are both widely grown, and are suitable for a pergola, or to grow against a house wall. Sun or partial shade *3m (10ft)*, but can be much taller.

Planting for scent

A garden without scent is like a meal without seasoning. All the elements appear to be there, but that extra spice is missing that lifts it from the ordinary and heightens the senses.

You can overdo the seasoning, however, so avoid planting too many fragrant plants of the same kind close together. One scent will compete with another, and the more subtle ones may be lost. Rather, make sure that plants with very fragrant flowers are chosen to flower in succession over a period of months. It will not matter if two fragrant shrubs are planted side by side if one flowers after the other has finished.

Mix plants that flower in the day with those that are scented at night – perhaps a rose that gives off its heady perfume during the day with a honeysuckle or night-flowering nicotiana that comes into its own once dusk falls.

Make use of plants with aromatic leaves that release their fragrance when brushed against or deliberately crushed.

Some of the plants suggested here are ornamental plants in their own right – roses and honeysuckles are highly decorative as well as fragrant – but find space for some plants which flower at night. Although they will add nothing to the daytime display they will certainly make up for lack of visual impact by their wonderful perfume after dark.

Chimonanthus praecox
See *Colour for the cold months.*

Choisya ternata
See *Everbright evergreens.* The green variety is just as good for fragrance.

Cytisus battandieri
Large deciduous shrub. Grey leaves. Pineapple-scented yellow flower in late spring and early summer. Not reliably hardy in cold areas, and best grown as a wall shrub *3 × 2.4m (10 × 8ft).*

Daphne mezereum
Deciduous shrub. Red, pink, purple or white flowers between late winter and mid spring *1.2 × 1m (4 × 3ft).*

Hamamelis mollis
See *Colour for the cold months.*

Jasminum officinale
See *Climbers and wall shrubs.*

Lavandula
See *Planting for quick results.*

Lonicera periclymenum
See *Climbers and wall shrubs.*

Mahonia 'Charity'
See *Everbright evergreens.*

Rosa
Roses are among the most fragrant of all shrubs, and you can grow their many forms in beds, borders, and as climbers. Use roses lavishly for a fragrant garden. Heights vary according to species.

ABOVE: *Stocks – varieties of* Matthiola incana *– are worth planting for their fragrance.*
LEFT: *One of the strongest spring fragrances comes from* Daphne mezereum *var.* rubra.

FRAGRANT ANNUALS

If you use a lot of summer bedding plants, be sure to include some fragrant ones such as stocks (*Matthiola incana*), and ornamental tobacco plants (nicotiana hybrids), though bear in mind that many of the compact, day-opening varieties of nicotiana have nothing like the powerful scent of the taller, evening-scented ones.

Night-scented stocks (*Matthiola bicornis*) are totally unattractive by day, so grow these as a gap-filler in a border where their day-time appearance doesn't matter.

Philadelphus
Deciduous shrubs. Several good species and hybrids, all with fragrant white flowers in early summer.

Sarcoccoca hookeriana humilis
See *Plants that prefer shade.*

ABOVE: *Lilacs (varieties of* Syringa vulgaris) *are among the most fragrant shrubs, and although some grow tall they are not too large for a small garden.*

Skimmia japonica
See *Autumn leaves and berries.*

Spartium junceum
Deciduous shrub. Yellow, pea–type flowers in summer *2.4 × 1.8m (8 × 6ft).*

Syringa vulgaris
Deciduous shrub, the popular lilac. The varieties have very fragrant flowers mainly in shades of blue, purple, mauve, and white, in late spring and early summer *2.4 × 1.5m (8 × 5ft).*

Viburnum x bodnantense
See *Colour for the cold months.*

Wisteria
See *Climbers and wall shrubs.*

SCENTED FOLIAGE

Use some of the scented-leaved geraniums (pelargoniums) on the patio. You can even plant some of them at the front of a border. Many herbs, such as pineapple sage, lemon balm, and lemon verbena, make acceptable patio plants in pots.

Among the shrubs with aromatic foliage are *Artemisia arborescens, Choisya ternata, Laurus nobilis, Rosmarinus officinalis,* and *Salvia officinalis.*

Eucalyptus can be grown in a small garden if you prune it back hard each spring to grow like a shrub.

RIGHT: *Wisterias are grown mainly for visual impact, but they are also fragrant.*

Attracting wildlife

You don't have to turn your garden into something that resembles a meadow – some might say overgrown and weedy garden – to attract wildlife.

Lots of shrubs, border and rock plants, and annuals and biennials will attract wildlife of many kinds, from birds, bees and butterflies to wasps and weevils. Not all are welcome, of course, but for the few that you don't want to attract you will certainly gain many beautiful and beneficial animals that will help to control the pests.

You will, of course, need to create particular habitats if you want to encourage particular types of wildlife, such as a pond for aquatic creatures. And there is a lot to be said for leaving an area of grass long – perhaps where bulbs are naturalized if you want a horticultural justification – and if you let a few nettles grow behind the garden shed you will provide food plants for many kinds of caterpillars that will later grace your garden as butterflies.

Attracting wildlife in general often brings the bonus of more beneficial insects such as hoverflies and ladybirds, which will help to keep down pests such as aphids.

LEFT: Aucuba japonica 'Variegata'.

ABOVE: Berberis thunbergii 'Atropurpurea Nana'.

Shrubs

Aucuba (birds)
Berberis (birds, bees, butterflies)
Callicarpa (birds)
Ceanothus (bees)
Cistus (bees)
Cotoneaster (bees, birds)
Cytisus (bees)
Daphne (birds, bees)
Escallonia (bees)
Hebe (butterflies)
Hedera (bees, butterflies)
Hypericum (birds)
Ilex (birds)
Lavandula (bees, butterflies)
Leycesteria formosa (birds)

Ligustrum (bees, butterflies)
Lonicera periclymenum (butterflies)
Mahonia (birds)
Pernettya (birds)
Perovskia (bees)
Potentilla (bees)
Pyracantha (birds, bees)
Rhamnus frangula (bees, butterflies)
Ribes sanguineum (bees)
Skimmia (birds, bees)
Symphoricarpos (birds, bees)
Syringa (bees, butterflies)
Ulex (bees)
Viburnum (birds, bees)
Weigela (bees)

Border and rock plants
Achillea filipendulina (bees, butterflies)
Alyssum saxatile (butterflies)
Armeria maritima (bees, butterflies)
Aster novi-beglii (bees, butterflies)
Erigeron (bees, butterflies)
Nepeta (bees, butterflies)
Scabiosa caucasica (bees, butterflies)
Sedum spectabile (bees, butterflies)
Solidago (birds, bees, butterflies)
Thymus (bees, butterflies)

Annuals and biennials
Centaurea cyanus (bees, butterflies)
Dipsacus spp. (birds)
Helianthus annus (birds)
Hesperis matronalis (bees)
Limnanthes douglasii (bees)
Lunaria annua (birds)
Scabiosa annual (bees, butterflies)

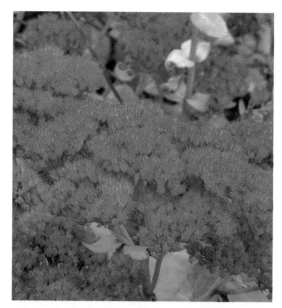

LEFT: Sedum *'Autumn Joy'*

BELOW: Solidago.

ABOVE: Alyssum saxatile.

OTHER WAYS TO ATTRACT WILDLIFE

A thick hedge attracts far more wildlife than a fence or wall. A prickly evergreen hedge like holly will provide good nest and roost sites for many birds.

An old log pile provides refuge for many beneficial insects and can make a nest site for small mammals.

The Kitchen Garden

Aᴍʙɪᴛɪᴏᴜs ᴋɪᴛᴄʜᴇɴ ɢᴀʀᴅᴇɴs ᴀʀᴇ sᴇʟᴅᴏᴍ achievable in a small space. Vegetables that are hungry for space such as potatoes and cabbages may lose out to flowers. But if you are content with smaller vegetables such as lettuces, carrots, beetroot, and dwarf beans, and can relegate tall climbing beans and expansive plants like globe artichokes to the mixed or herbaceous border, it is quite practical to grow a wide range of vegetables even where space is quite restricted.

Grow a whole range of vegetables, from lettuces to peas, in containers like windowboxes

ABOVE: *Raspberries are not an ideal crop for a small garden but they can be trained so that they don't take up too much space.*

TOP: *Fruit-growing is possible even on a roof or balcony garden . . . with a little imagination.*

OPPOSITE: *This picture shows an interesting way of providing supports for tall vegetables in a small kitchen garden.*

LEFT: *One of the upright-growing apple trees ideal for a small garden or limited space. This variety is 'Walz', planted in a bed of 'Surrey' ground cover roses.*

and growing bags. Even potatoes can be harvested from pots and growing bags and tomatoes of all types have been grown with great success in growing bags. This kind of small-scale vegetable gardening is demanding, and the yields always very modest for the effort involved, but if the idea of harvesting your own fresh vegetables just before you pop them into the pot appeals, you may find it worth the effort. It can certainly be fun.

If you have a reasonably sized garden – large enough to divide off a section for a kitchen garden – growing them in the ground is the most practical way to produce your vegetables, and much of the fruit.

Fruit trees and bushes are often ornamental and can be easily integrated into the flower garden. Trained fruit trees like espalier and fan apples look attractive even with bare branches in winter.

Herbs are much more easily accommodated than vegetables. Many are highly ornamental and lots of them make good container plants. Others look perfectly in place in a border. If you want to make a real feature of your herbs, make a herb garden a key part of your garden design.

Ornamental herbs

Formal herb gardens look impressive, but can be difficult to accommodate in a small space.

However, as the illustrations below show, there are alternatives.

Bear in mind that though herb gardens are packed with interest in summer, in winter you will be left with just a few evergreen shrubs and a handful of herbs that retain their foliage and are tough enough to survive unprotected. Alternatively, incorporate your herbs in an overall garden design that carries interest through all the seasons. Here are some other ways to incorporate herbs in a small garden.

A collection in a container

A herb pot can hold half a dozen or more different herbs. Do not start to harvest until plants are growing strongly, then keep harvesting little and often to produce compact yet well-clothed plants.

Shrubby plants like bay and rosemary can be grown in tubs to decorate the patio or to display by the front or back door.

Windowbox herbs

Herbs can be grown in windowboxes and troughs provided you choose compact plants such as thymes and marjorams. Ornamental, variegated mints also look good.

Growing bags

Growing bags are not elegant, but they are useful for rampant plants like mints, which would otherwise make a take-over bid for the border.

In among the flowers

Many herbs are so decorative that they don't look amiss in beds and borders, and indeed some are planted more for their ornamental than culinary uses.

Among the herbs that look good with other border plants are chives, fennel, marjoram, and lemon balm.

ABOVE: *Have fun with your small herbs. They can be arranged informally in pots, or grouped together as in the small wheelbarrow.*

RIGHT: *An attractive herb collection can be grown in a small raised bed, but bear in mind that many of these plants will grow much larger.*

HOW TO MAKE A HERB WHEEL

If you have an old cartwheel, just paint or varnish that and set it into the ground ready to plant. Few of us have access to cartwheels, however, but an acceptable second best can be made from bricks. Adjust the size of the wheel to suit your garden. Bricks are a convenient way to make the 'spokes', but you could use dwarf dividing 'hedges' of hyssop or thyme. Place an attractive terracotta pot in the centre as the hub of the wheel, and plant with herbs, or place an upright rosemary in the centre. A rosemary may become too large after a few years, but either keep it clipped to shape and size or replace it every second or third year.

1 Mark a circle about 1.5–1.8m (5–6ft) across, using a line fixed to a peg to ensure an even shape. If it helps, use a wine bottle filled with dry sand instead of a stick to mark out the perimeter. Excavate the ground to a depth of about 15cm (6in).

2 Place the bricks on end, or at an angle, around the edge. If you place them at a 45 degree angle it will create a dog-tooth effect; bricks placed on end will look more formal. Either lay them loose in compacted earth, or bed them on mortar.

3 Lay rows of brick, cross-fashion, as shown. If the diameter does not allow for them to be laid without gaps in the centre, stand an ornament or pot in the middle if you are not planting directly into the soil in that position.

4 Top up the areas between the spokes with good garden or potting soil.

5 Plant up each section, using plants that will balance each other in size of growth if possible. You could, for instance, grow a collection of different thymes.

6 For a smart finish, carefully cover the soil with fine gravel.

Fruit in a small space

The most satisfactory way to grow tree fruits such as apples and pears in a small garden or a confined space is trained as a cordon, fan or espalier against a wall or fence. Even some bush fruits such as gooseberries can be trained as cordons or double cordons against a fence.

ABOVE: *Wall-trained fruit trees take up relatively little space.*
RIGHT: *If you want apples in a small garden it is best to use one of the columnar varieties or to grow an ordinary variety on a trained system like this espalier 'Lord Lambourne'.*

Blackberries and hybrid berries can be trained against a fence or over an arch, but keep the growth contained and avoid allowing thorny shoots to overhang pathways.

It is even possible to grow apples in pots on the patio, but with the new flagpole-type varieties available that grow in a narrow column, you may prefer to plant these where space is limited. They will require much less watering and attention than ordinary varieties on dwarfing rootstocks in pots.

The initial training of espaliers, fans and cordons demands patience and skill. Unless you particularly like the challenge and can wait for two or three years longer, it is best to buy a ready-trained tree.

BUYING FRUIT TREES

Whether a fruit tree such as an apple, peach or cherry is suitable for a small garden depends not so much on the variety of the fruit but on the rootstock. This has a profound affect on the size of the tree (as well as how soon it starts to fruit). Always check the rootstock before you buy, and if in doubt ask whether it is suitably dwarfing for a small garden.

TRAINED FRUIT TREES

Trained trees look attractive and produce a heavy crop from a restricted space. But they require regular and methodical training, sometimes twice a year. If in doubt about how to prune a particular trained fruit, consult an encyclopedia or fruit book.

Espaliers are more ornamental than cordons (some shrubs, such as pyracanthas, are occasionally trained as espaliers using the same methods).

Cordons are usually trained at an angle of about 45 degrees, secured to support canes and wires fixed to stout posts or to a fence. Many plants can be planted in a small space, and soft fruits such as gooseberries and red and white currants can be trained in this way, saving the space taken up by a bush form.

Fans can be free-standing, tied to wires supported by posts, but they are usually planted against a wall or fence. In time a fan can be trained to cover a large area, such as a garage wall.

Step-overs are single-tiered espaliers, used as a fruiting edging, perhaps within the kitchen garden.

Potted fruit

Apples can be grown in pots provided you choose a very dwarfing rootstock. The same applies to peaches. You can experiment with other bush and tree fruits, but bear in mind that this is second best to growing them in the ground.

Flagpole apples

You can buy a range of apple trees that rarely produce long sideshoots, but instead grow upright and produce most fruiting spurs along the main vertical stem. These take up little space and won't cast a heavy shadow, so they are ideal for growing in a flower bed. The blossom is pretty in spring, and the ripening fruits are ornamental later in the year.

Rhubarb

Rhubarb is ornamental enough to be grown in the flower border. You can even grow it in a large pot as a foliage plant for the patio, though this is not the best way to achieve a heavy crop.

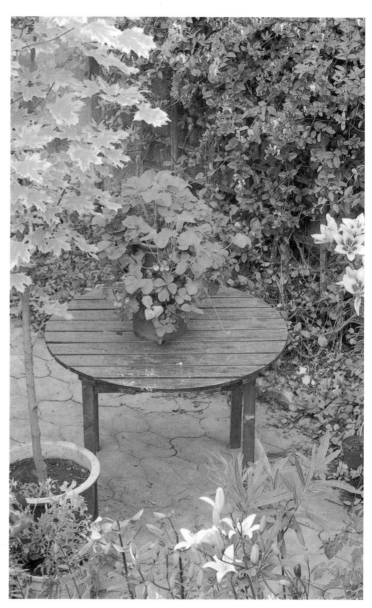

ABOVE: *There is always space for a few strawberries if you grow them in a container like this.*

ABOVE: *This rhubarb chard is growing in a flower bed.*

Strawberries

If you don't have much space for fruit, at least try growing strawberries. A strawberry barrel or a tower container will hold a lot of strawberries and provided you keep the container well watered it will be laden with fruit . . . which won't become splashed with mud if the weather is wet or awkward to pick. Also the fruit will be more difficult for slugs to reach.

Finding room for vegetables

If you are a dedicated vegetable grower you will probably want to turn over a large part of your garden to the task. However, this need not mean that the garden will be unattractive. Try growing vegetables in small beds, either in a patchwork pattern or a more formal ornamental potager. If you really are restricted for space, grow crops in containers, from growing bags to hanging baskets.

Whatever form your 'vegetable plot' takes, it should never be tucked away in a dull, sunless part of the garden. Most vegetables need good light and plenty of moisture to do well. Dry ground shaded by hedges and walls seldom produces succulent vegetables.

The deep bed system

If you are happy to devote a large area to vegetables, then you can grow them traditionally, in a rectangular plot divided into long straight rows, with paths for access between each one. Alternatively, you can use the deep bed system, where the plot is divided into small beds, about 1.2m (4ft) wide and, after the initial preparation, all the work is done from narrow paths at the sides.

This method has many advantages. It gives you a bigger area for growing vegetables, by cutting down the number of space-consuming

ABOVE: *This raised vegetable bed in a flower garden makes an interesting feature as well as a neat productive area.*

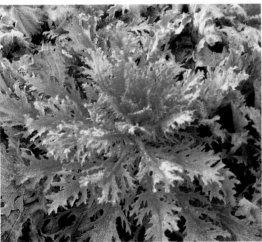

LEFT: *Ornamental kales are usually grown for their decorative effect, but they are edible if you get tired of looking at them. This variety is 'Coral Queen'.*

paths. Because the soil is dug deeply, and enriched with masses of bulky organic material, plant roots are encouraged to spread downwards rather than sideways. This allows you to grow plants much closer together than in a conventional row, giving you a bigger yield. Having prepared the beds, you can do all the cultivation without walking on the soil and compacting it. Soil structure and fertility are greatly improved because it is easier for worms and insects to work the manures and composts into the soil. Once the crops are underway, there is virtually no need for weeding since the plants are so close together they cover the soil surface, preventing weed growth.

Ornamental potagers

The term potager comes from jardin potager, simply being French for kitchen garden. But the term has come to refer primarily to a kitchen garden – usually with both fruit and vegetables – laid out ornamentally, perhaps with beds edged with low hedges like a parterre. Treated like this, your kitchen garden can become a prominent design element.

Growing bags

Growing bags are excellent for vegetables if all you have is a balcony or patio on which to grow them. It is quite feasible to grow lettuces, spinach, radishes, cucumbers, tomatoes, turnips, even self-blanching celery and potatoes, in growing bags.

Clearly, you won't keep the family fed with potatoes from a couple of growing bags, and the economics don't make much sense. But it is

ABOVE: *These are 'Totem' tomatoes growing in a 25cm (10in) pot.*
BELOW: *You can even grow tomatoes in a hanging basket.*

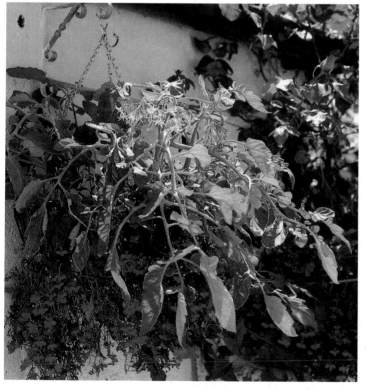

worth planting an early variety (you can move the bag into a protected area if frost threatens) so that you can enjoy those new potatoes straight from the garden.

Troughs, tubs and pots

Tomatoes are one of the most successful crops for a growing bag, and, provided you choose a suitable compact variety, they are equally successful in pots.

Courgettes (zucchini) and cucumbers are also a practical choice for a tub or large pot. Potatoes can be grown in a pot for a bit of fun, but you might be better planting an aubergine (eggplant) or pepper in it.

Windowboxes and hanging baskets

The only vegetable likely to do well in a hanging basket is the tomato, but you must choose a trailing or drooping variety, and control both watering and feeding.

Windowboxes offer more scope and, apart from tomatoes (use dwarf or trailing varieties), stump-rooted carrots, radishes, onions and lettuces are among the crops that do well.

Rather than grow a hearting lettuce, which leaves a gap as the whole head is harvested at once, try a non-hearting 'cut-and-come-again' variety that you can harvest in stages.

Flowers and vegetables

If you simply don't have the space to devote part of your garden to vegetables and herbs alone, consider integrating them with the existing ornamentals. Many vegetables are pretty in their own right – with striking foliage and flowers – and when grown in beds and borders, and intermixed with other decorative plants, they can work surprisingly well.

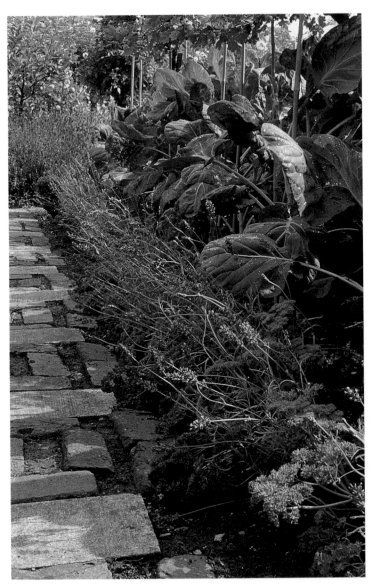

One of the enormous advantages of growing vegetables with flowers is that the diversity of plants helps to deter pests and diseases. Mixed planting provides a naturally balanced environment, where the flowers attract insects and other wildlife that feed on pests that feed on vegetables. Sowing marigolds among tomato plants, for example, will keep the tomatoes relatively free from attack by aphids, because the marigolds attract hover-flies, and their larvae like nothing better than an aphid feast.

Among the flowers
It is quite possible to incorporate vegetables as part of a formal bedding scheme. Red or purple rhubarb chard leaves, for example, contrast well with grey-foliaged bedding plants; carrot foliage looks attractive as a foil for bright summer bedding plants; and even one of the more decorative kinds of red-leaved lettuce will make a pretty edging for a summer bedding scheme. Unfortunately, the problem comes at harvest time, when gaps soon become rather conspicuous.

Vegetables are more acceptable as gap fillers in a herbaceous or mixed border. They fill the space admirably, and after harvesting the border is left no less attractive than it was originally. If you choose crops such as spinach or 'cut-and-come again' (oak leaf) lettuce, you can harvest the leaves without destroying the whole

LEFT: *Edging a vegetable plot with colourful flowers is the best solution if you want vegetables and ornamentals.*

ABOVE: *Rosemary (*Rosmarinus officinalis*) is a herb that tastes as good as it looks.*

ABOVE: *When young, purple sage (*Salvia officinalis 'Purpurascens'*) has tinged foliage.*

ABOVE: *Mint (*Mentha*) is highly invasive and should be planted in pots in the ground.*

plant. Other suitable candidates here are radishes, beetroot, asparagus peas, carrots, and leaf beet; but much depends on the size of your space and your imagination.

In a traditional cottage garden, where flowers rub shoulders with fruit, vegetables and herbs, the plants often merge into one another but the result can appear rather chaotic. If the rest of the garden is formal in style, dedicate just one area to mixed planting and make it a feature, separated with a hedge or screen.

Planting in blocks

Instead of having single vegetable plants dotted here and there among the flowers, try growing them in blocks or patches. The effect can be just as decorative, and the crops will certainly be easier to harvest, after which the space can easily be replanted. Plant the areas that had vegetables in summer with winter-flowering bulbs and spring bedding. That way, you will gain more ornamental value without sacrificing much in terms of crop.

With such small patches of ground, it takes no time at all to sow a batch of seed, tend delicate young

ABOVE: *Brushing past low-growing thymes (*Thymus*), such as this one with its delicate pink flowers, will release a pungent scent.*

plants, or keep weeds under control. Using this method, you may grow the same quantity of vegetables as in a conventional plot but the task will seem far less daunting.

Climbing vegetables

Most climbing vegetables are decorative in themselves, and you can treat them in much the same way as you would any ornamental annual climbers. Make a feature of ordinary or asparagus peas by

growing them against a free-standing trellis or a wall of canes and netting within the flower border. Train trailing forms of courgette (zucchini) over an archway or pergola. Or grow ridge cucumbers and scarlet runner beans on wigwams (tepees) of canes at the back of a border or along a series of rustic poles lining the path.

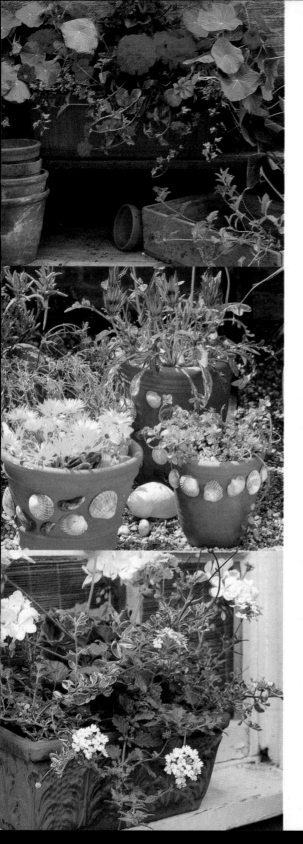

The Container Garden

- Decorating Containers • Colour Schemes
for Containers • Seasonal Planters
- Edible Collections • Scented Collections
- Difficult Situations • Inspirational
Containers • The Young Container
Gardener • Indoor Containers

Successful container gardening

CONTAINER GARDENING EXPANDS YOUR horticultural horizons. You do not need to be a full-time gardener with a large country garden to grow the tastiest herbs, lushest wild strawberries, or beautiful flowers for a summer evening. You don't even need any expert knowledge to be a successful container gardener – indeed, if you own a houseplant or a pot of parsley, you are already a container gardener.

The beauty of containers is that with the minimum amount of time and effort they will instantly jazz up a balcony or roof garden, extend the garden up to the back door, and liven up window-sills with colour, scent and form. They can also, of course, be used indoors, as spectacular table centrepieces, to brighten a corner of the room, or simply to add a little greenery and freshness.

The great advantage of gardening in containers is that, like furniture, they can be moved around to create a new look, with pride of place given to those plants that are performing best. Unlike plants growing in your garden, containers can simply be moved to wherever you want them: in the foreground when flowering, and then into the background once flowering is over. If you are unhappy with a particular arrangement or combination, you only have to move the pots to experiment and try something else.

Today, good quality container-grown plants are available all through the year, and skills such as seed sowing, potting-on and taking cuttings are not always essential, though many gardeners enjoy the process. There is nothing wrong with 'instant' gardening, it is simply a matter of choice. By buying plants that are nearing maturity, you can save the time-consuming and uncertain business of rearing the plants, and you can try out different shape and colour combinations before you buy the plants by simply grouping them together.

Of course, the plants are only a part of the equation, and you can be as creative as you like with your choice of containers. Shops and garden centres stock an ever-increasing range of containers to suit every budget, from magnificent Italian olive oil jars to humble plastic pots. Junk shops and flea markets are also a rich source of objects that can take on a new use as a planter – a blackened cooking pot with a hole in its base is useless for its original purpose, but is ideal as a container of character, and can be bought extremely cheaply. Similarly, an old basket can be completely transformed when filled with a fresh floral display. The range of possibilities is nothing short of amazing, both for the small-scale gardener and for gardeners who work with very large areas. Containers will add to the grace and majesty of even the grandest garden designs.

In the following pages you will find scores of imaginative and innovative themed ideas for beautiful containers, with recommendations of some of the best plants around for achieving them. Don't be dismayed if you can't find exactly the plants suggested. There is nearly always an excellent alternative, and new varieties with brighter colours and bigger, longer-lasting blooms keep appearing in the nurseries. With a bit of experience, you'll soon be able to create your own eye-catching arrangements. Whether you are a novice or an experienced gardener, container gardening is a highly accessible, enjoyable and colourful way to brighten up your surroundings.

OPPOSITE: *Plants are only a part of the equation, and decorative containers, such as this classic windowbox being prepared for use for instance, are readily available.*

Getting Started

To enjoy your container garden from its inception, begin by
choosing the best-shaped container for each planting and one
that will show off the plants to their full advantage. Plants
suitable for container gardening can be planted in the right
compost (soil mix), in standing pots or in baskets or half-pots
fixed to a wall as hanging gardens. Then, with regular
feeding and watering (keeping a watchful eye open for
signs of pests and diseases) you should have a success on
your hands.

ABOVE: *The soft petals and subtle
colour gradations of the violas make
them the perfect match for the pearly
interiors of the shells.*

OPPOSITE: *Even garden tools and
empty containers can make decorative
ornaments to complement a
beautifully arranged window box.*

The best plants for containers

Annuals and Biennials

Whether you raise them yourself from seed in the greenhouse or on the kitchen window-sill, or buy them in strips from the garden centre for an instant effect, fast-growing annuals and biennials will quickly and cheaply fill baskets and boxes and flower prolifically all summer to produce eye-catching effects. Choose compact varieties that will not need support. Trailing annuals such as lobelia, nasturtiums and dwarf sweet peas are all invaluable for hanging baskets. Some perennial species, including petunias, pelargoniums and busy Lizzies (impatiens), are normally grown as annuals.

Tender Perennials

Beautiful tender and half-hardy plants such as osteospermums, verbenas, pelargoniums, petunias and fuchsias are ideal for containers, where their showy flowers can be fully appreciated. Raise new plants from cuttings for next season. If you buy young, tender plants from the garden centre in the spring, don't be tempted to put newly planted boxes or baskets outside until all danger of frost is past.

ABOVE: *Trailing nasturtiums make a glorious display, providing colour from early summer.*

LEFT: *Petunias and pelargoniums are tender perennials, which are often grown as annuals.*

BELOW: *Containers of spring bulbs such as these yellow tulips cannot fail to delight.*

Evergreen Perennials

Evergreen non-woody perennials such as ajugas, berge-nias and *Carex oshimensis* 'Evergold' are always useful for providing colour and foliage in the winter, but look best as part of a mixed planting.

For single plantings, try *Agapanthus africanus* or *A. orientalis* with their blue flowers on tall stems. For a more architectural shape, consider one of the many different eryngiums (sea holly). *E. agavifolium* is par-ticularly attractive, and has greenish-white flowers in late summer.

Border Perennials

Few people bother to grow perennials in containers, but if you have a paved garden, or would like to intro-duce them to the patio, don't be afraid to exper-iment. Dicentras, agapanthus, and many ornamental grasses are among the plants that you might want to try, but there are very many more that you should be able to succeed with – and they will cost you nothing if you divide a plant already in the border.

Bulbs

Bulbs, particularly the spring varieties make ideal container plants. Bulbs should be planted at twice the depth of their own length. They can be packed in as tight as you like, and even in layers, so that you get a repeat-show-ing after the first dis-play. Note that when planting lilies (the white, scented, fail-safe *Lilium regale* is a fine choice if you have never tried them before), they need excellent drainage, so put in an extra layer of grit at the bottom. And to prevent spear-ing the bulb later on with a plant support, insert this in the compost at the same time.

Shrubs for Tubs

Camellias are perfect shrubs for tubs, combining
attractive, glossy evergreen foliage with beautiful
spring flowers. *Camellia* x *williamsii* and *C. japonica*
hybrids are a good choice. Many rhododendrons and
azaleas are also a practical proposition, and if you
have a chalky (alkaline) soil this is the best way to
grow these plants – provided you fill the container
with an ericaceous compost (soil mix).

Many hebes make good container plants (but not
for very cold or exposed areas), and there are many
attractively variegated varieties. The yellow-leaved
Choisya ternata 'Sundance' and variegated yuccas
such as *Yucca filamentosa* 'Variegata' and *Y. gloriosa*
'Variegata' are also striking shrubs for containers.

For some winter interest, try *Viburnum tinus*.

Topiary for Pots

Topiarized box is ideal for a pot. However, it is relatively slow growing at about 30cm (12in) a year.
It may be best to buy a mature, ready-shaped plant,
although you miss the fun of doing the pruning.

ABOVE: *If your garden cannot support lime-hating
rhododendrons, do not despair. They can easily be
grown in pots, in ericaceous compost (soil mix), giving colour from autumn, through winter, to summer.*

LEFT: *Pots on plinths and fruit trees in tubs create
a marvellous architectural effect, with plenty of
striking verticals.*

Trees for Tubs

Trees are unlikely candidates for containers, particularly
for small gardens. Fortunately, the restricted root-run
usually keeps them compact and they never reach
the proportions of trees planted in the ground. Even in
a small garden, some height is useful.

Choose trees that are naturally small if possible.
Laburnums, crab apples (and some of the upright-
growing and compact eating apples on dwarfing rootstocks), *Prunus* 'Amanogawa' (a flowering cherry with
narrow, upright growth), and even trees as potentially
large as *Acer platanoides* 'Drummondii'
(a variegated maple) will be happy in a large pot or tub
for a number of years. Small weeping trees also look
good. Try *Salix caprea pendula* or *Cotoneaster*
'Hybridus Pendulus' (which has cascades of red berries
in autumn). Even the pretty dome-shaped, grey-leaved
Pyrus salicifolia 'Pendula' is a possibility.

These must have a heavy pot with a minimum inside
diameter of 38cm (15in), and a loam-based compost
(soil mix). Even then they are liable to blow over in
very strong winds unless you pack some other hefty
pots around them during stormy weather.

Providing year-round colour

Containers are traditionally used for creating extra, lavish colourful effects in summer. With a little thought and careful planning you can enjoy delightful containers all year round.

First Signs of Spring

Early spring bulbs burst into life as soon as winter loosens its grip. Even on chilly, rainy days, pots planted with small bulbs – snowdrops, crocuses, scillas and *Iris reticulata* – will provide splashes of clear colour on the patio or window-sills, and can be briefly brought indoors, if you like, for an early taste of spring. Primulas and polyanthus look great in containers, too. If you grow lily-of-the-valley in the garden, pot up a few roots and bring them inside: they'll come into bloom weeks early.

ABOVE AND LEFT:
Plants might not flourish in the garden border all year round, but you can still have some delightful plants every day of the year. Here, small pots of lily-of-the-valley, dwarf irises, crocuses and primroses brighten up a warm day in early spring.

Summer Blooms

Summer is, of course, the highlight of the container gardener's year, giving the opportunity for lovely creative plantings. Deciding which plants to use is an enjoyable task.

RIGHT: *For a really eye-catching container, be different. A large potted mix, featuring summer bedding plants topped by a lanky white fuchsia, is encircled by a rustic woven sheep feeder. The effect is heightened by tufts of grass packed into the gaps.*

FAR RIGHT: *A flamboyant show of billowing annuals.*

Autumn Highlights

Grow one or two autumn-glory shrubs in tubs that you can bring out when you need a final burst of colour on the patio.

Ceratostigma willmottiamum has compact growth and lovely autumn foliage tints while still producing blue flowers. Berries can also be used as a feature, and you can usually buy compact gaultherias already bearing berries in your garden centre.

ABOVE: *Potted chrysanthemums (here flanked by ericas) are an easy and excellent way of prolonging bright summer colours into autumn.*

Winter Colour

Some winter-flowering shrubs can be used in tubs, such as *Viburnum tinus* and *Mahonia x media* 'Charity'. Try being bold with short-term pot plants such as Cape heathers (*Erica hyemalis* and *E. gracilis*) and winter cherries (*Solanum capsicastrum* and similar species and hybrids). You will have to throw them away afterwards, but they will look respectable for a few weeks even in cold and frosty winter weather.

HOW TO PROTECT PLANTS FROM FROST

Many of the most dramatic summer patio shrubs – like daturas and oleanders – must be taken into a frost-free place for the winter. Others that are frost-tolerant but of borderline hardiness in cold areas, like the bay (*Laurus nobilis*), or that are vulnerable to frost and wind damage to the leaves (such as *Choisya ternata* 'Sundance') need a degree of winter protection. It is a pity to lose these magnificent patio plants for the sake of a little forethought as autumn draws to a close. Shrubs that are fairly tough and need little protection from the worst weather can be covered with horticultural fleece, or bubbly plastic. If you use fleece, you may be able to buy it as a sleeve (ideal for winter protection for shrubs in tubs).

1 Insert four or five canes around the edge of the pot. Cut the plastic to size. Allow for an overlap over the pot.

2 Wrap it around the plant, allowing a generous overlap. For particularly vulnerable plants, use more than one layer. Securely tie the protection around the pot. For very delicate plants, bring the material well down over the pot, to keep the root-ball warm. Leave the top open for ventilation and to permit watering if necessary.

GARDENER'S TIP

If covering with fleece, tie the top together (moisture will be able to penetrate, and tying the top will help to conserve warmth).

OPPOSITE: *Smooth, topiarized box balls and pyramids catch the eye at any time of year. You can buy them ready styled or, better still, raise your own cuttings and shape them as you wish.*

Colour-theme plantings

Create impact in the garden by colour-theming seasonal planting to tune in with their surroundings. This works best with plants in containers as the containers can be chosen to tone and blend with the walls, then planted with flowers in complementary colours. Once the blooms are over, they can be replaced by new plantings for the next season. You do not always have to match the colours; you may decide to use contrasting colours instead. In this way, the garden looks fresh and bright all year round and you have several scene changes to enjoy as the seasons pass.

ABOVE: *The blue-green and purple tones of ornamental cabbage look fabulous in a galvanized grey bucket, set against the blue-green of a painted fence.*

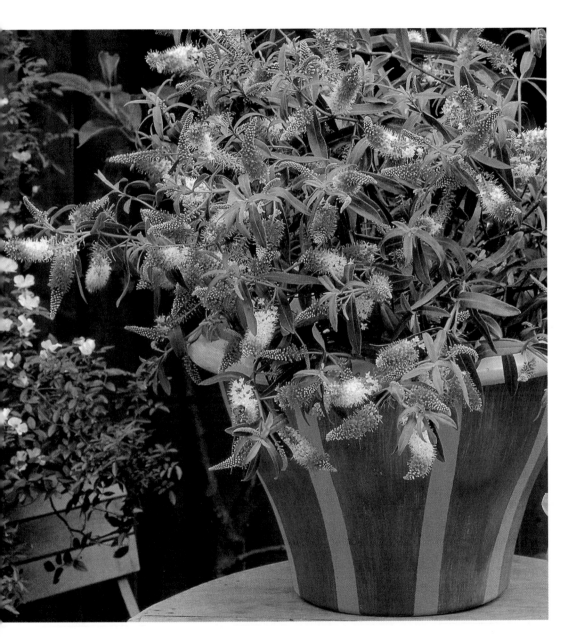

OPPOSITE: *An orange-yellow poppy and cream-coloured violas look stunning planted in beige pots, set against the warm ochre shades of a brick wall.*

ABOVE: *This pot has been painted in stripes to link the green background and pink blooms of a wonderful hebe.*

Colour-splash plantings

Just as you can decorate the inside of your home with colourful flower arrangements, so you can do the same outside. Use pots of flowering plants to provide a colourful splash in a prominent part of the garden or to decorate the outdoor living area when entertaining. Create an immediate colour impact by choosing a colour theme and teaming containers and plants in toning shades. Try painting some terracotta pots specially to match your favourite flowers. You could also make a tablescape for a special occasion, using a variety of containers and seasonal flowering plants in hot clashing colours or in cool shades of blue, purple and white.

ABOVE: *Simple and magical, it is as though the rich colouring of the tulips has leaked out of the petals and dripped down the side of the pots.*

ABOVE: *Even a couple of ordinary terracotta garden pots hanging on the wall make interesting decorative detail, especially when they are both planted with a froth of white blooms.*

LEFT: *This vivid arrangement of winter-flowering pansies in a trug can be moved around to provide colour wherever it is needed.*

ABOVE: *Bright, bold, hothouse colours are very effective in groups.*
Try to find equally brightly coloured planters and containers.

Creating cameo gardens

If you are lucky enough to have a spare part of the garden where nothing is going on, liven it up by introducing a set theme. It can be witty and original, or have a theme to merge with the rest of the garden. Or it could even be a special private area packed with all your favourite pots.

Cameo gardens can provide a surprise in a small corner, embellish an under-used area or even provide a miniature project for children, who love to have a space of their own. The idea is to find a theme – herbs, perhaps, or pansies, miniature vegetables or lavender – then make up a 'sampler', providing a different container for each variety. Alternatively, you can make the containers the theme, choosing watering-cans, culinary pots, pans and colanders, enamelware or terracotta in different shapes and sizes. Another idea is to design a miniature formal garden, perhaps taking inspiration from the classic Italian style. Choose a piece of small statuary as a focal point, then clip some young box plants into a miniature hedge surround and fill in with dwarf lavender.

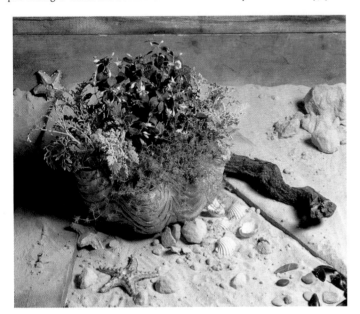

LEFT: *For a seaside-type garden, use a stone-coloured pot and grey-leaved plants to blend in with the sandy background.*

Pots for Privacy

To be able to relax totally in the garden, you need to satisfy two basic requirements: privacy and shelter. Without the benefit of enclosed spaces, especially in built-up areas, these considerations can be problematic. However, there are ways of achieving them. Trellis can be fixed on top of walls and fences to create extra height. You can then grow decorative climbers to provide a wonderful natural wallpaper. And within this enclosure you can create a special atmosphere with the use of gorgeous pots. In fact, pots score over plants in beds because they can be swapped round with other containers in the rest of the garden, giving a constant change of scenery.

One way of conveying privacy is by furnishing this area like a real room. A row of shelves for a collection of, say, pelargoniums, pouring out rich red and magenta flowers and subtler hues. Verbenas make an excellent alternative, and can either be left to tumble, or trained up miniature wigwams (teepees) of green sticks to provide a side-show in blues, mauves and purples, interspersed with white. Violas are equally small-scale and domestic, with the added advantage that, being placed at eye level, their amazingly exquisite, detailed patterning can be fully appreciated. But perhaps the best container plants for outdoor shelving, or even an old, brightly painted open kitchen display unit, are auricula primulas.

Auriculas impart a strong Victorian feel (although they were actually introduced in the late 16th century) with their ornate faces, which are so exquisite that they used to be displayed inside an empty picture frame. One by itself is always an eye-catcher, leaving the viewer demanding more. Visit a specialist nursery to see a wide range.

Scented Pots

An enclosed area with no wind is the perfect place to grow scented pot plants where the perfume can hang in the air. You can have anything from marzipan to the smell of melting, rich brown chocolate. Just place the pots around a chair, sit back and relax.

Daphne odora 'Aureomarginata' makes a perfect shrub for a tub. It grows quite slowly to about 1.5m (5ft), and has purplish flowers, and the most ravishing scent imaginable. Feed well, place in the sun, and add plenty of grit to the soil for quick drainage.

Jasminum officinale is a fast, vigorous climber; it will quickly race up the side of a house or, with a restricted root run, can be trained round a large frame. Give it a hot sunny spot, water well, and inhale. Lilies have equally strong scents. The range is huge, running from the highly popular and reliable *Lilium regale* to the various, multi-coloured hybrids like 'Black Dragon' and 'Green Dragon', to the stunning strain called Imperial Crimson, with white flowers speckled red. Good drainage is the secret of success.

For a talking point, choose the unusual but wonderful *Cosmos atrosanguineus* which has dark maroon flowers and a whiff of chocolate on hot, sunny days. For marzipan, try an old-fashioned heliotrope like 'Princess Marina'. And for an unusual small black flower and the scent of summer fruits, plant up *Salvia discolor*.

RIGHT: *Thyme-filled gardens have a distinguished history, and have been popular since the medieval period. The trick is to choose a selection, with round and needle-like leaves, to create a rich tapestry in shades of green, gold and silver.*

Novel Themes

Edible gardens are always popular, and besides growing potted fruit trees and strawberries, it is worth experimenting with different kinds of salad. Lettuces now come in a wide range of shapes and colours and the more ornamental forms of herbs like basil and sage are just as delicious as the green varieties.

You can also grow a range of potted plants with different textured foliage. Smooth and svelte, sharp and pointed, rubbery and mounded, are all available. When next visiting a garden centre, do not just go in with your eyes open but with a stroking, extended hand. Plants appeal to more senses than one.

ABOVE: *A marvellous concoction made from the simplest of easily gathered materials. A scattering of wet beach pebbles frames a circular pattern, backed up by a group of small pots and chimney pots, planted with a wide selection of succulents.*

TOP: *Serried ranks of watering-cans in the soft greys of weathered, galvanized metal make a beautiful feature in themselves. Planted up with hostas and violas, they become a highly original cameo garden.*

ABOVE: *This terracotta garden is focused around tall, long-tom pots planted with hostas, ivies and clematis let loose so that it behaves like a trailer, rather than a climber. Old drain covers and edging tiles add character.*

LEFT: *Potted plants always give plenty of impact when arranged in groups and one way to display them is on old baker's shelves in rows and rows of pots.*

RIGHT: *Themed gardens do not come much better than this. A sensational group of battered, wizened old boots double up as containers. The sumptuous profusion of pelargoniums in full blast obviously couldn't be happier.*

Living table decorations

Outdoor table decorations are easy to put together and are at their most successful when they complement their surroundings. Simply gather together some of the smaller pots from around the garden, you may plunder the garden for a few cut flowers or foliage to add, or even add fruit and vegetables to complete the effect. The concentration in one place of what grows in naturally looser arrangements throughout the garden focuses the overall look.

BELOW: *Spring narcissi are perfectly in scale for a table setting. And with so many varieties having strong scents, there's nowhere better to appreciate them while relaxing over a long cold drink.*

RIGHT: *Ornamental cabbages, complemented by individual cabbage leaves used decoratively on the napkins and a miniature arrangement in a small jar, make an unusual centrepiece.*

BELOW: *A wire basket with raffia interwoven round its base gathers together pots of verbena surrounded by tiny pots of variegated ivy. The end result is an outdoor casualness perfectly in accord with its surroundings.*

LEFT: *In summer, a couple of potted strawberry plants are transformed into an original decoration when arranged in a wire jug with some extra ripe fruits.*

The right location

Finding the right place for the right plant is the key to successful container gardening. One way of tackling the problem is to see container plants as a way of extending the garden into areas where plants do not normally grow. Once you have made a list of such areas, and it is always far longer than you would initially imagine, decide which kind of plants you would like growing there – climbers, scented plants, or plants to screen unsightly areas.

BELOW: *A classical, clipped, mop-head bay tree* (Laurus nobilis) *makes a smart entrance, and adds to the sense of formality. Its geometric shape is cleverly offset by a massed underplanting of lovely pink-flowering fuchsias.*

RIGHT: *An excellent way of livening up a typical suburban porch. Tropical, strap-shaped leaves add height and structure to a mass of smaller evergreens.*

Entrance Containers

A bare porch can be made to look far more welcoming and attractive by the addition of one large plant in a pot or urn. In warm, sheltered parts of the country you could try growing an exotic scented plant like one of the more tender daphnes (eg the evergreen *D. bholua* 'Jacqueline Postill') in a bright, south-facing spot.

If space is limited, you could hang smaller, ornate terracotta pots on the wall, one above the other, each with attractive, trailing growth. Or fix one or two hanging baskets just outside the porch, to provide aerial colour. But if you live in a particularly cold area, stick to summer bedding plants in the growing season, and for the rest of the year be content with one large, attractive urn. Even when unfilled, it can still be quite a feature.

Containers for Corners

Bare corners are all too often taken for granted, a kind of necessary evil. But there is no reason why they cannot add to the garden's glamour. Corners that are paved or covered with stony shingle make the perfect stage for a group of pots whose foliage and flowers mix and mingle, creating striking effects.

The key principle is to place the smaller plants at the front where they can be seen, with the medium-high plants behind, and the tallest at the back. Alternatively, choose a small group of elegant containers, using the plants in a more restrained way. A trailer growing from a pedestal container with a cluster of distinctive smaller plants round the base can be as stunning as a large group.

BELOW: *Antique stone urns like this are ideal for sharp corners where they create a special feature and help soften a stark 90 degree angle with curves, colour and interest.*

1 This shady area next to a driveway has been gravelled to break up the effect of a large area of paving but still looks bleak and uninteresting.

2 Plants in containers have transformed this corner. Even though the plants may not completely conceal the wires and downpipe, there is now so much else to interest the eye that they are easily overlooked.

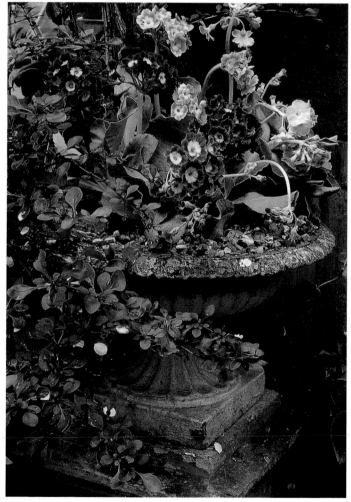

Pots for Steps and Walls

Steps and wall tops are too often left bare when they actually make a perfect platform for a row of colourful pot plants. The outside steps rising up to the top floor of a barn, for example, like a series of rising plinths, make a perfect stage for a series of pot plants, each tumbling colour onto the step below.

ABOVE LEFT: *The severe, formal Georgian entrance to this town house is wonderfully softened by the use of a row of containers on a ledge, packed with white-flowering fuchsias. Note how they complement the colour scheme.*

ABOVE: *Miniature violas, one plant to a pot, make an enchanting decoration for old stone steps.*

1 This terrace of brick and stone is attractive in its own right, but is not as colourful as it might be.

2 The addition of a variety of containers with flowering plants completes the picture and adds colour and depth to the scene.

Containers as Screens, and with Arbours and Arches

Where you have a garden eyesore, such as a crumbling outhouse or drainage pipe, use ingenuity and imagination to hide it. You do not need to go overboard. A large pot containing a prolific marguerite (argyranthemum) will produce hundreds of daisy-like blooms all summer. You could even grow this plant as a standard, with a mop-head of growth on a 90cm (3ft) high single stem. A planted container, whether hanging or on the ground, is a lovely finishing touch to a garden arch or arbour.

TOP: *This arbour would look very bare without its glorious hanging basket of petunias.*

ABOVE: *A pair of formal containers planted with fuchsia standards, complement this garden archway perfectly.*

LEFT: *A colourful windowbox is used here to mark the edge of a border.*

Types of Container

One of the challenges of container gardening is finding the right container for the right setting. You can now quite readily buy a whole range of lovely containers, for example, waist-high, Italian olive oil jars make a terrific focal point – big and bold and stylish. At the other end of the scale, you can be as imaginative as you like. You could use a Wellington boot or an old shoe for an engaging, quirky touch. In between, of course, the choice is huge: rustic terracotta, voguish metal or brightly painted cans, Mediterranean style.

It is important to consider the final setting when you are buying a container. A rustic tub may look charming under the window of a thatched cottage, but inappropriate outside a formal town house. Bear proportions in mind and, for example, choose a windowbox that exactly fits the sill. It is also worth noting that the weight of a container, when filled with compost (soil mix) and freshly watered, will be considerably greater than when empty. Think twice before packing your roof terrace or balcony with heavy pots: the structure may not be able to cope. And never leave a container on a window-sill from where it could fall down into the street.

Stone troughs

NOT SO READILY AVAILABLE BUT DEFINITELY WORTH LOOKING AT.
Advantages – durable and attractive.
Disadvantages – very heavy and expensive.

Pots and barrels

VERSATILE AND PRACTICAL.
Advantages – maintenance-free and versatile.
Disadvantages – heavy to move.

Wooden windowboxes

GIVE A WOODEN CONTAINER AN ORIGINAL LOOK WITH YOUR OWN COLOUR SCHEME.
Advantages – you can change the look to suit any new planting scheme.
Disadvantages – the boxes require occasional maintenance.

Terracotta windowboxes

AVAILABLE IN A WIDE RANGE OF SIZES AND STYLES.
Advantages – look good and appear even better with age.
Disadvantages – heavy, and may be damaged by frost.

Galvanized tin

TIN HAS MOVED FROM THE UTILITARI-
AN TO THE FASHIONABLE.

Advantages – an interesting variation from the usual materials.

Disadvantages – drainage holes
required.

Lightweight fibre windowboxes

PLAIN AND PRACTICAL.

Advantages – look rustic, and have a rich
brown colour.

Disadvantages – short life-span.

Baskets

CAN BE USED AS WINDOWBOXES
PROVIDED THEY ARE GENEROUSLY
LINED WITH MOSS BEFORE PLANTING.

Advantages – lightweight and
attractive.

Disadvantages – plant pots must
be removed for watering, or the
base of the basket will be soaked
and rot.

Types of hanging baskets

Before you choose the plants and plan how to
arrange them, decide first what style of hanging
basket you are going to display them in. Garden
centres stock a huge variety, which are all easy
to work with and hang. Hanging baskets are
made from plastic-coated wire, wrought-iron and
galvanized wire.

Hanging baskets

VARIED AND PRACTICAL.

Advantages – look lovely planted.

Disadvantages – need to be
lined before use.

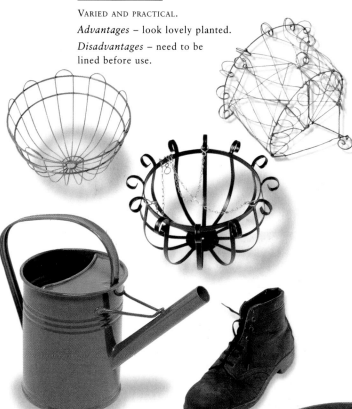

Novelty containers

HUGELY UNDERRATED. USE ANYTHING FROM
WATERING-CANS OR TYRES TO SHOES.

Advantages – witty and fun.

Disadvantages – possible short life-span.

Choosing composts (soil mixes)

Composts (soil mixes) come in various formulations to suit different plant requirements. A standard potting compost is usually peat-based and is suitable for all purposes. Peat and peat substitutes are relatively light in weight and therefore the best choice for hanging baskets. Regular watering is vital when using peat-based composts, as it is very difficult to moisten them again if they have been allowed to dry out completely. Different composts can be mixed together for specific plant needs.

Standard compost (soil mix)

The majority of composts available at garden centres are peat-based with added fertilizers.

Container compost (soil mix)

A peat-based compost with moisture-retaining granules and added fertilizer, specially formulated for windowboxes and containers.

Ericaceous compost (soil mix)

A peat-based compost with no added lime, essential for rhododendrons, camellias and heathers in containers.

Peat-free compost (soil mix)

Manufacturers now offer a range of composts using materials from renewable resources such as coir fibre. They are used in the same way as peat-based composts.

Loam-based compost (soil mix)

Uses sterilized loam as the main ingredient, with fertilizers to supplement the nutrients in the loam. Although much heavier than peat-based compost, it can be lightened by mixing with peat-free compost. Ideal for long-term planting as it retains nutrients well.

THE ESSENTIAL FERTILIZER ELEMENTS

All plant fertilizers contain three key elements, nitrogen (N), phosphorous (P), and potassium/potash (K), with extra trace elements. These three promote, respectively, foliage growth, flower development, and fruit ripening and root development.

When buying a packet of fertilizer you can easily check the balance of the ingredients. It is printed as an "NPK" ratio, for instance 12:5:12. But don't be fooled into thinking that a reading of 24:10:24 is stronger, giving twice the value. It won't, of course, as the ratio is the same. A fertilizer with a ratio of 10:5:10 provides a sound, balanced diet. (You can purchase meters from garden centres that give a guide to the nutrient levels in the soil but they are not, to date, particularly accurate.)

Besides feeding, you can also trick some plants into a prolific display of flowering. Plants packed into small containers, with restricted (but not crippling) root space, feel that they are in danger of dying. Their immediate response is to do what all flowering plants are programmed to do – flower and set seed to continue the species.

Feeding container plants

It is not generally understood that most potting composts (soil mixes) contain sufficient food for only six weeks of plant growth. After that, the plants will slowly starve unless more food is introduced. There are several products available, all of which are easy to use. Many of the projects in this book use slow-release plant food granules because they are the easiest and most reliable way of ensuring your plants receive sufficient food during the growing season. For these granules to be effective the compost needs to remain damp or the nutrients cannot be released.

Slow-release Plant Food Granules

These will keep your container plants in prime condition and are very easy to use. One application lasts six months, whereas most other plant foods need to be applied fortnightly. Follow the manufacturer's recommended dose carefully; additional fertilizer will simply leach away.

BELOW: *A variety of plant foods (clockwise from top left): liquid foliar feed, two types of pelleted slow-release plant food granules, a general fertilizer and loose slow-release plant food granules.*

TOP: *Slow-release plant food granules can be added to the compost (soil mix) in the recommended quantity before filling the container and planting it.*

ABOVE: *When adding fertilizer granules to the soil, sprinkle them on to the surface of the compost (soil mix) and rake into the top layer. Pelleted granules should be pushed approximately 2cm (³/4in) below the surface.*

Planting pots and planters

Planting up a container of any size could not be easier, as long as you follow a few basic rules. First, terracotta pots need a layer of material at the bottom to help the water drain away quickly. Plastic pots usually have sufficient drainage holes. Second, always plant into the appropriate size pot; that is, slightly larger than the root-ball. Putting a small plant into a large pot is counter productive. The plant will put on good root growth at the expense of flowers and foliage. Since the hungry root system will drink up water rapidly in summer, check regularly that the soil is not too dry.

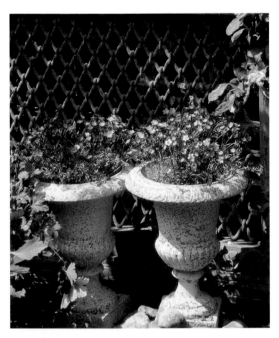

ABOVE: *Beautiful, elegant urns do not always need the finest flowering plants. As these twin pots show, even a modest planting works well. Indeed, it is often preferable because it does not detract from the gorgeous containers.*

Maintaining Plants

Large plants can grow in surprisingly small containers. They will not grow to the same height as if they were given a free root run, but should be impressive nonetheless. If possible, remove the top layer of soil every year, and replace it with fresh compost (soil mix). There comes a time, however, when most plants finally outgrow their containers. What then? You can replace the mature plant with a cutting and start again. Alternatively, stick instead to plants that are slow-growing, or which will not rapidly fill their pots with roots. Or root prune.

Root pruning is a remarkably easy technique, which involves removing the plant from the pot in spring, when it is beginning to put on good growth. Either slice away the exterior of the root-ball quite boldly, or snip at it with secateurs. Then replace in the existing pot, filling the gap with fresh compost.

Overwintering

Remember that while tender plants may just survive winter outside in your area, with their roots protected deep below ground, those in pots are much less likely to survive. The roots will be just the thickness of the pot away from encircling snow or icy winds. Bring these plants indoors or, if there's no room, take cuttings before the end of the season.

Planting in Terracotta

Terracotta containers are always popular, but need some preparation before planting.

1 With terracotta it is essential to provide some form of drainage material in the base of the container. When planting in large pots or boxes, recycle broken-up polystyrene (plastic foam) plant trays as drainage material. Lumps of polystyrene are excellent for this use and as they retain warmth they are of additional benefit to the plant.

2 In smaller pots the drainage material can be broken pieces of pot, known as crocks, or gravel.

Planting in Plastic

When buying plastic pots or boxes, check that the drainage holes are open. Some manufacturers mark the holes but leave it to the purchaser to punch or drill them out as required.

Plant Supports

Climbing plants in containers will need support. This can be provided by one or more canes which are pushed into the pot, a free-standing plant frame or a trellis fastened to a wall behind the container.

Planting in Wicker Baskets

If you wish to use a more unconventional container as a windowbox you may need to seal it with a sheet of plastic to prevent leakage.

1 Line the basket with a generous layer of moss which will prevent the compost (soil mix) leaking away.

2 Fill the basket with compost (soil mix), and mix in plant food granules or any organic alternative.

Saucers and Feet

Saucers are available for plastic and clay pots. They act as water reservoirs for the plants, and are used under houseplants to protect the surface they are standing on. Clay saucers must be fully glazed if they are used indoors or they will leave marks. Clay feet are available for terracotta pots. They will prevent the pot becoming waterlogged, but this also means that in a sunny position the pot will dry out very quickly and may need extra watering.

Plastic plant saucers can be used to line and protect containers which are not waterproof, such as this wooden apple-basket.

Planting hanging baskets

When you want colour high up or relating closely to the building, the easiest way is to create a hanging garden, either in baskets or in wall-mounted containers. A purpose-made hanging basket is designed so that as the flowers grow, they cascade through the side and spill over the edge in a joyous show of colour, covering the whole basket. An alternative is to make the basket or container part of the display. Ordinary shopping baskets, buckets, agricultural containers, even kitchen equipment such as colanders, pots and pans, can be used.

Planting and Positioning Hanging Baskets

One hanging basket, alone on a wall, can look rather insignificant. Far better to plant up baskets in pairs, either with similar plants to create an echoing effect, or with clashing, contrasting colours. For a really stunning effect, entirely cover a wall with baskets, but remember that they are very demanding, and will need prolific watering in a dry mid-summer.

If the container is large and in danger of getting too heavy for its support, one trick is to put a layer of broken-up expanded polystyrene (plastic foam), from plant trays or electrical goods packaging, in the bottom of the container. This is lighter than the equivalent amount of compost (soil mix) and provides good drainage. Containers should have drainage holes, and baskets will need lining to stop the soil from being washed out while

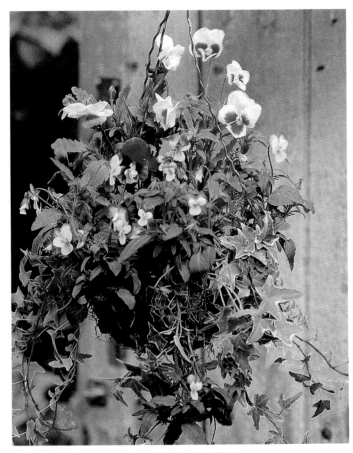

you are watering. Liners can be home-made from pieces of plastic sheet cut to size, with a layer of moss tucked between the basket and plastic for a more decorative look. Alternatively, you can use a proprietary liner, made from paper pulp, to fit purpose-made hanging baskets, or coconut matting – which comes in a variety of shapes and sizes to adapt to all kinds of baskets.

Whichever type of container you choose, it needs to be filled with a good compost, and adding fertilizer granules and water-retaining gel can also help promote lush results and make care and maintenance a little easier.

RIGHT: *Hanging baskets filled with pansies create a lovely focal point of gentle colour.*

Preparing Hanging Baskets

The key to successful hanging baskets is in the preparation. Time taken in preparing the basket for planting will be rewarded with a long-lasting colourful display. Slow-release plant food granules incorporated into the compost (soil mix) when planting ensure that the plants receive adequate nutrients throughout the growing season. It is essential to water hanging baskets every day, even in overcast weather, as they dry out very quickly. There are various ways to line a hanging basket.

Choosing a Lining

1 When buying a hanging basket, make sure that the chains are detachable. By unhooking one of the chains, they can be placed to one side of the basket, allowing you to work freely. Either rest the basket on a flat surface, or sit it on a flowerpot.

2 Traditionally, hanging baskets are lined with sphagnum moss. This looks very attractive and plants can be introduced at any point in the side of the basket. As sphagnum moss tends to dry out rather faster than other liners, it is advisable to use a compost (soil mix) containing water-retaining gel with this lining.

3 Coir fibre liners are a practical substitute for moss. Although not as good to look at, the coir will soon be hidden as the plants grow. The slits in the liner allow for planting in the side of the basket.

4 Cardboard liners are clean and easy to use. They are made in various sizes to fit most hanging baskets.

5 Press out the marked circles on the cardboard liner if you wish to plant into the side of the basket.

Underplanting a Hanging Basket

Underplanting helps to achieve a really lush-looking basket and soon conceals the shape of the container under flowers and foliage.

1 Line the lower half of the basket with a generous layer of moss.

2 Rest the root-ball on the moss and gently guide the foliage through the side of the basket.

3 Add more moss to the basket, tucking it carefully around the plants to ensure that they are firmly in place. Add a further row of plants near the top edge of the basket, if required, and continue to line the basket with moss, finishing off with a collar of moss overlapping the rim of the basket. Fill with compost (soil mix).

Watering container plants

Watering plants in containers is an acquired art, and an incredibly important one. You cannot leave it entirely to nature because rain tends to bounce off the leaves of the bushiest plants, soaking not into the pot but into the adjoining ground.

Outside, pot plants dry out very quickly on roasting hot days. Unlike plants in the ground, their roots are encircled by heat; some thirsty plants might even need two waterings a day, so keep checking. You have to get the balance right between over- and under-watering.

Trial and error is one way, but there are a few key tips, one of the best and simplest being to stick your finger deep into the soil to test for dryness. If you are unsure, wait until you see the first signs of wilting, then give the plant a thorough drink, letting the water drain out of the bottom of the pot. And always water plants either first thing in the morning or, better still, late at night, so that the moisture does not quickly evaporate. At all costs, try to avoid over-watering, which is a bigger killer than pests and diseases combined.

The best water is either rainwater or cold, boiled water, but it is not essential to use these unless your tap water is very hard, or you are growing lime-hating plants such as camellias. Don't allow your potted plants to become waterlogged. If there is any water remaining in the saucer half an hour after watering, tip it away.

Windowboxes and Pots

Don't rush the watering. Though you might think one soaking is enough for a big window box, it might only wet the top layer of compost (soil mix). Wait until the water sluices out of the bottom. Container composts include a water-retaining gel and if the compost remains wet in cold weather it can cause the roots to rot.

Hanging Baskets

Summer hanging baskets need daily watering even in overcast weather and on a hot day should be watered morning and evening. Once they have been allowed to dry out it can be difficult for the compost (soil mix) to re-absorb water. In these circumstances it is a good idea to immerse hanging baskets in a large bucket or bowl of water. Winter and spring hanging baskets should be watered only when the soil is dry.

LEFT: *Houseplants enjoy being sprayed with water, but in hard water areas you should use rainwater or bottled water.*

Water-retaining Gel

One of the main problems for most container gardeners is the amount of watering required to keep the plants thriving in the growing season. Adding water-retaining gels to compost (soil mix) will certainly help reduce this task. Sachets of gel are available from garden centres.

1 Pour the recommended amount of water into a bowl.

2 Scatter the gel over the surface, stirring occasionally until it has absorbed the water.

3 Add to your compost (soil mix) at the recommended rate, and mix the gel in thoroughly before using it for planting.

MULCHES

A mulch is a layer of protective material placed over the soil. It helps to retain moisture, conserve warmth, suppress weeds and prevent soil splash on foliage and flowers.

Bark chippings

Bark is an extremely effective mulch and as it rots down it conditions the soil. It works best when spread at least 7.5cm (3in) thick and is therefore not ideal for small containers. It is derived from renewable resources.

Clay granules

Clay granules are widely used for hydroculture, but can also be used to mulch houseplants. When placing a plant in a *cachepot*, fill all around the pot with granules. When watered, the granules absorb moisture, which is then released slowly to create a moist microclimate for the plant.

Gravel

Gravel makes a decorative mulch for container plants, and also provides the correct environment for plants such as alpines. It is available in a variety of sizes and colours which can be matched to the scale and colours of the plants used.

Stones

Smooth stones can be used as decorative mulch for large container-grown plants. You can save stones dug out of the garden or buy stones from garden centres. They also deter cats from using the soil as a litter tray.

Propagating plants

Most containers and plants are available from garden centres but raising your own plants from seed or cuttings is far easier than you may think and can be very rewarding. Buying young plants from mail order catalogues is an increasingly popular way of starting a collection.

Seed Sowing

One of the cheapest ways of getting a mass planting is by growing plants from seed. It is fun, can be easy (when growing marigolds, for instance), and you don't need a high-tech greenhouse. Furthermore, if you get hooked on the plants, you can collect your own ripe seed in the autumn for a spring sowing the following year.

Cuttings

If you want to increase your stock of the plants you are already growing in the garden, you can get quick results by taking spring cuttings.

When the cuttings have rooted – this will be immediately obvious because they suddenly perk up – wait for the roots to fill the pot, and then transfer to individual pots.

1 Fill the seed tray with seed compost (soil mix). Gently firm and level the surface by pressing down on the compost using a tray of the same size. When sowing large seeds, such as sunflowers or marigolds, use a dibber (dibble), cane or pencil to make holes for each seed. Plant the seeds and cover with compost.

2 When sowing small seeds they should be thinly scattered on the surface of the compost (soil mix) and then covered with just enough sieved sand and compost to conceal them. Firm the surface, using another tray. Water from above, using a fine rose on a watering-can, or by standing the tray in water until the surface of the compost is moist.

1 Remove the new softwood growth when it is about 10cm (4in) long, just above a leaf node.

2 Using a sharp knife, trim the cutting just below a node and trim away the lower leaves.

3 Enclose the seed tray in a plastic jar or bag to conserve moisture and cover with a black plastic bag, as most seeds germinate best in a warm dark place.

4 Check daily and bring into the light when the seedlings are showing.

3 Dip the end of the stem in hormone rooting powder, and plant up in a small container, using cuttings compost (soil mix).

4 Fill the pot with cuttings, water, and place in a warm, bright place, out of scorching sunlight.

5 To create a moist microclimate for the cuttings, it's a good idea to enclose the pot completely in a plastic bag. Secure it with an elastic band around the pot.

Mail Order

Send off each year for the latest seed and plant catalogues. You will invariably find a wider range than you can buy in a garden centre. Young plants are packed into special packages, which minimize damage during transit, but as they are restricted and in the dark they are initially weakened and some care is necessary to encourage vigorous growth.

1 Open the package with care. Leaves will probably unfold from the confined space. Each plant should be intact and clearly labelled.

2 Lift the plants out of their travelling box. Labels tucked underneath the root-ball reduce the necessity for handling it directly and helps to keep the compost (soil mix) intact.

3 Plant in a small pot. If the plants seem very wilted, remove some of the larger leaves.

Potting-On

After several weeks your young plants, whether grown from seed, mail order stock or cuttings, will need potting-on. This simply means giving the young plant its own larger, individual container.

1 Young plants are ready to move into larger pots when the roots start to emerge through the holes in the base of the pot. Gently remove the root-ball from the pot to check. If there is more than one seedling in the pot, carefully tease away each individual root-ball. (Some plants hate to have their roots disturbed. The information on the seed packet will tell you this. These seeds are best sown individually in peat pots or modular trays.) Lower the root-ball of the plant into a pot marginally bigger than the existing one.

2 Holding the plant carefully so as not to damage the stem, gently pour potting compost (soil mix) around the root-ball, firming lightly.

3 Dibble the compost (soil mix) down the side of the pot to eliminate air spaces. It does not matter if the stem of the seedling is buried deeper than it was previously, as long as the leaves are well clear of the soil. Water, using a can with a fine rose.

Pests and diseases

Container plants are every bit as susceptible to aphid and slug attacks as those grown in the garden. But they are generally easier to keep an eye on, so the moment you see a pest attack, take action. Most pests multiply at a staggering rate, and once a plant has been vigorously assaulted, it takes a long time to recover.

Common Pests

Aphids

These sap-sucking insects feed on the tender growing tips. Most insecticides are effective against aphids such as greenfly or blackfly (shown above). Choose one that will not harm ladybirds.

Mealy bugs

These look like spots of white mould. They are hard to shift and regular treatment with a systemic insecticide is the best solution.

Caterpillars

The occasional caterpillar can be picked off the plant and disposed of as you see fit, but a major infestation can strip a plant before your eyes. Contact insecticides are usually very effective.

Red spider mite

An insect that thrives indoors in dry conditions. Constant humidity will reduce the chance of an infestation, which is indicated by the presence of fine webs and mottling of the plant's leaves. To treat an infestation, pick off the worst affected leaves and spray the plants with an insecticide.

Vine weevils

These white grubs are a menace. The first sign of an infestation is the sudden collapse of the plant because the weevil has eaten its roots. Systemic insecticides or natural predators can be used as a preventative, but once a plant has been attacked it is usually too late to save it. Never re-use the soil from an affected plant. The picture above shows an adult weevil.

Snails

Snails cannot generally reach hanging baskets, but are more of a problem in wall baskets and windowboxes: they tuck themselves behind the container during daylight and venture out to feast at night. Use slug pellets or venture out yourself with a torch and catch them.

Whitefly

These tiny white flies flutter up in clouds when disturbed from their feeding places on the undersides of leaves. Whitefly are particularly troublesome in conservatories, where a dry atmosphere will encourage them to breed. Keep the air as moist as possible. Contact insecticides will need more than one application to deal with an infestation, but a systemic insecticide will protect the plant for weeks.

Common Diseases

Black spot – most commonly seen on roses; dark spots on leaves occur before they fall. Burn all affected foliage, and treat with a fungicide.
Botrytis – immediately evident as a pernicious, furry grey mould. Remove and burn all affected parts, and treat with a fungicide.
Powdery mildew – most likely to affect potted fruit trees. Remove and burn affected parts. Treat with a fungicide.
Rust – high humidity causes orange/dark brown pustules on the stem. Remove and burn affected parts. Treat with a fungicide.
Viruses (various) – the varied symptoms include distorted, mis-shapen leaves, and discoloration. Vigorous anti-aphid controls are essential. Destroy affected foliage.

Pest Control

There are three main types of pest control available to combat common pests.

Systemic insecticides

These work by being absorbed by the plant's root or leaf system, and killing insects that come into contact with the plant. This will work for difficult pests, such as the grubs of vine weevils which are hidden in the soil, and scale insects which protect themselves from above with a scaly cover.

Contact insecticides

These must be sprayed directly on to the insects to be effective. Most organic insecticides work this way, but they generally kill all insects, even beneficial ones, such as hoverflies and ladybirds. Try to remove these before spraying the infected plant.

Biological control

Commercial growers now use biological control in their glasshouses; this means natural predators are introduced to eat the pest population. Although not all are suitable for the amateur gardener, they can be used in conservatories for dealing with pests such as whitefly.

NATURAL PREDATORS

Aphidius – a wasp that lays eggs in young aphids; on hatching they devour the host.
Aphidoletes – a gall midge that devours aphids.
Bacillus thuringinesis – a bacterium that kills caterpillars.
Cryptolaemus montrouzieri – an Australian ladybird that eats mealy bug. It is activated by a temperature of 20°C (68°F).
Encarsia formosa – a parasitic wasp that lays eggs in the larvae of whitefly. The young wasps eat their hosts.

Metaphycus – a parasitic wasp, activated by a temperature of 20°C (68°F), that kills off soft scales.
Phasmarhabditis – a nematode that kills slugs provided the temperature of the soil is above 5°C (41°F).
Phytoseiulus persimilis – attacks red spider mite provided the temperature is 20°C (68°F).
Steinernema – kills vine weevils by releasing a bacterium into them. Needs a temperature of 12°C (53°F).

Decorating Containers

*One of the joys of container gardening is decorating your own pots,
giving them exactly the right colour scheme to suit the plants and their surroundings.
Decorating pots is an undervalued and under-explored art. The majority of
plant pots sold in garden centres are plain brown, which people assume is the
colour they have to be. As the following projects show, plant pots are like
empty canvases. You can turn them into bright, colourful containers
with a Mediterranean feel, or much subtler pots in the softest of tones. It is also worth
experimenting with more unusual containers such as tin cans and buckets.*

ABOVE: *Terracotta pots decorated with simple geometric shapes in yellow and green make perfect containers for spring bulbs.*

Tin can plant nursery

Seedlings can be decorative in themselves, so prick them out from their seed trays into a collection of shiny aluminum cans mounted on to a plaque. They can grow there until they are ready to be planted out. The plaque itself looks wonderful made from ordinary aluminum cans, but if you want to add a bit more colour, scour the shelves of delicatessens for some unusual printed cans and enjoy some culinary treats at the same time.

MATERIALS

Piece of board, about
  60 x 30cm (24 x 12in)
Undercoat
Coloured gloss paint
Decorating brush
Can opener
Variety of empty
  aluminium cans with
  the labels removed

Metal snippers
Pliers
Nail
Hammer
Tin tacks

1 Apply an undercoat followed by a coat of gloss paint to the board, allowing each coat to dry completely.

2 Use the can opener to remove the top of each can if this has not already been done. Wash out the cans thoroughly.

3 Using metal snippers, cut down the side of each can and cut off half of the bottom.

4 Open out the sides with pliers and snip a V-shape into each one. Pierce the bottom of each can, using a nail and hammer.

5 Try out the arrangement of the cans on the board. Then, using one tin tack at each side point of the cans, nail into position.

Mexican painted pots

A series of traditional folk-art motifs painted over stripes of vibrant colours gives simple pots a rich Mexican look. Enhance the effect by allowing some of the untreated terracotta colour show through, especially if you use pots with a fluted top like this one. Planted up with pelargoniums in hot summer colours, and stacked together, they make a lively garden feature.

MATERIALS

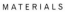

Terracotta pot with fluted-top
Masking tape
White undercoat
Small decorating brush
Artist's gouache paints
Fine and medium artist's brushes
Polyurethane matt varnish

1 Mark the stripes on the pot using masking tape. Cut some lengths into narrower widths to get variation in the finished design. Bear in mind that the areas covered by masking tape will remain natural terracotta.

2 Paint the body of the pot with undercoat, avoiding the fluted rim. Allow to dry completely.

3 Paint the coloured stripes with gouache paints, changing colour after each band of masking tape. Allow to dry completely.

4 Peel off the masking tape to reveal coloured stripes alternating with terracotta stripes.

5 Using the fine artist's brush and white undercoat, paint simple motifs over the stripes. When completely dry, coat with matt varnish.

Verdigris bucket

There is something irresistible about the luminous, blue-green tones of verdigris. It is a colour that always complements plants and is not difficult to reproduce on a cheap galvanized bucket. To make the rust bucket shown behind the verdigris one, follow the steps below, but substitute rust-coloured acrylic paint for the aqua paint.

MATERIALS
....

Galvanized bucket
Medium-grade sandpaper
Metal primer
Small decorating brush
Gold paint
Amber shellac
Artist's acrylic paint in white
  and aqua-green
Water for mixing
Natural sponge
Polyurethane matt varnish

1 Sand the bucket, then prime with metal primer. Allow to dry for 2–3 hours. Paint with gold paint and allow to dry for 2–3 hours.

2 Paint with amber shellac and allow to dry for 30 minutes. Mix white acrylic paint with aqua-green and enough water to make a liquid consistency.

3 Sponge on the verdigris paint and allow to dry for 1–2 hours. Apply a coat of varnish.

Lead chimney

The wonderful chalky tones of lead have made it a popular material for garden containers down the centuries. However, lead is incredibly heavy and very expensive, so here is a way of faking it, using a plastic, terracotta-coloured chimney and some simple paint effects.

MATERIALS

Plastic, terracotta-
  coloured chimney
Sandpaper
Acrylic primer
Large artist's brush

Emulsion (latex) paint in
  charcoal grey and white
Acrylic scumble glaze
Water
Decorating brush
Polyurethane matt varnish

1 Sand the chimney to give it a key. Paint with one coat of acrylic primer and allow to dry for 1–2 hours.

2 Apply one coat of charcoal-grey emulsion and allow to dry for 2–3 hours.

3 Tint the scumble glaze with white emulsion and thin with water. Paint over the chimney randomly. Wash over with water and allow to dry.

4 Add more of the white scumble mixture to parts of the chimney for extra colour and 'age'. Varnish with polyurethane matt varnish when dry.

A shell windowbox

Decorated windowboxes provide a delightful finish to windows, almost bringing the garden into the house. Being flat-fronted, they are also easier to decorate than round pots. Here, mussel shells lend impact to a co-ordinated planting of lavender and violas. Experiment with different shapes, using some mussel shells face-up and others face-down.

MATERIALS

Small terracotta windowbox
Mussel shells
Glue gun and all-purpose glue sticks
Crocks or pebbles
Compost (soil mix)
Water-retaining gel
Slow-release plant food granules
2 lavender plants
Tray of young viola plants

1 When you are satisfied with your design, fix the shells in position on the windowbox, using a glue gun.

2 Place crocks or pebbles over the drainage holes inside the windowbox.

3 Partly fill the box with compost (soil mix), adding water-retaining gel and plant food granules as you go.

4 Place the lavenders at the back of the box. Press extra compost (soil mix) in front of them until it is the right height for the violas. Plant the violas on this raised bed.

5 Press more compost (soil mix) firmly around all the plants and water generously.

The Planting Projects

Containers can provide colourful focal points in a small
garden; they can ensure year-round interest when planted
with evergreens; on a small balcony or roof terrace they can
be gardens in themselves; they can celebrate a special
occasion like a wedding or Christmas; or even
supply the cook with herbs or vegetables. Try some of the
following projects, but let them fuel your own ideas and
imagination too.

ABOVE: *Containers are invaluable in a
small garden as they can fill up any
spare space. Individually these
containers do not look special, but
grouping them creates a focal point.*

OPPOSITE: *A wooden windowbox,
planted with a simple combination of
bright red and yellow, can create a
lovely relaxed, rustic feel, whether in
the country or in the heart of a city.*

Colour Schemes for Containers

The artistry of container gardening lies in the way in which you arrange and combine all your raw materials: not just the plants themselves, but the container and the site you choose for it. Above all, sensitive colour co-ordination can make the difference between a planting scheme that is just pretty and one that draws gasps of admiration. The plants and the container need to enhance each other: lavender with blue violas in a stone urn, for instance, or fiery nasturtiums in terracotta pots. Think about the background, too – the colour of the surrounding walls, the paint on the window frame – and make the picture work as a whole.

Single-colour schemes can be striking, emphasizing the contrasting forms of the flowers and foliage, but so can strong contrasts of colour or tone. Let the glowing palette presented on the following pages inspire you to new heights of creativity.

ABOVE: *Pure white petunias and lobelia planted with a touch of grey foliage make a sophisticated display.*

A delicate antique basket

An antique basket is not essential for this scheme, but the bowl shape makes an interesting variation. A small variety of dahlia, known as a dahlietta, has large white flowers that blend with trailing verbenas and a begonia. Silver-leaved marguerites, with soft pink flowers, add a subtle touch of colour.

VERBENA

DAHLIETTA

ARGYRANTHEMUM

MATERIALS

36cm (14in) hanging basket
Sphagnum moss
Compost (soil mix)
Slow-release plant food granules

PLANTS

White Begonia semperflorens
3 white dahliettas
3 white trailing verbenas
3 marguerites (Argyranthemum
  'Flamingo')

BEGONIA

1 Line the basket with moss and fill with compost (soil mix). Work a teaspoon of slow-release plant food granules into the top of the compost.

2 Plant the begonia in the centre and position and plant the dahliettas around the begonia.

3 Plant a verbena to one side of each of the dahliettas. Plant the marguerites, angling them so they will trail over the edge of the basket. Water well and hang in a sunny position.

GARDENER'S TIP

Regular dead-heading of the flowers will keep the basket in tip-top condition. The slow-release plant food granules will give the flowers a regular supply of nutrients provided the basket is not allowed to dry out.

PLANT IN LATE SPRING OR EARLY SUMMER

An all-white windowbox

A painted wooden windowbox filled with a white pelargonium, verbenas, marguerites, bacopa, and silver senecio is an ideal combination for a summer wedding celebration in the garden.

MATERIALS

45cm (18in) slatted wooden windowbox
Sphagnum moss
Compost (soil mix)
Slow-release plant food granules

PLANTS

White pelargonium
2 white marguerites (argyranthemums)
2 white trailing verbenas
2 Senecio cineraria 'Silver Dust'
White bacopa

SENECIO

BACOPA

PELARGONIUM

MARGUERITE

VERBENA

1 It is a good idea to line slatted wooden containers with moss before planting to prevent the compost from leaking out when the box is watered.

2 Fill the moss-lined window-box with compost (soil mix), mixing in 2 teaspoons of slow-release plant food granules. Plant the pelargonium in the centre of the windowbox towards the back.

3 Plant the marguerites on either side of the pelargonium.

4 Plant the trailing verbenas in the two back corners of the windowbox.

5 Plant the senecios in the front two corners of the windowbox to frame the bacopa.

6 Plant the bacopa centrally in the front of the box. Water the arrangement thoroughly and stand in a sunny position.

GARDENER'S TIP

To prolong the life of wooden containers it is advisable to empty them of compost before winter and store them under cover until spring.

PLANT IN LATE SPRING OR EARLY SUMMER

White flowers and painted terracotta

There are plenty of inexpensive windowboxes available, but they do tend to look rather similar. Why not customize a bought windowbox to give it a touch of individuality? This deep blue painted windowbox creates an interesting setting for the cool white pelargonium and verbenas.

MATERIALS

45cm (18in) terracotta windowbox painted blue
Crocks (broken pots) or other suitable drainage material
Compost (soil mix)
Slow-release plant food granules

PLANTS

White pelargonium
2 variegated felicias
2 white trailing verbenas

FELICIA

VERBENA

PELARGONIUM

1 Cover the base of the window box with a layer of crocks (broken pots) or similar drainage material.

2 Fill the windowbox with compost (soil mix). Add 2 teaspoons of slow-release plant food granules. Plant the pelargonium in the centre of the windowbox.

3 Plant a felicia on either side of the pelargonium at the back of the container. Plant a verbena on either side of the pelargonium at the front of the windowbox. Water well and stand in a sunny position.

GARDENER'S TIP

White pelargoniums need regular dead-heading to look their best. Old flowerheads discolour and quickly spoil the appearance of the plant.

PLANT IN LATE SPRING OR EARLY SUMMER

Wedding fuchsias

MATERIALS

Wire basket
Sphagnum moss
Garden twine

PLANTS

3 Fuchsia 'Happy Wedding Day'
3 busy Lizzies (impatiens)
(optional)
3 white lace-cap hydrangeas
(optional)

FUCHSIA

'Happy Wedding Day' is a modern fuchsia which produces very large, round flowers. The lax growth makes it highly suitable for use in a decorative wire basket. As its name suggests, this fuchsia is ideal for a wedding display. Other white-flowered plants can be used to make a really imposing display, and to reinforce the lively impact of the fuchsia's fresh white bells.

1 Make a hand-sized pad of sphagnum moss and start to cover the outside of the plastic pot containing the fuchsia.

2 Use a long piece of twine to start tying the moss in place. Leave the ends loose.

3 Continue working around the pot, using small pads of moss.

4 Use the long ends of the piece of twine to secure the moss as you work round the pot.

5 Completely cover the pot with moss. Repeat for the other plants. Group the pots together for a finished display.

GARDENER'S TIP

To ensure that you have a vigorous display with lots of flowers on the wedding day, you will need to stop the plants at least eight weeks before. This involves pinching out the sideshoots and growing tips with your fingers. It will encourage extra bushy growth, and the development of even more flower buds.

PLANT IN SPRING OR SUMMER

A silver and white wall basket

The helichrysum's silvery foliage and cool blue lavender flowers give a delicate colour scheme which would look good against a weathered background.

MATERIALS

30cm (12in) wall basket
Sphagnum moss
Compost (soil mix)
Slow-release plant food granules

PLANTS

2 lavenders (Lavandula dentata var. candicans)
Osteospermum 'Whirligig'
2 Helichrysum petiolare

OSTEOSPERMUM

LAVENDER

HELICHRYSUM

GARDENER'S TIP

The lavender used in this project is fairly unusual – if you wish, you can substitute a low-growing variety such as 'Hidcote'.
Keep the helichrysum in check by pinching out its growing tips fairly regularly or it may take over the basket.

PLANT IN SPRING

1 Line the basket with moss and half-fill it with compost (soil mix).

2 Mix in a half-teaspoon of plant food granules. Plant the lavenders in each corner.

3 Plant the osteospermum in the centre of the basket then add the helichrysums on either side.

4 Angle the plants to encourage them to trail over the side of the basket. Fill with compost (soil mix). Water the basket and hang.

An informal wall basket

The strong pink of the dahlietta flower is echoed in the leaf colouring of the pink-flowered polygonums in this country-style basket. Silver thymes and white lobelias provide a gentle contrast.

MATERIALS

36cm (14in) wall basket
Sphagnum moss
Compost
Slow-release plant food granules

PLANTS

5 white lobelias
3 Polygonum 'Pink Bubbles'
2 thymes (Thymus 'Silver Queen')
1 pink dahlietta (miniature dahlia)

LOBELIA

THYME

POLYGONUM

DAHLIETTA

GARDENER'S TIP

To prevent the thyme getting leggy, trim off all the flowerheads after flowering – this will help to maintain a dense, well-shaped plant.

PLANT IN SPRING

1 Line the back and the base of the basket with moss, and position three lobelias around the side of the basket near the base.

2 Plant two of the polygonums into the side of the basket above the lobelia. Rest the root-balls on the moss, and gently feed the foliage through the basket.

3 Fill the basket with compost (soil mix). Add a half-teaspoon of slow-release plant food granules into the top of the compost. Plant the thymes into the corners of the basket, angling them so that they tumble over the sides.

4 Plant the dahlietta in the middle of the basket and the remaining polygonum in front of the dahlietta. Plant the remaining lobelias. Water well and hang in a sunny position.

A medley of pinks

In this basket-weave stone planter sugar-pink petunias are planted with ivy-leaved pelargoniums and shaggy-flowered pink dianthus with a deep-red eye. None of these plants requires much depth for its roots and, provided the plants are fed and watered regularly, they will be happy.

MATERIALS

*60cm (24in) window box
Gravel
Compost (soil mix)
Slow-release plant food granules*

PLANTS

*2 pink-flowered ivy-leaved
  pelargoniums
3 sugar-pink petunias
6 pink dianthus*

DIANTHUS

PETUNIA

PELARGONIUM

1 Fill the base of the windowbox with a layer of washed gravel or similar drainage material.

2 Fill the window box with compost (soil mix), adding in 2 teaspoons of plant food granules.

3 Plant the two pelargoniums 10cm (4in) from either end of the window box.

4 Plant the petunias, evenly spaced, along the back edge of the windowbox.

5 Plant four dianthus along the front edge, and the other two on either side of the central petunia.

6 Spread a layer of gravel around the plants; this is decorative and also helps to retain moisture. Water well and stand in a sunny position.

GARDENER'S TIP

Once the summer is over, the petunias and pelargoniums will need to be removed, but the dianthus will overwinter quite happily. Cut off any flower stems and add a fresh layer of gravel.

PLANT IN LATE SPRING OR EARLY SUMMER

A wall basket in shades of pink

Trailing rose-pink petunias provide the main structure of this wall basket and are combined with two colourful verbenas and white alyssum. On their own, the pale petunia flowers could look somewhat insipid but they are enhanced by the deeper tones of the verbenas.

MATERIALS

36cm (14in) wall basket
Sphagnum moss
Compost (soil mix)
Slow-release plant food granules

PLANTS

4 white alyssum
2 cascading rose-pink petunias
2 Verbena 'Pink Parfait' and 'Carousel', or similar

ALYSSUM

VERBENA

PETUNIA

1 Line the back of the basket and half-way up the front with moss. Plant the alyssum into the side of the basket, resting the rootballs on the moss and feeding the foliage through the sides.

2 Fill the basket with compost (soil mix) and work a half-teaspoon of slow-release plant food granules into the top. Plant the petunias in each corner.

3 Plant the verbenas one in front of the other, in the middle of the basket. Water thoroughly and hang in a sunny position.

GARDENER'S TIP

If, like these petunias, some of the plants are more developed than others, pinch out the growing tips so that all the plants grow together and one variety will not smother the others.

PLANT IN LATE SPRING OR EARLY SUMMER

'Balcon' pelargoniums

Traditionally planted to cascade from balconies in many European countries, these lovely pelargoniums are now increasingly and deservedly popular. They are seen at their best when planted alone, as in this basket, where the only variation is of colour.

MATERIALS

40cm (16in) hanging basket
Sphagnum moss
Compost (soil mix)
Slow-release plant food granules

PLANTS

5 'Balcon' pelargoniums
('Princess of Balcon' and 'King of Balcon' were used here:
the former is now often known as 'Roi des Balcons Lilas',
and the latter as 'Hederinum')

'BALCON' PELARGONIUMS

GARDENER'S TIP

Take cuttings from non-flowering stems in the autumn to use in next year's basket. Pelargonium cuttings root easily and the young plants can be kept on a window-sill until spring.

PLANT IN LATE SPRING OR EARLY SUMMER

1 Fully line the basket with moss. Fill with compost (soil mix). Work a teaspoon of slow-release plant food granules into the top layer of the compost.

2 Plant one of the pelargoniums in the centre of the basket.

3 Plant the other four pelargoniums round the edge of the basket, and remove any supporting canes to encourage the plants to tumble over the side. Water well and hang the basket up in a sunny spot.

Sugar and spice

The candy-floss colour of the petunias is enriched by combining them with deep crimson ivy-leaved pelargoniums. Slower-growing silver-leaved snapdragons and a variegated pelargonium will add further colour later in the summer.

MATERIALS

36cm (14in) hanging basket
Sphagnum moss
Compost (soil mix)
Slow-release plant food granules

PLANTS

3 snapdragons (Antirrhinum *'Avalanche') (optional)*
Ivy-leaved Pelargonium *'Blue Beard'*
Ivy-leaved Pelargonium *'L'Elégante' (optional)*
3 pink petunias

SNAPDRAGON

PELARGONIUMS

PETUNIA

GARDENER'S TIP

It is a good idea to include a number of different plants. This creates a more interesting picture and ensures that if one plant does not thrive, as happened to the snapdragons in this basket, the other plants will still make a good display.

PLANT IN LATE SPRING OR EARLY SUMMER

1 Line the lower half of the basket with moss. Plant the snapdragons in the side of the basket, resting the root-balls on the moss and guiding the foliage through the side of the basket.

2 Line the remainder of the basket with moss, tucking it carefully around the underplanted snapdragons.

3 Fill the basket with compost (soil mix), working a teaspoon of slow-release plant food granules into the top layer of compost. Plant the *Pelargonium* 'Blue Beard' at the back of the basket.

4 Plant the *Pelargonium* 'L'Elégante' at the front of the basket. Plant the petunias around the pelargoniums. Water thoroughly and hang in a sunny position.

Three tiers of colour

Scented petunias, delicate white marguerites and starry isotoma make a stunning layered arrangement. Use veined petunias, as they have the strongest scent.

MATERIALS

36cm (14in) terracotta window box
Crocks (broken pots) or other suitable drainage material
Compost (soil mix)
Slow-release plant food granules

PLANTS

2 white marguerites (argyranthemums)
3 petunias
3 isotoma

ISOTOMA

MARGUERITE

PETUNIA

GARDENER'S TIP

Try to position flowers where they can be seen at dusk, when their colours become far more intense and are a treat not to be missed.

PLANT IN LATE SPRING OR EARLY SUMMER

1 Cover the base with crocks (broken pots). Fill with compost (soil mix), working in 2 teaspoons of plant food granules.

2 Plant the marguerites on either side of the centre towards the back of the windowbox.

3 Plant one petunia in the centre and the other two at each end of the windowbox.

4 Plant the isotoma along the front edge of the windowbox. Water the arrangement well and stand in a sunny position.

Divine magenta

The gloriously strong colour of magenta petunias is combined with blue *Convolvulus sabatius*, heliotropes, which will bear scented deep purple flowers, and a variegated scented-leaf pelargonium, which will add colour and fragrance later in the summer.

MATERIALS

45cm (18in) basket
Sphagnum moss
Compost (soil mix)
Slow-release plant food granules

PLANTS

Scented-leaf Pelargonium
 'Fragrans Variegatum'
3 purple heliotropes
3 Convolvulus sabatius
5 trailing magenta-flowered
 petunias

HELIOTROPES

PELARGONIUM

CONVOLVULUS

PETUNIA

1 Carefully line the hanging basket with a thick layer of moss.

2 Fill the basket with compost (soil mix), working a teaspoon of slow-release plant food granules into the top layer.

3 Plant the scented-leaf pelargonium in the middle of the hanging basket.

4 Plant the heliotropes, evenly spaced, around the central pelargonium.

5 Plant the blue convolvulus, evenly spaced, around the edge of the basket.

6 Plant the petunias in the spaces between the convolvulus and the heliotropes.

GARDENER'S TIP

Baskets with flat bases like this one can be stood on columns rather than hung from brackets. This is a useful solution if fixing a bracket is difficult.

PLANT IN LATE SPRING OR EARLY SUMMER

A peachy pink wall basket

The vivid flowers of the petunias and pelargonium contrast dramatically with the greeny-yellow lamiums. This basket is seen to best effect against a dark background.

LAMIUM

PETUNIA

PELARGONIUM

MATERIALS

30cm (12in) wide wall basket
Sphagnum moss
Compost (soil mix)
Slow-release plant food granules

PLANTS

3 Lamium 'Golden Nuggets'
Peach/pink zonal Pelargonium
  'Palais', or similar
3 petunias

1 Line the back and lower half of the front of the basket with moss. Plant the lamiums by resting the root-balls on the moss, and feeding the foliage through the side of the basket. Line the rest of the basket with moss.

2 Fill the basket with compost (soil mix). Work half a tea-spoon of slow-release plant food granules into the top layer. Plant the pelargonium in the centre of the basket against the back edge.

3 Plant one petunia in each corner and the third in front of the pelargonium. Water well and hang on a sunny wall.

GARDENER'S TIP

For a gentler colour scheme, the lamium can be replaced with the silver-grey foliage of *Helichrysum microphyllum*.

PLANT IN LATE SPRING OR EARLY SUMMER

A small pelargonium basket

Ivy-leaved pelargoniums are lovely plants for hanging baskets, and one plant will fill a small basket like this by the middle of summer. The silver-leaved helichrysum and lilac diascias add the finishing touches to this pretty pink-and-silver theme.

MATERIALS

25cm (10in) hanging basket
Sphagnum moss
Compost (soil mix)
Slow-release plant food granules

PLANTS

2 Diascia 'Lilac Belle'
Ivy-leaved Pelargonium 'Super Rose'
2 Helichrysum microphyllum

DIASCIA

HELICHRYSUM

PELARGONIUM

GARDENER'S TIP

If you like some height in your hanging basket, use small canes to support some of the pelargonium's stems; if you prefer a cascading effect, leave the pelargonium unsupported.

PLANT IN LATE SPRING OR EARLY SUMMER

1 Line the bottom half of the hanging basket with moss.

2 Plant the diascias into the side of the basket by resting the root-balls on the moss, and gently feeding the foliage between the wires. Add some compost (soil mix).

3 Line the rest of the basket with moss, top up with compost (soil mix) and work a teaspoon of slow-release plant food granules into the top layer. Plant the pelargonium in the centre of the basket.

4 Plant the helichrysums on either side of the pelargonium. Water the basket well and hang in a sunny position.

Luxury basket

Fuchsia 'Pink Galore' is a beautiful cultivar for a luxury hanging basket. The dark glossy green foliage is a perfect foil for the very full, soft rose-pink flowers. A plastic basket with a fixed reservoir has been used to facilitate growth and watering, and the curtain of stems will soon hide the basket from view.

FUCHSIA

MATERIALS

36cm (14in) plastic hanging basket with fixed reservoir
Compost (soil mix)
Slow-release plant food granules

PLANTS

5 Fuchsia 'Pink Galore'

1 To avoid the plants becoming tangled in the chain, pull it to one side while planting up the basket.

2 Put a layer of compost (soil mix) with a half-teaspoon of slow-release plant food granules into the bottom of the basket.

3 Arrange four of the plants around the edge of the basket in a symmetrical pattern. Place the last plant centrally.

4 Remove each fuchsia plant from its pot, and gently ease the root-ball into the compost (soil mix).

5 Carefully fill the spaces between the plants with more mixture of compost (soil mix) and plant food granules. Firm the compost with your hands.

6 Tease the stems and the foliage around the chains as they are lifted into position.

GARDENER'S TIP

Always use an odd number of plants to achieve the best effect.
A plant placed centrally will prevent a gap appearing as the plants begin to cascade downwards.

PLANT IN EARLY SUMMER

Pleasing with pinks

Many different alpine pinks are available which will be equally at home in pots, hanging baskets or at the front of the flowerbed. They all love a well-drained, sunny site and will provide lots of colour and scent throughout June and often into July.

MATERIALS

- *Moss*
- *Plastic lining cut generously to fit the depth of the basket*
- *Old crocks (broken pots) or other suitable drainage material*
- *Compost (soil mix)*
- *33cm (13in) diameter wire basket*

PLANTS

1 alpine pink plant Dianthus 'Whatfield Can-Can'
1 alpine pink plant Dianthus 'Whatfield Magenta'
1 alpine pink plant Dianthus 'Calypso Star'
1 alpine pink plant Dianthus 'Dainty Dame'

DIANTHUS

GARDENER'S TIP

This pretty wire basket has been painted blue to complement the colours used in the planting scheme. It provides a beautiful background for a simple arrangement of various alpine pinks.

PLANT IN LATE SPRING

1 Cover the base and sides of the basket with a generous layer of moss. Cut several 2.5cm (1in) slits in the bottom of the plastic liner to allow excess moisture to drain away.

2 Place the plastic liner in position. Cut off any excess or leave to tuck in at the end of the planting. Add a layer of drainage material and then enough compost (soil mix) to bring level to within 5cm (2in) of the rim of the basket.

3 Arrange the four alpine pinks around the edge of the basket. Water well. Firm in the plants. Add more compost (soil mix) and moss if necessary.

In the pink

The common name for *Dianthus deltoides* is the pink. Its delightful deeply coloured flowers and silvery grey foliage work very well in a hanging basket combined with prostrate thymes, pink-flowered verbena and an osteospermum.

MATERIALS

36cm (14in) hanging basket
Sphagnum moss
Compost (soil mix)
Slow-release plant food granules

PLANTS

6 Dianthus deltoides
Osteospermum *'Pink Whirls'*
Verbena *'Silver Anne'*
3 thymes (Thymus 'Pink Chintz'
or similar prostrate variety)

PINKS

THYME

VERBENA

OSTEOSPERMUM

GARDENER'S TIP

Pinch out the growing tips regularly to prevent plants such as the osteospermum growing too vigorously upwards and unbalancing the look of the basket. It will be bushier and more in scale with the other plants as a result.

PLANT IN SPRING

1 Line the bottom half of the basket with moss and fill with compost (soil mix). Plant three of the pinks into the side of the basket, resting the root-balls on the compost and feeding the leaves carefully through the wire.

2 Line the rest of the basket with moss and fill with compost (soil mix). Work a teaspoon of slow-release plant food granules into the top of the compost. Plant the osteospermum in the centre of the basket.

3 Plant the verbena to one side of the osteospermum on the edge of the basket and the thymes, evenly spaced, around the unplanted edge.

4 Plant the remaining three pinks between the thymes and the verbena. Water well and hang in a sunny position.

Bright splashes of colour

MATERIALS

*76cm (30in) plastic windowbox
with drainage holes*
Compost (soil mix)
Slow-release plant food granules

PLANTS

2 yellow gazanias
3 Alaska nasturtiums
3 Brachycome 'Lemon Mist'
*2 yellow snapdragons
(antirrhinums)*

The leaves of the Alaska nasturtium look as if they have been splattered with cream paint. In this box they are planted with yellow-flowered snapdragons, gazanias and brachycome daisies.

BRACHYCOME

NASTURTIUM

SNAPDRAGONS

GAZANIA

GARDENER'S TIP

Nasturtiums are among the easiest plants to grow from seed. Start them off about 4–6 weeks before you plant your windowbox, potting them on to keep them growing vigorously.

PLANT IN THE SPRING

1 Fill the windowbox with compost (soil mix) and add 2 teaspoons of plant food. Plant the gazanias either side of the centre.

2 Plant the nasturtiums at either end and in the centre of the windowbox.

3 Plant the three brachycome plants, evenly spaced, along the front of the windowbox.

4 Plant the two snapdragons on either side of the central nasturtium. Water thoroughly and stand in a sunny position.

Fire and earth

The earth tones of this small decorative terracotta window-box are topped with the fiery reds and oranges of the plants – the fuchsia with its orange foliage and tubular scarlet flowers, the orange nasturtiums and the red claw-like flowers of the feathery-leaved lotus.

MATERIALS

36cm (14in) terracotta windowbox
Clay granules or other suitable drainage material
Compost (soil mix)
Slow-release plant food granules

PLANTS

Fuchsia 'Thalia'
3 orange nasturtiums
2 Lotus berthelotii

NASTURTIUM

FUCHSIA

LOTUS

1 Cover the base of the window-box with drainage material. Fill with compost (soil mix) and a teaspoon of plant food granules.

2 Plant the fuchsia in the centre of the windowbox.

3 Plant the nasturtiums along the back of the windowbox.

4 Plant the two lotuses in the front of the windowbox on either side of the fuchsia. Water thoroughly, leave to drain, and stand in a sunny position.

GARDENER'S TIP

This stunning fuchsia is worth keeping for next year. Pot it up in the autumn, cut back by half and overwinter on a window-sill or in a heated greenhouse.

PLANT IN LATE SPRING OR EARLY SUMMER

Fruit and flowers

Bright red petunias become even more vibrant when inter-planted with variegated helichrysums and underplanted with alpine strawberries. With their delicate trailing tendrils, the strawberry plants soften the lower edge of the basket.

MATERIALS

30cm (12in) hanging basket
Sphagnum moss
Compost (soil mix)
Slow-release plant food granules

PLANTS

3 alpine strawberry plants
3 bright red petunias
3 Helichrysum petiolare
'Variegatum'

HELICHRYSUM

ALPINE STRAWBERRY

PETUNIA

GARDENER'S TIP

The tendrils, or runners, sent out by the strawberries are searching for somewhere to root. If you can fix a pot in a suitable spot, pin the plantlet into the compost (soil mix) while it is still attached to the parent plant. As soon as it has rooted it can be cut free.

PLANT IN LATE SPRING OR EARLY SUMMER

1 Line the lower half of the basket with moss.

2 Plant the alpine strawberries by resting the root-balls on the moss, and guiding the leaves through the side of the basket.

3 Line the rest of the basket with moss and fill with compost (soil mix). Work in a teaspoon of slow-release plant food granules. Plant the petunias, evenly spaced, in the top of the basket.

4 Interplant the petunias with the helichrysums. Water thoroughly and hang in full or partial shade.

Flame-red flowers in terracotta

The intense red flowers of the pelargoniums, verbena and nasturtiums are emphasized by a few yellow nasturtiums and the variegated ivy, but cooled slightly by the soothing blue-green of the nasturtium's umbrella-shaped leaves.

NASTURTIUM

VERBENA

IVY

PELARGONIUM

MATERIALS

50cm (20in) terracotta window box
Crocks (broken pots) or other suitable drainage material
Compost (soil mix)
Slow-release plant food granules

PLANTS

2 red zonal pelargoniums
2 nasturtiums – 1 red, 1 yellow
Red verbena
2 variegated ivies

1 Place a layer of crocks (broken pots) or other suitable drainage material in the base of the windowbox.

2 Fill the container with compost (soil mix), adding 3 teaspoons of slow-release plant food granules.

3 Plant the pelargoniums either side of the centre of the windowbox.

4 Plant a nasturtium at each end of the windowbox, in the back corners.

5 Plant the verbena in the centre of the windowbox.

6 Plant the ivies in front of the nasturtiums in the corners. Water well, leave to drain, and place in a sunny position.

GARDENER'S TIP

Nasturtiums are prone to attack by blackfly. Treat at the first sign of infestation with a suitable insecticide and the plants will remain healthy.

PLANT IN LATE SPRING OR EARLY SUMMER

Sunny daisies and violas

Osteospermum daisies are sun-worshippers, keeping their petals furled in cloudy weather. In this windowbox they are combined with yellow violas and tumbling white bacopas.

VIOLA

BACOPA

OSTEOSPERMUM

MATERIALS

45cm (18in) fibre windowbox
Polystyrene or other suitable drainage material
Compost (soil mix)
Slow-release plant food granules

PLANTS

Osteospermum *'Buttermilk'*
3 yellow violas
2 white bacopas

1 Line the base of the box with polystyrene or other suitable drainage material and fill with compost (soil mix).

2 Mix in 3 teaspoons of plant food granules. Plant the osteospermum in the centre.

3 Plant two of the violas at each end of the windowbox and the third in front of the osteospermum.

4 Plant the two bacopas on either side of the osteospermum. Stand in a sunny spot and water thoroughly.

GARDENER'S TIP

Pinch out the growing tips of the osteospermum regularly to encourage a bushy rather than a leggy plant.

PLANT IN SPRING

A floral chandelier

MATERIALS

36cm (14in) hanging basket
Sphagnum moss
Compost (soil mix)
Slow-release plant food granules

PLANTS

3 yellow lantanas, 2 variegated,
* 1 green-leaved*
2 Bidens ferulifolia
5 African marigolds (tagetes)

The chandelier shape is a result of combining the spreading bidens with upright lantanas and marigolds. Since the variegated-leaf lantanas proved very slow to establish, a more vigorous green-leaved form was added later. As the season progresses, the strongly marked leaves of the variegated plants will become more dominant.

AFRICAN MARIGOLDS

LANTANA

BIDENS

1 Line the basket with moss. Fill it with compost (soil mix), working a teaspoon of plant food granules into the top layer. Plant the lantana in the centre.

2 Plant the two bidens opposite one another at the edge of the basket.

3 Plant the African marigolds around the lantana plants. Water thoroughly and hang in a sunny position.

GARDENER'S TIP

To complete the chandelier, make candle holders by twisting thick garden wire around the base of yellow candles and add them to the hanging basket.

PLANT IN LATE SPRING OR EARLY SUMMER

Vibrant reds and sunny yellows

This basket is an exciting mix of glowing colours and contrasting leaf shapes. A bright red verbena and the pineapple-scented salvia tumble from the basket, intertwined with red and yellow nasturtiums and a striking golden grass.

NASTURTIUM

VERBENA

SALVIA

GOLDEN
GRASS

MATERIALS

36cm (14in) hanging basket
Sphagnum moss
Compost (soil mix)
Slow-release plant food granules

PLANTS

4 trailing nasturtiums
Golden grass Hakonechloa
  'Alboaurea', or similar
Salvia elegans
Verbena 'Lawrence Johnston'

1 Line the bottom half of the basket with moss.

2 Plant three of the nasturtiums into the side of the basket by resting the root-balls on the moss, and carefully feeding the leaves through the basket.

3 Line the rest of the basket with moss and fill with compost (soil mix). Work a teaspoon of plant food granules into the compost. Plant the golden grass to one side of the basket.

4 Plant the salvia a third of the way round the edge of the basket from the grass.

5 Plant the verbena at an equal distance from the salvia and the golden grass.

6 Plant the remaining nasturtium in the centre. Water well and hang in a sunny position.

GARDENER'S TIP

Nasturtiums are wonderful plants for hanging baskets – vigorous, colourful and undemanding – but they can be disfigured by blackfly. Spray at the first sign of an infestation with an insecticide which will not harm beneficial insects.

PLANT IN LATE SPRING OR EARLY SUMMER

Summer carnival

The orange markings on the throats of some of the mimulus flowers look wonderful with the orange-flowered pelargonium in this colourful basket. By the end of the season, trails of lysimachia leaves will form a waterfall of foliage around the base.

MATERIALS
....
36cm (14in) basket
Sphagnum moss
Compost (soil mix)
Slow-release plant food granules

PLANTS
....
Orange-flowered zonal
  pelargonium
3 Lysimachia nummularia 'Aurea'
3 mimulus

LYSIMACHIA

MIMULUS

PELARGONIUM

GARDENER'S TIP

Dead-head the flowers regularly to encourage repeat flowering, and if the mimulus start to get leggy, cut back the offending stems to a leaf joint. New shoots will soon appear.

PLANT IN LATE SPRING OR EARLY SUMMER

1 Line the basket with moss and fill it with compost (soil mix), working a teaspoon of slow-release plant food granules into the top layer. Plant the pelargonium in the centre of the basket.

2 Plant the lysimachia, evenly spaced, around the edge of the basket, angling the plants so they will trail over the sides.

3 Plant the mimulus between the lysimachia. Water the hanging basket thoroughly and hang in a sunny spot.

Tumbling violas

Violas can be surprisingly vigorous plants and, given the space, will happily tumble over the edge of a wall basket. Combined with curly-leaved parsley and the daisy-like flowers of asteriscus the effect is delicate but luxuriant.

MATERIALS

30cm (12in) wall basket
Compost (soil mix)
Sphagnum moss
Slow-release plant food granules

PLANTS

5 parsley plants
5 yellow violas
Asteriscus 'Gold Coin'

PARSLEY

ASTERISCUS

VIOLA

1 Line the back and lower half of the front of the basket with sphagnum moss.

2 Plant three of the parsley plants into the sides of the basket by resting the root-balls on the moss, and feeding the foliage through the wires.

3 Add another layer of moss and plant two of the viola plants in the side of the basket using the same method.

4 Finish lining the basket with moss and fill with compost (soil mix), working a half-teaspoon of slow-release plant food granules into the top layer. Plant the asteriscus in the centre of the basket, and surround with the remaining parsley and viola plants.

GARDENER'S TIP

To keep the violas flowering all summer they need regular dead-heading – the easiest way to do this is to give the plants a trim with a pair of scissors rather than trying to remove heads individually.

PLANT IN SPRING

Mediterranean mood

The lantana is a large shrub which thrives in a Mediterranean or sub-tropical climate, but it is increasingly popular in cooler climates as a half-hardy perennial in borders and containers. This multi-coloured variety has been planted with yellow bidens and orange dahliettas.

DAHLIETTA

BIDENS

LANTANA

MATERIALS

36cm (14in) hanging basket
Sphagnum moss
Compost (soil mix)
Slow-release plant food granules

PLANTS

Orange/pink lantana
3 orange dahliettas (miniature dahlias)
3 Bidens aurea

1 Line the basket with moss. Fill the basket with compost (soil mix), working a teaspoon of slow-release plant food granules into the top layer. Plant the lantana in the centre of the basket.

2 Plant the dahliettas, evenly spaced, around the lantana.

3 Plant the bidens between the dahliettas. Water thoroughly and hang in a sunny position.

GARDENER'S TIP

To encourage a bushy plant, pinch out the growing tips of the lantana regularly. Like many popular plants, the lantana is poisonous, so treat it with respect and do not try eating it.

PLANT IN LATE SPRING OR EARLY SUMMER

A sunny wall basket

MATERIALS

30cm (12in) wall basket
Sphagnum moss
Compost (soil mix)
Slow-release plant food granules

PLANTS

2 Lysimachia congestiflora
3 *Alaska nasturtiums*
3 *mixed colour African marigolds*
   (tagetes)

LYSIMACHIA

NASTURTIUM

AFRICAN
MARIGOLDS

The vibrant yellows, oranges and reds of the flowers in this basket glow richly amongst the variegated leaves of the nasturtiums. As the season progresses the underplanted lysimachia will bear deep yellow flowers and add another layer of colour.

1 Line the back of the basket and half-way up the front with moss. Plant the lysimachia by resting the root-balls on the moss and feeding the foliage between the wires.

2 Line the rest of the basket and fill with compost (soil mix), adding in a half-teaspoon of plant food granules. Plant the nasturtiums along the back.

3 Plant the African marigolds in front of the nasturtiums. Water the basket well and hang it up in a sunny spot.

GARDENER'S TIP

If you have a large area of wall to cover, group two or three wall baskets together.
This looks very effective, especially when they are planted with the same plants.

PLANT IN SPRING

Dark drama

The intense purple of the heliotrope usually dominates other plants, but here it is teamed with a selection of equally dramatic colours – *Dahlia* 'Bednall Beauty', with its purple foliage and dark red flowers, black grass and red and purple verbenas – to make a stunning display.

MATERIALS

60cm (24in) terracotta
windowbox
Polystyrene (plastic foam) or
other suitable drainage material
Compost (soil mix)
Slow-release plant food granules

PLANTS

Heliotrope
2 Dahlia 'Bednall Beauty'
Black grass (Ophiopogon
planiscapus 'Nigrescens')
2 purple trailing verbenas
2 red trailing verbenas

BLACK GRASS

VERBENAS

DAHLIA

HELIOTROPE

1 Fill the bottom of the windowbox with broken polystyrene (plastic foam) or other suitable drainage material.

2 Fill the windowbox with compost (soil mix), adding in 3 teaspoons of slow-release plant food granules. Plant the heliotrope centrally at the back of the windowbox, gently teasing apart the roots, if necessary.

3 Plant the dahlias in the back corners of the windowbox.

4 Plant the black grass in front of the heliotrope.

5 Plant the purple verbenas at the back between the heliotrope and the dahlias.

6 Plant the red verbenas at the front in either corner. This is a large container so it is best to position it before watering. Put it where it will benefit from full sun, then water thoroughly.

GARDENER'S TIP

Dahlias can be overwintered by digging up the tubers after the first frosts, cutting the stems back to 15cm (6in) and drying them off before storing in slightly damp peat in a frost-free shed. Start into growth again in spring and plant out after all danger of frost is past.

PLANT IN LATE SPRING OR EARLY SUMMER

A cascade of lilac and silver

Petunias and violas are surrounded by a cascading curtain of variegated ground ivy and silver-leaved senecio in this softly coloured hanging basket.

MATERIALS

30cm (12in) hanging basket
Sphagnum moss
Compost (soil mix)
Slow-release plant food granules

PLANTS

3 deep blue violas
3 soft blue petunias
Variegated ground ivy (Glechoma hederacea 'Variegata')
3 Senecio cineraria 'Silver Dust'

SENECIO

IVY

PETUNIA

VIOLAS

GARDENER'S TIP

If the ground ivy becomes too rampant and threatens to throttle the other plants, prune it by removing some of the stems completely and reducing the length of the others.

PLANT IN LATE SPRING OR EARLY SUMMER

1 Line the lower half of the basket with moss. Plant the violas in the side by resting the root-balls on the moss, and carefully guiding the foliage between the wires. Line the rest of the basket with moss and fill with compost (soil mix), working a teaspoon of slow-release plant food granules into the top layer.

2 Plant the three petunias, evenly spaced, in the top of the basket. Plant the ground ivy on one side to trail over the edge of the basket.

3 Plant the three senecios between the petunias. Water well and hang in a sunny position.

Violas and verbenas

Deep blue violas are surrounded by trailing purple verbenas to make a simple but attractive basket. Trailing verbena is a particularly good hanging-basket plant with its feathery foliage and pretty flowers.

VERBENA

VIOLAS

MATERIALS

30cm (12in) hanging basket
Sphagnum moss
Compost (soil mix)
Slow-release plant food granules

PLANTS

9 blue violas
3 purple trailing verbenas

1 Line the lower half of the basket with moss. Plant five of the violas into the side of the basket by resting the root-balls on the moss and guiding the foliage through the side of the basket.

2 Line the rest of the basket with moss and fill with compost (soil mix), working a teaspoon of slow-release plant food granules into the top layer. Plant the verbenas around the basket edge.

3 Plant the remaining violas in the centre of the basket. Water well and hang in partial sun.

GARDENER'S TIP

If the violas grow too tall, pinch out the main stems of the plants to encourage the spreading side shoots.

PLANT IN SPRING

An instant garden

There is not always time to wait for a windowbox to grow and this is one solution. Fill a container with potted plants and, as the season progresses, you can ring the changes by removing those that are past their best and introducing new plants.

HELICHRYSUM

PETUNIA

LAVENDER

CONVOLVULUS

BACOPA

MATERIALS
64cm (25in) galvanized tin windowbox
Clay granules
5 1-litre (5in) plastic pots
Compost (soil mix)

PLANTS
Lavender (Lavandula pinnata)
2 blue petunias
Convolvulus sabatius
Blue bacopa
Helichrysum petiolare
Viola 'Jupiter'

GARDENER'S TIP
When using a container without drainage holes, take care not to overwater or the roots will become waterlogged.
Check after heavy rain, too, and empty away any excess water.

PLANT IN LATE SPRING OR EARLY SUMMER

1 Fill the base of the container with clay granules or similar drainage material.

2 Pot up the lavender into one of the pots.

3 Pot up one of the petunias with the convolvulus.

4 Pot up the other petunia with the bacopa.

5 Pot up the helichrysum.

6 Pot up the viola and arrange the pots in the windowbox.

Showers of flowers

Deep, velvety purple pansies
and purple sage are surrounded
by pink nemesias and tumbling
purple verbenas in a pretty
basket hung, here, in the corner
of a thatched summerhouse.

MATERIALS
....
40cm (16in) hanging basket
Sphagnum moss
Compost (soil mix)
Slow-release plant food granules

PLANTS
....
3 purple verbenas
Purple sage
3 deep purple pansies
6 Nemesia 'Confetti'

VERBENA

SAGE

PANSY

NEMESIA

GARDENER'S TIP

In summer, pansies tend to flag
in hot sun, especially in
hanging baskets. They will do
best where they are in the
shade during the hottest part
of the day.

PLANT IN SPRING

1 Line the lower half of the
basket with moss. Plant the
verbenas in the side of the basket.
Line the rest of the basket and fill
with compost (soil mix), adding in
a teaspoon of plant food granules.

2 Plant the sage in the middle
of the basket.

3 Plant the pansies around the
sage, spacing them evenly. Add
more compost (soil mix) around
the pansies and press in firmly.

4 Plant three nemesias at the
back of the pansies, and three
nemesias between the pansies.
Water and hang in light shade.

A pretty stencilled planter

This small stencilled wooden windowbox is full of blue flowers. In a particularly pretty mix, petunias are intertwined with brachycome daisies and trailing convolvulus. A pair of brackets hold it in place under the window.

MATERIALS

40cm (16in) wooden windowbox
Clay granules or other suitable
*   drainage material*
Compost (soil mix)
Slow-release plant food granules

PLANTS

3 blue petunias
2 blue brachycome daisies
Convolvulus sabatius

BRACHYCOME

PETUNIA

CONVOLVULUS

1 Line the base of the windowbox with clay granules or other suitable drainage material. Fill the windowbox with compost (soil mix), working in a teaspoon of slow-release plant food granules.

2 Plant the three petunias, evenly spaced, towards the back of the box. Plant the brachycome daisies between the petunias.

3 Plant the convolvulus centrally at the front of the box. Water thoroughly and position in full or partial sun.

GARDENER'S TIP

If you are stencilling a wooden container for outside use, do not forget to seal the wood after decorating it. In this instance, a matt wood varnish in a light oak tint has been used.

PLANT IN LATE SPRING OR EARLY SUMMER

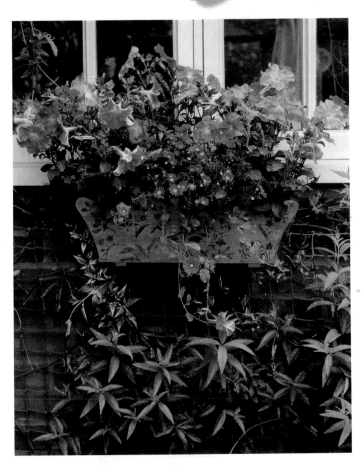

Marguerites and pimpernels

We are more familiar with the wild scarlet pimpernel, but in this windowbox its blue relative, anagallis, has been planted to climb among the stems of the yellow marguerites and snapdragons. Blue-flowered variegated felicia and golden helichrysum complete the picture.

MATERIALS

76cm (30in) plastic windowbox
Compost (soil mix)
Slow-release plant food granules

PLANTS

2 yellow marguerites
4 blue anagallis
3 variegated felicias
2 Helichrysum petiolare 'Aureum'
4 yellow snapdragons
   (Antirrhinum)

MARGUERITE

ANAGALLIS

HELICHRYSUM

SNAPDRAGONS

FELICIA

1 Check the drainage holes are open in the base and, if not, drill or punch them open. Fill the windowbox with compost (soil mix), working in 3 teaspoons of slow-release plant food granules.

2 Plant the marguerites on either side of the centre, towards the middle of the windowbox.

3 Plant two of the anagallis in the back corners of the windowbox and two at the front, on either side of the marguerites.

4 Plant one felicia in the centre of the box and the other two on either side of the anagallis.

5 Plant the helichrysum in the front corners of the window-box to trail over the edges.

6 Plant two of the snapdragons on either side of the central felicia and two on either side of the marguerites. Water thoroughly, drain, and stand in a sunny or partially sunny position.

GARDENER'S TIP

Dead-head the marguerites, snapdragons and felicias to keep them flowering all summer. When planting the marguerites, pinch out the growing tips to encourage bushy plants.

PLANT IN SPRING

Shades of mauve

AGERATUM

ISOTOMA

HELICHRYSUM

SCABIOUS

MATERIALS

40cm (16in) hanging basket
Sphagnum moss
Compost (soil mix)
Slow-release plant food granules

PLANTS

6 blue ageratum
Blue scabious
3 Helichrysum petiolare
3 blue Isotoma axillaris

Some unlikely plants, such as this powder-blue scabious, can do very well in a hanging basket, especially when combined, as it is here, with isotoma and ageratum in the same colour, and the trailing silver foliage of helichrysum.

1 Line the lower half of the basket with moss. Plant three ageratum by resting the root-balls on the moss, and carefully guiding the foliage through the wires.

2 Add a further layer of moss and plant the other three ageratum into the side of the basket at a higher level.

3 Fill the basket with compost (soil mix), working a teaspoon of slow-release plant food granules into the top layer. Plant the scabious in the centre of the basket.

4 Plant the helichrysums, evenly spaced, around the edge of the basket. Plant the isotoma between the helichrysums. Water well and hang in a sunny position.

GARDENER'S TIP

At the end of the season the scabious can be removed from the basket and planted in the border to flower for many years to come.

PLANT IN LATE SPRING

Sapphires for spring

Deep blue pansies are surrounded by gentian-blue anagallis and underplanted with golden helichrysums in this richly coloured basket.

MATERIALS

30cm (12in) hanging basket
Sphagnum moss
Compost (soil mix)
Slow-release plant food granules

PLANTS

3 Helichrysum petiolare 'Aureum'
3 deep blue pansies
3 blue anagallis

ANAGALLIS

HELICHRYSUM

PANSY

1 Line the lower half of the basket with moss before planting the helichrysums in the sides of the basket.

2 Rest the root-balls on the moss, and carefully guide the foliage through the wires.

3 Line the rest of the basket with moss and fill with compost (soil mix), working a teaspoon of plant food into the top layer. Plant the pansies, evenly spaced, in the top of the basket.

4 Plant the anagallis between the pansies. Water the basket thoroughly and hang in partial sun.

GARDENER'S TIP

The golden-green colour of *Helichrysum petiolare* 'Aureum' is far stronger if the plants are not in full sun. Too much sun tends to fade the colouring.

PLANT IN SPRING

Seasonal planters

There's no need to confine your ideas to summer planting schemes, however
exuberant. You can keep boxes and hanging baskets looking vibrant and beautiful all
year round. It's a lovely reassurance that spring is on its way to see the earliest
spring bulbs bursting into flower right outside your window, and judiciously planted pots
can often be slipped into temporary gaps in the borders to bridge the seasons.
One of the joys of container gardening is that you can put together combinations that
will look their best in spring, summer or autumn, then swap them around to take
centre stage at the appropriate time.

You may also have containers you don't want to move: if a stately classical urn is a
focal point in your garden, give it all-year-round interest with an evergreen shrub
or a beautifully clipped piece of topiary; you can ring seasonal changes by underplanting
with spring and summer bedding plants.

ABOVE: *A colourful spring display in a moss-lined basket.*

Daffodils and wallflowers

A weathered wooden tub planted in the autumn with daffodil bulbs and wallflower plants will provide a colourful spring display. Alternatively, you can buy pots of daffodils and wallflowers in bud in the early spring and plant them for an instant show.

MATERIALS

36cm (14in) wooden tub
Polystyrene or other drainage
    material
Compost (soil mix)
Slow-release plant food granules

PLANTS

24 daffodil bulbs or 4 1-litre
    (5in) pots of daffodils
3 bushy wallflower (Cheiranthus)
    plants

DAFFODIL

WALLFLOWER

GARDENER'S TIP

To save the bulbs for next year, allow the leaves to die right back and then dig up and store in a cool dry place.

PLANT BULBS IN THE
AUTUMN OR PLANTS IN BUD
IN SPRING

1 Break the polystyrene (plastic foam) into large pieces and fill the bottom third of the tub to provide drainage and to save on the quantity of compost (soil mix) used.

2 Add compost (soil mix) until the tub is half-full and arrange 12 of the daffodil bulbs evenly over the surface. Cover the bulbs with compost.

3 Arrange the remaining 12 bulbs on the surface of the compost (soil mix). Remove the wallflower plants from their pots and place on the compost. Don't worry if the plants cover some of the bulbs, they will grow round the wallflowers. Fill the tub with compost, pressing down firmly around the wallflowers to ensure that they do not work loose in windy weather. Sprinkle a tablespoon of plant food granules on to the surface and work into the top layer of compost.

Miniature spring garden

Terracotta pots filled with crocuses, irises and primroses
nestling in a bed of moss, make a delightful scaled-down spring
garden which would fit on the
smallest balcony
or even a window-sill.

IRIS

MOSS

CROCUS

PRIMROSE

MATERIALS

Terracotta seed tray
2 terracotta pots, 13cm (5in) high
Crocks (broken pots)
Compost (soil mix)
Bun moss

PLANTS

3 primroses
Pot of Iris reticulata
Pot of crocuses

1 Cover the drainage holes of
the seed tray and the two pots
with crocks (broken pots).

2 Half-fill the seed tray with
compost (soil mix). Before
planting the primroses, loosen the
roots by gently squeezing the root-
ball and teasing the roots loose.

3 Arrange the primroses in the
seed tray and fill with compost
(soil mix) around the plants,
pressing down around the plants
to ensure they are firmly planted.

4 Arrange the bun moss around
the plants so that all the
compost (soil mix) is hidden.

5 Remove the irises from their
plastic pot and slip them into a
terracotta pot. Bed them in with a
little extra compost (soil mix) if
necessary, and then arrange moss
around the base of the stems.

6 Repeat this process with the
crocuses and then water all the
containers and arrange them
together.

GARDENER'S TIP

Once the irises and crocuses are past their best, hide them behind other pots to die down and dry out
before starting them into growth again in the autumn.

PLANT IN EARLY SPRING

Spring flowers in an instant

An arrangement of pots of spring flowers is surrounded with bark to give the appearance of a planted windowbox. As soon as the flowers are over, the pots can be removed and left to die back, and the container is ready for its summer planting.

MATERIALS

40cm (16in) terracotta windowbox
Bark chippings

PLANTS

Pot of daffodils
Pot of yellow tulips
4 yellow pansies in pots

PANSY

DAFFODIL

TULIP

GARDENER'S TIP

Once the flowers have finished and the pots have been removed from the windowbox, the pots of bulbs can be tucked away in a corner of the garden ready to flower again next year.

PLANT IN LATE WINTER OR EARLY SPRING

1 Position the pot of daffodils at the right-hand end of the windowbox.

2 Position the pot of tulips at the left-hand end of the windowbox.

3 Fill the centre and around the pots with bark chippings until the windowbox is half-full.

4 Position the pansies between the tulips and the daffodils, and add bark until all the pots are concealed. Water moderately and stand in any position.

A spring display of auriculas

An old strawberry punnet carrier makes an attractive and unusual windowbox in which to display some beautifully marked auriculas planted in antique terracotta pots. A large flower basket or wooden trug would look just as good as this marvellous old wooden carrier.

MATERIALS

8 8–10cm (3–4in) old or antique-
 style terracotta pots
Crocks (broken pots) or other
 suitable drainage material
Compost (soil mix)
50cm (20in) wooden carrier

PLANTS

8 different auriculas (Primula
auricula)

AURICULAS

GARDENER'S TIP

A window-sill is an ideal position to see auriculas at their best. It is difficult to admire the full drama of their markings if they are at ground level. When they have finished flowering, stand the pots in a shady corner or a cold frame.

PLANT IN EARLY SPRING

1 Place a crock over the drainage hole of a pot.

2 Remove an auricula from its plastic pot and plant it firmly with added compost (soil mix).

3 Stand the newly planted auricula in the wooden carrier.

4 Repeat the process for the other plants to fill the carrier. Water thoroughly and stand in light shade.

Display in a copper tub

A battered old washing boiler makes an attractive and characterful container for a display of white tulips, underplanted with purple violets and evergreen periwinkles.

MATERIALS

60cm (24in) copper boiler
20cm (8in) plastic pot
Compost (soil mix)

PLANTS

20 white tulip bulbs
* or tulips in bud*
5 purple violets
2 periwinkles
* (Vinca minor)*

VIOLET

TULIP

PERIWINKLE

GARDENER'S TIP

Lift the tulips when they have finished flowering and hang them up to dry in a cool airy place. They can be replanted late in autumn to flower again next year. Provided you pick off the dead heads, the violets will flower all summer. For a summer display, lift the central violet and plant a standard white marguerite in the centre of the container.

PLANT BULBS IN AUTUMN OR PLANTS IN BUD IN SPRING. PLANT THE VIOLETS AND PERIWINKLES IN SPRING

1 Place the upturned plastic pot in the base of the tub before filling it with compost (soil mix). This will save on the amount of compost used, and will not have any effect on the growth of the plants as they will still have plenty of room for their roots.

3 Do the underplanting in early spring. The compost (soil mix) will have settled in the container and should be topped up to within 7.5cm (3in) of the rim. Remove the violets from their pots. Gently tweak the root-balls and loosen the roots to aid the plants' growth.

5 Plant a periwinkle on either side of the central violet, again loosening the root-balls.

2 If you are planting tulip bulbs, half-fill the container with compost (soil mix), arrange the bulbs evenly over the surface and then cover them with a good 15cm (6in) of compost. This should be done in late autumn.

4 Plant one violet in the centre and four around the edges. Scoop out the soil by hand to avoid damaging the growing tips of the tulips beneath the surface.

6 If you are planting tulips in bud, the whole scheme should be planted at the same time, interplanting the tulips with the violets and periwinkles. Position in sun or partial shade.

Scented spring planter

Lilies-of-the-valley grow very well in containers and they will thrive in the shade where their delicate scented flowers stand out amongst the greenery. Surrounding the plants with bun moss is practical as well as attractive as it will stop the soil splashing back on to the leaves and flowers during fierce spring showers.

MATERIALS

Tinware planter
Clay granules
Compost (soil mix)
Bun moss

PLANTS

6–8 pots of lily-of-the-valley

LILY OF THE VALLEY

1 Fill the bottom of the planter with 5cm (2in) of clay granules to improve drainage.

2 Cover the granules with a layer of compost (soil mix) and arrange the lily-of-the-valley plants evenly on the compost.

3 Fill in around the plants with more compost (soil mix), making sure to press firmly around the plants so that they won't rock about in the wind. Now cover the compost with bun moss, fitting it snugly around the stems of the lily-of-the-valley, as this will also help keep the plants upright.

GARDENER'S TIP

If you want to bring your planter indoors to enjoy the scent of the flowers, use a container without drainage holes in the base, but be very careful not to overwater. Once the plants have finished flowering replant them in a pot with normal drainage holes or in the garden. They are woodland plants and will be quite happy under trees.

PLANT IN EARLY SPRING

Woodland garden

You do not need your own woodland area for this garden, just a shady corner and an attractive container to hold a selection of plants that thrive in damp shade. The plants are buried in bark chippings in their pots and will relish these conditions as they closely imitate their natural habitat.

MATERIALS

50cm (20in) glazed pot
Bark chippings

FERNS

BLUEBELL

ANEMONE
BLANDA

PLANTS

Pot of bluebells
3 hardy ferns
Pot of Anemone blanda

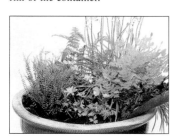

1 Fill the container three-quarters full with bark chippings. Plant your largest pot (in this case the bluebells) first. Scoop a hollow in the bark and position the pot so that the base of the leaves is approximately 5cm (2in) below the rim of the container.

2 Cover the pot with bark so that the plastic is no longer visible and the plant is surrounded by chippings.

3 Arrange the ferns so that they relate attractively to one another. Fill the spaces between the ferns with bark.

4 Add the *Anemone blanda* at the front of the container where its flowers will be seen to best advantage, and then top up the whole arrangement with bark. Stand the container in light shade and water.

GARDENER'S TIP

After the bluebells and anemones have finished flowering, lift them out of the container in their pots and set them aside in a shady corner to rest. They can be replaced by other woodland plants such as wild strawberries or periwinkle.

PLANT IN EARLY SPRING

A garland of spring flowers

Miniature daffodils, deep blue pansies, yellow polyanthus and variegated ivy are planted together to make a hanging basket that will flower for many weeks in early spring, lifting the spirits with its fresh colours and delicate woodland charm.

MATERIALS

30cm (12in) hanging basket
Sphagnum moss
Compost (soil mix)
Slow-release plant food granules

PLANTS

3 variegated ivies
5 miniature daffodil bulbs 'Tête-à-Tête' or similar, or a pot of daffodils in bud
3 blue pansies
2 yellow polyanthus

POLYANTHUS

IVY

PANSY

MINIATURE DAFFODIL

1 Line the lower half of the basket with moss.

2 Plant the ivies into the side of the basket by resting the root-balls on the moss, and guiding the foliage through the basket so that it will trail down.

3 Line the rest of the basket with moss and add a layer of compost (soil mix) to the bottom of the basket. Push the daffodil bulbs into the compost.

4 Fill the remainder of the basket with compost (soil mix), working a teaspoon of slow-release plant food granules into the top layer. Plant the pansies, evenly spaced, in the top of the basket.

5 Plant the polyanthus between the pansies. Water the basket and hang in sun or shade. If planting daffodils in bud, remove them from the pot and place in the centre of the basket before arranging the ivies and filling with compost (soil mix).

GARDENER'S TIP

When dismantling the arrangement, plant the variegated ivies in the garden. They look particularly good tumbling over walls, or threading their way through and linking established shrubs. Prune hard if they get out of hand and become too invasive.

PLANT IN AUTUMN IF GROWING DAFFODILS FROM BULBS; IN LATE WINTER OR EARLY SPRING FOR READY-GROWN DAFFODILS

A basket of contrasts

The deep green and burgundy foliage of *Fuchsia* 'Thalia' will be even more startling later in summer when the bright red pendant flowers stand out against the leaves and compete with the glowing colours of the nemesias. The yellow-green helichrysums provide a cooling contrast.

MATERIALS

30cm (12in) wall basket
Sphagnum moss
Compost (soil mix)
Slow-release plant food granules

PLANTS

3 Helichrysum petiolare 'Aureum'
Fuchsia 'Thalia'
4 nemesias in red, yellow and orange tones

NEMESIA

HELICHRYSUM

FUCHSIA

1 Line the back of the basket and the lower half of the front with moss. Fill the lower half of the basket with compost (soil mix).

2 Plant two of the helichrysum plants into the side of the basket by resting the root-balls on the moss, and carefully feeding the foliage through the wires.

GARDENER'S TIP

Dead-head the nemesias regularly to ensure that they continue flowering throughout the summer.

PLANT IN LATE SPRING OR EARLY SUMMER

3 Line the rest of the basket with moss and top up with compost (soil mix). Work a half-teaspoon of slow-release plant food granules into the top layer. Plant the fuchsia in the centre.

4 Plant the remaining helichrysum in front of the fuchsia. Plant two nemesias on each side of the central plants. Water the basket well and hang in full or partial sun.

Delicate summer flowers

CONVOLVULUS

BRACHYCOME

PANSIES

Pale orange pansies contrast beautifully with the lavender-blue convolvulus, and the pastel yellow brachycome daisies link the whole scheme together.

MATERIALS

30cm (12in) hanging basket
Sphagnum moss
Compost (soil mix)
Slow-release plant food granules

PLANTS

3 orange pansies
3 Brachycome 'Lemon Mist'
2 Convolvulus sabatius

1 Line the basket with moss and fill with compost, mixing a teaspoon of slow-release plant food granules into the top layer. Plant the pansies around the edge.

2 Plant the brachycome daisies between the pansies.

3 Place the convolvulus plants in the centre of the basket so that the tendrils can weave between the other plants. Water and hang in full or partial sun.

GARDENER'S TIP

Each time you water this basket be sure to remove any pansy flowers that are past their best. Once pansies start to set seed they quickly grow leggy and stop flowering.

PLANT IN SPRING

A mass of sweet peas

This large basket is filled with sweet peas surrounding a regal pelargonium. It is inter-planted with chives to provide a contrasting leaf shape and help deter pests. Their fluffy purple flowers will add a further dimension to the arrangement, and the leaves can be snipped off for use in the kitchen.

MATERIALS

40cm (16in) hanging basket
Sphagnum moss
Compost (soil mix)
Slow-release plant food granules

PLANTS

Regal Pelargonium 'Sancho Panza'
2–3 small pots or a strip of low-growing sweet peas such as 'Snoopea'
3 chive plants

SWEET PEAS

CHIVES

PELARGONIUM

1 Line the basket with a generous layer of moss.

2 Fill the basket with compost (soil mix) and work a teaspoon of slow-release plant food granules into the top layer. Plant the regal pelargonium in the centre of the basket.

3 Gently divide the sweet peas into clumps of about eight plants each.

4 Plant the sweet pea clumps around the edge of the basket.

5 Plant the chives between the sweet peas and the central pelargonium.

6 Fill any gaps with more moss. Water well and hang the basket in a sunny position.

GARDENER'S TIP

Sweet peas will bloom longer if you keep picking the flowers and be sure to remove any seed pods as they form. Similarly, the chives grow longer and are stronger if their flowerheads are removed before they seed.

PLANT IN LATE SPRING

Hot flowers in a cool container

Shocking-pink petunias and verbenas are the dominant plants in this windowbox which also features a softer pink marguerite and silver helichrysum. The dark green of the wooden windowbox is a pleasing foil for the vibrant flowers.

MATERIALS

76cm (30in) plastic windowbox
  with drainage holes
90cm (3ft) wooden windowbox
  (optional)
Compost (soil mix)
Slow-release plant food granules

PLANTS

Trailing pink marguerite
  (Argyranthemum 'Flamingo')
2 bright pink verbenas, such as
  'Sissinghurst'
3 shocking-pink petunias
4 Helichrysum petiolare
  microphyllum

MARGUERITE

VERBENA

PETUNIA

HELICHRYSUM

GARDENER'S TIP

To add height to this scheme, buy some 30cm (12in) green plant sticks. Push two into the soil behind each of the verbenas, and train them upwards.

PLANT IN LATE SPRING OR
EARLY SUMMER

1 Fill the plastic windowbox with compost (soil mix), adding in 3 teaspoons of slow-release plant food granules. Plant the marguerite centre front.

2 Plant the verbenas in the back corners of the windowbox.

3 Plant one of the petunias behind the marguerite, and the other two on either side of it.

4 Plant one helichrysum on each side of the central petunia, and the other two in the front corners of the windowbox. Water well and lift into place. Stand in a sunny position.

A lime-green and blue box

MATERIALS

*76cm (30in) plastic windowbox
with drainage holes*
Compost (soil mix)
Slow-release plant food granules

PLANTS

5 lime-green tobacco plants
2 scaevola
2 Helichrysum petiolare 'Aureum'
3 Convolvulus sabatius

Lime-green flowering tobacco and helichrysums contrast beautifully with the blue scaevolas and convolvulus in this windowbox of cool colours.

SCAEVOLA

TOBACCO

CONVOLVULUS

HELICHRYSUM

1 Fill the window box with compost (soil mix), working in 3 teaspoons of plant food granules. Plant the tobacco plants along the back of the windowbox.

2 Plant the two scaevolas approximately 10cm (4in) from each end, in front of the tobacco plants.

3 Plant the two helichrysums on either side of the centre of the windowbox next to the scaevolas.

4 Plant two of the convolvulus in the front corners of the box and the third in the centre front. Water thoroughly and position in light shade or partial sun.

GARDENER'S TIP

At the end of the season pot up the scaevolas and convolvulus. Cut right back and protect from frost.

PLANT IN LATE SPRING

A miniature cottage garden

This basket derives its charm from its simple planting scheme. Pot marigolds and parsley are planted with bright blue felicias to create a basket which would look at home on the wall of a cottage or outside the kitchen door.

PARSLEY

FELICIA

POT
MARIGOLDS

MATERIALS

36cm (14in) hanging basket
Sphagnum moss
Compost (soil mix)
Slow-release plant food granules

PLANTS

5 parsley plants
3 pot marigolds (Calendula 'Gitana', or similar)
3 felicias

1 Line the lower half of the basket with moss.

2 Plant the parsley into the sides of the basket by resting the root-balls on the moss, and gently feeding the foliage through the wires.

3 Line the rest of the basket with moss, carefully tucking it around the roots of the parsley.

4 Fill the basket with compost (soil mix), mixing a teaspoon of slow-release plant food granules into the top layer.

5 Plant the three pot marigolds, evenly spaced, in the top of the basket.

6 Plant the felicias between the marigolds. Water well and hang in full or partial sun.

GARDENER'S TIP

Regular dead-heading will keep the basket looking good, but allow at least one of the marigold flowers to form a seedhead and you will be able to grow your own plants next year.

PLANT IN SPRING

Foliage basket

An old basket makes an ideal container for this interesting group of foliage plants. The different leaf shapes and colours are emphasized when they are grouped together. Including flowers would detract from the architectural quality of the plants.

MATERIALS
....
30cm (12in) basket
Sphagnum moss
Loam-based compost (soil mix)
Slow-release plant food granules
Bark chippings

PLANTS
....
Phormium tenax
  Mexican orange blossom
  (Choisya ternata)
  Carex brunnea *'Variegata'*

PHORMIUM

CAREX

MEXICAN
ORANGE BLOSSOM

GARDENER'S TIP

A planted basket makes an ideal gift for a friend, especially when you have chosen the plants yourself. Include a label, giving the names of the plants and how to care for them.

PLANT AT ANY TIME OF THE YEAR

1 Line the basket with moss. Place the phormium at the back and position the orange blossom next to it.

2 Add the carex and fill between the plants with compost (soil mix) enriched with a tablespoon of slow-release plant food granules.

3 Mulch around the plants with bark chippings. Water well and place in partial shade.

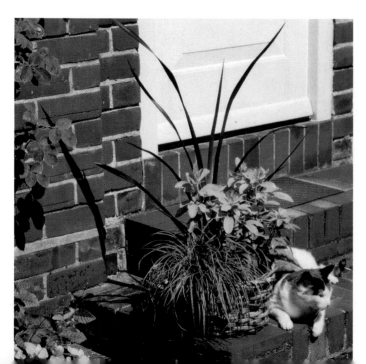

Layers of flowers

MATERIALS

36 cm (14 in) fibre windowbox
Drainage material
Compost (soil mix)
Slow-release plant food granules

PLANTS

2 white tobacco plants
Variegated Pelargonium
  'l'Elégante'
2 pink busy Lizzies (impatiens)
3 white lobelias

This windowbox is unusual as the colours are in distinct layers, with upright white flowering tobacco above pink busy Lizzies, and tumbling white variegated pelargonium and lobelias. The fibre windowbox is concealed by a decorative twig container.

LOBELIAS

TOBACCO

PELARGONIUM

BUSY
LIZZIE

1 Put some drainage material in the base of the windowbox; fill with compost (soil mix), mixing in 2 teaspoons of plant food granules. Plant the flowering tobacco near the back edge.

2 Plant the pelargonium at the front of the windowbox, in the centre.

3 Plant the busy Lizzies at each end of the windowbox.

4 Plant one of the lobelias between the flowering tobacco, and the other two on either side of the pelargonium.

GARDENER'S TIP

Somehow, rogue blue lobelias have appeared among the white plants. This sort of thing often happens in gardening and, as in this case, the accidental addition can turn out well.

PLANT IN SPRING

Full of cheer

Vivid red pelargoniums and verbenas are combined with cheerful yellow bidens and soft green helichrysums in this planter, which brightens the exterior of an old barn.

MATERIALS

76cm (30in) plastic windowbox
Compost (soil mix)
Slow-release plant food granules

PLANTS

3 scarlet pelargoniums
2 Bidens ferulifolia
2 red trailing verbenas
2 Helichrysum petiolare 'Aureum'

HELICHRYSUM

PELARGONIUM

BIDENS

VERBENA

GARDENER'S TIP

Regular dead-heading and an occasional foliar feed will keep the pelargoniums flowering prolifically all summer.

PLANT IN SPRING

1 The easiest way to make drainage holes in a plastic planter is with an electric drill.

2 Fill the windowbox with compost (soil mix), working in 2 teaspoons of slow-release plant food granules.

3 Plant the pelargoniums, evenly spaced, in the windowbox.

4 Plant the two bidens on either side of the central pelargonium to spill over the front of the planter.

5 Plant the two verbenas on either side of the central pelargonium towards the back of the planter.

6 Plant the helichrysums in the front corners. Water thoroughly and stand the box in a sunny position.

An antique wall basket

This old wirework basket is an attractive container for a planting scheme which includes deep pink pansies, a variegated ivy-leaved pelargonium with soft pink flowers, a blue convolvulus and deep pink alyssum.

MATERIALS

30cm (12in) wall basket
Sphagnum moss
Compost (soil mix)
Slow-release plant food granules

PLANTS

5 rose-pink alyssum
Pelargonium 'L'Elégante'
3 deep pink pansies
Convolvulus sabatius

PELARGONIUM   ALYSSUM

CONVOLVULUS

PANSY

GARDENER'S TIP

Wall baskets look good among climbing plants, but you will need to trim the surrounding foliage if it gets too exuberant.

PLANT IN LATE SPRING OR EARLY SUMMER

1 Line the back of the basket and the lower half of the front with moss. Plant the alyssum into the side by resting the root-balls on the moss, and guiding the foliage through the wires.

2 Line the remainder of the basket with moss and fill with compost (soil mix), working a half-teaspoon of plant food granules into the top layer. Plant the pelargonium at the front of the basket.

3 Plant the pansies around the pelargonium. Plant the convolvulus at the back of the basket, trailing its foliage through the other plants. Water well and hang in partial sun.

A cottage terracotta planter

Charming, cottage-garden plants tumble from this terracotta windowbox in a colourful display. The sunny flowers of the nemesias, marigolds and nasturtiums mingle with the cool, soft green helichrysums and blue-green nasturtium leaves.

MATERIALS

36cm (14in) terracotta
  windowbox
Crocks (broken pots) or other
  suitable drainage material
Compost (soil mix)
Slow-release plant food granules

PLANTS

3 pot marigolds (calendulas)
2 Helichrysum petiolare 'Aureum'
2 nasturtiums
2 Nemesia 'Orange Prince'

MARIGOLD

HELICHRYSUM

NASTURTIUM

NEMESIAS

1 Cover the base of the container with crocks (broken pots) and fill with compost (soil mix), adding 2 teaspoons of plant food granules. Plant the marigolds along the back.

2 Plant the two helichrysums in the front corners of the windowbox.

3 Plant the nasturtiums between the marigolds at the back of the container.

4 Plant the nemesias between the helichrysums. Water well and stand in partial sun.

GARDENER'S TIP

The golden-leaved helichrysum retains a better colour if it is not in full sun all day. Too much sun makes it looks rather bleached.

PLANT IN SPRING

A touch of gold

Yellow lantana and the yellow-flowered variegated-leaf nasturtium provide colour from early summer onwards, and later in the season the black-eyed Susan will be covered in eye-catching flowers. Hang this exuberant basket high on a sunny wall so that the trailing plants can make as much growth as they like.

NASTURTIUM

BLACK-EYED SUSAN

LANTANA

MATERIALS

30cm (12in) hanging basket
Sphagnum moss
Compost (soil mix)
Slow-release plant food granules

PLANTS

3 Alaska nasturtiums
Yellow lantana
3 black-eyed Susans (Thunbergia alata)

1 Line the lower half of the basket with moss.

2 Plant the nasturtiums into the side of the basket by resting the root-balls on the moss, and carefully guiding the leaves through the wires.

3 Line the rest of the basket with moss. Fill the basket with compost (soil mix), working a teaspoon of slow-release plant food granules into the top layer.

4 Plant the lantana in the centre of the basket.

5 Plant the black-eyed Susans around the lantana. Water well and hang in a sunny position.

GARDENER'S TIP

Save some of the nasturtium seeds for next year's baskets and pots – they are among the easiest of plants to grow and some of the seeds are quite likely to find their own way into nearby cracks and crevices.

PLANT IN LATE SPRING OR EARLY SUMMER

A wild one

Native plants are those that have grown naturally in the countryside for thousands of years. Some of the most colourful ones are cornfield flowers, but many are quite rare now. To enjoy them this summer, sow a pot full of wild flowers to stand on your doorstep.

FLOWER POT

MATERIALS

Pebbles
Very large flower pot
Garden soil

WILD FLOWER SEEDS

PLANTS

PEBBLES

Packet of wild flower seeds

GARDEN SOIL

1 Put a few pebbles in the base of the pot for drainage.

2 Fill the pot with garden soil, taking out any bits of roots or large stones.

3 Make sure the surface is level, then sprinkle a large pinch of flower seeds evenly on top.

4 Cover the seeds lightly with soil, just so you can't see them any more, and water them in with a gentle sprinkle.

GARDENER'S TIP

Remember to keep watering as the flowers grow!
Pots need much more watering than beds because the water drains away.

PLANT IN EARLY SPRING

A pastel composition

Pure white pelargonium blooms emerge from a sea of blue felicias, pinky-blue brachycome daisies and verbenas in this romantic basket.

PELARGONIUM

MATERIALS

36cm (14in) hanging basket
Sphagnum moss
Compost (soil mix)
Slow-release plant food granules

PLANTS

2 pink verbenas
2 Brachycome 'Pink Mist'
Blue felicia
White pelargonium

VERBENA

BRACHYCOME

FELICIA

1 Line the basket with moss and fill with compost (soil mix). Work a teaspoon of plant food granules into the top layer.

2 Plant the verbenas opposite each other at the edge of the basket, so that the foliage will tumble over the sides.

3 Plant the brachycome daisies around the edge of the basket. Plant the felicia off-centre in the middle of the basket.

4 Plant the pelargonium off-centre in the remaining space in the middle of the basket. Water thoroughly and hang in a sunny position.

GARDENER'S TIP

White pelargonium flowers discolour as they age; be sure to pick them off to keep the basket looking at its best.

PLANT IN LATE SPRING OR EARLY SUMMER

Daisy chains

The soft yellow of the marguerites' flowers is emphasized by combining them with yellow-leaved helichrysum and bright blue felicia in this summery basket.

MARGUERITE

HELICHRYSUM

FELICIA

MATERIALS

40cm (16in) hanging basket
Sphagnum moss
Compost (soil mix)
Slow-release plant food granules

PLANTS

3 variegated felicias
3 yellow marguerites
  (argyranthemums)
3 Helichrysum petiolare 'Aureum'

GARDENER'S TIP

Pinch out the growing tips
of the marguerites regularly to
encourage bushy plants.

PLANT IN LATE SPRING OR
EARLY SUMMER

1 Line the lower half of the basket with moss. Plant the felicias into the sides of the basket by resting the root-balls on the moss, and carefully guiding the foliage through the wires.

2 Line the rest of the basket with moss. Fill with compost (soil mix), working a teaspoon of plant food granules into the top layer. Plant the marguerites in the top of the basket.

3 Plant the helichrysums between the marguerites, angling the plants to encourage them to grow over the edge of the basket. Water well and hang in full or partial sun.

Begonias and fuchsias

Fuchsias are wonderful hanging basket plants as they flower prolifically late into the autumn. By the end of summer, when the other plants may start to look a bit straggly, the fuchsia will be at its best with a glorious display of colour.

MATERIALS

36cm (14in) hanging basket
Sphagnum moss
Compost (soil mix)
Slow-release plant
    food granules

PLANTS

2 Diascia *'Ruby Field'*
3 Helichrysum microphyllum
Fuchsia *'Rose Winston'* or
    similar soft pink
3 deep pink begonias

BEGONIA

DIASCIA

HELICHRYSUM

FUCHSIA

1 Line the lower half of the basket with moss and arrange the diascias and helichrysums in the basket to decide where to plant each one. Ensure they do not become tangled in the wires.

2 Plant the two diascias into the sides of the basket by resting the root-balls in the moss, and gently feeding the foliage through the wires.

GARDENER'S TIP

If some of the plants in the basket begin to look straggly in comparison with the fuchsia, cut them right back and give a liquid feed – they will grow with renewed vigour and provide a wonderful autumn show.

PLANT IN LATE SPRING OR EARLY SUMMER

3 Line the rest of the basket with moss, partly fill with compost (soil mix) and plant the three helichrysums into the side of the basket near the rim.

4 Fill the basket with compost (soil mix). Work a teaspoon of plant food granules into the top layer of compost. Plant the fuchsia in the centre of the basket.

5 Finally, plant the three begonias around the fuchsia. Water well and hang the basket in full sun or partial shade.

Pot of sunflowers

Sunflowers grow very well in
pots provided you are not
growing the giant varieties.
Grow your own from seed;
there are many kinds to choose
from, including the one with
double flowers used here.

MATERIALS

30cm (12in) glazed pot
Polystyrene (plastic foam) or
  similar drainage material
Equal mix loam-based compost
  (soil mix) and container
  compost
Slow-release plant food granules

PLANTS

3 strong sunflower seedlings,
approximately 20cm (8in) tall

SUNFLOWER
SEEDLING

GARDENER'S TIP

Allow at least one of the sunflower
heads to set seed. As the plant
starts to die back, cut off the seedhead
and hang it upside-down to ripen.
Reserve some seeds for next year
and then hang the seedhead outside
for the birds.

PLANT SEEDS IN SPRING
AND SEEDLINGS IN SUMMER TO
FLOWER IN LATE SUMMER

1 Line the base of the pot with
drainage material and fill with
the compost (soil mix). Scoop out
evenly spaced holes for each
seedling and plant, firming the
compost around the plants.

2 Scatter 1 tablespoon of plant
food granules on the surface
of the compost (soil mix). Place in
a sunny position, out of the wind,
and water regularly.

Alpine sink

An old stone sink is a perfect container for a collection of alpine plants. The rock helps to create the effect of a miniature landscape and provides shelter for some of the plants. The sink is set up on the stand of an old sewing machine so that the plants can be admired easily.

MATERIALS
....

Stone sink or trough 76 x 50cm (30 x 20in)
Crocks (broken pots) or other suitable drainage material
Moss-covered rock
Loam-based compost (soil mix) with $1/3$ added coarse grit
Washed gravel

PLANTS
....

Achillea tomentosa
Veronica peduncularis
Hebe
Ivy
Sedum ewersii
Aster natalensis
Alpine willow (Salix alpina)
Arabis ferdinandi-coburgi
  'Variegata'

HEBE

SEDUM

ACHILLEA

IVY

VERONICA

1 Cover the drainage hole of the sink with crocks (broken pots). Position the rock. Do this before adding the soil to create the effect of a natural rocky outcrop. Pour the compost (soil mix) into the sink.

2 Plan the position of your plants so that the end result will have a good balance of shape and colour. If the sink is very shallow you will need to scoop out the soil right to the base before planting but alpine plants are used to shallow soil. Make sure that the bottom leaves of low-growing plants are level with the soil. Too low and they will rot; too high and they will dry out.

3 When all the plants are in place, carefully pour washed gravel all around them to cover the whole soil area. Water and place in full or partial sun.

Flowers for late summer

Although this windowbox is already looking good, towards the end of the summer it will really come into its own – by then the vibrant red and purple flowers of the pelargonium, salvias and lavenders will be at their most prolific.

MATERIALS

60cm (24in) wooden planter, stained black
Polystyrene (plastic foam) or other suitable drainage material
Compost (soil mix)
Slow-release plant food granules

PLANTS

Pelargonium *'Tomcat'*
2 *Lavenders* (Lavandula pinnata)
2 Salvia *'Raspberry Royal'*
2 *blue brachycome daisies*
Convolvulus sabatius
6 *rose-pink alyssum*

ALYSSUM

CONVOLVULUS

BRACHYCOME

LAVENDER

SALVIA

PELARGONIUM

1 Line the base of the container with polystyrene (plastic foam) or similar drainage material. Fill the windowbox with compost (soil mix), working in 3 teaspoons of slow-release plant food granules. Plant the pelargonium at the back of the windowbox, in the centre.

2 Plant the two lavenders in the rear corners of the box.

3 Plant the salvias at the front on either side of the pelargonium.

4 Plant the brachycome daisies in the front corners of the windowbox.

5 Plant the convolvulus in the centre, in front of the pelargonium.

6 Fill the spaces with the alyssum. Water well and place in a sunny position.

GARDENER'S TIP

Both the lavenders and the salvias are highly aromatic, so if possible position this box near a door or a path, so that you can enjoy the fragrance as you brush against the plants.

PLANT IN EARLY SUMMER

Autumn hanging basket

Towards the end of the season the colours of summer hanging baskets do not always marry happily with the reds and golds of autumn. This is the time to plant a richly coloured hanging basket for winter.

MATERIALS

30cm (12in) hanging basket
Plastic pot
Sphagnum moss
Equal mix loam-based compost
  (soil mix) and container compost
Slow-release plant food granules

PLANTS

4 winter-flowering pansies
3 variegated ivies
Euonymus fortunei ('Emerald
  and Gold' was used here)
2 dahlias

DAHLIA

PANSY

IVY

EUONYMUS

1 Support the hanging basket on a pot. Unhook the chain from one fixing point so that it hangs down one side of the basket. Line the base and bottom half of the basket with a generous layer of sphagnum moss.

2 Pour in compost (soil mix) until it is level with the top of the moss. Plant a layer of three pansies and three ivies, passing the foliage through the wire of the basket, so that the root-balls of the plants are resting on the compost.

3 Line the rest of the basket with moss and top up with compost (soil mix), firming it around the roots of the ivies and pansies. Then plant the remaining plants in the top of the basket, with the euonymus in the centre and the remaining pansy and dahlias surrounding it. Scatter a tablespoon of slow-release plant food granules on to the compost and water the hanging basket well. Re-attach the chain and hang the basket in full or partial sun.

GARDENER'S TIP

Although special composts (soil mixes) with water-retaining gel are a boon for summer baskets, they can get water-logged in later months. Mix equal parts of loam-based and container composts for autumn and winter planting.

PLANT IN SPRING OR SUMMER TO FLOWER IN AUTUMN

Heather windowbox

This is a perfect project for an absolute beginner as it is extremely simple to achieve. The bark windowbox is a sympathetic container for the heathers, which look quite at home in their bed of moss.

MATERIALS
....

30cm (12in) bark windowbox
Crocks (broken pots) or other
  suitable drainage material
Ericaceous compost (soil mix)
Bun moss

PLANTS
....

Heathers

HEATHERS

1 Put a layer of crocks or other suitable drainage material in the bottom of the box.

2 Remove the heathers from their pots and position them in the windowbox.

GARDENER'S TIP

Do not be tempted to use ordinary compost (soil mix) as it contains lime which, with few exceptions, is not suitable for the majority of heathers.

PLANT IN AUTUMN

3 Fill the gaps between the plants with the compost (soil mix), pressing it around the plants. Water in well.

4 Tuck the bun moss snugly around the plants so that no soil is visible. Place in full or partial sun.

Evergreens with extra colour

They may be easy to look after but all-year-round window-boxes can start to look a bit lifeless after a couple of seasons. It does not take much trouble to add a few seasonal flowers and it makes all the difference to a display.

MATERIALS

76cm (30in) plastic windowbox
Compost (soil mix)
Slow-release plant food granules

PLANTS

Hebe 'Baby Marie'
Convolvulus cneorum
Potentilla 'Nunk'
Variegated ivies
2 Diascia 'Ruby Field'
Pink marguerite (Argyranthemum 'Flamingo')

IVY

CONVOLVULUS

POTENTILLA

MARGUERITE

DIASCIA

HEBE

1 Check the drainage holes are open in the base and, if not, drill or punch them open. Fill the windowbox with compost (soil mix), adding in 3 teaspoons of slow-release plant food granules. Plant the hebe in the centre.

2 Plant the convolvulus near one end of the windowbox.

3 Plant the potentilla near the other end of the windowbox.

4 Plant the two ivies at the front corners of the windowbox.

5 Plant the diascias on either side of the hebe at the front of the windowbox.

6 Plant the marguerite between the hebe and the convolvulus at the back. Water well and stand in full or partial sun.

GARDENER'S TIP

At the end of the summer, remove the diascias and marguerite, feed the remaining plants with more granules, and fill the spaces with winter-flowering plants such as pansies or heathers.

PLANT IN SPRING

Classic topiary

MATERIALS

4 large terracotta pots
Bark chippings
Crocks (broken pots) or other
suitable drainage material
Equal mix loam-based compost
(soil mix) and container compost
Slow-release plant food granules

PLANTS

4 box trees (Buxus sempervirens)
in different topiary shapes

BOX TREES (*BUXUS SEMPERVIRENS*)

The clean lines of the topiary are matched by the simplicity of the terracotta pots. Since the eye is drawn to the outlines of the box plants, decorated pots would be a distraction.

1 If the plant has been well looked after in the nursery it may not need potting on yet. In this case simply slip the plant in its pot into the terracotta container.

2 To conserve moisture and conceal the plastic pot, cover with a generous layer of bark chippings.

3 To repot a box tree, first place a good layer of crocks or other drainage material in the bottom of the pot. Remove the tree from its plastic pot and place it in the terracotta container. Surround the root-ball with compost (soil mix), pushing it well down the sides.

4 Scatter a tablespoon of plant food granules on top of the compost (soil mix) and top with a layer of bark chippings. Water well and position in sun or partial shade.

GARDENER'S TIP

Don't get carried away when you trim topiary. Little and often, with an ordinary pair of scissors, is better than occasional dramatic gestures with a pair of shears.

PLANT AT ANY
TIME OF THE YEAR

Trug of winter pansies

Winter pansies are wonderfully resilient and will bloom bravely throughout the winter as long as they are regularly dead-headed. This trug may be moved around to provide colour wherever it is needed, and acts as a perfect antidote to mid-winter gloom.

MATERIALS

Old wooden trug
Sphagnum moss
Compost (soil mix)
Slow-release plant
 food granules

PLANTS

15 winter-flowering pansies
(violas)

PANSIES

1 Line the trug with a layer of sphagnum moss. Fill the moss lining with compost (soil mix).

2 Plant the pansies by starting at one end and filling the spaces between the plants with compost (soil mix) as you go. Gently firm each plant into position and add a final layer of compost mixed with a tablespoon of plant food granules around the pansies. Water and place in a fairly sunny position.

GARDENER'S TIP

Not everyone has an old trug available, but an old basket, colander, or an enamel bread bin could be used instead. Junk shops and flea markets are a great source of containers that are too battered for their original use, but fine for planting.

PLANT IN AUTUMN TO FLOWER IN WINTER

Evergreen garden

Evergreen plants come in many shapes, sizes and shades. Grouped in containers they will provide you with year-round interest and colour.

MATERIALS

Terracotta pots of various sizes
Crocks (broken pots) or similar drainage material
Equal mix loam-based compost (soil mix) and container compost
Plant saucers
Gravel
Slow-release plant food granules

PLANTS

False cypress (Chamaecyparis lawsoniana *'Columnaris';* C. pisifera *'Filifera Aurea'*)
Berberis darwinii
Berberis thunbergii *'Atropurpurea Nana'*
Pachysandra terminalis
Bergenia

FALSE CYPRESS

BERGENIA

BERBERIS

PACHYSANDRA

GARDENER'S TIP

Include some golden or variegated foliage amongst your evergreens and choose contrasting leaf forms to make a striking group.

PLANT AT ANY
TIME OF THE YEAR

1 Large shrubs, such as this conifer, should be potted into a proportionally large container. Place plenty of crocks (broken pots) at the base of the pot. If the plant is at all potbound, tease the roots loose before planting in its new pot. Fill around the root-ball with compost (soil mix), pressing it down firmly around the edges of the pot.

2 Smaller plants, like bergenia, should be planted in a larger pot than the original. Place crocks in the base of the pot, position the plant and then fill around the edges with compost (soil mix). Repeat with the remaining plants.

3 Plants will stay moist longer if they are stood in saucers of wet gravel. This group of plants will do well positioned in partial shade. Water regularly and feed with slow-release plant food granules in the spring and autumn.

Year-round windowbox

In the same way that a garden has certain plants that provide structure throughout the year, this window box has been planted so that there is always plenty of foliage. Extra colour may be introduced each season by including small flowering plants, such as heathers.

MATERIALS

90cm (3ft) wooden windowbox, preferably self-watering
Equal mix loam-based compost (soil mix) and container compost
Slow-release plant food granules
Bark chippings

PLANTS

Skimmia reevesiana 'Rubella'
2 Arundinaria pygmaea
2 Cotoneaster conspicuus
2 periwinkles (Vinca minor 'Variegata')
6 heathers

ARUNDINARIA

PERIWINKLE   COTONEASTER   SKIMMIA   HEATHER

1 If you are using a self-watering container, feed the wicks through the base of the plastic liner. Slip the liner into the wooden windowbox.

2 Before you start planting, plan the position of the plants so that the colours and shapes look well balanced. Remove the plants from their pots, tease loose their roots if they look at all potbound and position in the windowbox. Top up with compost (soil mix).

3 Once the structure plants are in place you can add the colour; in this case, the heathers. Scoop out a hole for each heather and then plant, pressing firmly around each one. Scatter two tablespoons of plant food granules over the surface.

4 Top-dress the windowbox with a layer of bark chippings; this will help to conserve moisture. Water thoroughly.

GARDENER'S TIP

Plants do not need watering in winter, unless they are sheltered from the rain. Even then they should be watered sparingly and not in frosty weather. Self-watering containers should be drained before winter to prevent frost damage.

PLANT AT ANY TIME OF THE YEAR

Winter cheer

Many windowboxes are left unplanted through the winter, but you can soon brighten the house or garden during this season with an easy arrangement of pot-grown plants plunged in bark.

MATERIALS

40cm (16in) glazed windowbox
Bark chippings

PLANTS

2 miniature conifers
2 variegated ivies
2 red polyanthus

POLYANTHUS   CONIFER

IVY

1 Water all the plants. Place the conifers, still in their pots, at each end of the windowbox.

2 Half-fill the windowbox with bark chippings.

3 Place the pots of polyanthus on the bark chippings between the two conifers.

4 Place the pots of ivy in the front corners of the windowbox. Add further bark chippings to the container until all the pots are concealed. Water only when plants show signs of dryness. Stand in any position.

GARDENER'S TIP

When it is time to replant the windowbox, plunge the conifers, still in their pots, in a shady position in the garden. Water well through the spring and summer and they may be used again next year.

PLANT IN EARLY WINTER

Classic winter colours

Convolvulus cneorum is an attractive small shrub with eye-catching silver-grey leaves, which last through winter, and white flowers in spring and summer. Planted with ice-blue pansies, it makes a softly subtle display from autumn to spring.

MATERIALS

30cm (12in) hanging basket
Sphagnum moss
Compost (soil mix)

PLANTS

8 silver/blue pansies (Viola
'Silver Wings', or similar)
Convolvulus cneorum

CONVOLVULUS

PANSIES

1 Half-line the basket with moss and fill with compost (soil mix) to the top of the moss. Plant four of the pansies into the side of the basket by placing their root-balls on the compost, and gently guiding the leaves through the side of the basket.

2 Line the rest of the basket with moss and top up with compost (soil mix). Plant the convolvulus in the basket centre.

3 Plant the remaining four pansies around the convolvulus. Water well and hang in sun or partial shade.

GARDENER'S TIP

At the end of the winter cut back any dead wood or straggly branches on the *Convolvulus cneorum*, and give a liquid feed to encourage new growth. Small shrubs such as this may be used in hanging baskets for one season, but will then need planting into a larger container or the border.

PLANT IN AUTUMN

Gothic ivy

Twisted willow branches set into a chimney pot offer an attractive support for ivy, and will provide welcome interest in the winter.

MATERIALS

Chimney pot
Compost (soil mix)
90cm (3ft) wire netting

PLANTS

4–5 branches of twisted willow
Large ivy (Hedera helix var. hibernica was used here)

IVY

1 Place the chimney pot in its final position (in shade or half-shade) and half-fill with compost (soil mix). Fold or crumple the wire netting down into the chimney pot so that it rests on the compost.

2 Arrange the willow branches in the chimney pot, pushing the stems through the wire netting.

3 Rest the ivy, in its pot, on the wire netting amongst the willow branches. Fill the chimney pot with compost (soil mix) to within 10cm (4in) of the rim. Cut loose any ties and remove the cane.

4 Arrange the stems of ivy over the willow branches and water. To start with it may look rather contrived, but as the ivy settles into its new surroundings it will attach itself to the willow.

GARDENER'S TIP

You may find that some of your twisted willow branches take root in the compost (soil mix). Plant a rooted branch in the garden where it will grow into a tree. It will eventually be quite large so do not plant it near the house.

PLANT AT ANY TIME OF THE YEAR

Golden Christmas holly

Evergreen standard holly trees are splendid container plants. This golden holly in a gilded pot has been dressed up for Christmas with bows and baubles.

HOLLY

MATERIALS

40cm (16in) terracotta pot
Gold spray-paint
Crocks (broken pots) or
  similar drainage material
Composted manure
Loam-based compost (soil mix)
Pine cones
90cm (3ft) wired ribbon
Tin Christmas decorations

PLANTS

Golden holly

1 Spray the pot with gold paint and leave to dry. Place a good layer of drainage material in the base. Cover with a 7.5cm (3in) layer of composted manure and a thin layer of loam-based potting compost (soil mix). Remove the holly from its existing container and place in the gilded pot.

2 Surround the root-ball with compost (soil mix), pressing down firmly to ensure that the tree is firmly planted, and cover the surface with pine cones.

3 Tie the ribbon into a bow around the trunk of the tree. Spray the decorations gold and hang in the branches. Water the tree to settle it in, but do not do this on a frosty day.

GARDENER'S TIP

In the autumn, plant some corms of *Iris reticulata* or similar small bulbs in the compost (soil mix) surrounding the tree for a delightful spring display.

PLANT IN AUTUMN, WINTER OR SPRING

An evergreen wall basket

Pansies will flower throughout the winter. Even if they are flattened by rain, frost or snow, at the first sign of improvement in the weather their heads will pop up again to bring brightness to the dullest day. They have been planted with ivies to provide colour from early autumn through to late spring.

MATERIALS

30cm (12in) wall basket
Sphagnum moss
Compost (soil mix)

PLANTS

2 golden variegated ivies
2 copper pansies (viola)
Yellow pansy (viola)

PANSIES

IVY

GARDENER'S TIP

Winter baskets do not need regular feeding and should only be watered in very dry conditions. To prolong the flowering life of the pansies, dead-head regularly and pinch out any straggly stems to encourage new shoots from the base.

PLANT IN AUTUMN

1 Line the basket with moss. Three-quarters fill the basket with compost (soil mix) and position the ivies with their root-balls resting on the compost. Guide the stems through the sides of the basket so that they trail downwards. Pack more moss around the ivies and top up the basket with compost.

2 Plant the two copper pansies at either end of the basket.

3 Plant the yellow pansy in the centre. Water well and hang in shade or semi-shade.

Edible Collections

What could be nicer than reaching out of the kitchen window to gather fresh herbs from the window-sill, or eating succulent tomatoes or strawberries grown on the balcony? If you don't have room for a vegetable patch, even if you don't have a garden at all, you can still enjoy home-grown produce if you plant it in containers. Go for compact varieties of beans and tomatoes, and choose lettuces such as 'Salad Bowl' so that you can pick just what you need and leave the plants to go on growing. You will be able to grow a wide range: you could even try a few early potatoes in a pot, for the first and most delicious crop of the year.

Kitchen-garden containers can be beautiful, too. Alpine strawberries are both decorative and delicious tumbling out of a hanging basket, and you can grow herbs for their looks as well as their flavour, choosing variegated mints, red-leaved basil or purple sage to contribute to the visual feast.

ABOVE: *Herbs thrive on a sunny windowsill.*

Herbs in the shade

Although the Mediterranean herbs need lots of sunshine, there are many others which prefer a cooler situation to look and taste their best. This windowbox, ideal for just outside the kitchen door or window, has an interesting variety of mints, sorrel, chives, lemon balm and parsley.

MATERIALS

50cm (20in) terracotta
  windowbox
Polystyrene (plastic foam) or
  other suitable drainage material
Compost (soil mix)
Slow-release plant food granules,
  pelleted chicken manure, or
  similar organic plant food

PLANTS

Lemon balm
3 mints (black peppermint, silver
  mint and curly spearmint were
  used here)
Sorrel
Chives
Parsley

LEMON BALM

MINTS

CHIVE

SORREL

PARSLEY

MINT

1 Line the base of the container with polystyrene (plastic foam) or similar drainage material. Top up with compost (soil mix). Work in 3 teaspoons of plant food granules or organic alternative.

2 Plant the lemon balm and two of the mints along the back of the windowbox.

3 Plant the third mint, the sorrel and the chives along the front. Finally, plant the parsley in the centre. Position the box in light shade and water thoroughly.

GARDENER'S TIP

Use the freshly picked mint to make refreshing teas. Pour hot boiled water over a few washed leaves and infuse for five minutes.

PLANT IN EARLY SPRING

Vital ingredients

A lovely present for an enthusiastic cook, this windowbox contains chervil, coriander, fennel, garlic, purple sage, French tarragon, savory, origanum and basil.

MATERIALS

45cm (18in) wooden windowbox
Crocks (broken pots) or other
*   suitable drainage material*
Compost (soil mix)
Slow-release plant food granules,
*   pelleted chicken manure, or*
*   similar organic plant food*

PLANTS

French tarragon
Chervil
Garlic
Coriander (cilantro)
Purple sage
Basil
Fennel
Savory
Origanum

FENNEL

GARLIC

SAVORY

BASIL

ORIGANUM

CORIANDER

CHERVIL

FRENCH TARRAGON

PURPLE SAGE

GARDENER'S TIP

There are now various kinds of basil seed available (some specialists sell at least 12), with varieties ranging from Greek to Indonesian. The key point when growing them is to remove the flower buds the moment they appear as the leaves will quickly lose their flavour once the flowers open.

PLANT IN SPRING

1 Line the base of the container with a layer of drainage material. Fill the windowbox with compost (soil mix). Work in a teaspoon of plant food granules or an organic alternative.

2 Before planting the herbs, arrange them in the windowbox in their pots.

3 Plant the back row of herbs in the windowbox first.

4 Plant more herbs at the front of the windowbox. Water well and stand in a sunny position.

Wine case herb garden

Add a coat of varnish to an old wine case to make an attractive and durable container for a miniature herb garden. The container can be placed near the kitchen door or on a balcony.

MATERIALS

Wooden wine case
Pliers
Sandpaper
Paintbrush
Light oak semi-matt varnish
Crocks (broken pots) or similar
  drainage material
Compost (soil mix) with $\frac{1}{3}$
  added coarse grit
Slow-release plant food granules
  or pelleted chicken manure
Bark chippings

PLANTS

Selection of 7 herbs, such as sage, chives, parsley, mint, tarragon, lemon thyme and creeping thyme

SAGE

PARSLEY

CHIVES

GARDENER'S TIP

Some herbs like cool, partial shade while others like hot, dry, free-draining soil. A mixed herb garden will thrive for only one growing season.

PLANT IN SPRING

1 Remove any wire staples from around the edges of the box and sand down the rough edges. Apply two coats of varnish on the inside and outside of the box, allowing the varnish to dry thoroughly between coats. When dry, cover the base of the box with a layer of crocks or similar drainage material.

2 Before planting, decide how you are going to arrange the plants in the container to achieve a pleasing balance of colour, height and shape.

3 Fill the box with compost (soil mix) and plant from one end of the box to the other. Loosen the root-balls, as this will help the plants to root into the surrounding compost.

4 When the planting is complete, scatter 2 tablespoons of plant food granules or pelleted chicken manure on the compost (soil mix) surface. Firm in the plants and mulch with bark chippings to retain moisture. Water well.

The good life

This windowbox will not exactly make you self-sufficient, but it is surprising how many different vegetables can be grown in a small space. It is perfect for anyone who likes the taste of home-grown vegetables but does not have a garden to grow them in.

MATERIALS

76cm (30in) plastic windowbox
Compost (soil mix)
Slow-release plant food granules, pelleted chicken manure or similar organic plant food

PLANTS

Garlic
3 Chinese leaves (Bok Choy)
4 plugs of beetroot (see Gardener's Tip)
Pepper plant
3 dwarf French (fine) beans
3 plugs of shallots

BEETROOT

CHINESE LEAVES

GARLIC

FRENCH BEAN

PEPPER

SHALLOTS

1 Check the drainage holes are open in the container's base. Fill the windowbox with compost (soil mix), working in 2 teaspoons of slow-release plant food granules or an organic alternative. Start planting from one end.

2 Starting at the right-hand end of the windowbox, first plant the garlic. Next plant the Chinese leaves (Bok Choy).

3 Follow these with the plugs of beetroot.

4 Plant the pepper plant next, just to the left of the centre.

5 Now plant the three dwarf French bean plants.

6 Finally, plant the shallot plugs in the left-hand corner. Water well and stand in full or partial sun.

GARDENER'S TIP

It is now possible to buy plugs of small vegetable plants at garden centres. There is no need to separate the plants provided there is sufficient room between the clumps.

PLANT IN SPRING

A taste for flowers

It is often said that something "looks good enough to eat", and in this instance it is true. All the flowers in this windowbox may be used for flavour and garnishes.

MATERIALS

36cm (14in) terracotta
windowbox
Crocks (broken pots) or other
suitable drainage material
Compost (soil mix)
Slow-release plant food granules,
pelleted chicken manure or
similar organic plant food

PLANTS

Chives
2 nasturtiums
2 pansies (viola) with well-
marked "faces"
2 pot marigolds (calendula)

CHIVE

NASTURTIUM

PANSY

MARIGOLDS

GARDENER'S TIP

To keep all the plants producing flowers, dead-head regularly. Once a plant has set seed it considers its work done and will produce fewer and fewer flowers.

PLANT IN EARLY SPRING

1 Cover the base with a layer of crocks (broken pots) or similar drainage material. Fill with compost (soil mix), working in 2 teaspoons of plant food granules or an organic alternative. Plant the chives in the right-hand corner.

2 Plant one of the nasturtiums in the left-hand corner and the other centre-front.

3 Plant one pansy at the back next to the chives, and the other at the front to the left of the central nasturtium.

4 Plant one of the marigolds at the back between the pansy and nasturtium, and the other one just behind the central nasturtium.

A hanging garden of herbs

A basket of herbs is both decorative and useful, especially when hung near the kitchen door or window. Herbs benefit from regular picking to encourage the plants to produce lots of tender new shoots throughout the summer. Some herbs can be very vigorous so be sure to choose compact varieties for your hanging basket.

MATERIALS

30cm (12in) hanging basket
Sphagnum moss
Compost (soil mix)
Slow-release plant food granules

PLANTS

5 parsley
French tarragon
Sage
Rosemary (prostrate form)
2 basil

PARSLEY

FRENCH
TARRAGON

BASIL

ROSEMARY

SAGE

GARDENER'S TIP

Fortunately, the strongly aromatic nature of most herbs does dissuade pests, but if you should have any problems be sure to use a safe organic pesticide. Soapy washing-up water can be used against greenfly.

PLANT IN SPRING

1 Line the lower half of the basket with moss. Plant the parsley, resting the root-balls on the moss and feeding the leaves through the sides of the basket.

2 Line the rest of the basket with moss and fill with compost (soil mix). Work a teaspoon of plant food granules into the top. Plant the tarragon.

3 Plant the sage. Plant the prostrate rosemary, angling it slightly to encourage it to grow over the side of the basket.

4 Finally, plant the two basil plants and water well before hanging in partial sun. A regular liquid feed is recommended.

Butler's tray kitchen garden

Not many of us have the space or time to maintain a kitchen garden, but this table-top selection of plants will give you a taste of the delights to be had, and might even inspire you to try the real thing.

MATERIALS

Terracotta pots of various sizes
Crocks (broken pots) or other
* suitable drainage material*
Compost (soil mix)
Butler's tray
Thick plastic sheet
Clay granules

PLANTS

Selection of kitchen garden plants, such as pot marigolds (calendula), basil, nasturtium, miniature tomato, strawberry and French tarragon

STRAWBERRY

TARRAGON

TOMATO

NASTURTIUM

MARIGOLD   BASIL

1 If the plants have well-developed root systems, like this marigold, they will benefit from being planted in a larger pot. Place crocks (broken pots) in the bottom of the pots for drainage. Gently tease loose some of the roots before you repot the plant.

2 You may be able to divide a single basil plant when repotting, enabling you to fill two pots. The miniature tomato and the strawberry should be planted in larger pots to allow plenty of room for root development.

3 Nasturtiums flower better in poor soil. Once you have planted them, leave them to their own devices. Give them a little water but no plant food or you will get lots of leaves and very few flowers.

4 Line your tray with a thick plastic sheet and cover it with clay granules. These retain moisture and create a damp micro-climate for the plants. Arrange your plants on the tray, place in a sunny position and water and feed (except the nasturtiums) regularly.

GARDENER'S TIP

The marigolds and nasturtiums are not purely decorative, the flowers and leaves of both are edible and can be used in salads.

PLANT IN LATE SPRING OR EARLY SUMMER

Beans and parsley in a basket

A hanging basket planted with dwarf beans and parsley can be surprisingly productive and will outwit all but the most acrobatic of snails.

MATERIALS

36cm (14in) hanging basket
Sphagnum moss
Compost (soil mix)
Slow-release plant food granules

PLANTS

7 parsley plants
3 dwarf (fine) bean plants

PARSLEY

DWARF BEAN

1 Line the lower half of the basket with moss and half-fill with compost (soil mix).

2 Plant the parsley into the sides, resting the root-balls on the compost (soil mix) and feeding the leaves through the wires.

3 Gently separate the bean plants from one another.

4 Line the upper half of the basket with moss and add more compost (soil mix). Add a teaspoon of slow-release plant food granules into the top layer. Plant the beans in the compost. Water the basket thoroughly and hang in partial sun.

GARDENER'S TIP

Fruit and vegetable hanging baskets need quite a lot of attention to crop well. They should be kept moist at all times and need a liquid feed once a week. If you are going to be away, move the basket into the shade, where it will not dry out so quickly.

PLANT IN SPRING

Wild strawberry basket

Wild strawberries can be grown in a basket and enjoyed anywhere, whether in the countryside or a small city garden.

1 Line the base and sides of the basket with a generous layer of sphagnum moss.

2 Fill the lined area with compost (soil mix). Scoop out a hollow for each strawberry plant, and firm the compost around the root-ball as you plant.

3 Scatter a tablespoon of plant food granules on the surface of the compost (soil mix).

4 Tuck more moss around the edges and under the leaves to conserve moisture and stop the fruit touching the soil. Water and place in full or partial sun.

GARDENER'S TIP

Propagate strawberry runners by pinning the plantlets into small pots of compost (soil mix). A loop of wire or a hairpin placed on either side of the plantlet will hold it firmly in place until it has rooted. Then simply cut the runner and you have a new strawberry plant.

PLANT IN SPRING TO FRUIT
IN SUMMER

Good enough to eat

All the plants in this basket bear an edible crop: the tomato fruit, nasturtium flowers and parsley leaves. You could even impress your family or guests with a 'hanging basket salad', using all three together.

MATERIALS

36cm (14in) hanging basket
Sphagnum moss
Compost (soil mix)
Slow-release plant food granules

PLANTS

6 parsley plants
3 trailing nasturtiums
3 'Tumbler' tomatoes, or similar

PARSLEY

TRAILING
NASTURTIUM

TOMATO

GARDENER'S TIP

If you would prefer to grow your plants organically, plant this basket using an organic compost (soil mix) and use natural plant foods such as pelleted chicken manure or a liquid seaweed feed.

PLANT IN LATE SPRING OR EARLY SUMMER

1 Line the lower half of the basket with moss.

2 Plant three parsley plants into the side of the basket by resting the root-balls on the moss, and feeding the leaves through the side of the basket.

3 Line the basket to just below the rim and fill with compost (soil mix). Work a teaspoon of plant food granules into the top of the compost. Plant three nasturtium plants into the side of the basket, just below the rim.

4 Finish lining the basket with moss, being careful to tuck plenty of moss around the nasturtiums.

5 Plant the tomato plants in the top of the basket.

6 Plant the remaining three parsley plants amongst the tomatoes in the top of the basket. Water well and hang in a sunny position. Liquid feed regularly.

Summer fruits

The red of ripening strawberries is matched by vibrant red pelargonium flowers in this unusual arrangement. Alpine strawberry plants make a good contrast, with their delicate fruit and tendrils.

ALPINE
STRAWBERRY

STRAWBERRY

PELARGONIUM

MATERIALS

36cm (14in) hanging basket
Sphagnum moss
Compost (soil mix)
Slow-release plant food granules
  or organic plant food

PLANTS

3 'Maxim' strawberry plants, or
  similar
Pelargonium 'Miss Flora', or
  similar
3 alpine strawberry plants

1 Line the basket with moss.

4 Plant the alpine strawberries in between the larger strawberry plants. Water well, and hang in partial or full sun.

GARDENER'S TIP

After the large strawberries have fruited, cut back all their foliage to encourage the formation of next year's flowers. The pelargonium and alpine strawberries will stop the basket looking too bare while the new foliage is growing.

PLANT IN SPRING

2 Fill the basket with compost (soil mix). Work a teaspoon of slow-release plant food granules into the top layer of compost. Plant the strawberry plants around the side of the basket.

3 Plant the pelargonium in the centre of the basket.

Home-grown salads

These compact but heavy-fruiting tomato plants have been specially bred to be grown in containers. Teamed with lettuce, radishes, chives and parsley, they provide all the ingredients for a fresh garden salad.

GARDENER'S TIP

Keep the tomato plants watered at all times, and liquid feed with a proprietary tomato food or liquid seaweed fertilizer.

PLANT IN SPRING

MATERIALS

76cm (30in) plastic windowbox
Compost (soil mix)
Slow-release plant food granules, pelleted chicken manure or similar organic plant food

PLANTS

3 'Tumbler' tomatoes
Chives
4 lettuces, 'Little Gem' (Romaine hearts) or 'Corsair'
2 'Salad Bowl' lettuces
4 parsley plants
Radish seed

TOMATO

LETTUCE

CHIVES

LETTUCE

PARSLEY

1 Check the drainage holes are open in the base of the windowbox and, if not, drill or punch them open. Fill with compost (soil mix), working in 2 teaspoons of slow-release plant food granules or organic alternative. Plant the tomatoes, evenly spaced, along the centre.

2 Plant the chives in front of the middle tomato plant. Plant the 'Little Gem' (Romaine hearts) or 'Corsair' lettuces diagonally to one another between the tomato plants.

3 Plant the 'Salad Bowl' lettuces in the front corners. Plant the parsley plant diagonally opposite one another alongside the 'Little Gem' or 'Corsair' lettuces.

4 Scatter radish seed between the plants and gently rake into the soil. Water thoroughly and stand in a sunny position.

Scented Collections

Scent gives a lovely extra dimension to container planting schemes, especially for planters that are sited at "nose" level, such as windowboxes. On warm days the aromas will drift in through open windows. Use plants with scented leaves for a really lasting effect: herbs such as lavender and mint are invaluable foils for larger-flowered plants and will fill the air with fragrance. The scented-leaf pelargoniums are perfect container plants and you can choose from a wide variety of lovely variegations and leaf shapes as well as perfumes that range from lemon and mint to rose. Their charming pink flowers are an added bonus. Put scented plants in containers near paths and doorways, where their rich fragrances will be released each time you brush past them. A fragrant plant in a pot by the front door makes a special welcome for visitors.

ABOVE: *Lavender is always a favourite for its delightful scent. Here it is combined with scaevolas and trailing convolvulus.*

Scented windowbox

The soft silvers and blues of the flowers and foliage beautifully complement this verdigris windowbox. The scent of the lavender and petunias will drift magically through open windows.

MATERIALS

60cm (24in) windowbox
Gravel or similar drainage material
Equal mix loam-based compost (soil mix) and container compost
Slow-release plant food granules

PLANTS

2 lavenders
2 pale blue petunias
4 deep blue petunias
4 Chaenorhinum glareosum (or lilac lobelia)
6 Helichrysum petiolare

PETUNIA

CHAENORHINUM

HELICHRYSUM

LAVENDER

GARDENER'S TIP

To keep a densely planted container like this looking its best it is necessary to feed regularly with a liquid feed, or more simply to mix slow-release plant food granules into the surface of the compost (soil mix) to last the whole summer. Cut back the lavender heads after flowering to ensure bushy flowering plants again next year.

PLANT IN LATE SPRING OR EARLY SUMMER

1 Fill the bottom 5cm (2in) of the windowbox with drainage material and half-fill with compost (soil mix). Position the lavender plants, loosening the soil around the roots before planting, as they will establish better this way.

2 Now arrange the flowering plants around the lavender, leaving spaces for the helichrysums between them.

3 Finally, add the helichrysums and fill between the plants with compost (soil mix), pressing firmly so that no air gaps are left around the roots. Place in a sunny position and water regularly.

Regal rosemary

This spring hanging basket can be created using many different combinations of flowers and herbs.

MATERIALS

35cm (14in) diameter wire
   hanging basket
Moss
Circle of plastic sheeting (can be
   cut from the compost bag), the
   size of a side plate
Compost (soil mix)

PLANTS

1 golden lemon balm plant
1 variegated applemint plant
1 eau-de-cologne mint plant
2 viola plants Viola 'Penny'
3 golden feverfew plants
1 marjoram plant
2 red daisy plants
5 parsley plants
1 rosemary plant
2 cowslip plants
1 pink daisy plant

LEMON BALM
PLANT

APPLEMINT

VIOLA

FEVERFEW

PARSLEY

MARJORAM

ROSEMARY

1 Line the base of the basket with a generous layer of moss. Cover with the circle of plastic sheeting and a thin layer of compost (soil mix). Plant the bottom layer of herbs with the lemon balm in the centre and the two mints to each side, leaving a gap of about 8–10cm (3–4in) between the lemon balm and the mint.

2 Add a collar of moss around each plant and bring the wall of moss one-third of the way up the sides of the basket. Add compost (soil mix) to a depth of about 5cm (2in). Plant the two violas in the gaps between the lemon balm and mints. Plant two golden feverfew at the same level but further round the sides. Secure each plant with more moss, bringing the level two-thirds of the way up the sides of the basket.

3 Plant an upper ring with the marjoram, feverfew and a daisy around the front, and two parsley plants either side. Bring the wall of moss to about 2.5cm (1in) above the rim of the basket, which allows for the moss to settle as the top planting is completed and the basket is watered.

4 Plant the rosemary towards the centre back of the basket, with the cowslips on either side and the daisies in front. Plant the three parsley plants around the edge of the basket. Fill in any gaps with compost (soil mix). Water well and firm in the plants. Add more compost and moss if necessary.

GARDENER'S TIP

Many daisies, violas and parsleys can be bought very reasonably as small plants growing in strips of polystyrene (plastic foam) cells. These work out much cheaper than individual pots of plants. Another advantage is that their roots are smaller and therefore easier to push through the sides of the basket. Don't be afraid to use herbs already growing in the garden. Golden feverfew may have self-seeded in abundance and mints and marjorams will divide easily at this time of year.

PLANT IN EARLY SPRING

A nose-twitcher windowbox

One of the French country names for the nasturtium means 'nose-twitcher' and refers to the peppery smell of the plant. It has been planted here with the equally aromatic and colourful ginger mint and pot marigold.

MATERIALS

25cm (10in) terracotta windowbox
Crocks (broken pots) or other drainage material
Compost (soil mix)
Slow-release plant food granules

MARIGOLD

NASTURTIUM

GINGER MINT

PLANTS

Variegated ginger mint
Nasturtium, Tropaeolum 'Empress of India',
* or similar*
Pot marigold, Calendula 'Gitana', or similar

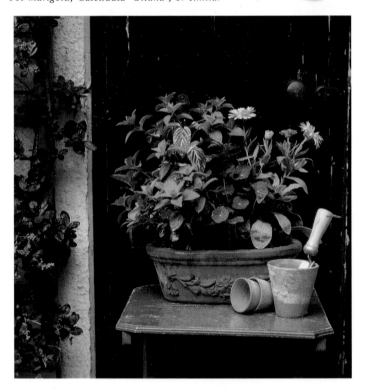

GARDENER'S TIP

A small windowbox like this one can double as a table-centre for an outdoor meal.

PLANT IN SPRING

1 Cover the base of the window-box with a layer of crocks (broken pots). Fill the container with compost (soil mix), working in a half-teaspoon of slow-release plant food granules.

2 Plant the ginger mint on the right of the container.

3 Plant the nasturtium in the centre.

4 Plant the marigold on the left of the container. Water well and stand in full or partial sun.

Sweet-smelling summer flowers

Scented pelargonium and verbena are combined with heliotrope and petunias to make a windowbox that is fragrant as well as a visual pleasure.

MATERIALS

40cm (16in) terracotta windowbox
Crocks (broken pots) or other suitable drainage material
Compost (soil mix)
Slow-release plant food granules

PLANTS

Scented-leaf Pelargonium *'Lady Plymouth'*
3 soft pink petunias
Heliotrope
2 Verbena 'Pink Parfait'

HELIOTROPE

PETUNIA

VERBENA

PELARGONIUM

GARDENER'S TIP

At the end of the summer the pelargonium can be potted up and kept through the winter as a houseplant. Reduce the height of the plant by at least a half and it will soon send out new shoots.

PLANT IN LATE SPRING OR EARLY SUMMER

1 Cover the base of the window-box with a layer of crocks (broken pots). Fill with compost (soil mix), working in 2 teaspoons of plant food granules. Plant the pelargonium to the right of centre, towards the back.

2 Plant a petunia in each corner and one in the centre at the front of the windowbox.

3 Plant the heliotrope to the left of the pelargonium.

4 Plant one verbena behind the heliotrope and the other in front of the pelargonium. Water well and place in a sunny position.

Sweet-scented lavender

In this large basket an unusual lavender is planted amongst *Convolvulus sabatius* and the fan-shaped flowers of scaevola in cool, toning shades of blue. Underplanting with trailing plants ensures that the flowers cascade down the sides of the basket.

MATERIALS

40cm (16in) hanging basket
Sphagnum moss
Compost (soil mix)
Slow-release plant food granules

PLANTS

3 Convolvulus sabatius
2 *scaevolas*
2 *lavenders* (Lavandula dentata *var.* candicans)

LAVENDER

CONVOLVULUS

SCAEVOLA

1 Line the lower half of the basket with moss.

2 Plant two of the convolvulus into the side of the basket by resting the root-balls on the moss, and carefully guiding the foliage between the wires.

3 Plant one of the scaevolas into the side of the basket in the same way.

4 Line the rest of the basket with moss, taking care to tuck it around the underplanting.

5 Fill the basket with compost (soil mix), working a teaspoon of plant food granules into the top layer. Plant the lavenders opposite one another in the top.

6 Plant the remaining convolvulus and scaevola plants in the spaces between the lavenders. Water thoroughly and hang in a sunny position.

GARDENER'S TIP

If you are unable to obtain *Lavandula dentata*, the varieties called 'Hidcote' or 'Munstead' are readily available and make suitable substitutes.

PLANT IN SPRING

Scented pelargoniums

There is a wonderful variation in leaf size, shape and colouring, as well as an incredible diversity of scents, amongst the *Pelargonium* family. Choose the fragrances you like best and put the plants where you will brush against them to release their fragrance.

MATERIALS

40cm (16in) terracotta
   windowbox
Crocks (china) or other suitable
   drainage material
Compost (soil mix)
Slow-release plant food granules

PLANTS

4 scented-leaf pelargoniums

PELARGONIUMS

GARDENER'S TIP

During the summer, pick and dry the leaves of these pelargoniums for use in pot-pourri or in muslin bags to scent linen. If you have a greenhouse or conservatory, move the windowbox inside for the winter and water sparingly until spring.

PLANT IN SPRING

1 Cover the base of the window-box with crocks (broken pots) or other suitable drainage material. Fill with compost (soil mix), working in 2 teaspoons of slow-release plant food granules. Plant the first pelargonium at the right-hand end of the container.

2 Choose a plant with contrasting leaf colour and shape, and place this next to the first pelargonium towards the front edge of the windowbox.

3 Plant the third pelargonium behind the second.

4 Finally, plant the fourth pelargonium at the left-hand end of the container. Water well and position in full or partial sun.

A butterfly garden

We should all do our bit to encourage butterflies into our gardens and this windowbox filled with sedum, marjoram, thyme and origanum should prove irresistible. All these plants are perennials and can be over-wintered in the windowbox.

MATERIALS

60cm (24in) stone windowbox
Crocks (broken pots) or other
    suitable drainage material
Compost (soil mix)
Slow-release plant food granules

PLANTS

Sedum 'Ruby Glow'
Marjoram
Lemon thyme (Thymus
    citriodorus)
Common thyme (Thymus
    vulgaris)
Origanum

LEMON
THYME

ORIGANUM

MARJORAM

COMMON
THYME

SEDUM

GARDENER'S TIP

You can imitate the look of an old stone windowbox by painting a new one with a dilute mixture of liquid seaweed plant food and water. This encourages moss to grow and ages the stone.

PLANT IN SPRING

1 Cover the base of the window box with a layer of crocks (broken pots). Fill with compost (soil mix), mixing in 3 teaspoons of slow-release plant food granules.

2 Plant the sedum off-centre to the left of the windowbox and the marjoram to the left of the sedum.

3 Plant the lemon thyme in the centre front and the common thyme in the back right-hand corner of the container.

4 Plant the origanum in the front right-hand corner of the windowbox. Water well and place in a sunny position.

Star-jasmine in a villandry planter

The soft, seductive scent of the star-jasmine makes this a perfect container to place by the side of a door where the scent will be appreciated by all who pass through.

STAR-
JASMINE

MATERIALS

50cm (20in) villandry planter or similar, preferably self-watering
Equal mix loam-based compost (soil mix) and standard compost
Slow-release plant food granules
Bark chippings

PLANTS

Star-jasmine (Trachelospermum jasminoides)

1 Feed the wicks through the holes in the base of the liner.

2 Fill the water reservoir in the base of the planter to the top of the overflow pipe, and place the liner inside the planter.

3 Fill the bottom of the liner with compost (soil mix) while pulling through the wicks so that they reach the level of the roots.

4 Remove the jasmine from its pot, gently tease the roots loose and stand it in the planter.

NOTE Steps 1–3 are for self-watering planters only.

5 Add compost (soil mix) and firm it around the root-ball of the jasmine. Scatter 2 tablespoons of plant food granules on the surface, and gently work them into the top layer of compost with the trowel.

6 Mulch around the plant with a layer of bark chippings, then water. Check the reservoir of the self-watering container once a week and top up if necessary. Conventional pots should be watered daily in the early morning or evening during hot weather.

Citrus scents

Lemon verbena is a deciduous shrub from Chile and Argentina where it grows up to 3m (10ft) high. It has one of the most powerfully scented of all leaves – just one touch will leave the aroma lingering for quite a while. Here orange- and lemon-scented geraniums make an attractive partnership with lemon verbena.

MATERIALS

Windowbox, 40cm (16in) long by 15cm (6in) wide and deep
Crocks (broken pots) or similar drainage material
Compost (soil mix)

PLANTS

1 scented geranium plant Pelargonium 'Prince of Orange'
1 scented geranium plant Pelargonium crispum 'Variegatum'
1 lemon verbena plant Aloysia triphylla

1 Cover the base of the container with 2.5cm (1in) of drainage material and add 5cm (2in) of compost (soil mix).

2 Plant the variegated geranium at one end of the box, the lemon verbena in the centre and the orange-scented geranium at the other end. Add compost to within 2.5cm (1in) of the rim. Water well and firm the plants.

GERANIUM

LEMON VERBENA

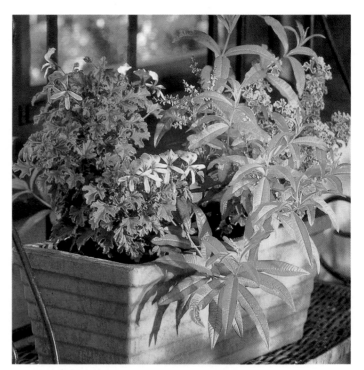

GARDENER'S TIP

Keep the compost (soil mix) moist from late spring through the summer. It should be left drier throughout the cooler days of winter. Use or remove all flowers to promote further flower production. Overwinter in a greenhouse or conservatory. Pot into a bigger container the following year.

PLANT IN EARLY SUMMER

Geranium inspirations

Scented geraniums are renowned for their fragrant leaves. Lemon-, spice-, peppermint- and orange-scented varieties all exist, and they are all surprisingly powerful. Take cuttings of non-flowering shoots in spring or autumn. Tender geraniums 'Attar of Roses' and 'Capitatum' share this pot with a mature lemon verbena plant which has been potted on several times.

MATERIALS

Pot, 40cm (16in) wide by 30cm (12in) deep
Crocks (broken pots) or similar drainage material
Compost (soil mix)

PLANTS

1 lemon verbena plant Aloysia triphylla
1 scented geranium plant Pelargonium 'Attar of Roses'
1 scented geranium plant Pelargonium 'Capitatum'

GERANIUM

LEMON
VERBENA

1 Cover the base of the container with 5cm (2in) of drainage material and add about 20cm (8in) of compost (soil mix).

2 Plant the lemon verbena towards the centre back with the geraniums to the front on either side.

3 Add enough compost to bring level to within 2.5cm (1in) of the rim. Water well and firm the plants.

GARDENER'S TIP

Scented geraniums will be killed by frost so they need the protection of a greenhouse or window-sill indoors through the winter. They should be kept fairly dry during this period. In summer, they can remain indoors or be planted in pots outside.

PLANT IN EARLY SUMMER

Difficult Situations

*A shady pathway or a bare corner of the patio may cry out for plants to enliven it,
but it can be hard to know what to grow there. The areas near the house
walls are usually very dry, and may be in shade for most of the day. On the other hand,
paved areas can be so hot and sunny that many plants would not be able to
survive without scorching. Here are some solutions to furnishing the more difficult parts
of the garden. With imaginative use of dramatic foliage and careful
choice of shade-tolerant flowering plants, you can light up the darkest areas
with exciting and colourful arrangements. It really is possible to achieve a flower-filled
hanging basket on a north-facing wall. For windy corners, choose varieties with
wiry stems, such as bidens, that will not suffer from being blown about, and for hot
spots go for sun-lovers like osteospermum or mesembryanthemum.*

ABOVE: *Ferns thrive in shady spots and can add a burst of colour to even
the darkest corner of the garden.*

Busy Lizzies in bloom

There are not many shade-loving plants as colourful and prolific as the busy Lizzie. These plants will very happily bloom all summer long in a hanging basket on a north-facing wall, or in any shady or partially shaded position.

MATERIALS

30cm (12in) hanging basket
Sphagnum moss
Compost (soil mix)
Slow-release plant food granules

PLANTS

6 rose-pink lobelias
3 pale pink busy Lizzies
  (impatiens)
3 white busy Lizzies
3 dark pink busy Lizzies

LOBELIA

BUSY LIZZIES

1 Line the lower half of the basket with moss and plant three lobelias through the side of the basket near the bottom.

2 Carefully feed the foliage through the sides of the basket. Line the basket with some more moss.

3 Plant one busy Lizzie of each colour. Line the rest of the basket with moss and partly fill with compost (soil mix). Work in a teaspoon of plant food granules. Plant the remaining three lobelias into the side of the basket near the top edge. Add more compost.

4 Plant the remaining busy Lizzies in the top of the basket. Water thoroughly and hang in partial or full shade.

GARDENER'S TIP

In wet or windy weather, busy Lizzies can look a bit battered, but once the weather improves, five minutes spent removing dead or damaged flowers will soon restore the basket to its former glory.

PLANT IN LATE SPRING OR EARLY SUMMER

Shady characters

All the plants used in this windowbox are perfectly happy in the shade. A periwinkle with variegated leaves and blue spring flowers is planted with blue-leaved hostas and summer-flowering busy Lizzies in a windowbox that will brighten a gloomy corner for many months.

MATERIALS

45cm (18in) fibre windowbox
Crocks (broken pots) or other suitable
  drainage material
Compost
Slow-release plant food granules

PLANTS

Variegated periwinkle (Vinca minor
  'Aureovariegata')
3 Hosta 'Blue Moon'
5 white busy Lizzies (impatiens)

HOSTA

BUSY LIZZIE

PERIWINKLE

1 Cover the base of the window-box with a layer of drainage material. Fill the windowbox with compost (soil mix), mixing in 2 teaspoons of plant food granules.

2 Plant the periwinkle in the centre of the windowbox.

3 Plant two of the hostas in the back corners of the window-box and the third in front of, or slightly to one side of, the periwinkle.

4 Plant the busy Lizzies in the remaining spaces.

GARDENER'S TIP

To keep the busy Lizzies looking their best, pick off the dead flowers and leaves regularly or they will stick to the plant and spoil its appearance.

PLANT IN LATE SPRING

Full of ferns

A damp shady corner is the perfect position for a basket of ferns. Provided they are regularly fed and watered, and the ferns are cut back in late autumn, this basket will give pleasure for many years. These are hardy ferns, but the idea can be adapted for a conservatory or bathroom using less hardy plants such as the maidenhair fern.

MATERIALS
....
36cm (14in) hanging basket
Sphagnum moss
Compost (soil mix)
Slow-release plant food granules

PLANTS
....
4 different ferns (dryopteris,
athyrium, Matteuccia
struthiopteris *and* Asplenium
scolopendrium *'Crispum')*

FERNS

2 Fill the basket with compost (soil mix). Mix a teaspoon of slow-release plant food granules into the top of the compost.

3 Before removing the ferns from their pots, arrange them in the basket to ensure that you achieve a balanced effect. Plant the ferns and water well.

GARDENER'S TIP

Strange as it may seem, finely chopped banana skins are a favourite food of ferns. Simply sprinkle around the base of the stems and watch the ferns flourish.

PLANT IN SPRING

Bronze and gold winners

Bronze pansies and mimulus and golden green lysimachias take the medals in this striking arrangement, with richly coloured heuchera adding to the unusual mixture of tones. This arrangement will work most successfully in a partially shaded situation.

MATERIALS

40cm (16in) hanging basket
Sphagnum moss
Compost (soil mix)
Slow-release plant food granules

PLANTS

Heuchera *'Bressingham Bronze'*
3 bronze-coloured pansies (viola)
3 bronze-coloured mimulus
3 Lysimachia nummularia *'Aurea'*

LYSIMACHIA

MIMULUS

PANSY

HEUCHERA

1 Line the basket with moss.

2 Fill the basket with compost (soil mix), working a teaspoon of plant food granules into the top layer of compost.

3 Plant the heuchera in the middle of the basket.

4 Plant the pansies, evenly spaced around the heuchera.

5 Plant the three mimulus between the pansies.

6 Plant the lysimachias around the edge of the basket. Water well and hang in light shade.

GARDENER'S TIP

At the end of the season the heuchera can be planted in the border or in another container. It will do best in partial shade, as full sun tends to scorch and discolour the leaves.

PLANT IN SPRING

Shady corner

Shady corners are often thought of as problematical, when in fact there is a wealth of wonderful plants that thrive in these situations, such as the hosta, hydrangea and fern used in this arrangement.

MATERIALS

3 terracotta pots of various sizes
Crocks (broken pots) or other
suitable drainage material
Composted manure
Equal mix standard compost (soil
mix) and loam-based compost

PLANTS

Hosta sieboldiana elegans
Variegated hydrangea
Polystichum fern

HYDRANGEA

POLYSTICHUM

HOSTA

GARDENER'S TIP

The hosta is a beautiful foliage plant much loved by slugs and snails which chew unsightly holes in the leaves. To prevent this, smear a broad band of petroleum jelly below the rim of the container and the leaves will remain untouched.

**PLANT AT ANY TIME
OF THE YEAR**

1 Plant the hosta in a pot large enough for its bulky root system, and with space for further growth. Place crocks (broken pots) at the bottom of the pot and then put in a layer of manure before adding the potting compost (soil mix). Follow this procedure with the hydrangea as well.

2 Plant the fern in a terracotta pot slightly larger than its existing pot. It should not need transplanting for 2–3 years.

3 The hydrangea makes a great deal of growth during the summer and could get very top-heavy. Plant in a sturdy pot with plenty of space for root growth.

A space in the sun

Since osteospermum, portulaca and diascia are all sun-lovers this is definitely a basket for your sunniest spot, where the plants will thrive and the colours will look their best.

PORTULACA

DIASCIA

OSTEOSPERMUM

MATERIALS

36cm (14in) hanging basket
Sphagnum moss
Compost (soil mix)
Slow-release plant food granules

PLANTS

6 peach portulaca
Osteospermum *'Buttermilk'*
*3 Diascia 'Salmon Supreme', or
similar*

1 Line the lower half of the basket with moss. Plant three portulaca by resting the root-balls on the moss, and guiding the foliage between the wires.

2 Add more moss to the basket, tucking it carefully around the portulaca.

3 Partly fill the basket with compost (soil mix). Work a teaspoon of plant food granules into the top layer. Plant the remaining three portulaca just below the rim of the basket.

4 Line the rest of the basket with moss. Plant the osteopermum centrally. Plant the diascias around the osteospermum. Water thoroughly and hang in a sunny spot.

GARDENER'S TIP

Keep pinching out the growing tips of the osteospermum to ensure a bushy plant.

PLANT IN LATE SPRING OR EARLY SUMMER

A dazzling display

The succulents in this windowbox will provide a vivid splash of colour throughout the summer, and will cope very well on a hot dry window-sill. Mesembryanthemum, kalanchoe and portulaca all love the sunshine and will grow happily in this small windowbox.

PORTULACA

MESEMBRYANTHEMUMS

MATERIALS

36cm (14in) plastic windowbox
Compost (soil mix)
Slow-release plant food granules

PLANTS

Kalanchoe
2 portulaca
3 mesembryanthemum

KALANCHOE

1 Check the drainage holes are open in the base and, if not, drill or punch them open. Fill the windowbox with compost (soil mix), working in a teaspoon of slow-release plant food granules.

2 Plant the kalanchoe in the centre of the windowbox.

3 Plant the two portulaca in the front corners of the windowbox.

4 Plant one mesembryanthemum in front of the kalanchoe and the other two behind the two portulaca. Water well and stand in a sunny position.

GARDENER'S TIP

Since mesembryanthemum flowers open in response to direct sunlight, it is essential to place them in a position where they are in full sun for as long as possible every day.

PLANT IN LATE SPRING OR EARLY SUMMER

Desert belles

An attractively weathered windowbox is the container used for this dramatic collection of succulents. With their architectural leaf shapes and wonderful range of colouring they would look particularly good in a modern setting.

MATERIALS

40cm (16in) terracotta
  windowbox
Crocks (broken pots) or other
  suitable drainage material
Compost (soil mix)
Gravel
Slow-release plant food granules

PLANTS

Aloe
Crassula ovata
Echeveria elegans
Sansevieria trifasciata

ECHEVERIA

CRASSULA

SANSEVIERIA

ALOE

GARDENER'S TIP

Move the windowbox to a conservatory or frost-free greenhouse for the winter. Water sparingly only if plants show signs of shrivelling.

PLANT IN LATE SPRING OR
EARLY SUMMER FOR OUTDOOR
USE, OR ANY TIME OF YEAR
FOR A CONSERVATORY

1 Place a layer of crocks (broken pots) or other suitable drainage material in the base of the container. Fill with compost (soil mix), mixing in a teaspoon of slow-release plant food granules. Plant the aloe at the right-hand end of the windowbox.

2 Plant the crassula next to the aloe, the echeveria at the back of the windowbox, and the sansevieria in front.

3 Surround the plants with a layer of gravel. Water well to establish and thereafter water sparingly. Place in full sun.

Inspirational Containers

Sometimes a container is so characterful it dictates its own planting scheme. A wooden tub with an oriental feel, for example, is a perfect container for a delicate Japanese maple – a restrained yet stunning combination. Or the shape of the pot may echo that of the flowers, such as lilies planted in a curvaceous urn. Old wooden boxes and trugs call for cottage-garden mixtures to enhance their old-fashioned charm. If you can find striking and original containers like these, seek out plants that suit them and show them to their best advantage.

There are also ideas here for truly dramatic effects; a plunging cascade of variegated foliage, a black-and-white pot with black and white flowers to match, ivy trained into a formal topiary shape and a fountain of fuchsias.

ABOVE: *Ivy trained around a shaped hoop adds height and interest to this pot of petunias.*

Old favourites

Dianthus, violas and candytuft are delightful cottage-garden plants that make a pretty display during late spring and early summer. Although by the time we took our photograph the candytuft was over, the other flowers were still putting on a good show.

MATERIALS

40cm (16in) painted wooden windowbox
Crocks (broken pots) or other suitable drainage material
Compost (soil mix)
Slow-release plant food granules

PLANTS

Dianthus
Candytuft (iberis)
2 violas

DIANTHUS

CANDYTUFT

VIOLAS

GARDENER'S TIP

Once the flowers are over, cut back the plants and plant them out in the garden. There is still time to replant the windowbox with summer plants.

PLANT IN EARLY SPRING

1 Cover the base of the container with a layer of drainage material. Fill with compost (soil mix), working in a teaspoon of plant food granules.

2 Plant the dianthus slightly to the right of the centre of the windowbox.

3 Plant the candytuft to the left of the centre of the window-box beside the dianthus.

4 Plant a viola at each end. Water well and stand in a mixture of sun and shade.

Colourful evergreens

Evergreen cordyline with its dramatic red spear-shaped leaves, a green hebe and a golden conifer have been mixed with blue-green hostas in a permanent planting, which is given seasonal interest by the addition of red-flowered New Guinea impatiens.

MATERIALS

76cm (30in) plastic windowbox
Compost (soil mix)
Slow-release plant food granules

PLANTS

Red cordyline
Golden conifer Chamaecyparis pisifera *'Sungold'*
Hebe *'Emerald Green'*
Hosta *'Blue Moon'*
Golden grass Hakonechloa *'Aureola'*
2 red-flowered New Guinea impatiens

CORDYLINE

HOSTA

IMPATIENS   HEBE

CONIFER

GOLDEN GRASS

GARDENER'S TIP

At the end of the summer replace the impatiens with pansies, polyanthus or heathers.

PLANT IN SPRING

1 Check the drainage holes are open in the base and, if not, drill or punch them open. Fill the windowbox with compost (soil mix), adding in 3 teaspoons of plant food granules. Plant the cordyline left of centre and the conifer at the right-hand end.

2 Plant the hebe in the centre of the windowbox. Plant the hosta between the hebe and the conifer.

3 Plant the golden grass at the left-hand end of the window-box. Plant the impatiens between the golden grass and the cordyline, and next to the hosta. Water well and stand in partial sun.

A trough of alpines

A selection of easy-to-grow alpine plants is grouped in a basket-weave stone planter to create a miniature garden. The mulch of gravel is both attractive and practical as it prevents soil splashing on to the leaves of the plants.

MATERIALS

40cm (16in) stone trough
Crocks (broken pots)
Compost (soil mix)
Slow-release plant food granules
Gravel

PLANTS

Sempervivum
Alpine aquilegia
White rock rose (helianthemum)
Papaver alpinum
Alpine phlox
Pink saxifrage
White saxifrage

SEMPERVIVUM

PAPAVER
ALPINUM

SAXIFRAGES

ALPINE PHLOX

ROCK ROSE

ALPINE AQUILEGIA

1 Cover the base of the trough with crocks (broken pots). Fill the container with compost (soil mix), working in a teaspoon of plant food granules and extra gravel for improved drainage.

2 Arrange the plants, still in their pots, in the trough to decide on the most attractive arrangement. Complete the planting, working across the trough.

3 Scatter a good layer of gravel around the plants. Water thoroughly and stand in a sunny position.

GARDENER'S TIP

Tidy the trough once a month, removing dead flowerheads and leaves, adding more gravel if necessary. A trough like this will last a number of years before it needs replanting.

PLANT IN SPRING

The apothecary's box

Many plants have healing qualities and, while they should always be used with caution, some of the more commonly used herbs have been successful country remedies for centuries.

CHAMOMILE

FENNEL

MATERIALS

Wooden trug
Crocks (broken pots) or other suitable drainage material
Compost (soil mix)
Pelleted chicken manure

MARIGOLD

PLANTS

Lavender – for relaxation
Rosemary – for healthy hair and scalp
Chamomile – for restful sleep
Fennel – for digestion
Feverfew – for migraine
3 pot marigolds (calendula) – for healing

FEVERFEW

LAVENDER

ROSEMARY

1 Place drainage material in the trug and fill with compost (soil mix), working in 2 teaspoons of fertilizer. Plant a central lavender.

2 Plant the rosemary in the front right-hand corner of the trug.

3 Plant the chamomile in the back left-hand corner.

4 Plant the fennel in the back right-hand corner.

5 Plant the feverfew in the front left-hand corner.

6 Plant the marigolds in the remaining spaces. Water well and stand in full or partial sun.

GARDENER'S TIP

Herbs should not be used to treat any medical condition without first checking with your medical practitioner.

PLANT IN THE SPRING

Daring reds and bold purples

The colour of the fuchsia's flowers is echoed by the deep purple and crimson petunias. The stark white windowbox provides the perfect contrast to make a bold display.

GARDENER'S TIP

At the end of the season the catmint plants can be trimmed back and planted in the garden. The fuchsia and campanulas can be cut back and potted up to be overwintered in a frost-free greenhouse.

PLANT IN SPRING

MATERIALS

76cm (30in) plastic windowbox
90cm (3ft) wooden windowbox (optional)
Compost (soil mix)
Slow-release plant food granules

PLANTS

Fuchsia 'Dollar Princess'
2 low-growing catmint (Nepeta mussinii)
2 white-flowered Campanula isophylla
2 crimson petunias
2 purple petunias

CAMPANULA

CATMINT

PETUNIAS

FUCHSIA

1 Check the drainage holes are open in the base and, if not, drill or punch them open. Fill the windowbox with compost (soil mix), working in 3 teaspoons of slow-release plant food granules. Plant the fuchsia in the centre.

2 Plant a catmint at each end of the windowbox. Plant the campanulas next to the catmint.

3 Plant the crimson petunias on either side of the fuchsia at the back and the purple one in front.

4 Water thoroughly and allow to drain. Lower the plastic windowbox into place inside the wooden windowbox, if using. Stand in a sunny position.

Chinese water garden

In China, glazed pots are frequently used as small ponds in courtyards.
This pot contains a water lily, a flowering rush and an arum lily.

MATERIALS

Water lily basket
Piece of hessian
Aquatic compost (soil mix)
Large bucket
70cm (28in) glazed pot
Putty (optional)
Bricks

PLANTS

Compact water lily
(Nymphaea tetragona)
Flowering rush
(Butomus umbellatus)
Arum lily (Zantedeschia
aethiopica)

FLOWERING
RUSH

WATER LILY

ARUM LILY

1 Line the basket with hessian, insert the water lily and top up with aquatic compost (soil mix). Lower the basket into a bucket of water to settle the compost.

2 If the glazed pot has a drainage hole, plug it with putty and leave to harden overnight. Use bricks to create platforms for the two potted plants.

3 Before filling the pot with water, position the rush so that its pot will be fully submerged and the arum lily so that the pot will be half-submerged.

4 Fill the pot with water and gently lower the water lily into position – its leaves should float on the surface. This water garden will do best in a sunny position.

GARDENER'S TIP

This arrangement is not recommended for anyone with small children; they can drown in a surprisingly small amount of water.

PLANT IN LATE SPRING OR
EARLY SUMMER

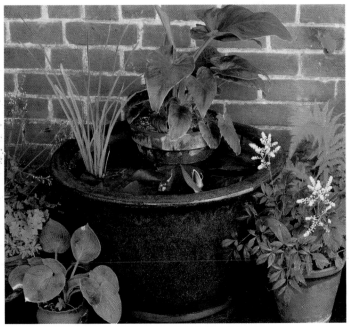

Colourful cooking pot

Junk shops are a rich source of old pots and pans which can make characterful containers for plants when their kitchen days are over.

MATERIALS

30cm (12in) cooking pot
Gravel
Equal mix loam-based
*   compost (soil mix) and*
*   container compost*
Slow-release plant food granules

IVY

INULA

PLANTS

Ceratostigma plumbaginoides
Inula *'Oriental Star'*
Golden ivy

CERATOSTIGMA

GARDENER'S TIP

These plants are all perennials. When the ceratostigma and inula have finished flowering, plant them in a border where they will flower again next year.

PLANT IN SPRING OR EARLY SUMMER

1 Make one or two drainage holes in the base of the pot and add a 5cm (2in) layer of gravel.

2 Remove the ceratostigma from its pot and plant it at one side of the container.

3 Add the inula and the ivy, and fill in between the plants with compost (soil mix), firming them in position as you work. Scatter a tablespoon of plant food granules over the surface of the compost. Water and place in the sun.

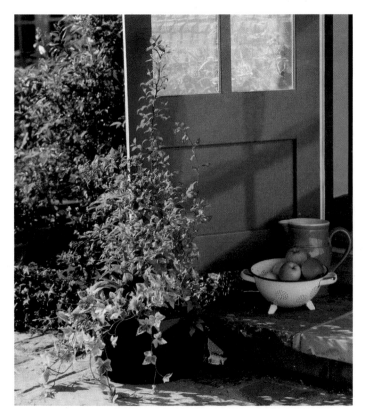

Black-and-white arrangement

Linking the colour of the container with the plants creates a harmony of design, which is given extra dramatic impact when the colours used are black and white.

MATERIALS

Terracotta pot, 30cm (12in) high
Masking tape
Paint brush
Matt white and black paint
Crocks (broken pots) or other
  suitable drainage material
Compost (soil mix)
Slow-release plant food granules
Fine gravel

PLANTS

White osteospermum
Black grass (Ophiopogon planiscapus 'Nigrescens')
3 Viola 'Molly Sanderson'

BLACK GRASS

VIOLA

OSTEOSPERMUM

1 Mark out a checkered pattern on the pot with masking tape.

2 Paint the top and bottom row of checks white and the rim and the middle row black. Remove the tape.

3 Cover the drainage holes at the bottom of the pot with crocks (broken pots) and half-fill with compost (soil mix). Plant the osteospermum at the back.

4 Place the black grass next to the osteospermum and top up the container with compost (soil mix). Plant the three violas in a group.

5 Scatter a tablespoon of plant food granules on the surface of the compost (soil mix) and mulch with fine gravel. Water and stand in a sunny position.

GARDENER'S TIP

Experiment with other colourful themes. You could try a sky blue-and-white check container planted with a morning glory, or a bright red and green pot planted with a red pelargonium.

PLANT IN SPRING OR EARLY SUMMER

Topiary ivy with white petunias

Use wire topiary frames (available at most garden centres) to train ivy or other climbing plants into interesting shapes. The ivy will take some months to establish a strong outline; in the meantime, miniature white petunias complete the picture.

MATERIALS

45cm (18in) oval terracotta
  windowbox
Crocks (broken pots) or other
  suitable drainage material
Compost (soil mix)
Slow-release plant food granules
Wire topiary frame
Pins made from garden wire
Plant rings

PLANTS

2 variegated ivies
4 miniature white petunias

IVIES

PETUNIA

1 Place a layer of drainage material in the base of the windowbox. Fill the windowbox with compost (soil mix), working in 2 teaspoons of slow-release plant food granules.

2 Plant the two ivies, one in front of the other in the centre of the windowbox.

3 Position the topiary frame in the centre of the windowbox and use pins to hold it in place.

4 Wrap the stems of ivy around the stem of the frame, and then around the frame itself.

5 Cut away any straggly stems and use plant rings to secure the ivy to the frame.

6 Plant the petunias around the topiary ivy. Water thoroughly and stand in light shade.

GARDENER'S TIP

Maintain the shape of the ivy with regular trimming and training – 5 minutes once a week will create a better shape than 15 minutes once a month.

PLANT IVY AT ANY TIME OF YEAR, PETUNIAS IN SPRING

Wild delights

Cowslips are now readily available either as seed or as growing plants and they can be grown in borders, grassland or containers. The wild flower seeds tend to produce much smaller plants than cultivated cowslips, which are the ones more often sold as plants in garden centres. The dainty heads of yellow cowslips look charming growing alongside pretty blue violas and the delicate creamy markings of variegated mint. They make a versatile combination.

MATERIALS

A medium-sized wicker basket 45cm (18in) long, 30cm (12in) wide and 15cm (6in) deep was used here. It has been given three coats of yacht varnish both inside and outside to preserve it for outdoor use.
Crocks (broken pots) or other similar drainage material
Black plastic lining
Compost (soil mix)

PLANTS

4 cowslip plants Primula veris
4 viola plants Viola 'Penny'
1 large variegated applemint plant Mentha suaveolens 'Variegata'

VIOLA

APPLEMINT

GARDENER'S TIP

Once planted, lift the basket from underneath. The handle will not be strong enough to support the weight of the filled basket.

PLANT IN EARLY SPRING

1 Line the basket with black plastic refuse sack trimmed to fit and cut four slits in the base to allow excess water to drain through.

2 Cover the base of the container with 2.5cm (1in) drainage material and add compost (soil mix) to a depth of about 5cm (2in).

3 Plant two cowslips in the corners on one side of the basket and position the third under the opposite handle. Then arrange three violas in opposite positions.

4 Plant the mint in the centre with another cowslip and viola on either side. Fill in any gaps with compost (soil mix), bringing the compost to within 2.5cm (1in) of the top of the container. Water well. Firm in the plants and add more compost if necessary. Tuck in any excess plastic beneath the rim of the basket. Stand in full or partial sun.

Dramatic foliage

GROUND IVY

NEMESIA

BEGONIA

BLACK GRASS

VIOLA

*Viola 'Bowles' Black' is combined with black grass – ophiopogon –
and the dramatically coloured Begonia rex. Pale pink nemesias and
variegated ground ivies provide an
effective contrast.*

MATERIALS

*36cm (14in) hanging basket
Sphagnum moss
Compost (soil mix)
Slow-release plant food granules*

PLANTS

Begonia rex
Black grass (Ophiopogon planiscapus
'Nigrescens')
2 variegated ground ivies (Glechoma
hederacea *'Variegata')*
2 Nemesia denticulata 'Confetti'
2 Viola 'Bowles' Black'

1 Line the basket with moss and
fill it with compost (soil mix),
working a teaspoon of plant food
granules in the top layer of
compost. Plant the begonia at the
back of the basket. Plant the black
grass in front of the begonia.

2 Plant the ground ivies at either
side of the basket, angling the
plants so that the foliage tumbles
down the sides of the basket.

3 Plant the nemesias on either
side of the begonia. Plant the
violas on either side of the black
grass. Water the basket well and
hang in light shade.

GARDENER'S TIP

At the end of the season the begonia can be potted up and kept indoors as a
houseplant and the black grass can be planted in an outdoor container.

PLANT IN LATE SPRING OR EARLY SUMMER

Foliage wall pot

The bushy growth of *Fuchsia magellanica* 'Alba Variegata' is ideal for displaying as a crown of leafy hair in a head-shaped wall pot. This copy of an ancient Grecian head will add a classical touch to a modern garden.

FUCHSIA

MATERIALS

Grecian head wall pot
Expanded clay granules

PLANTS

Fuchsia magellanica 'Alba
  Variegata'

1 Check that the wall pot has a hook or can be hung up. The hanging point will need to be sufficiently strong to carry the weight of a moist pot.

2 Add expanded clay granules to the base of the wall pot to lift the top of the plant to the right level.

3 Place the plant in its pot inside the wall pot.

4 Arrange the foliage to make a convincing leafy crown of hair for the head.

GARDENER'S TIP

Check the base of the pot for drainage holes. If there are no holes, you will need to remove the pot each time you water it, allowing the compost to drain before replacing it.

PLANT AT ANY TIME OF YEAR

Filigree foliage

The purply-black leaves of this heuchera are all the more stunning when surrounded by the delicate silver-and-green filigree foliage of senecio, the tender *Lavandula pinnata* and the soft lilac-coloured flowers of the bacopa and the brachycome daisies. The plants are grown in a white plastic planter which is concealed inside an elegant wooden windowbox.

MATERIALS

76cm (30in) plastic windowbox
Compost (soil mix)
Slow-release plant food granules
90cm (3ft) wooden windowbox
   (optional)

PLANTS

Heuchera *'Palace Purple'*
2 lavenders
2 blue brachycome daisies
3 Senecio cineraria 'Silver Dust'
2 blue bacopa

SENECIO

LAVENDER

BRACHYCOME

BACOPA

HEUCHERA

1 Check drainage holes are open in the base of the planter and, if not, drill or punch them out. Fill the windowbox with compost (soil mix), mixing in 2 teaspoons of plant food granules. Plant the heuchera in the centre.

2 Plant the two lavenders on either side of the heuchera.

3 Plant the two brachycome daisies at each end of the windowbox.

4 Place the three senecios at the front of the box between the brachycomes.

5 Plant the two bacopa between the senecio and the heuchera.

6 Water thoroughly and lift into place in the wooden window-box, if using. Place in full or partial sun.

GARDENER'S TIP

Wooden windowboxes can be assembled so they are self-watering where access is difficult for daily watering. A variety of self-watering containers are available and come with full instructions for their use.

PLANT IN SPRING

Fuchsia wall fountain

A dry terracotta wall fountain makes a lovely innovative planting pot. *Fuchsia* 'Daisy Bell' is particularly suited to growing in such a fountain or in a hanging basket. Its growth is trailing, lax and self-branching, and it produces numerous flowers freely throughout the summer.

MATERIALS

Terracotta wall fountain
Bricks
Clay granules
Peat-free compost (soil mix)

PLANTS

3 Fuchsia *'Daisy Bell'*

FUCHSIA

1 Prop the wall fountain securely upright using the bricks. Make sure that the planting bowl is held straight, so that you can create a balanced arrangement.

2 Fill with expanded clay granules and compost (soil mix). Add a water-retaining gel if you are concerned about the rapid water-loss from terracotta.

3 Arrange the plants while still in their pots.

4 Plant them when you are satisfied with your arrangement, adding extra compost (soil mix) to cover the root-balls. Finally, add a layer of clay granules to the top of the compost as a mulch to prevent excessive water loss through evaporation.

GARDENER'S TIP

When planting a wall pot, avoid using a fuchsia cultivar that needs regular stopping to encourage branching. Choose a variety like 'Daisy Bell' which is naturally abundant and bushy.

PLANT IN EARLY SPRING OR EARLY SUMMER

Illusions of grandeur

A small plastic windowbox takes on unexpected grandeur when filled with rich, velvety purples and pinks, and placed in a stylish setting.

MATERIALS

30cm (12in) plastic windowbox
Compost (soil mix)
Slow-release plant food
granules

GARDENER'S TIP

Dead-head the violas regularly to keep them flowering, and pinch out any straggly stems.

PLANT IN SPRING

PLANTS

Heliotrope
2 Viola 'Bowles' Black'
Blue verbena
4 lilac lobelias

HELIOTROPE

VERBENA

LOBELIA

VIOLA

1 Check the drainage holes are open in the base and, if not, drill or punch them open. Fill the container with compost (soil mix), mixing in a teaspoon of plant food granules. Plant the heliotrope in the centre at the back.

2 Plant the violas at either end of the windowbox in the back corners. Plant the verbena centrally in front of the heliotrope.

3 Plant two of the lobelias on either side of the verbena and the others between the heliotrope and the violas. Water thoroughly and stand in partial shade.

Mediterranean garden

The brilliant colours of the Mediterranean are recreated with these painted pots. While the plants thrive in the climate of the Mediterranean, they also perform perfectly in less predictable weather.

MATERIALS

4 terracotta pots of various sizes
Paint brush
Selection of brightly coloured
    emulsion paints
Masking tape
Crocks (broken pots)
Loam-based compost (soil
    mix) with 1/3 added grit
Gravel

PLANTS

Prostrate rosemary
Aloe (optional)
Golden thyme
Large red
    pelargonium

ROSEMARY

ALOE

PELARGONIUM

1 Paint the pots with solid colours or with patterns using two coats if necessary. The terracotta absorbs the moisture from the paint, so they will dry very quickly.

2 Paint the rim of one pot with a contrasting colour.

3 Create a zig-zag pattern using masking tape and painting alternate sections.

4 Place crocks (broken pots) in the bottom of the pots and then position the plants, firming them in place with extra compost. The compacted roots of the rosemary will benefit from being teased loose before planting.

5 The aloe does not need a large pot. Plant it in a pot just slightly larger than the one you bought it in.

6 Plant the thyme and pelargonium in separate pots. Finish the plants with a top-dressing of gravel, water well and place in a sheltered sunny corner.

GARDENER'S TIP

For commercial reasons the plants you buy will probably have been grown in a peat compost (soil mix), although they prefer a loam-based compost. Gently loosen the peat around their roots and mix it with the loam-based compost before potting up in the new mixture.

PLANT IN LATE SPRING OR EARLY SUMMER

Japanese-style planter

A wooden apple barrel makes an inexpensive container for this Japanese maple. The tree is surrounded by moss and stones to create the effect of a Japanese garden. This planted container is designed to be very lightweight and would be ideal for a roof terrace or balcony.

MATERIALS

Apple barrel or similar wooden tub
Plastic saucer to fit the bottom of
  the container
Slow-release plant food granules
Polystyrene (plastic foam) packing material
Bun moss
Large stones

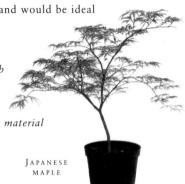

JAPANESE
MAPLE

PLANT

Japanese maple (Acer palmatum var. dissectum)

GARDENER'S TIP

The tree should be checked annually to see if it needs repotting. If roots are showing through the base of the pot this is a sure sign that the tree should be moved into a larger one. If weight is not a consideration use clay granules instead of polystyrene (plastic foam).

PLANT AT ANY TIME OF THE YEAR

1 Place the plastic saucer in the base of the container.

2 Stand the tree in its pot in the saucer. Scatter half a tablespoon of plant food granules on the surface of the compost (soil mix). Fill the area around the pot with polystyrene (plastic foam).

3 Cover the surface of the perlite or polystyrene with bun moss interspersed with stones. Place in full or partial sun and water regularly.

Regency lily urn

The shape of this urn is based on the shape of the lily flower, so it makes an appropriate container for this lovely mix of lilies, lavenders, pink marguerites and helichrysums.

LILY

LAVENDER

MARGUERITE

HELICHRYSUM

MATERIALS

Suitably shaped urn
Gravel
Loam-based compost (soil mix) with ⅓ added grit
Slow-release plant food granules

PLANTS

2 white lilies
2 lavenders (Lavandula 'Hidcote')
2 pink marguerites (argyranthemums)
3 Helichrysum petiolare

1 Place a 5cm (2in) layer of gravel at the bottom of the urn and half-fill with compost (soil mix). Place the lilies in the centre.

2 Arrange the lavenders and marguerites around the lilies.

3 Plant the helichrysums around the edge of the urn so that they cascade over the rim as they grow. Fill between the plants with additional compost (soil mix) enriched with a tablespoon of plant food granules. Water well and place in a sunny position.

GARDENER'S TIP

Cut back the lavender heads when they have finished flowering, leave the lilies to die down naturally, and dead-head the marguerites regularly to keep them flowering all summer. The helichrysums and marguerites are not frost hardy, but the lavenders and lilies should bloom again next year.

PLANT IN SPRING

Standard fuchsia

Fuchsia 'Tom West' is an
excellent hardy variety which
was raised in 1853. Here,
underplanted with variegated
ivy, and benefiting from the
large Chinese-style glazed pot,
the display has a very modern
chic appeal.

MATERIALS

*Large glazed pot, at least 70cm
(28in) diameter
Crocks (broken pots)
Peat-free compost (soil mix)
Slow-release plant food granules*

PLANTS

1 half-standard Fuchsia *'Tom
West'
6 variegated ivies*

FUCHSIA

IVY

1 Cover the drainage hole in the
base of the pot with the crocks
(broken pots). This prevents it
from becoming blocked and
facilitates the free drainage of
excess water.

2 Almost fill the pot with peat-
free compost (soil mix). Add
slow-release plant food granules to
the compost.

3 Remove the half-standard
fuchsia from its pot, and lower
it gently on to the compost so that
the top of its root-ball is slightly
lower than the lip of the pot.

4 Add more compost (soil mix).
Plant the variegated ivies
around the base of the fuchsia. Fill
in the gaps between the root-balls,
and tease the ivies' stems and
foliage across the compost surface.
Water to settle the compost.

GARDENER'S TIP

The variegated foliage of 'Tom West' develops a lovely rich
pink colouring when grown in a sunny position. The
best foliage colour is on the young growth, so regular pinching
out of new stem tips will ensure a colourful plant.

PLANT IN EARLY SPRING OR EARLY SUMMER

Galvanized-bath garden

An old tin bath makes an ideal planter; it is large and deep enough to take quite large plants. Here, foxgloves and euphorbias are underplanted with violets, making an attractive early summer display.

EUPHORBIA

FOXGLOVE

VIOLET

MATERIALS

Tin bath, 60cm (24in) wide
Gravel or similar drainage material
Equal mix loam-based compost (soil mix) and standard compost
Slow-release plant food granules

PLANTS

3 foxgloves (digitalis)
2 euphorbia
3 violets (viola)

1 If the bath does not have drainage holes, you should make some in the base, and then cover it with a 10cm (4in) layer of gravel or similar drainage material. Half-fill the bath with the compost (soil mix), and position the foxgloves.

2 Next add the euphorbia, teasing loose the roots to enable growth if they are at all potbound. Fill between the plants with compost (soil mix), firming around the root-balls.

3 Finally, plant the violets around the edges, where they can tumble over the sides as they grow. Water and place in a shady position.

GARDENER'S TIP

Buy your foxgloves before they have formed their flower spikes; they will transplant better and you will have the pleasure of watching them grow. Do not cut the stems down after flowering; when you can hear the seeds rattling, simply shake them over any corner of the garden where you would like foxgloves to grow.

PLANT IN AUTUMN OR SPRING

Chimney pot clematis

It is well known that clematis love to have their heads in the sun and their roots in the shade. A chimney pot creates the perfect environment as it provides exactly these conditions. Ideally, the clematis should be planted in soil with the chimney pot placed over it, but with a little care, pot-grown plants will do well for a few years.

CLEMATIS

MATERIALS

2 x 20cm (8in) plastic pots
Gravel or other suitable drainage material
Equal mix loam-based compost (soil mix) and container compost
Slow-release plant food granules
60cm (24in) chimney pot

PLANTS

Clematis 'Prince Charles'

1 Fill one of the plastic pots with gravel.

2 Plant the clematis in the other plastic pot, filling around the root-ball with the compost (soil mix). Scatter a tablespoon of plant food granules over the surface of the compost. (The two pots will be positioned one on top of the other inside the chimney pot, as shown.)

3 Place the chimney pot over the pot of gravel and then carefully lower the clematis into position. It will need a sunny position and regular watering.

GARDENER'S TIP

Clematis can suffer from clematis wilt: suddenly whole stems will start to wilt and die. Cut all affected growth away from the plant and spray the remaining plant fortnightly with a product containing Benolyl.

PLANT IN SPRING

A topiary planting

BOX PYRAMID

BOX BALL

BACOPA

Topiary box plants remain in their pots in this windowbox. A mulch of bark conceals the pots and retains moisture, and small pots of white bacopa add another dimension to the sculptured design.

MATERIALS

64cm (25in) terracotta planter
Bark chippings

PLANTS

Box pyramid in 5 litre (9in) pot
2 box balls in 5 litre (9in) pots
5 pots white bacopa

1 Water all the plants thoroughly. Stand the box pyramid in its pot in the centre of the container.

2 Stand the box balls on either side of the pyramid.

3 Fill the container with bark chippings to hide the pots.

4 Plunge the pots of bacopa in the bark at the front of the container. Stand in light shade. Water regularly.

GARDENER'S TIP

Provided the box plants are not root-bound they will be quite happy in their pots for a year. If the leaves start to lose their glossy dark green colour, it is a sign that they need a feed. Sprinkle a long-term plant food on the surface of the pots and boost with a liquid feed.

PLANT BOX AT ANY TIME OF THE YEAR,
AND BACOPA IN SPRING

The Young Container Gardener

Most children become enthusiastic gardeners as soon as they have a patch of soil they
can really call their own, and this applies equally to containers. What is more,
if they can make or decorate their container before planting it up, they'll get a real sense
of achievement. These projects use easily available plants and seeds that can be
bought quite cheaply and are reliable and free-flowering, given a little care and
attention. There are suggestions for easy-to-grow vegetables and a small pond
made from a toy-box that will quickly become a haven for wildlife. Youngsters will have
every reason to be proud of the results.

ABOVE: *An old pair of boots can make a fun container for brightly
coloured flowers.*

Watering-can planter

An old watering-can makes an attractive container, especially when it is painted and stencilled. When planted with an evergreen plant, such as the ivy used here, it will provide an eye-catching year-round display.

MATERIALS

Old watering-can
Paint brush
Eggshell paint, for the base coat
Stencil design
Masking tape
Stencil brush
Stencil paints, for the decoration
Fine paint brush
Bark chippings
Slow-release plant food granules

PLANT

Ivy

1 Paint the watering-can with the base colour. Apply two coats if necessary and leave each coat to dry thoroughly before painting the next.

2 Fasten the stencil design in place with masking tape. When stencilling, the brush should not hold much paint; dab it on newspaper to get rid of the excess. Use two or three colours to give your design a more three-dimensional effect.

GARDENER'S TIP

Other galvanized tin containers such as tin baths and buckets may also be painted and used.

PLANT AT ANY TIME OF THE YEAR

3 Use the fine paint brush to paint the rim of the can. You could pick out additional detailing if you wish.

4 When all the paint is quite dry, fill the watering-can with bark chippings.

5 Scoop out a hollow in the chippings and insert the ivy in its pot. Scatter some slow-release plant food granules on the surface. Arrange the tendrils so that they trail over the handle and spout of the watering-can. Water, pouring any excess water out through the spout. Place the watering-can in a shady spot or hang it from a hook in a cool corner.

Seaside garden

Even if you live miles from the sea you can create your own garden in
a sunny corner with some seashells, succulents and driftwood.

MATERIALS

Seashells
Self-hardening clay
4 terracotta pots of various sizes
Loam-based compost (soil mix)
  with 1/3 added grit
Gravel
Driftwood

PLANTS

Gazania
3 mesembryanthemum
2 crassula
Upright lampranthus
2 trailing lampranthus

LAMPRANTHUS

GAZANIA

1 Fill the shells with clay,
leaving some unfilled to cover
the compost (soil mix).

2 Press the shells onto the
terracotta pots and leave the
clay to harden overnight.

3 Plant the gazania in one of the
larger pots.

4 Plant the three
mesembryanthemums as a
group in one pot.

5 Plant the crassulas together in
a fairly small pot. These plants
grow naturally in poor soils and
do not mind overcrowding.

6 The upright and trailing
lampranthus have similar
colour foliage and flower but quite
different shapes so they make an
interesting contrast when planted
together. Cover the compost (soil
mix) in each pot with a layer of
gravel and then add seashells and
pieces of driftwood. Group
together in a sunny position.

Small is beautiful

Not everyone has room for a large hanging basket, especially when the plants have reached maturity, but there is sure to be space for a small basket like this one which will flower cheerfully all summer long.

MATERIALS

25cm (10in) hanging basket
Sphagnum moss
Compost (soil mix)
Slow-release plant food granules

PLANTS

4 nasturtiums
2 Lysimachia nummularia 'Aurea'
3 pot marigolds (calendula)

NASTURTIUM

LYSIMACHIA

MARIGOLDS

GARDENER'S TIP

Small baskets dry out very quickly so be sure to water frequently. To give a really good soak you can immerse the basket in a bucket of water, but be careful not to damage the trailing plants.

PLANT IN SPRING

1 Line the lower half of the basket with moss. Plant three of the nasturtiums into the side of the basket by resting the root-balls on the moss and carefully guiding the leaves through the sides of the basket.

2 Line the rest of the basket with moss and fill with compost (soil mix), working half a teaspoon of slow-release plant food granules into the top layer. Plant the lysimachia opposite one another at the edge of the basket.

3 Plant the pot marigolds in the top of the basket.

4 Plant the remaining nasturtium in the middle of the basket. Water well and hang in a sunny postion.

Terrific tyres

Old car tyres get a new and completely different lease of life with a lick of paint. They make perfect containers for all sorts of plants and are ideal for a first garden.

BEDDING PLANTS

MATERIALS

Coloured emulsion paints
Paint brush
2 car tyres
Compost (soil mix) and garden soil
Newspaper

PLANTS

Selection of bedding plants
  such as cosmos
  pelargoniums, pansies
  (viola), and pot marigolds
  (calendula)

1 Use ordinary emulsion to paint the tyres – any colours look good, the brighter the better.

2 Put one tyre on top of another and fill with potting compost or equal quantities of garden soil and compost (soil mix). To cut down on the amount of compost, stuff newspaper into the tyres.

3 Put the tallest plants in first – this is a cosmos. Surround it with smaller plants like pelargoniums, pansies and marigolds.

4 Plant some delicate trailing plants to grow over the edge. Start your tyre garden off by giving it a lot of water. Keep watering through the summer and do not let it get too dry.

GARDENER'S TIP

You can get old tyres for free at most garages. For something cheap and fast growing, try growing pumpkin plants.
PLANT IN SPRING OR EARLY SUMMER

Blooming old boots

This is a blooming wonderful way to recycle an old pair of boots, the bigger the better. It just goes to show that almost anything can be used to grow plants in, as long as it has a few holes in the bottom for drainage. Try an old football, a sports bag, or even an old hat for plant containers with lots of character.

MATERIALS
Knife
Old pair of working boots
Compost (soil mix)

PLANTS
Selection of bedding plants such as impatiens, pelargoniums, verbenas, pansies and lobelias

BEDDING
PLANTS

1 Using a knife very carefully, make some holes in between the stitching of the sole for drainage. It helps if there are holes there already.

2 Fill the boots with compost (soil mix), pushing it right down so there are no air spaces.

3 Plant flowers like pelargoniums, that can cope with hot dry places, and verbenas which will trail over the edge.

4 Squeeze in a pansy with a contrasting flower colour and a trailing lobelia plant. Lobelia grows in the smallest of spaces and will delicately tumble over the edge.

5 The boots need watering every day in the summer, and bloom even better if some plant food is mixed into the water once a week.

SAFETY NOTE
Children should always be supervised when using any sharp objects.

PLANT IN SPRING

A watery world

No garden is complete without the sight and sound of water. Great for toe-dipping on a hot sunny day, this mini-pond is too small for fish but a welcome watering spot for thirsty birds. Any large container can be used to make a mini-pond, as long as it is watertight. A toy-tidy, like this one, is ideal.

MATERIALS

Large, wide container
Gravel
Lead from a wine bottle top
Flower pot

PLANTS

2 aquatic plants such as golden sedge and monkey flower
Strands of oxygenating weed
Small floating plants such as water lettuce and floating ferns

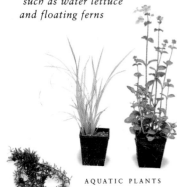

AQUATIC PLANTS

OXYGENATING WEED

FLOATING PLANTS

GARDENER'S TIP

Keep shallow containers in a semi-shady area to avoid excess evaporation. Plant up an adjoining mix of tulips and alliums for a spring and early summer display.

PLANT IN SPRING

1 Put a layer of gravel in the bottom of a large, wide container and fill with water almost to the top.

2 Lower the aquatic plants (which should be in net pots when you buy them) gently into the water around the edge.

3 Bend a piece of lead around the base of pieces of oxygenating weed to weigh them down. Pot the bunch into a flower pot and put a layer of gravel on the surface.

4 Lower the pot into the mini-pond, then add a few floating plants. Sink the pond into a hole in the garden so that it keeps cool.

Tasty treats!

You do not need a large garden to grow fruit and vegetables – it is possible to grow some in just a windowbox. Strawberries and bush or trailing tomatoes are small enough, so are radishes and lettuces. Nasturtium leaves and flowers are edible, with a hot, peppery taste. They look lovely in a salad.

MATERIALS

76cm (30in) plastic windowbox
Compost (soil mix)

PLANTS

2 tomato plants
2 strawberry plants
Radish seeds
Lettuce seeds
Nasturtium seeds

STRAWBERRY PLANTS

LETTUCE SEEDS

NASTURTIUM SEEDS

RADISH SEEDS

TOMATO PLANT

1 Fill the windowbox with compost (soil mix) to just below the rim. Plant the tomatoes in the back corners of the windowbox.

2 Plant the strawberries, about 30cm (12in) away from the tomatoes.

3 Sow radish and lettuce seeds 1cm (½in) apart. After the young radishes have been harvested, the lettuces can grow into their space.

4 Sow some nasturtium seeds in the corners so that they can grow up and trail over the edge. Water thoroughly.

GARDENER'S TIP

To get a plant out of a pot, turn it upside down with the stem between your fingers. With the other hand, firmly squeeze the bottom of the pot to release the root-ball.

PLANT IN SPRING

Garden with a buzz

To encourage beautiful butterflies and buzzing bees into the
garden, grow a few of their
favourite plants to tempt them
in from miles around. Many
butterflies are now becoming
scarce, so every butterfly-
friendly plant that you can
grow will help them to survive.
Bees and butterflies like lots
of sunshine so put the barrel or
planter in a sunny spot.

MATERIALS

Pebbles
Large planter or half barrel
Compost (soil mix) or equal
  quantities of garden soil and
  compost

PLANTS

Selection of suitable plants such
  as phlox, aster, lavender,
  verbena, blue lobelia, scabious

PLANTS

GARDENER'S TIP

Other excellent plants are broom,
catmint, delphinium, nasturtium,
ox-eye daisy, petunia, primrose,
stock, sweet William and thrift.

PLANT IN SPRING

1 Put a few pebbles in the
bottom of the barrel or planter
for drainage, then fill with
compost (soil mix) or an equal
mixture of soil and compost.

2 Plant phlox and aster in the
middle as they will grow the
tallest.

3 Plant lavender and verbena
around the edge.

4 Plant blue lobelia in the front,
so it tumbles over the edge.
Water the container.

Fuchsias for tots

Several fuchsia cultivars are excellent plants for children to grow. These fuchsias can be bought at the start of the summer in small pots or in polystyrene trays. Transferred to small, brightly painted pots on a window-sill, or in a light corner in the children's room, they will flower continuously through the summer.

FUCHSIA

MATERIALS

7.5cm (3in) terracotta pots
Paint brush
Bright acrylic or emulsion paints
Crocks (broken pots)
Compost (soil mix)

PLANTS

Fuchsia 'Happy' and F. 'Tom Thumb'

1 Paint the pots with bright primary colours in stripes or bold patterns. The paints used here are thick and water-resistant. If you use ordinary emulsion, you may need a couple of coats to achieve a bold effect. To achieve geometric patterns, use masking tape to mask out specific areas before painting. Let the paint dry before you continue.

2 Place small crocks (broken pots) in the bottom of the pots to cover the drainage hole and facilitate quick drainage.

3 Remove the fuchsias from their plastic pots and place one in each terracotta pot. Add more compost (soil mix) down the sides of the pot.

4 Use the blunt end of the paint brush to ease the compost (soil mix) into the gap between the plant's root-ball and the pot. Tamp down the compost firmly but not too tightly. Water the pots and allow to drain.

PLANT IN EARLY SPRING,
OR EARLY SUMMER

Spring into action

On misty, autumn days spring might seem a long time away, but young gardeners have to think ahead. If you want a cheerful pot of flowers to greet you early next year, now is the time to get planting. There are hundreds of different types of spring-flowering bulbs to choose from, and mixed and matched with forget-me-nots, daisies, pansies or wallflowers, you cannot go wrong.

MATERIALS

Large flower pot
Small stones
Compost (soil mix)

PLANTS

Tulip bulbs
Wallflowers
    (cheiranthus)
Forget-me-nots,
    daisies or
    pansies (violas)

FORGET-ME-NOT

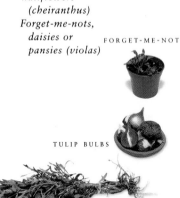

TULIP BULBS

WALLFLOWERS

GARDENER'S TIP

The plants will not need heavy watering over the autumn and winter, but they will need an occasional drink so keep an eye on the pot in case it dries out.

PLANT IN AUTUMN

1 Use the biggest pot that you have got and put a few stones over the hole in the bottom for drainage. Fill the pot two-thirds full with compost (soil mix).

2 Plant about 5 tulip bulbs. Cover the bulbs with handfuls of compost (soil mix).

3 Using your hands to make holes, plant three wallflowers evenly spaced out. If you dig up a tulip bulb by mistake, just pop it back in again.

4 Fill any gaps with forget-me-nots, daisies or pansies, or a mixture. Give all the plants a good watering.

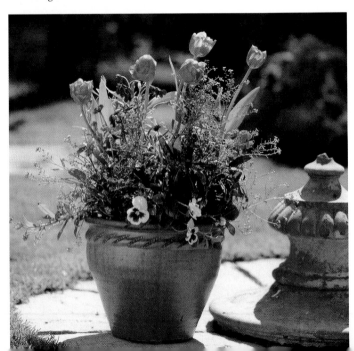

Cactus garden

Planting a bowl of cacti may take a little care and patience, but it is worth the effort since children love cacti. Once planted, the cacti ask nothing more than benevolent neglect.

MATERIALS

25cm (10in) terracotta bowl
Cactus compost (soil mix)
Newspaper
Cactus gravel

PLANTS

Euphorbia submammilaris
Rebutia muscula
*Rose pincushion (*Mammilaria zeilmanniana)
Cheiridopsis candidissima
Astrophytum ornatum
Prickly pear (Opuntia)

REBUTIA   EUPHORBIA   PRICKLY PEAR

CHEIRIDOPSIS

ASTROPHYTUM

ROSE PINCUSHION

GARDENER'S TIP

If there are young children in your household be sure to choose the site of your cactus garden with care. If cacti are too aggressive for you, plant succulents instead: they require the same treatment, but are free of thorns.

PLANT AT ANY TIME OF THE YEAR

1 Fill the bowl with cactus compost (soil mix) to within 5cm (2in) of the rim. Prepare a thickly folded strip of newspaper to help you handle the cacti.

2 Before planting, decide on your arrangement of the plants by standing them, in their pots, in the bowl.

3 Ease the plants from their pots, surround them with a newspaper collar and lift into place. Handle more ferocious plants carefully, and leave the really prickly cacti until last or you will stab yourself on them as you are planting the rest.

4 Fill in around the plants with extra compost (soil mix) if needed. Add a finishing touch with a top-dressing of fine cactus gravel. Stand in good light and water sparingly.

Indoor Containers

Plants do furnish a room, and the same considerations apply to the effective use of containers indoors as in the garden: find containers that suit their surroundings and the plants you have chosen for them; plant them imaginatively and group them for impact. Foliage plants will form the backbone of most arrangements, rather as trees and shrubs do in the garden. Flowering plants won't be so long-lasting indoors, but are always the centre of attraction while they are in bloom. Decorative pots intended to go outdoors can be used very successfully indoors too. Baskets make good plant holders if you line them with plastic. Your indoor plants will appreciate good light (although direct sunlight through glass is too powerful for most species) and a moist atmosphere: stand the pots in saucers of wet gravel and give them a daily misting to help keep them looking their best.

ABOVE: *Introduce flowering plants to your indoor collections to brighten up your home.*

Indoor table-top garden

Many indoor plants have dramatically coloured flowers and foliage. In this arrangement the purple flowers of the African violet are echoed by the velvety leaves of the gynura. The delicate fronds of the maidenhair fern and the dark green foliage of the button fern add interest with their contrasting shape and colour.

MATERIALS

30cm (12in) terracotta seed tray
Crocks (broken pots)
Houseplant compost (soil mix)
Slow-release plant food granules
Clay granules

PLANTS

Maidenhair fern (adiantum)
African violet (saintpaulia)
Gynura
Button fern (Pellaea rotundifolia)

AFRICAN VIOLET

MAIDENHAIR FERN

GARDENER'S TIP

Terracotta transmits moisture and will mark a table-top if it is in direct contact with it.
Cut 2.5 cm (1in) sections from a cork and glue them to the four corners of the seed tray.
A plastic tray smaller than the seed tray can then be slipped underneath it to catch any drips.

PLANT AT ANY TIME OF THE YEAR

1 Cover the drainage holes in the bottom of the seed tray with crocks (broken pots).

2 Arrange the plants before removing them from their pots. Plant the tallest plant first, then add the others around it.

3 Fill any gaps with compost (soil mix) and scatter a table-spoon of plant food granules on the surface. Mulch between the plants with clay granules to help retain moisture. Water and place in a light position, but out of direct sunlight. Spray regularly with water.

Bottle it up

Bottle gardens are great fun to make, and if you choose a stoppered bottle you will probably be able to grow some of those tricky plants that demand very high humidity. Don't worry too much about choosing the right plants, however. If you are prepared to replace plants when they outgrow their space, just concentrate on the plants that please you. You will have to improvise tools for your bottle garden by lashing old pieces of cutlery to garden canes.

SMALL FOLIAGE PLANTS

MATERIALS

Large glass bottle with cork
Fine gravel
Paper or thin cardboard
Charcoal
Compost (soil mix)
Knife, fork, spoon and
cotton reel attached to canes

PLANTS

Small foliage plants

1 Place some fine gravel in the bottom of the bottle. If the neck is narrow you can make yourself a funnel from paper or thin cardboard to scatter it evenly over the base.

2 Add a thin layer of charcoal. This will help to absorb impurities and reduce the risk of the bottle smelling if there is too much moisture.

3 Spread a layer of compost (soil mix) over the base, and level it. Using your improvised trowel, make a hole for the plant.

4 Firm each plant in well. If you can't reach with your hand, use a cotton reel pushed on to the end of a cane to tamp down the compost (soil mix).

5 Work around the whole bottle until it is fully planted. Then mist the plants. Aim the spray at the sides of the bottle if compost (soil mix) is clinging to the glass and spoiling the effect. Leave the plants and compost moist but not soaking wet.

6 If using a stoppered bottle you will have to balance the atmosphere over a week or two. You may need to keep inserting or removing the cork for periods (see opposite).

GARDENER'S TIP

Place the cork firmly in position and leave it for a day or two. Some misting of the glass, especially in the morning,
is quite normal – but if it never clears there is too much moisture, so leave the cork off for a day and try again.
If no condensation appears at all, it is probably too dry – mist again, then return the cork. It will take trial and error at
first, but once the atmosphere is balanced you can leave the bottle for months without attention, although you will have
to prune or remove plants that become too large.

PLANT IN SPRING

Palm court

Palms look graceful and elegant. They usually look best in isolation or among other palms, rather than in a group of mixed plants. Display them so that their classic shape can be appreciated. Allow these aristocrats space to make a statement.

MATERIALS

Decorative pot with drainage hole
Polystyrene (plastic foam) or other suitable
* drainage material*
Compost (soil mix), loam-based if plant is large
Bark chippings

1 Unless your palm is small, choose a large pot. As it will be conspicuous, choose an attractive, decorative one that does the plant justice. Start by placing a layer of polystyrene (plastic foam) or other drainage material in the bottom.

PALM

PLANT

Palm, appropriate for size of pot

2 Stand the palm in the pot and surround the root-ball with container compost (soil mix), pressing it firmly around the plant. Scatter a tablespoon of plant food granules on the surface.

3 Cover the compost (soil mix) with a layer of bark and water. Place in a position that receives good light, but no more than a couple of hours of direct sunlight each day. Water regularly during growing season, but allow the compost to dry out between waterings during the winter.

GARDENER'S TIP

Palms can look splendid in isolation, but they usually look more impressive in a collection. Display plants of different sizes to add interest, and place small ones on pedestals in front of taller ones in large pots. Like most houseplants, the palm will benefit from being stood outside during warm summer rain. A good soaking shower removes dust from the leaves and gives the plant the benefit of a drink of untreated water.

PLANT IN SPRING

Colourful kitchen herbs

PARSLEY

Make a bright cheerful statement by using painted cans as containers for your kitchen herbs, often now available in pots from most supermarkets.

CORIANDER

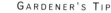

BASIL

MATERIALS
Empty food cans
White spirit
Masking tape
Paint brush
Gloss paint

PLANTS
Dill
Chives
Parsley
Coriander
(cilantro)
Basil

GARDENER'S TIP

Large painted cans make colourful planters in the garden. Ask your local restaurant or school for some of the catering size cans that they normally throw away.

PLANT AT ANY TIME OF THE YEAR

1 Thoroughly wash and dry the cans. Use white spirit to remove any residual spots of glue. Wrap masking tape round the lips of the cans so that half of it protrudes above the rims.

2 Fold the protruding masking tape inside the rims of the cans.

3 Paint the cans and leave them to dry.

4 Depending on the colours you choose, some of them may need more than one coat. Leave to dry completely.

5 Place each plant, pot and all, in a separate can. Stand in a light position and water if the compost (soil mix) dries out.

Sweet scents for a conservatory

This simple, very informal planting would thrive in a conservatory. A pretty combination of scented-leaf pelargonium, deep blue miniature petunias, purple trailing verbenas and exuberant tumbling ground ivies.

VERBENA

GROUND IVY

MATERIALS
30cm (12in) plastic windowbox
Compost (soil mix)
Slow-release plant food granules

PLANTS
Scented-leaf Pelargonium 'Lady Plymouth'
2 variegated ground ivies (Glechoma hederacea 'Variegata')
2 deep purple trailing verbenas
2 deep blue 'Junior' petunias

PETUNIA

PELARGONIUM

1 Check drainage holes are open; if not, drill or punch them out. Fill the windowbox with compost (soil mix), working in a teaspoon of plant foot granules. Plant the pelargonium in the centre.

GARDENER'S TIP
If the ground ivy gets too rampant, cut it back. Root some pieces and plant out in the spring to run wild over a wall.

PLANT IN SPRING

2 Plant the ground ivies at each end, and the two verbenas at the back of the box between the pelargonium and ground ivies.

3 Plant the petunias between the pelargonium and ground ivies at the front of the box. Water thoroughly and stand in a sunny position.

Water-loving plants

The sweet flag is a marsh plant which loves the moist conditions in most bathrooms. Planted in gravel in a stylish glass pot or vase, it is easy to see when the water needs topping up.

SWEET FLAG

MATERIALS

20cm (8in) glass vase or pot
Gravel

PLANTS

1 large or 2 small sweet flags
(Acorus gramineus 'Variegatus')

1 Fill the bottom half of the container with gravel.

2 Take the plants out of their existing pots and place them on the gravel.

3 Fill the pot with gravel to the base of the leaves and half-fill the container with water. Place on a light window-sill and never allow the plants to dry out.

GARDENER'S TIP

The umbrella plant (*Cyperus alternifolius*) will also thrive in these conditions.

PLANT AT ANY TIME OF THE YEAR

Combined effects

Displaying houseplants in groups creates a humid microclimate, which the plants prefer to the dry atmosphere of most homes. The humidity is increased by standing the pots in saucers of wet gravel kept moist by regular watering. Choose plants of contrasting shapes and sizes for the most striking effect.

MATERIALS

4 pots of various sizes with
*   saucers*
Crocks
Compost
Gravel

PLANTS

Lilies
Maidenhair fern
*   (adiantum)*
Cretan fern
Variegated creeping fig
*   (Ficus pumila)*

1 Place the crocks in the bottom of the pots. Check the proportion of pot to plant.

2 Remove the lilies from their plastic container and position in the pot.

3 Fill gaps around the root-balls with compost (soil mix), pressing down firmly to avoid any air spaces.

4 Remove the foliage plants from their containers and plant in the other pots, topping up with compost (soil mix).

5 Water the plants thoroughly. Fill the saucers with gravel. Stand the pots in their saucers and position the plants in good light, but away from direct sun. Keep the gravel in the saucers damp, and water the plants when the compost (soil mix) dries out.

LILY

MAIDENHAIR
FERN

CREEPING
FIG

CRETAN
FERN

GARDENER'S TIP

Bear in mind the background of your display when choosing your plants. Large architectural leaves and strong plain colours won't get lost against a busy wallpaper, whereas lots of variegations and colour are better against a plain background.

PLANT AT ANY TIME OF THE YEAR

Beautiful baskets

A basket is a great way to display a small group of houseplants. You don't need a lot of plants to make a superb show, and when one is past its best you can just remove it and pop in a replacement.

MATERIALS

Basket
Plastic sheet
Compost (soil mix)
Sphagnum moss,
* dried or fresh*

PLANTS

5–6 small plants such as saintpaulia (African violet), chlorophytum, adiantum, exacum, impatiens

BUSY LIZZY
ADIANTUM
SAINTPAULIA
CHLOROPHYTUM
EXACUM

1 To protect the basket (and your furniture) from the effects of moisture, line it with a piece of plastic cut to size.

2 Add a layer of compost (soil mix) to retain moisture, and provide a humid atmosphere around the plants.

3 Remove the plants from their pots and place in the basket. It may be necessary to add or remove some compost (soil mix) from the bottom to bring each plant to the right height.

4 Make sure you are entirely happy with the arrangement of the plants, then trickle a little more compost (soil mix) between them to fill in the gaps.

5 Use dried or fresh moss to fill any spaces between the plants.

GARDENER'S TIP

You could leave the plants in the individual pots for convenience.

PLANT AT ANY TIME OF YEAR

Indoor topiary

Proper topiary is not practical indoors, but you can cheat a little and achieve a similar effect by training ivy over a frame. Start with an easy shape like the lollipop shown here, and once you are proficient you can experiment with all kinds of imaginative shapes. Buy a wire frame or make your own.

MATERIALS

Pot large enough to accommodate frame
Crocks (broken pots)
Compost (soil mix)
Wire frame

PLANTS   IVY

2–3 small-leaved variegated ivies

1 Place crocks (broken pots) over the drainage hole and cover with a layer of compost (soil mix).

2 Insert the wire frame, placing it centrally, and top up with more compost (soil mix) to secure it.

3 Insert the ivies around the edge of the pot. The more plants you use, the more quickly the frame will be covered.

4 Leave a few shoots to trail over the edge of the pot, but thread the rest through the frame. Within a few months the frame will probably be completely hidden by the new growth. Thread new shoots through bare areas, and pinch back any that are too long. Regular pinching back of long shoots will help to retain the shape once the frame has been covered.

GARDENER'S TIP

Once you have mastered this lollipop shape, try making an animal (teddy bear or rabbit). If you can't find a ready made template, then make your own wire shape. Alternatively, try something more ambitious like a large cup and saucer, or even a tennis racket.

PLANT IN EARLY SPRING

Terrarium display

SELECTION OF
SMALL HOUSE
PLANTS

Terrariums are similar to bottle gardens and come in a variety of shapes. Many of them are not sealed, so the atmosphere is less humid. They provide a more ornamental way to display plants. If access is easy, you may want to consider a few flowering plants to provide colour.

MATERIALS

Terrarium
Expanded clay granules
Gravel
Compost (soil mix)

PLANTS

Selection of small
plants

1 Place a layer of clay granules, followed by gravel, in the base to reduce the risk of the compost (soil mix) becoming water-logged. Use either gravel or clay granules if you cannot get both.

2 Add the compost (soil mix), making the layer several centimetres deep if possible. If this is not practical due to the design of the terrarium, you will need to reduce the depth of the root-balls.

3 If your centrepiece plant is too large, try a little judicious pruning with scissors.

4 You should be able to plant and firm the plants by hand. Plant the back, or the least accessible area first.

5 Place the plants most likely to require regular pruning or pinching back in the most accessible positions.

6 Plant your centrepiece, firming it in well.

GARDENER'S TIP

Be sure that you select slow-growing small-leaved plants, or what began as an airy, well-presented display could end up as a miniature jungle.

PLANT IN EARLY SPRING

Mixed blessings

A bowl of mixed plants almost always looks better than the same number dotted around in individual pots. Garden centres and florists often sell mixed bowls, but you can probably make one more cheaply using a container that you already have – and you can ring the changes with different plants.

FOLIAGE AND
FLOWERING PLANTS

MATERIALS

Bowl with drainage hole
Crocks (broken pots)
Compost (soil mix)
Spare pot the same size as
*   centrepiece plant pot*

PLANTS

Collection of mixed foliage and
*   flowering plants*

1 Cover the drainage hole with crocks (broken pots). Part-fill the container with compost (soil mix).

2 It is a good idea to have a showy centrepiece plant – insert an empty pot temporarily so that you are sure to leave enough space.

3 Place the other plants around the centrepiece, rearranging them as necessary while still in their pots. Do not start planting until you are happy with the results.

4 Remove the plants from their pots and plant. Finally, insert the centrepiece. If it is likely to be a long-term occupant, remove it from its pot. If you are likely to have to replace it after a few weeks – as is common with flowering plants once they finish blooming – keep it in its container.

GARDENER'S TIP

For a lively, varied mix use a combination of small bushy, vertical, and trailing plants. Tradescantias are a good choice for the last category, particularly since they come in a wide range of bright colours, including greens, creams and bronze.

PLANT AT ANY TIME OF YEAR

Start a collection

Once houseplants become more of a consuming hobby than a passing pleasure, you will begin to look for more ways to feed your passion. One option is to start a collection of a particular type of plants, whether a large and diverse group such as cacti, or a smaller, interesting group like saintpaulias (African violets).

SAINTPAULIAS

MATERIALS

Baskets or containers of various sizes
Florist's foam
Moss

PLANTS

Collection of plants, such as saintpaulias (African violets)

1 Start by grouping your plants to find an arrangement that pleases you.

2 The design will look more interesting if you can create a cascade effect using florist's foam to build up different levels.

3 Build up the back of the display on florist's foam first.

4 Fill in the space in front in steps. Try the plants for size so that you can use more foam beneath the pots if needed.

GARDENER'S TIP

To find the best range of plants, do not rely on the average garden centre. You must hunt out a specialist nursery where they will have a far more imaginative and superior collection: everything to satisfy the enthusiast.

PLANT IN EARLY SPRING

5 Arrange the plants to look as though they could be growing as a natural group and not in straight rows. Fill the spaces between the pots with moss.

Orchid basket

MILTONIA

PLANTS

Miltonia or
phalaenopsis
orchid

Orchids are no longer the rare exotic plants that they used to be and most garden centres now stock some. A few inexpensive materials and a little time will create a stylish container to show these lovely flowers at their very best.

MATERIALS

Plastic-lined twig basket,
  15cm (6in) diameter
Gravel
Sphagnum moss
3 x 40cm (16in) canes
Raffia

1 Pour a 2.5cm (1in) layer of gravel into the base of the basket and line with moss.

2 Slip the orchid (still in its pot) into the basket.

3 Push the canes into the moss at the edge of the basket so that they are held firmly in place.

4 Tie a length of raffia between each cane, finishing off with a neat knot.

GARDENER'S TIP

Orchids do not like to stand in water, but they do like a humid atmosphere. A layer of gravel underneath the pot acts as a reservoir for excess water which creates humidity. The orchid will also benefit from being sprayed with water.

PLANT AT ANY TIME
OF THE YEAR

Plant crazy

These highly decorative and unusual planters are enhanced by the careful choice of plants which provide the royal head-dresses. The queen's tresses float delicately above the crown, whilst the king's tumble downwards.

MATERIALS

2 decorative pots
Gravel
Compost (soil mix)

PLANTS

Chandelier plant
(Kalanchoe
tubiflora)
Creeping fig
(Ficus pumila)

CREEPING FIG

CHANDELIER
PLANT

1 Pour a 5cm (2in) layer of gravel into the bottom of the pots.

2 Place the chandelier plant into the planter; if there is any space around the root-ball, fill with compost (soil mix) and gently firm the plant in position.

3 After you have planted the creeping fig in the other planter, arrange the sprays of leaves so that they resemble hair. As the plant grows it will need an occasional haircut to keep it under control. Water regularly and stand in a light position.

GARDENER'S TIP

If you are going away for a few days during the summer months, give your houseplants a holiday in the garden. Stand them on a tray lined with a thick layer of damp newspaper, positioned in a shady corner, where they will not dry out.

**PLANT AT ANY TIME
OF THE YEAR**

Period fuchsias

Fuchsias were first cultivated in Europe in the 1780s. Many cultivars bred in the 1800s can still be found in cultivation today. Fuchsia 'Bland's New Striped' was first seen in cultivation in 1872, and 'Claire de Lune' in 1880. Growing plants from a particular period will add an exciting historic flavour to any collection.

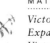

MATERIALS
....
Victorian copper pot
Expanded clay granules
Victorian-style planter
Crocks (broken pots)
Compost (soil mix)

PLANTS
....
Fuchsia *'Claire de Lune'*
Fuchsia *'Bland's New Striped'*

1 Put a layer of expanded clay granules into the base of the Victorian copper pot. This will help to create a humid atmosphere around the plants.

2 Place the *Fuchsia* 'Claire de Lune' in the copper pot, arranging the branches and foliage to fall around the sides.

3 Cover the drainage hole in the bottom of the Victorian-style planter with terracotta crocks.

4 Fill the pot with compost (soil mix).

5 Remove *F.* 'Bland's New Striped' from its pot. The network of fresh, healthy roots shows that the plant is strong and vigorous.

6 Plant in the compost (soil mix). Cover the root-ball and firm the compost with your hands.

GARDENER'S TIP

Orange flowers are often considered to be a modern advance in fuchsia cultivars, but 'Lye's Unique' has salmon-orange flowers, and originated in 1886. Other old varieties to look out for include 'Charming', a hardy bush which was developed in 1877.

PLANT IN EARLY SPRING OR EARLY SUMMER

Copper-bottomed begonia

The stunningly marked leaves of this begonia are shown to great advantage in this old copper pot. The pot was an inexpensive purchase from a flea market, and was cleaned before use.

MATERIALS

Copper pot, 20cm (8in) diameter
Lemon
Slow-release plant food granules
Clay granules

PLANT

Begonia

BEGONIA

1 Rub the tarnished pot with half a lemon. The acidity of the juice will quickly clean the pot, but don't overclean it or it will look brand new and lose some of its character.

2 Place the begonia, in its plastic pot, in the copper container. Scatter a teaspoon of plant food granules on the surface of the compost (soil mix).

3 Surround the plant with clay granules. Place in a light, but not sunny, position and water regularly.

GARDENER'S TIP

Other houseplants recommended for this treatment are streptocarpus, gynura and cyclamen.

PLANT AT ANY TIME OF THE YEAR

Dramatic datura

The angel's trumpet or *Datura* (strictly speaking, it should now be known as *Brugmansia*), a popular conservatory plant, will grow enormous in time, provided it is planted in a large container and given regular food and water. The plant will benefit from a period outdoors during the summer, but will grow indoors for the rest of the year.

MATERIALS

Deep planter, at least 40cm (16in) diameter
Polystyrene (plastic foam) or similar drainage material
Gloves
Equal mix loam-based compost (soil mix) and container compost
Slow-release plant food granules

PLANTS

Angel's trumpet (Brugmansia suaveolens)
4 white busy lizzies (impatiens)

ANGEL'S TRUMPET

BUSY LIZZIE

1 Fill the base of the container with lightweight polystyrene (plastic foam) or similar drainage material. Wear gloves to lift the angel's trumpet into the container.

2 Pour compost (soil mix) round the edges of the plant, pressing down firmly around the root-ball. Scatter 2 tablespoons of plant food granules on the surface.

3 Plant the busy Lizzies around the base of the angel's trumpet, and remember to water frequently.

GARDENER'S TIP

All parts of the angel's trumpet are poisonous, and it should be handled with care. Standing it outside in summer is recommended as the scent of the flowers can have a narcotic effect in confined spaces. It is not recommended in households with small children. While it is sensible to be cautious, it is also a fact that many commonly cultivated plants are poisonous. For example, with the exception of its tubers, the potato plant is poisonous, as are dieffenbachia and oleander.

PLANT IN SPRING

Plant guide

TREES AND SHRUBS FOR CONTAINERS

Acer palmatum
Apple (dwarf)
Bay
Berberis thunbergii 'Atropurpurea Nana',
    B. darwinii
Box
Camellia
Ceratostigma plumbaginoides
Chamaecyparis pisifera
Choisya ternata
x *Citrofortunella microcarpa**
Convolvulus cneorum
*Cordyline**
Cotoneaster conspicuus
*Datura**
Euonymus fortunei
Fuchsia
Hebe
Holly
Hydrangea
*Lantana**
Lavender
Potentilla
Rhododendron
Rosemary
Rose
Skimmia

CLIMBERS FOR CONTAINERS

Bougainvillea*
Clematis alpina, C. macropetala
*Cobaea scandens**
Gynura*
Ivy
Jasmine
Stephanotis*
Thunbergia alata
Trachelospermum jasminoides

HARDY PLANTS FOR PERMANENT PLANTING IN CONTAINERS

Anemone blanda
Aquilegia alpina
Arabis ferdinandi-coburgi 'Variegata'
Asplenium crispum
Athyrium niponicum
Berberis thunbergii 'Atropurpurea Nana',
    B. darwinii
Bergenia
Box
Ceratostigma plumbaginoides
Chamaecyparis pisifera 'Filifera Aurea', 'Sungold'
Choisya ternata
Convolvulus cneorum
Cotoneaster conspicuus
Crocus
Day lily
Dianthus
Dryopteris filix-mas
Euonymus fortunei 'Emerald and Gold'
Euphorbia
Foxglove
Hebe
Helianthemum
Heuchera 'Palace Purple', 'Bressingham Bronze'
Holly
Hosta
Hydrangea
Inula
Iris reticulata
Ivy
Lamium
Lavender
Lily-of-the-valley
Narcissus
Nepeta mussinii
Ophiopogon planiscapus 'Nigrescens'
Pachysandra terminalis
Polygonum affine

Polystichum acrostichoides
Potentilla
Primula auricula
Rosemary
Salix alpina
Sedum ewersii
Sedum 'Ruby Glow'
Sempervivum
Skimmia japonica 'Rubella'
Thyme
Trachelospermum jasminoides
Veronica peduncularis
Vinca minor

TRAILING PLANTS FOR HANGING BASKETS

Ageratum*
*Begonia semperflorens**
*Bidens ferulifolia**
Brachyscome iberidifolia
*Campanula isophylla**
*Chaenorhinum glareosum**
*Convolvulus sabatius**
Erigeron mucronatus
Felicia*
Fuchsia (lax varieties)*
Gazania*
Glechoma hederacea
*Helichrysum petiolare**
Lampranthus*
Lantana*
Lobelia*
*Lotus berthelotii**
Lysimachia nummularia
Nasturtium
Osteospermum*
Pelargonium*
Petunia*
Sedum ewersii
*Senecio maritima**
Sweet peas
Verbena*
Vinca minor

SPRING-FLOWERING PLANTS FOR CONTAINERS
Anagallis
Anemone blanda
Aquilegia
Arabis ferdinandi-coburgi 'Variegata'
Bluebells
Crocus
Day lily
Euphorbia
Forget-me-not
Iris reticulata
Lily-of-the-valley
Narcissus
Polyanthus
Primroses
Primula auricula
Snowdrops
Tulips
Vinca minor
Viola
Wallflower

AUTUMN AND WINTER COLOUR
Arabis ferdinandi-coburgi 'Variegata'
Berberis thunbergii 'Atropurpurea Nana',
   B. darwinii
Bergenia
Ceratostigma plumbaginoides
Chamaecyparis pisifera 'Sungold'
Convolvulus cneorum
Euonymus fortunei
Euphorbia
Ferns
Heuchera 'Palace Purple', 'Bressingham Bronze'
Hakonechloa macra 'Alboaurea'
Hebe
Holly
Iris unguicularis
Ivy
Pachysandra terminalis
Polygonum affine
Salvia greggii
Sedum 'Ruby Glow'
Vinca minor

PLANTS FOR SHADE
Anemone blanda
Begonia semperflorens
Bergenia
Box
Campanula isophylla
Chamaecyparis pisifera
Digitalis
Euonymous
Euphorbia
Ferns
Glechoma hederacea
Heuchera
Holly
Hosta
Hydrangea
Impatiens*
Ivy
Lily-of-the-valley
Narcissus
Ophiopogon planiscapus
Pachysandra terminalis
Primrose
Primula auricula
Skimmia
Sorrel
Thunbergia alata
Trachelospermum jasminoides
Vinca minor
Viola

PLANTS FOR HOT CONDITIONS
Aloe*
Alyssum
Argyranthemum*
Arundinaria pygmaea
Crassula ovata*
Diascia*
*Erigeron mucronatus**
Gazania*
Hakonechloa macra 'Aureola'
Helianthemum
Inula
Lavender
*Lotus berthelotii**
Mesembryanthemum
Osteospermum*

PLANTS WITH DECORATIVE FOLIAGE
Berberis thunbergii
Bergenia
Chamaecyparis pisifera
Choisya ternata

Convolvulus cneorum
Euonymus fortunei
Euphorbia
Fuchsia magellanica
Glechoma hederacea
Hebe
Hedera helix 'Hibernica'
*Helichrysum petiolare**
Heuchera
Holly
Hosta 'Blue Moon'
*Lotus berthelotii**
Lysimachia nummularia
Nasturtium 'Alaska'
Pachysandra terminalis
Pelargonium, ivy-leaved
Salvia officinalis
Senecio maritima
Thymus 'Silver Queen', 'Archer's
   Gold'
Vinca minor

FRAGRANT PLANTS
Alyssum
*Bidens atrosanguinea**
Cheiranthus
Choisya ternata
x *Citrofortunella microcarpa**
Dianthus
Heliotrope
Jasmine
Lavender
Lilies
Lily-of-the-valley
Nicotiana
Pelargonium, scented-leaved varieties*
Rosemary
Sweet pea
Thyme
Trachelospermum jasminoides
Viola odorata

Gardener's Records

Every garden is unique. They all vary in shape and size, and they have different soils, aspects and plants. They are looked after by very different people. For some people gardening is a necessary chore, for others it is a fascinating hobby, and an endless challenge to improve the garden and grow better plants. Through trial and error, you can create the garden of your dreams, with the certain knowledge that if something goes wrong you will definitely have another chance to get it right the following year.

ABOVE: *Grouping plants makes a high impact feature. Replace plants when they have passed their best, to keep it looking good.*

OPPOSITE: *A supply of fresh material for recipes is one of the rewards of growing your own herbs.*

The lawn

The lawn is probably the most important single element of the garden and they do need looking after. They need mowing at least once a week during the summer, possibly more in the middle of spring when the grass is growing quickly. They need feeding and weed control, autumn care to eliminate moss, and raking and spiking (aerating) in the winter or spring.

The first essential for any lawn is a mower that suits the amount of grass you have to cut. It is easiest to apply fertilizer and weedkiller in liquid form and it is worth renting a scarifier during the winter to clear out the dead grass.

RIGHT:*A curving border adds interest and perspective to a lawn and gives the garden a greater feeling of depth.*

	Year	Year	Year
Sown _____	Weed/Mosskiller applied		
Turfed _____	Scarified/Raked		
	Reseeded		
Sown _____	Weed/Mosskiller applied		
Turfed _____	Scarified/Raked		
	Reseeded		

LEFT:*Large concrete paving slabs are one way of saving wear on a small lawn which has constant traffic. Make sure that the path or stepping stones are in scale with the garden, otherwise they might look obtrusive.*

Shrubs

Shrubs are the mainstay of every garden. They are tolerant, undemanding and colourful, and, when established, they require little more than a mulch in the spring and – usually – some occasional pruning when they outgrow their allotted space.

RIGHT: *Old-fashioned shrub roses have enjoyed a great revival of popularity in recent years.*

Species ....

Source .... Planted ....

Year .... Year .... Year ....
Pruned ....
Mulched ....

Species ....

Source .... Planted ....

Pruned ....
Mulched ....

Species ....

Source .... Planted ....

Pruned ....
Mulched ....

Species ....

Source .... Planted ....

Pruned ....
Mulched ....

Species ....

Source .... Planted ....

Pruned ....
Mulched ....

Species ....

Source .... Planted ....

Pruned ....
Mulched ....

Climbers

Climbers are one of the best ways to extend a small garden upwards. They cover the walls in flowers and obscure unsightly fences. Although climbers provide a wonderful natural canopy, bear in mind that the support must be high enough for trailing shoots not to become a nuisance below. This is particularly important with climbing roses, as the thorns are a potential hazard.

RIGHT: *Wisteria is one of the loveliest climbers of all in early summer.*

Species _____   Year _____ Year _____ Year _____

Source _____   Pruned _____
Planted _____   Mulched _____

Species _____

Source _____   Pruned _____
Planted _____   Mulched _____

Species _____

Source _____   Pruned _____
Planted _____   Mulched _____

Species _____

Source _____   Pruned _____
Planted _____   Mulched _____

Annuals and bedding plants

Annuals and bedding plants provide instant colour in the garden. They brighten the summer in towns and cities all over the world, enlivening planters and windowboxes, and if you have room they are well worth planting in a bed on their own or among the permanent plants in the herbaceous or mixed border.

RIGHT: *Here a windowbox is used to stunning effect with a colour-coordinated display of bedding plants.*

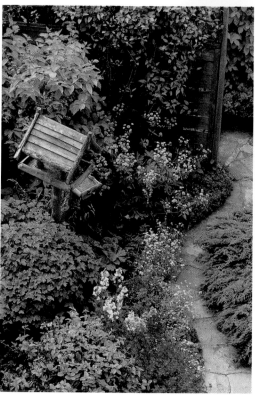

ABOVE: *Annuals and bedding plants are often used to fill in the gaps in a border of more established plants.*

Species _____
Sown _____ Planted out _____

Species _____
Sown _____ Planted out _____

Species _____
Sown _____ Planted out _____

Species _____
Sown _____ Planted out _____

Species _____
Sown _____ Planted out _____

Species _____
Sown _____ Planted out _____

Species _____
Sown _____ Planted out _____

Species _____
Sown _____ Planted out _____

Species _____
Sown _____ Planted out _____

Species _____
Sown _____ Planted out _____

Species _____
Sown _____ Planted out _____

Species _____
Sown _____ Planted out _____

Bulbs and tubers

The bulbs of spring are one of the first signs that the wheel of the seasons has turned and that warmer summer days are on their way. There is something charming about these early flowers, the yellow of the winter aconites, the nodding heads of the snowdrops and the teasing upright crocuses opening their heads to receive the sun's rays then closing up when it goes behind the clouds. Daffodils and narcissus are the most spectacular bulbs, covering gardens with yellow fields of colour. But there are also summer bulbs such as lilies, galtonias, scillas and chionodoxas. Then there are also the tubers, gladioli, begonias and, most important of all, the dahlias.

RIGHT: *Hyacinths, one of the best loved and popular bulbs, often grown as gifts at Christmas time as a foretaste of the coming spring.*

Species _____   Year _____ Year _____ Year _____

Source _____   Fed _____

Planted _____   Divided _____

Species _____

Source _____   Fed _____

Planted _____   Divided _____

Species _____

Source _____   Fed _____

Planted _____   Divided _____

Species _____

Source _____   Fed _____

Planted _____   Divided _____

Species _____   Year _____ Year _____ Year _____

_____

Source _____   Fed _____

Planted _____   Divided _____

Species _____

_____

Source _____   Fed _____

Planted _____   Divided _____

Species _____

_____

Source _____   Fed _____

Planted _____   Divided _____

Species _____

_____

Source _____   Fed _____

Planted _____   Divided _____

ABOVE: *What you should look for when buying tubers: a healthy pot tuber (left) and a healthy tuber (right).*

Species ....   Year .... Year .... Year ....

Source ....   Fed   ....
Planted ....   Divided ....

Species ....

Source ....   Fed   ....
Planted ....   Divided ....

Species ....

Source ....   Fed   ....
Planted ....   Divided ....

Species ....

Source ....   Fed   ....
Planted ....   Divided ....

ABOVE: *Plastic pots are surprisingly acceptable if the flowers are stunning, such as these vibrant spring bulbs.*

OPPOSITE: *Place pots of L. regale lilies near seats to enjoy the fragrance to the full.*

Fruits

If you have space in your garden, do consider growing some fruit. This may present a challenge: to grow fruit successfully you need plenty of space. You can certainly grow raspberries up a wall, or espalier apple and pear trees along the fence. There are many excellent varieties available grafted on to miniature rootstocks for this purpose.

If you do have room you can make a fruit cage in which to grow strawberries and raspberries. But beware of the birds: you will need to net all your fruit or the birds will get to them before you can.

RIGHT: *Strawberries epitomize the long warm days of early summer and can be grown in containers as well as in the ground.*

Year _____ Year _____ Year _____

Type _____	Planted _____
Variety _____	Pruned _____
Source _____	Mulched _____
	Sprayed _____
	Picked _____

Type _____	Planted _____
Variety _____	Pruned _____
Source _____	Mulched _____
	Sprayed _____
	Picked _____

Type _____	Planted _____
Variety _____	Pruned _____
Source _____	Mulched _____
	Sprayed _____
	Picked _____

Type _____	Planted _____
Variety _____	Pruned _____
Source _____	Mulched _____
	Sprayed _____
	Picked _____

Vegetables

There is absolutely nothing so good as fresh young vegetables, and the fact that they have been grown and freshly picked by you makes the pleasure of eating them that much greater. Those Arran Pilot early potatoes, and new sugar snap peas cooked in the pod, young asparagus in the spring, ping-pong-ball-sized beetroot, are all quite delicious and immeasurably superior to anything you might buy at the supermarket.

RIGHT: *A pile of home-grown vegetables will inspire any cook and tempt any appetite.*

Year _____ Year _____ Year _____

Vegetable _____ Sown _____

Variety _____ Thinned _____

                                                                     Harvested _____

Vegetable _____ Sown _____

Variety _____ Thinned _____

                                                                      Harvested _____

Vegetable _____ Sown _____

Variety _____ Thinned _____

                                                                      Harvested _____

Vegetable _____ Sown _____

Variety _____ Thinned _____

                                                                      Harvested _____

Vegetable _____ Sown _____

Variety _____ Thinned _____

                                                                      Harvested _____

Vegetable _____ Sown _____

Variety _____ Thinned _____

                                                                      Harvested _____

Vegetable _____ Sown _____

Variety _____ Thinned _____

                                                                      Harvested _____

Herbs

Try to find some room in your garden to grow a few herbs. No cook should be without a supply of fresh mint, parsley, marjoram, rosemary, chives and thyme, and, if you are more ambitious, tarragon, basil and coriander (cilantro). Don't be put off growing herbs for lack of space – most can be grown very success-fully in containers.

RIGHT: *A selection of herbs in small individual pots, these are just the right size for planting together in a large pot. Make sure that there is room enough for them to grow.*

Year _____ Year _____ Year _____

Type	Sown
Variety	Thinned
	Picked
Type	Sown
Variety	Thinned
	Picked
Type	Sown
Variety	Thinned
	Picked
Type	Sown
Variety	Thinned
	Picked
Type	Sown
Variety	Thinned
	Picked
Type	Sown
Variety	Thinned
	Picked

Seeds

If you have the patience, raising plants from seeds will not only save you money, but can be an immensely satisfying process. If you are lucky enough to have a greenhouse, you will be able to grow almost all the plants you need, but even without one, many will grow quite happily, either outside, in the case of hardy varieties, or on a window-sill indoors.

RIGHT: *If your seeds fail, you can usually buy replacement seedlings from a commercial greenhouse or garden centre.*

	Year _____	Year _____	Year _____
Type _____	Sown _____		
Variety _____	Thinned _____		
Type _____	Sown _____		
Variety _____	Thinned _____		
Type _____	Sown _____		
Variety _____	Thinned _____		
Type _____	Sown _____		
Variety _____	Thinned _____		
Type _____	Sown _____		
Variety _____	Thinned _____		
Type _____	Sown _____		
Variety _____	Thinned _____		
Type _____	Sown _____		
Variety _____	Thinned _____		
Type _____	Sown _____		
Variety _____	Thinned _____		

Cuttings

It is relatively easy to raise new plants by taking cuttings. Pelargoniums, clematis and many shrubs can be raised from softwood or semiripe cuttings taken in spring and summer. Other trees and shrubs can be raised from hardwood cuttings that are taken in autumn. Chrysanthemum cuttings can be taken in the greenhouse in winter.

RIGHT: *Rooted cuttings ready for planting out in position in spring.*

		Year _____	Year _____	Year _____
Plant _____	Taken _____			
	Planted out _____			
Plant _____	Taken _____			
	Planted out _____			
Plant _____	Taken _____			
	Planted out _____			
Plant _____	Taken _____			
	Planted out _____			
Plant _____	Taken _____			
	Planted out _____			
Plant _____	Taken _____			
	Planted out _____			
Plant _____	Taken _____			
	Planted out _____			
Plant _____	Taken _____			
	Planted out _____			

	Year	Year	Year

Plant ....

Taken ....

Planted out ....

Plant ....

Taken ....

Planted out ....

Plant ....

Taken ....

Planted out ....

Plant ....

Taken ....

Planted out ....

Plant ....

Taken ....

Planted out ....

Plant ....

Taken ....

Planted out ....

Plant ....

Taken ....

Planted out ....

Plant ....

Taken ....

Planted out ....

Plant ....

Taken ....

Planted out ....

Plant ....

Taken ....

Planted out ....

Plant ....

Taken ....

Planted out ....

ABOVE: *Hormone rooting powder usually contains a fungicide and so will help prevent rotting, as well as encouraging root growth.*

Weather

It is in a gardener's interest to note the main details of the weather each year. There are two good instruments which can be used. The first is a thermometer. Note the temperature, either each day, or in extremes of heat or cold. For instance, if you know that for 16 consecutive days in the winter the temperature did not rise above freezing-point, it will not surprise you to find that a number of plants have died when spring arrives.

The other useful instrument is a rain gauge. Place this in an open position in the garden with uninterrupted access to the sky. This does need to be checked every morning when it is wet to keep a record of the amount of rain that falls.

RIGHT: *Remember to feed the birds during cold weather, some may be depending on you to help them through the winter.*

	Rainfall	Sunshine	Average Temperature	Comments
January				
February				
March				
April				
May				
June				
July				
August				
September				
October				
November				
December				

	Rainfall	Sunshine	Average Temperature	Comments
January				
February				
March				
April				
May				
June				
July				
August				
September				
October				
November				
December				

Tools and machinery

Lawnmower		Guarantee	
Supplier			
Telephone No.		Serviced	
Rotivator (Tiller)		Guarantee	
Supplier			
Telephone No.		Serviced	
Other Machines		Guarantee	
Supplier			
Telephone No.		Serviced	

Plant suppliers

Name		Name	
Address		Address	
Telephone No.		Telephone No.	
Name		Name	
Address		Address	
Telephone No.		Telephone No.	
Name		Name	
Address		Address	
Telephone No.		Telephone No.	

ABOVE: *Always keeping your equipment well-maintained will help ensure that you will have fewer repair bills.*

ABOVE: *Depending on the size of your garden, you may need a shed. Think carefully about the use of the shed before you buy.*

Index

A

Abelia x grandiflora 191, 204
Abies balsamea 'Nana' 176
Abies cephalonia 'Meyer's Dwarf' 176, 176
abstract ornaments 115
Acaena microphylla 138
Acanthus spinosus 202, 210, 210
Acer palmatum atropurpureum 156
Acer platanoides 'Drummondii' 237
Achillea filipendulina 159, 196, 219
    A. filipendulina 'Gold Plate' 159, 202

Achillea ptarmica 'The Pearl' 162
Achillea tomentosa 138
Actinidia kolomikta 214, 214
Aethionema grandiflorum 191
afternoon sun plants 191
Agapanthus 158, 196
    A. africanus 236
    A. orientalis 236
Agave americana 21
Ajuga reptans 77, 156, 192, 192, 236
Akebia quinata 190
Alchemilla mollis 154, 156
alpines 47, 78, 89, 127, 138–9, 302–3,
    361, 421
Alyssum montanum 138
Alyssum saxatile 78, 89, 138, 159, 196,
    219, 219
Amelanchier canadensis 206
Amelanchier laevis 168, 169
Anagallis 324, 325
Anchusa azurea 202
Anemone blanda 'White Splendour' 162
Anemone x hybrida 'Honorine Joubert' 162
Angelica archangelica 210, 210
animal figures 115
animals 18, 218, 219
annuals 7, 18, 143, 197, 209, 214, 219, 236
Antennaria dioica 'Rosea' 138
Anthemis punctata subsp.
    cupaniana 162, 162
Anthemis tinctoria 159

anthuriums 55
aphids 218, 268
Aponogeton distachyos 131
apples 108, 220, 221, 225, 237
Aquilegia alpina 202
Arabis caucasica 138
Arabis ferdinandi-coburgi 'Variegata' 138
Aralia elata 'Variegata' 170, 170
arbours 22, 29, 56, 125, 255
arches 23, 25, 27, 103, 104–5, 229, 255
architectural plants 210-11
arctotis 209
Arenaria balearica 138
Argyranthemum (marguerites) 255, 324,
    325, 358
Armeria maritima 77, 81, 138, 219
Artemisia absinthium 158
Artemisia arborescens 196, 217
Artemisia ludoviciana 154, 158, 158
Aruncus dioicus 204, 205
Arundinaria viridistriata (syn. Pleioblastus
    auricomus, P. viridistriatus) 170, 208
Arundo donax 213
Asarina 107
asparagus 228
aspect 54–5, 190–1
Asplenium scolopendrium 194
Aster alpinus 138
Aster novi-belgii 219
    A. novi-belgii 'Royal Ruby' 160
Astilbe 131, 192
    A. 'Elizabeth Bloom' 204
    A. x arendsii 204
Astrantia major 192, 192
aubergines 227
Aubrieta 89, 138, 154
Aucuba japonica 164, 170, 172, 174, 192,
    202, 204, 206, 218
    A. japonica 'Variegata' 218
auriculas 246, 333
autumn 66–7, 166–7, 168–9
    plantings 240, 359–67
awnings 124
Azalea 19, 200, 237
Azolla caroliniana 131

B

backyards 21, 39, 50–1
balconies 25, 28, 38, 54–5, 233
bamboo 28
bamboo fencing 93
barbecues 45
barrels 256, 458, 440
basements 39, 50–1
baskets 233, 257, 462
    edible plantings 389
    indoor displays 472
    pink 302
    summer plantings 348
    vibrant colour 312
    white and silver 279, 284, 285
bathroom plants 469
beans 18, 107, 220, 229, 388

beds 19, 116, 136, 142–3, 146–7
    feeding and fertilizing 186–7
    maintenance 180
beech 86
bees 218, 458
beetroot 220, 228
Begonia 359, 482
benches 7, 45
Berberis 206, 206, 218
    B. corallina 201
    B. darwinii 164, 190
    B. thunbergii 159, 168, 174
    B..thunbergii 'Atropurpurea Nana'
        86, 218
    B. wilsoniae 168
    B. x stenophylla 87, 190, 204
Bergenia 81, 164, 174, 192, 236
    B. cordifolia 47, 190
    B. purpurascens 156
berries 7, 240
Betula 19, 167
biennials 219, 236
birds 7, 19, 24, 64, 218, 219
    birdbaths 7, 19, 26, 114, 114, 148
black spot 269
bluebells 19
boots 249, 454, 455
borders 19, 142–3, 145, 146–7, 148–9, 219
    colour schemes 158–63, 166–7
    dwarf conifers 157, 165, 175, 176–7

evergreens 164–5
    feeding and fertilizing 186–7
    heathers 178–9
    low-maintenance plants 174–5
    maintenance 180
    planting 150–1
    staking plants 182
    variegated foliage 170–1
botrytis 269
bottle garden 464, 465
Bougainvillea 21
bowls 461, 476
bricks 43, 45, 46, 75, 88

bricklaying 90–1
Brunnera macrophylla 192, *193*
bubble fountains 126
Buddleia 11
  B. davidii 172, 196, 206
built-in furniture 120
bulbs 7, 19, 47, 53, 55, 68–9, 89, 143, 236, 238
butterflies 7, 19, 218, 219, 403, 458
Buxus 22, 87, 142, 213
  B. sempervirens 'Aureovariegata' 170, 192
  B. sempervirens 'Suffruticosa ' 86

C
cacti 21, 54, 461
Calendula officinalis 18
Callicarpa 218

Calluna vulgaris 52, 201, *201*
Caltha palustris 130, 131
Camellia 160, 164, 192, 201
  C. japonica 190, 237
  C. x williamsii 190, 237
cameo gardens 246–7
Campanula 202
  C. carpatica 138
  C. cochleariifolia 138
  C. garganica 138
Campsis radicans 191, *191*
Campsis x tagliabuana
  'Madame Galen' 191
candles 50, 118–19
Canna indica 191
Cardamine pratensis 'Flore Pleno' 204
Carex morrowi 'Evergold' 170
Carex oshimensis 'Evergold' 236
carrots 220, 227, 228
cars 39, 46
Caryopteris x clandonensis 172, 196
  C. x clandonensis 'Heavenly Blue' 202
cascades 128
Casiope 201
Catalpa bignonioides 'Aurea' 210
caterpillars 268

Ceanothus 158, 214, 218
  C. impressus 191
  C. x burkwoodii 158, 164
  C. x deleanus 'Gloire de Versailles' 191
Cedrus deodara 'Golden Horizon' 176
celery 227
Centaurea cyanus 219
Cerastium tomentosum 138
Ceratostigma plumbaginoides 168
Ceratostigma willmottianum 206, 240
Chaenomeles 206
  C. japonica 204-5
  C. x superba 190
chain link fencing 93
Chamaecyparis lawsoniana 'Aurea Densa' 176, *177*
Chamaecyparis lawsoniana 'Bleu Nantais' 176
Chamaecyparis obtusa 'Nana Gracilis' 176
Chamaemelum nobile (chamomile) 41, 70, 78
children 22, 448–61
chimney pots 274, 375, 445
Chimonanthus praecox 166, 216
chives 222
choices checklist 15
Choisya ternata 163, 172, 174, 190, 216, 217
  C. ternata 'Sundance' 159, 164, 236
Chrysanthemum 160, 166, 166, 209
  C. x superbum (syn. *C. maximum*) 162, *162*
circles 32–3, 60
  making a miniature pebble circle 79
Cistus 162, 202, *203*, 218
  C. x corbariensis 172
  C. x cyprius 191
  C. x pulverulentus 'Sunset' 191
claire-voyée 100
Clematis 107, 108, 109, 110, 125, *189*, 214, 445
  C. alpina 109, 190
  C. montana 101, *101*, 190
  C. 'Nelly Moser' 190
  C. 'Prince Charles' 445
  C. tangutica 190
  C. 'The President' 214
  C. viticella 108
Cleome 209
Clerodendrum trichotomum 168
Clianthus puniceus 208
climbers *18*, 23, 28, 101, 106, 111, 188, 214–15
  annual 107
  arbours 125
  pillars 110
  shrubs 109
  trees 108
climbing vegetables 228–9
closeboard fencing 92
clover 71
Cobaea scandens 107, 109
cobbles 75
Colchicum 68, 154
  C. speciosum 166
collections 497

colour 29, 55, 143, 242–3, 244–5, 278
  autumn 166–7, 168–9
  black and white 427
  blue and purple 320, *321*, 323, 324, *325*
  blue and silver 158–9
  lime-green and blue 345
  pink 287, *288*, 289, 290, 291–3, 294, 295, 296, 297, 298, 299, 300, 302
  red 160–1, 310, 311
  variegated 170-1
  vibrant 301, 304, 306, 308, 309, 310, *311*, 312, 313, 314, 315, 316, *317*
  white 162–3, 279, 280, *281*, 282, 283, 284, *285*, 286
  yellow and gold 159, 310, *311*, 354, 355, 412, *413*
Colutea arborescens 196, *196*
compost 67, 235, 258
compost areas 14, 22, 30
conifers 47, 49, 179
construction 37, 52
container ponds 126, 128, 456
containers 233, 270, 278
contours 35
Convolvulus cneorum 162, 196
cooking pots 426
copper pots 480, *481*, 482
cordons 224
Cordyline australis 208, *208*, 210
corner sites 41, 253
Cornus 167
  C. alba 52, 168, *168*
  C. alba 'Elegantissima' 170
  C. alba 'Sibirica' 167
  C. canadensis 163, 201

  C. controversa 'Variegata' 210
  C. mas 166
  C. stolonifera 'Flaviramea' 167, 174
Cortaderia selloana 'Aureolinata' 156
Corydalis lutea 138
Cosmos atrosanguineus 247
Cotinus coggygria 52, 174, *174*
Cotoneaster 174, 218

C. dammeri 81, 165
C. frigidus 206
C. horizontalis 168, 174, 190
C. 'Hybridus Pendulus' 237
cottage gardens 18, 47, 228, 346
Cotula coronopifolia 71
Cotula squalida 77
courgettes 227, 229
courtyard gardens 17, 25, 25
Crambe cordifolia 205, 211
crazy paving 77
crevice plants 77
Crinodendron hookerianum 190
Crocosmia 191
C. 'Lucifer' 160, 161
Crocus 47, 68, 154, 238
C. speciosus 166
C. tommasinianus 166, 166
cucumbers 227, 229
curved borders 146
cuttings 266
Cyclamen coum 166
Cyclamen hederifolium (syn.
C. neapolitanum) 166
Cynara cardunculus 181
Cytisus battandieri 216
Cytisus multiflorus (syn. C. albus) 162
Cytisus x kewensis 172

D
Daboecia cantabrica 200, 201
Dahlia 160
Daphne bholua 'Jacqueline Postill' 252
Daphne mezereum 216, 216, 218
Daphne odorata 'Aureomarginata' 247
Datura (syn. Brugmansia) 21, 211, 211, 483
decking 54, 59, 80
deep beds 226
Delphinium 158, 158, 202
designing plans 32–7, 150–1
Deutzia scabra 190
D. scabra 'Plena' 191, 202
diagonals 32–3, 60–1
Dianthus 78, 160, 191, 202–3
D. barbatus 'Scarlet Beauty' 203

D. deltoides 138, 138
Dicentra 236
D. spectabilis 192
Digitalis 190
D. grandiflora (syn. D. orientalis) 205
Dipsacus 219
diseases 235, 268–9
ditches 100
Dodecathon meadia 190
drawing plans 34–5, 36–7
drives 39, 46, 47, 48, 49
dry stone walling 89, 89
Dryas octopetala 138, 191
dustbins 30
dwarf conifers 89, 157, 165, 175, 176–7

E
eating outdoors 6, 24, 42, 124–5, 250–1
Eccremocarpus scaber 107, 109, 110, 191
Echinacea purpurea 191
Echinops ritro 191, 196
edges 47, 59, 60–1, 77, 147
Eichhornia crassipes 130
Elaeagnus pungens 206
E. pungens 'Maculata' 164, 165,
170, 174
E. x ebbingei 206
E. x ebbingei 'Gilt Edge' 206
E. x ebbingei 'Limelight' 170
electrical installations 117
Elodea canadensis 131, 134
entrances 252, 254
Epimedium grandiflorum 201
Epimedium perralderianum 156, 192
Eranthis hyemalis 68
erecting fences 94–5
Erica 165, 166, 201
E. carnea 52, 164, 173, 174
E. gracilis 240
E. hyemalis 240
Erigeron 219
Erinus alpinus 138
Eryngium agavifolium 236
Eryngium variifolium 197
Erysimum cheiri (syn. Cheiranthus
barbatus) 203, 329
Escallonia 84, 160, 218
E. macrantha 65
espaliers 50, 101, 221, 224
eucalyptus 11, 217
Eucryphia glutinosa 162
Euonymus fortunei 52, 81, 165, 170,
190, 214
E. fortunei 'Emerald Gaiety' 108
E. fortunei 'Emerald 'n' Gold' 52, 156
Euphorbia 27
E. griffithii 190
evergreens 7, 46, 55, 81, 164–5, 236, 366,
367, 370, 376, 377, 420
exotic style 21, 51, 55, 189, 208–9

F
fans 221, 224
Fatsia japonica (syn. Aralia sieboldii) 156,
157, 175, 208, 211

feeding 186–7
container plants 235, 259
feet on containers 261
fences 7, 84, 92–3, 94–5, 101
fennel 222
ferns 19, 50, 51, 408, 411
borders 194–5
fertilizers 186–7, 258, 259
Festuca glauca 154–5, 156, 158

flooring 54, 78–9
flowers with vegetables 228–9
focal points 7, 19, 20, 26–7, 51,
102–3, 189
foliage 7, 55, 215, 348, 408, 432, 433,
434, 435
borders 156–7
scented 217
formal style 16–17, 86, 142
Forsythia 87
F. suspensa 190
F. x intermedia 159, 207
Fothergilla major 169, 201
fountains 126, 128, 436
Fremontodendron 'California Glory' 191
Fritillaria 68
F. imperialis 69, 191
front gardens 39, 46–7, 48–9, 85
frost 54, 236, 240
fruit 7, 221, 224–5, 228, 378, 386,
389, 392
fruit trees 101, 221, 224
Fuchsia 160, 236, 252, 284, 285, 298,
299, 359, 436, 442, 443, 459, 480, 481
F. magellanica 'Versicolor' 170, 173
furniture 21, 57, 103, 120–1, 122–3

G
Galanthus 238
G. nivalis 47, 69, 155, 190
garden flares 118, 118
garden layouts 28, 32–3, 42, 46–7, 48–9,
60–1, 144
Garrya elliptica 190, 207, 215, 215
gates 27, 85

Genista tinctoria 172, 173, 197
Gentiana acaulis 138
Gentiana septemfida 138
Gentiana sino-ornata 138, 201
Geranium 407
    G. cinereum 'Ballerina' 191
    G. 'Johnson's Blue' 191
    G. subcaulescens 'Splendens' 138
    G. x oxonianum 108
gerberas 209
gilded pots 119
Gladiolus 160–1
globe artichokes 220

gnomes 115
grass borders 156–7
grass substitutes 70–1
gravel 20, 41, 46, 47, 49, 58, 82–3
Griselinia littoralis 175, 212, 213
ground cover 11, 58, 59, 81, 152
growing bags 221, 222, 227
Gunnera manicata 208, 211
Gypsophila 203
    G. paniculata 155, 162
    G. repens 138

H
ha-has 100
Hakonechloa macra 'Alboaurea' 156, *157*
Halimiocistus sahucii 162
Hamamelis mollis 166, 190, 216
hanging baskets 227, 257, 262–3, 264, 408
    autumn plantings 359, 364
    blue and purple 318–19, 322, 326–7
    children's 452
    edible plantings 385, 388, 390,
        391, 392
    inspirational plantings 432
    pink 291–2, 294, 295, 297, 298,
        299, 300
    scented 396, *397*, 400, *401*
    shade 409, 410, 411, 412, *413*
    spring plantings 338, *339*
    summer plantings 341, 342, *343*, 346,
        347, 354, *355*, 357–8
    sun 415
    vibrant colour 309, 310, *311*, 314

winter plantings 374
hard landscaping 7, 11, *15*, 18, *59*
heathers 87, 178–9
Hebe 47, 165, 175, 197, 218, 237, *243*
    H. 'Midsummer Beauty' 173
    H. x franciscana 'Variegata' *165*, 170
Hedera helix (ivy) 55, 101, 109, *188*,
    125, 190, *207*, 215, 218, 375, 418,
    428, *429*
Hedera colchica 190
hedges 7, 16, 23, 28, 46, 86–7, 84, 219
height *38*, 102, 104, 106–7, 110–11,
    112–13, 237
Helenium 'Bruno' 161, *161*
Helenium 'Waldtraut 191
Helianthemum 'Fire Dragon' *138*, 161
    H. nummularium 196, 198, 203
Helianthus annuus (sunflower) 219, 360
Helichrysum italicum 191
Heliotropium 247
Helleborus 27, 192
    H. foetidus 190
    H. niger 167
    H. orientalis 167, *167*
Hemerocallis 131, 159, *159*, 161, 175
    H. 'Burning Daylight' 205
herbs 7, *10*, 17, 24, 87, 121, 217, 221,
    222–3, 228, 247, 378, 379–81,
    385–8, 390
    herb wheel, making 223
Hesperis matronalis 219
Heuchera 'Pewter Moon' 156-7
Hibiscus syriacus 175
    H. syriacus 'Blue Bird' 158
Hippophaë rhamnoides 52
hit-and-miss fencing 92
hoops 112-13
Hordeum jubatum 155
Hosta 58, 131, 157, 171, 191, 193, 248
    H. fortunei albopicta 170
    H. fortunei var. *hyacinthina* 156
houseplants 55, 209
Houttynia cordata 130, 171, *171*
    H. cordata 'Chameleon' 171
hoverflies 218
human figures 115
Humulus lupulus 108, 110, 125
    H. lupulus 'Aureus' 101, 191, 205, 215
Hydrangea 148
    H. macrophylla 52
    H. paniculata 'Grandiflora' 52
    H. petiolaris 108, 190, 215
Hypericum 218
    H. calycinum 159, 172, 173, 193
    H. 'Hidcote' 159, 190
    H. olympicum 138, 139
    H. x moserianum 'Tricolor' 171
hyssop 223

I
Iberis sempervivens 'Snowflake' 139
Ilex (holly) 149, 165, 169, 171, 175, 190,
    213, 218
    I. aquifolium 207
    I. aquifolium 'Aurea Marginata' *165*

I. x altaclarensis 'Lawsoniana' 207
Impatiens (busy Lizzies) 236, 409
Imperata cylindrica 'Rubra' 191
indoor gardens 463, 470–1, 476
indoor topiary 473
informal style 18–19, 86, 287
insects 18, 24, 218, 219
interlap fencing 92
Ipomoea 107, 109
    I. tricolor 'Heavenly Blue' 208, 209
Iris 127
    I. laevigata 130
    I. pallida 'Variegata' 171, *171*
    I. pseudacorus 131
    I. pseudacorus 'Variegatus' 171
    I. reticulata 238
    I. sibirica 131
    I. unguicularis 167, *167*
iron furniture 120
island beds 136, 144

J
Japanese style 20, *20*, 28, 32, 440
Jasminum 24, 109
    J. nudiflorum 167, 190, 215, *215*
    J. officinale 215, 216, 247
Jerusalem artichokes 212
Juncus effusus 'Spiralis' 130
Juniperus communis 'Compressa' 176
Juniperus horizontalis 176
Juniperus scopulorum/virginiana
    'Skyrocket' 211
Juniperus virginiana 'Sulphur Spray' (syn.
    J. chinensis 'Sulphur Spray') 176

K
Kalmia latifolia 201
Kerria japonica 'Pleniflora' 190
kitchen gardens 220–1

Kniphofia 175, *175*, 197, 208, 211
knot gardens 16–17
Kolkwitzia amabilis 191, 203

L
L-shaped gardens 41
Lablab purpureus (syn. *Dolichos lablab*) 107

labour-saving tips 15, 35
Laburnum 237
ladybirds 218
Lagenaria 107
lanterns 50, 118, *118*
Lathyrus grandiflorus 205
Lathyrus odoratus (sweet peas) 107, 109,

236, 342
Laurus nobilis (bay) 217, 222, 252
Lavandula 24, 47, 78, 87, 173, 197, 216,
    218, 394, 400, *401*
    L. angustifolia 155
    L. angustifolia 'Hidcote' 191
    L. stoechas 191
Lavatera olbia 52
lawns 15, 26, 58, 60–1, 64–5, 66–7,
    68–9, 69–70
    laying turf 63
    sowing grass seed 62
laying bricks and blocks 91
laying gravel beds 83
laying paving 73, 77
lead chimney 274
legal restrictions 39, 80, 84–5
Lemna 131, 133
lemon balm 217, 222
lettuces 220, 227, 228, 247
Leucanthemum x superbum (syn.
    Chrysanthemum maximum) 205
Leucojum aestivum 162
levels 15, 40, 42–3, 61
Leycesteria formosa 173, 173, 207, 218
lighting 7, 50, 103, 116–17
Ligustrum 171, 218
    L. ovalifolium 86, 207
    L. ovalifolium 'Aureum' 159, 212,
        213, *213*
Lilium 161, 162–3, 191, 208, *209*, 441
    L. regale 236, 247
Limnanthes douglasii 18, 219
Liriope muscari 175, 193
lily-of-the-valley 238
Lobelia 89, 236, 278
    L. cardinalis 161

long gardens 17, 19, 27, 39, 40
Lonicera (honeysuckle) 24, 108, 109,
    110, 125
    L. nitida 86, *86*
    L. nitida 'Baggesen's Gold' 159, 165,
        193, 212, 213
    L. periclymenum 190, 215, 216, 218
    L. pileata 52
    L. x brownii (syn. *L. sempervirens*)
        'Dropmore Scarlet' 203
    L. x japonica 212, 215
low-maintenance gardens 11, 20, 46, 174–5
Lunaria annua 219
Lupinus arboreus 173
Lychnis chalcedonica 161, *161*
M
Mahonia 218
    M. aquifolium 52, 193
    M. 'Charity' 165, 167, 173, 211, *211*,
        216, 240
    M. japonica 175, 190
mail order plants 267
maintenance
    beds and borders 180
    container plants 235, 259, 260
    low-maintenance gardens 11, 20,
        46, 174–5
    ponds 132–3
Malus (apples) 108, 220, 221, 225, 237
    M. 'John Downie' 169
    M. tschonoskii 169
marjoram 222
Matteucia struthiopteris 157, *194*
Matthiola bicornis 51, 216
Matthiola incana 216, *216*
mealy bugs 268
measuring garden site 34–5
mechanical aids 66
Meconopsis betonicifolia 201
Mediterranean style 7, 21, *21*, 89, 208–9,
    314, 438, *439*
Mentha (mint) 222, 229
Mexican painted pots *25*, 272
Mimulus 131
Mina lobata (syn. *Ipomoea lobata*) 107
mirrors 29
Miscanthus sacchariflorus 213
Miscanthus sinensis 'Silberfeder' 157
Molucella laevis 191
Monarda 'Cambridge Sacrlet' 161
morning sun plants 190
mulching 179, 183, 184–5, 265
Myriophyllum 131, 134

N
Narcissi 55, 68, 69, *250*, 329
narrow gardens 17, 19, 27, *39*, 40
natural predators on pests 269
neighbours 84–5, 116
Nepeta 219
    N. x faassenii 155, 158, 197
Nerine bowdenii 167, *167*
Nicotiana 51, *51*, 55
novelty containers 51, 233, 257
    boots *249*, 454, *455*

chimney pots 274, 375, 445
cooking pot 426
indoor plantings 479
tin bath 444
tyres 453
watering-can planter 449
wine case 381

O
oleanders 21
Olearia x haastii 52, 163, *163*, 207
onions 227
optical illusions 29
orchid basket 498
ornamental vegetables 226, 242, *251*
ornaments 19, 21, 103, 114–15, *116*
Orontium aquaticum 131
Osmanthus x burkwoodii (syn. *x Osmarea
    burkwoodii*) 207
Osteospermum 191, 197, 208, 236, 308
    O. jacundum 196
    O. 'Whirligig' *163*
oval beds 146
overwintering container plants 260
Oxalis adenophylla 139

P
Pachysandra terminalis 52, 81, *171*, 193
    P. terminalis 'Variegata' 171
palms 21, 466
panel fencing 92, 94
Papaver orientale 161, 191

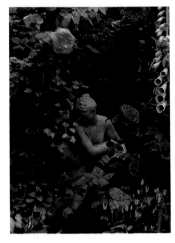

parsley 388
parterres 16-17
Parthenocissus 190
    P. henryana 190
passageways 39
Passiflora 109
paths 7, 15, 58, 64, 76–7
patios 28, 38, 42-3, 44–5
Paulownia tomentosa 211
paving 7, 15, 18, 21, 42, 43, 54, 58, 72–3,
    74–5, 76–7, 78–9

paved gardens 17
peas 220, 228
peat beds 136
pebbles 76, 78–9
pedestals 115
Pelargonium 21, 161, 236, 246, 249, 291, 297, 402
Pennisetum villosum (syn. *P. longistylum*) 157
Penstemon 191
peppers 227
perennials 7, 18, 89, 143, 236
pergolas 23, 44–5, 103, 104–5, 188, 229
Pernettya (gaultheria) 175, 218, 240
  P. mucronata 52, 169, *169*, 201
Perovskia atriplicifolia 158, 197
Persicaria bistorta 'Superba' (syn. *Polygonum bistorta*) 205

pests 235, 268–9
Petunia 236, 255, 278, 428, 429
Phalaris arundinacea 'Picta' 163
Philadelphus 52, *52*, 163, 207, 217
  P. coronarius 'Aureus' 86, 159, 173
Phlomis fruticosa 197, *197*, 202, 203
Phlox douglasii 138, *139*
Phlox paniculata 205
  P. paniculata 'White Admiral' 163
Phlox subulata 139
Phormium 21, 41, 101, 165, 171, 197, 205, 208, 211
  P. 'Dazzler' 161
  P. tenax 205
Picea abies 'Gregoryana' *176*, 177
Picea glauca 'Echiniformis' *177*
  Picea g. var. *albertiana* 'Alberta Globe' 177
  *Picea g.*var. *albertiana* 'Conica' 177
Picea pungens 'Globosa' 177
Picea pungens 'Montgomery' 177
picket fencing 93
pillars 110–11
pimpernels 324
Pinus mugo 'Corley's Mat' 177
Piptanthus laburnifolius 190
pithoi 27
planning designs 32–7, 150–1

plant size 7, 11, 151
plant supports 261
planting:
  conifer and heather mixed bed 179
  containers 261
  fern border 195
  ground cover 152
  herbaceous plants 151
  hedge 87
  ponds130–1
  rock garden 138–9
  shrubs 153
  waterlilies 130
plastic containers 261, 301, 324, 325, 344–5, 350, 366, *367*, 382, *383*
plastic fencing 93
plastic furniture 120
play areas 22
Pleioblastus auricomus (syn. *P. viridistriatus*) 157
plinths 115
pointed gardens 40
pollution-tolerant plants 206–7
Polyanthus 238
Polygonum baldschuanica (syn. *Fallopia baldschuanica*) 108, 125, 213, *213*, 215
ponds 19, 126, 128–9, 132–3, 134–5, 136
  miniature 425, 456
  planting 130–1
Pontederia cordata 130
Portulaca 209
post and chain fencing 93
potagers 226, 227
potatoes 221, 227
Potentilla 87, 218
  P. atrosanguinea 161
  P. fruticosa 159, 173, 175, 202, 203
  P. tabernaemontani 138
pots 256, 264
  autumn plantings 360
  children's plantings 459–60
  inspirational plantings 427, 438, *439*, 442, *443*, 445–6
  scented plantings 247, 336, 399, 407
  shade 414
  spring plantings 330, *331*, 333, 337
  summer plantings 356
  winter plantings 368, 370, 376
potting-on 267
powdery mildew 269
power tools 66
primroses 19
Primula 23, 131, 238, 246
privacy 7, 23, 52–3, 84, 88, 96, 246
propagating plants 266–7
pruning 11
Prunus 'Amanogawa' 237
Prunus subhirtella 'Pendula' (syn. *P.* 'Autumnalis Pendula')167
Pulsatilla vulgaris 139
pumps 134–5
Pyracantha 190, 215, *215*, 218
  P. 'Orange Glow' 169
Pyrus salicifolia 'Pendula' 237

R
radishes 227, 228
raised beds 45, 136
ramblers 96
ranch-style fencing 93, *95*
Raoulia ayustralis 138, *139*
rectangles 32–3, 60
red spider mite 268
refuse areas 7, 14
Reseda odorata 191
Rhamnus frangula 218
Rheum palmatum (rhubarb) 208, *209*, 225, 228
Rhodochiton atrosanguineum 107
rhododendrons 19, 237
Rhodohypoxis baurii 138, 201
Rhus typhina (syn. *R. hirta*) 169
Ribes sanguineum 175, 218
rock gardens 19, 49, 126–7, 218
Rodgersia pinnata 'Superba' *204*, 205
romance 35
Romneya coulteri 197
roof gardens 25, 28, 38, 39, 52–3, 233
Rosa 17, 24, 47, 86, 87, 108, 110, 129, 142, 154-5, 161, *188*, 215, 216
  R. 'American Pillar' 110, *111*
  R. 'Bourbon Queen' 155
  R. 'Cardinal Richelieu' 155
  R. 'Constance Spry' 155
  R. 'Dublin Bay' 98
  R. 'Kew Rambler' 110
  R. rugosa 155, 190
Rosmarinus officinalis 87, 165, *165*, 191,

191, 197, 217, 222, *223*, 229, 396
Rubus cockburnianus 'Golden Vale' 157
Ruscus aculeatus 193
rushes 127
rust 269
rustic poles, joining 105

S
safety considerations 52, 117, 118
Salix alba Chermesina 167
Salix caprea pendula 237
Salix helvetica 109, *109*

Salix matsudana 'Tortuosa' 211, *211*
salpiglossis 209
Salvia discolor 247
Salvia officinalis 217, 229
   S. officinalis 'Icterina' 171
   S. officinalis 'Purpurascens' 157
   S. officinalis 'Tricolor' 191
Salvia sclarea 181
Salvinia braziliensis 130
sandpits 22
Santolina chamaecyparissus 159, 165, 197
Sarcococca hookeriana humilis 193, *193*, 217
saucers 261
Saxifraga 139
   S. x umbrosa 193
Scabiosa 'Butterfly Blue' 203
Scabiosa causica 219
scale drawings 35, 150
scent 7, 24, 51, 70, 124, 188, 116–17, 233, 468
   foliage 217
   hanging baskets 396, *397*, 400, *401*
   pots 247, 336, 399, 407
   windowboxes 395, 397, 402–3, 406
Scilla 238
Scirpus 'Zebrina' 130
screening 7, 14, 23, 25, 28–9, 53, 55, 88–9, 98, 255
   plants 212–23
sculptural plants 210–11
sculptures 115
seaside garden style *246*, 450, *451*
seating areas 22, 23
seats 19, 41, 45, *102*, 122, *123*
   tree seats 41, 121

Sedum 138
   S. 'Autumn Joy' *219*
   S. lydium 138
   S. spathulifolium 'Cape Blanco' 139
   S. spectabile 197, *197*, 219
   S. spurium 139
seed sowing 62, 266
Sempervivum 138, 191
   S. ballsii 139

Senecio 'Sunshine' 86, 159, *165*, 173, 191
setts 75
shade 7, 11, 51, 188, 189, 408–14
   plants 190, 192–3
shapes 28, 32–3, 42, 46–7, 48–9, 60–1, 144
shared gardens 100
sheds 7, *13,14*, 22, 30
shelter 7, 23
shelving 31
shrubs 11, 14, 28, 40, 42, 45, 100, 108–9, 142–3, 153, 218, 237
   quick growing 172–3
sink gardens 136
   autumn plantings 361
Skimmia 218
   S. japonica 169, *169*, 193, 217
slopes 35, 43, 38
snails 133, 268
soft landscaping 141
soil 198–9
   acid 200–1
   alkaline (chalk) 202–3
   clay 204–5
   soil mixes 235, 258
Solanum bapsicastrum 240
Solanum jasminoides 110
Soleirolia soleirolia 58
Solidago 159, 219, *219*
Sorbus 169, *169*
sound 24, 50, 124
spinach 227, 228
Spiraea 'Arguta' 163
Spiraea japonica 52
Spiraea x bumalda 173, *173*
Spirogyra 133
spring plantings 238, 329–39
square gardens 41
Stachys lanata (syn. *S. byzantina*) 47, 157, 159, 197
staking border plants 182
star-jasmine 404
statues 26, 29, *103*, *115*
stems, colourful 167
Stephanotis floribunda 109
stepping stones 48, 49, 59
steps 42–3, 51, 254
Sternbergia lutea 167
stone gardens 20, 32
stop-overs 224
storage 30–1
Stratiotes aloides 131
strawberries 225, *251*, 305, 389, 392
streams 19
strelitzias 55
succulents 54, 247
summer plantings 238, 340–58
sun plants 191, 196–7, 408
sundials 26, *103*, 114
Symphoricarpos 218
   S. albus 193, *193*
Syringa 218
   S. vulgaris 203, *203*, 207, 217, *217*
   S. vulgaris 'Madame Lemoine" 163

T
table decorations 250-1
Tamarix tetranda 52, 207
Taxus baccata (yew) 86
   T. baccata 'Repandens' 177
   T. baccata 'Standishii' 177
temporary supports for climbers 106–7
terracotta containers 256, 260, 330, *331*, 333, 368, 370, 436, 446, *447*
   pots 21, 31, 223, 260, *270*, 368, 370, 386, *387*, 399, 414, 427, 438, *439*
   windowboxes 282, 293, 304, 306, *307*, 316, 332, 353, 379, 384, 398, 402, 417
terrarium 474, *475*
testing soil 199
Thuja 23

   T. occidentalis 'Ericoides' 177
   T. orientalis 'Aurea Nana' (syn. *Platycladus orientalis* 'Aurescens') 177
   T. orientalis 'Rosedalis' (syn. *Platycladus orientalis* 'Rosedalis') 177
   T. orientalis 'Sieboldii' *177*
Thunbergia alata 107
Thymus 218, 222, 229, 247
   T. serpyllum 70, 77, 78, 139
Tiarella cordifolia 193
tiles 21, 54, 75, 78, *78*, 79
Tillaea recurva 131
tin containers 257, 320, *321*
   bath 444
   spring plantings 336
   tin can plant nursery 271
tomatoes 221, 227, *227*, 386, 390, 393
topiary 237, *241*, 368, 428, 446, *447*
   indoor topiary 473
touch 24, 124, 247
town gardens 28–9
Trachelospermum jasminoides 404
Trachycarpus fortunei 21
Tradescantia x andersoniana 205
trees 11, 14, 28–9, 40, 45,47, 108–9,

167, 237
  fruit trees 101, 221, 224
  tree seats 41, 121
trellis 23, 28–9, 28, 30, 50, 96–7, 98–9, 212
triangulation 35
Trifolium repens 71
Trillium grandiflorum 201
tripods 27, 112–13
Tropaeolum (nasturtiums) 89, 110, 236
  T. majus 107, 109
  T. peregrinum (syn. *T. canariense*) 107, 109
  T. speciosus 190
tropical plants 208–9
troughs 56, 138, 256, 361
  inspirational plantings 421
trugs 418
  inspirational plantings 422, 423
  winter plantings 369
tubs 14, 236
  spring plantings 329, 334, 335
  trees and shrubs 237
  vegetables 227, 247
Tulipa 68, 161, 244
turf laying 63
turnips 227
tyres 453

U
Ulex 218
  U. europaeus 175, 197
umbrellas 124
urns 7, 25, 27, 252, 253, 260
  inspirational plantings 441
utilities 7, 14, 28, 30–1

V
variegated plants 170–1
vegetables 7, 220–1, 226–7, 378, 382, 383, 386, 388, 390, 393, 467
  ornamental 226, 242, 251
  tubs 227, 247
  windowboxes 457
  with flowers 228–9
verandas 54–5

Verbascum 203
Verbena 217, 236, 246, 251, 319, 406
verdigris bucket 273
Veronica prostrata 139
verticals 38, 102, 104, 106–7, 110–11, 112–13, 237
Viburnum 218
  V. davidii 175, 193
  V. plicatum 163
  V. tinus 86, 165, 167, 175, 237, 240
  V. x bodnatense 217
  V. x bodnatense 'Dawn' 167
villandry planter 404, 405
Vinca major 190
Vinca minor 'Variegata' 171, 171, 193
vine weevils 268
Viola 78, 235, 243, 246, 262, 308, 313, 319, 369
  V. x wittrockiana 155
viruses 269
Vitis coignetiae 44, 108, 191, 215

W
wall baskets 51
  pink 287, 290, 296
  silver and white 286
  summer plantings 340, 352
  vibrant colour 313, 315
  winter plantings 377
wall features 115, 128
wall fountains 436
wall pots 433
wall shrubs 50, 214–15
wall spouts 126
wallflowers 329
walls 7, 21, 23, 42, 84–5, 88–9, 98–9, 101, 138, 212, 254
washing lines 14
wasps 218
water features 19, 24, 49, 50, 116, 126–7
water plants 127
water snails 133
watering 53, 235, 264-5
watering-can planter 449
waterlilies 127, 130
  'Froebelli' 131
  'James Brydon' 131
  Laydekeri lilacea 131
  Pygmeae helvola 131
  'Rose Arey' 131
water lily basket 425
weeds 59, 64–5, 81, 183, 228
  pond weeds 133
weevils 218
Weigela 173, 173, 218
  W. florida 207
  W. florida 'Variegata' 171
white-flowered plants 51, 189
whitefly 269
wicker baskets 261
  inspirational plantings 430, 431
wildlife 7, 189, 218–19
wildlife gardens 18–19
wind 38, 55, 408

wind chimes 50
wind-tolerant plants 52
windbreak screens 53
windowboxes 51, 55, 220–1, 222, 225, 227, 256–7, 264
  autumn plantings 362, 363, 365–6
  blue and purple 320, 321, 323, 324, 325
  edible plantings 379–80, 382, 383, 384, 393
  inspirational plantings 419–20, 424, 428, 429, 434, 435, 437
  pink 288, 289, 293
  scented plantings 395, 397, 402–3, 406
  shell 275
  spring plantings 332
  summer plantings 344–5, 349–51, 353

  sun 416–17
  vegetables 457
  vibrant colour 301, 304, 306, 308, 316, 317
  white and silver 280, 281, 282, 283
  winter plantings 371, 372, 373
wine case 381
winter 134–5
  plantings 240, 368–77
Wisteria 215, 217, 217
wood anemones 19
wooden furniture 120
woodland gardens 19, 337

X
x Cupressocyparis leylandii 86

Y
Yucca 21, 21, 41, 101, 175, 197, 209, 211
  Y. filamentosa 'Variegata' 165, 237
  Y. gloriosa 'Variegata' 165

Z
Zantedeschia aethiopica 209, 209

Acknowledgements

The publishers would like to thank all those who provided locations, materials and equipment for the special photography in this book. Specially commissioned photographs were provided by the following:

Peter Anderson: 62, 63, 66, 67, 68, 132, 133, 134, 135, 154bl, 155tr, 156t, 156b, 157tr, 176, 177, 178, 182 top row, 182br, 183, 192, 193, 200r, 201r and 204br.

Sue Atkinson: 157tl, 157b, 160tr, 161tl, 162l, 163br, 196, 202l, 202r, 204, 205t, 205b, 206l, 229tr.

Jonathan Buckley: 27bl, 52l, 52r, 96c, 96r, 97, 98, 99, 106, 107, 108, 109, 110, 111, 112, 113, 163t, 163bl, 180, 197, 186, 190b, 191, 200l, 203, 206, 207bl, 207tr, 207br, 229tl, 229c and 229b.

John Freeman: 14, 16b, 17t, 19t, 20, 31br, 35, 38t, 39, 44b, 45t, 45b, 50b, 51b, 53b, 57, 58t, 59t, 61, 64t, 64b, 65tl, 65tr, 65bl, 69, 71, 73, 74, 75, 77, 81, 82, 83 top row, 83cl, 83bl, 84, 86t, 87 top row, 87c, 87bc, 87br, 89t, 90t, 91, 92tl, 92tr, 94, 95tl, 95 steps, 102, 103b, 104, 105 steps, 114, 115, 120, 127br, 128, 129, 130, 131tr, 136b, 137, 139 steps, 142, 145b, 146, 147, 148, 149b, 151, 152 steps, 153, 179, 182bl, 184, 185, 187, 188tr, 188br, 189b, 192, 193, 197, 220tr, 220br, 223, 227b, 236m, 236b, 237b, 238m, 240, 246, 254tl, 255br, 258, 260r, 261mr, 265r, 266, 267, 284, 298, 299, 329, 330, 331, 333, 334, 335, 336, 337, 348, 356, 360, 361, 364, 365, 368, 369, 370, 371, 372, 373, 375, 376, 381, 386, 387, 389, 395, 404, 405, 425, 426, 427, 433, 436, 438, 439, 440, 441, 442, 443, 444, 445, 449, 453, 454, 455, 456, 457, 458, 459, 460, 461, 466, 467, 469, 470, 471, 477, 478, 479, 480, 481, 482 and 483.

Don Last: 269r, 463, 464, 465, 472, 473, 474, 475, 476 and 477.

Marie O'Hara: 23l, 31t, 132 and 204br.

Debbie Patterson: 22, 23c, 23tr, 23b, 24l, 24r, 25tl, 25tr, 25b, 26, 27tl, 27tr, 27br, 28t, 28b, 29tl, 29tr, 29b, 30t, 30b, 31t, 78t, 78b, 79, 96l, 118b, 118t, 119, 122l, 122r, 123, 124, 125, 155b, 236t, 237t, 238t, 241, 242t, 244t, 244m, 245, 247, 250, 251, 255, 260l, 270, 271, 272, 273, 274 and 285.

The publishers would also like to thank the following picture libraries from allowing their photographs to be reproduced for this book:
Derek Fell: 19b, 53t, 55t, 55b, 95tr, 141, 221 and 226t.

The Garden Picture Library: 16t (Marijke Heuff), 54 (Ron Sutherland), 80 (John Duane), 116 (Jane Legate), 222t (Lynne Brotchie) and 222b (J S Sira).

Robert Harding: 42b.

The Harpur Garden Library: 10 (designed by Maggie Geiger, NYC), 15t (a garden in Canterbury), 15b (designed by Michael Balston), 17b (designed by Trevor Frankland), 21t (designed by John Patrick, VIC), 38b (designed by Anthony Noel, London), 42t (designed by Berry's Garden co., Golders Green), 43b (designed by Christopher Masson, London), 44t (designed by Malcolm Hillier, London), 56 (designed by Christpher Masson, London), 58b (designed by Wayne Winterrowd & Joe Eck, London), 59b

(designed by Anne Alexander-Sinclair), 60t (designed by Ernie Taylor, Great Barr), 60b (a garden in Tayside), 72t (designed by Berry's Garden Co., Golders Green), 76 (designed by Hilary McMahon for Costin's Nursery, RHS Chelsea), 85b (designed by Anthony Noel, London), 85t (Fudlers Hall, Mashbury), 88t (designed by Jan Martinez, Kent), 93b (designed by Bruce Kelly, NYC), 105br (designed by Arabella Lennox-Boyd), 126b (designed by Simon Fraser, London), 136t (Joe Elliot, Broadwell, Gloucs), 140 (designed by Beth Chatto), 141 (designed by Ernie Taylor, Great Barr), 144 (Bank House, Borwich) and 149t (Home Farm, Balscotte, Oxon).

Peter McHoy: 16b, 50t, 51t, 65br, 70t, 70b, 72, 77bl, 83br, 86b, 87bl, 88b, 89b, 92b, 93t, 100, 101t, 101b, 117, 131b, 137b, 138t, 138bl, 138br, 139t, 155tl, 158t, 158c, 158b, 159t, 159c, 159b, 161tr, 161b, 162r, 164t, 164b, 165t, 165c, 165b, 166t, 166b, 167t, 167c, 167b, 168t, 168b, 169t, 169bl, 169br, 170t, 170b, 171tl, 171tr, 171bl, 171br, 172t, 172b, 173tl, 173tr, 173b, 174t, 174b, 175, 192tc192b, 193t, 193m, 193b, 196l, 196r, 197t, 197b, 203tl, 203bl, 208t, 208b, 209tr, 209br, 209l, 210t, 210b, 211tl, 211tr, 211b, 212l, 212t, 213t, 213b, 214t, 214b, 215t, 215bl, 215br, 216t, 216b, 217t, 217b, 218, 219t, 219c, 219b, 220bl, 224r, 225r, 226b, 227t, 239, 244, 249, 252r, 268 and 269l.

Jacqui Hurst: 18, 103t, 126t, 127t, 127bl, 143t, 143b, 145t, 152tl, 188l, 189t and 228.

Lucy Mason: 131tl.

All container projects were created by Stephanie Donaldson and photographed by Marie O'Hara unless otherwise stated.
Project contributors:
Clare Bradley: 449, 453, 454, 455, 456, 457, 458, 460, 461, 464 and 465.

Blaise Cook: 246, 252l, 255br, 266, 267, 284, 298, 299, 433, 436, 442, 443, 459, 480 and 481.

Tessa Eveleigh: 236, 238t, 241, 242t, 244t, 244m, 245, 247, 248, 250, 251 and 255t.

Peter McHoy: 244, 249, 252r, 461, 463, 464, 465, 472, 473, 474, 475, 476 and 477.

Lesley Harle: 270.

Karin Hossack: 25, 271 and 272

Cleo Mussi: 79.

Liz Wagstaff: 119, 273 and 27.

t=top, b=bottom, m=middle, l=left, r=right

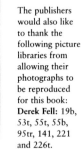